In the Brightness of Place

SUNY series in Contemporary Continental Philosophy
Dennis J. Schmidt, editor

In the Brightness of Place

Topological Thinking
in and after Heidegger

Jeff Malpas

SUNY PRESS

Cover image: Colin McCahon, *Kaipara Flat with a blue sky*, 1971, watercolor on paper, private collection. Reproduced by courtesy of the Colin McCahon Research and Publication Trust.

Published by State University of New York Press, Albany

© 2022 State University of New York

All rights reserved

Printed in the United States of America

No part of this book may be used or reproduced in any manner whatsoever without written permission. No part of this book may be stored in a retrieval system or transmitted in any form or by any means including electronic, electrostatic, magnetic tape, mechanical, photocopying, recording, or otherwise without the prior permission in writing of the publisher.

For information, contact State University of New York Press, Albany, NY
www.sunypress.edu

Library of Congress Cataloging-in-Publication Data

Name: Malpas, Jeff, author.
Title: In the brightness of place : topological thinking in and after
   Heidegger / Jeff Malpas.
Description: Albany : The State University of New York Press, [2022] |
   Series: SUNY series in contemporary continental philosophy | Includes
   bibliographical references and index.
Identifiers: LCCN 2022002684 (print) | LCCN 2022002685 (ebook) | ISBN
   9781438490038 (hardcover : alk. paper) | ISBN 9781438490021 (pbk. : alk.
   paper) | ISBN 9781438490045 (ebook)
Subjects: LCSH: Place (Philosophy) | Heidegger, Martin, 1889–1976.
Classification: LCC B105.P53 M38 2022 (print) | LCC B105.P53 (ebook) |
   DDC 114—dc23/eng/20220225
LC record available at https://lccn.loc.gov/2022002684
LC ebook record available at https://lccn.loc.gov/2022002685

10 9 8 7 6 5 4 3 2 1

In the summer of 1936, the bright experience of the place [*Ortschaft*] where my thinking had to stand came to me. It is this place for which I suspected I was searching in *Being and Time* . . .

—Martin Heidegger, *Anmerkungen I–V*

Contents

Acknowledgments		ix
Introduction: In the Brightness of Place		1
One	Out of History to Topology	7
Two	The "Anthropology" of the World	27
Three	On Not Naturalizing Heidegger	49
Four	Ontology and Hermeneutics	65
Five	Language and Place	83
Six	The Refusal of Metaphor	99
Seven	Finding Ourselves in the World	113
Eight	Technology and Spatialization	137
Nine	From Extremity to Releasement	163
Ten	Where Are We When We Think?	185
Epilogue	To the Other Beginning	209
Notes		227
Bibliography		281
Index		297

Acknowledgments

The material that makes up the contents of this volume was first presented at conferences or seminars in various places around the world, from Aarhus to Albuquerque, Lancaster to Ljubljana, Milan to Montreal, Stockholm to San Francisco. Among many others, I am particularly grateful to Andrew Benjamin, Eleni Bastea, Diego Bubbio, Ed Casey, Steve Crowell, Bogdan Costea, Hans Fink, Hans-Helmuth Gander, Peter Gratton, Jean Grondin, Sara Heinämaa, Laurence Hemming, Niall Keane, Dean Komel, Andrea Pinotti, Claude Romano, Hans Ruin, Sharon Rider, Dennis Schmidt, Camilla Serck-Hanssen, and Thomas Wentzer, all of whom have contributed in various ways to the ideas developed here.

This book is, in part, an outcome of a project funded by the Australian Research Council (ARC)—Place, Commonality, and the Human: Towards a New Philosophical Anthropology, undertaken, during 2016–2018, in collaboration with Andrew Benjamin, and the work from which the volume derives was also supported by funding from the Alexander von Humboldt Foundation.

None of the chapters that make up this volume has appeared previously in the form in which it does here. However, the volume does draw upon (and in some cases includes) material from the following essays—"In the Brightness of Place: Out of History to Topology," *Jenseits von Polemik und Apologie Die „Schwarzen Hefte"in der Diskussion*, ed. Alfred Denker and Holger Zaborowski, *Heidegger Jahrbuch* 12 (Freiburg: Karl Alber, 2020), 99–116; "The Beckoning of Language: Heidegger's Hermeneutic Transformation of Thinking," *Hermeneutic Heidegger*, ed. Ingo Farin and Michael Bowler (Evanston, IL: Northwestern University Press, 2016), 203–21; "'The House of Being': Poetry, Language, Place," *Paths in Heidegger's Later Thought*, ed. Günter Figal, Diego D'Angelo, Tobias

Keiling, and Guang Yang (Bloomington: Indiana University Press, 2020), 15–44; "The Spatialization of the World: Technology, Modernity, and the Effacement of the Human," *Phainomena* 27 (2018): 91–108; "From Extremity to Releasement: Place, Authenticity, and the Self," ed. Hans Pedersen and Lawrence Hatab, *The Horizons of Authenticity: Essays in Honor of Charles Guignon's Work on Phenomenology, Existentialism, and Moral Psychology* (Dordrecht: Springer, 2015), 45–62. "Re-Orienting Thinking: Philosophy in the Midst of the World," *Commonplace Commitments: Thinking Through the Legacy of Joseph P. Fell*, ed. Peter S. Fosl, Michael McGandy, and Mark Moorman (Lewisburg, PA: Bucknell University Press, 2016), 169–86. I am grateful to the original publishers for the opportunity to reuse the material in this way. I similarly acknowledge the kind permission of the publishers to use the quotation, appearing in translated form as the epigraph on p. v, from Martin Heidegger, *Anmerkungen I–V*, in *Schwarze Hefte* [Black Notebooks] *1942–1948* (Frankfurt am Main: ©Vittorio Klostermann GmbH, 2015), 191.

Sincere thanks are also due to Randall Lindstrom, who has been invaluable in assisting with the preparation of the material for this volume.

Last, but by no means least, I would like to express my gratitude to Ingo Farin, who has been and remains my most important philosophical interlocutor and who is not only an exceptional teacher and colleague but also an enthusiastic and engaged (though never uncritical) partner in the task of thinking.

Introduction

In the Brightness of Place

This volume, as with much of my work over the last thirty years, is organized around one simple idea: that all our thinking, especially in philosophy, is fundamentally oriented towards and determined by place—*topos*. Place, it should be noted, is not the same as *space*, even though the two are connected, nor it is to be set in opposition to *time*, even though the two can be distinguished.[1] Place encompasses space and time, without being reducible to either, so that space and time can be said to be derivative of place. What *place* names is an overarching *ontological* structure or event—the bounded opening in whose brightness things first come to presence—which is to say that it names the essential origin, ground, and framework for thinking, no matter how or where it arises. It also names that structure or event as it is given in any and every ordinary place.[2] The equivocity that is apparent here (which necessarily carries over into an equivocity affecting space and time also) reflects the essential character of place—an equivocity that derives from the *iridescence* that belongs to place as both extraordinary and ordinary, both familiar and strange, both ontological and ontic (to use the language of early Heidegger), both transcendent and immanent. The iridescent character of place means that place resists any attempt to reduce it to a metaphysical foundation, ground, or principle in the usual sense; resists even its reduction to the extraordinary, the strange, the transcendent, the ontological alone.

That place is something ordinary, even if it is also extraordinary, means that what is at issue in talk of place is that very place that is the place of our everyday life and existence—the place, *this* place, no matter when or where, in which we always already find ourselves, the place in and through which the world opens to us (since to be *in* the world is to be *placed*). Yet, that place is indeed ordinary in this way does not imply that place is always recognized, that it is easily understood, or that it is readily grasped. What Heraclitus says of nature or *physis*[3] applies equally to place or *topos*: place loves to hide. Despite the *iridescence* of place, despite the *brightness* of place, despite the *openness* of place, place remains often obscure, overlooked, neglected, forgotten. That this is so, however, is itself a consequence of the fundamental and disclosive character of place. As it is fundamental and disclosive, so place is often hidden by that which is disclosed in and through it—place withdraws in favour of that which it discloses. The attempt to overcome the withdrawal of place as well as its forgetting, and to do so philosophically, is at the heart of what is here referred to as *topological thinking*, or just *topology*—the "thoughtful saying" of place.

These opening comments, declarative as they are, summarize an account of place that has been developed over several previous books and many previous essays. It is not the aim of this volume simply to reiterate that account, and the reader who seeks some further, more specific elaboration and clarification of the claims made above is best advised to look to some of those previous books and essays. Although the underlying character of place is touched upon at various points in the pages that follow, this volume is not intended as a treatise solely or specifically on place.

Instead, its aims are twofold. First, it aims to explore the question of place in relation to a range of different issues or problems (the chapters are arranged in a fairly loose order and are accessible largely independently of one another): poetry, landscape, origin, nature, language, metaphor, emotion, reason, technology, authenticity, releasement, place, world (these being the most salient). Only the first chapter is a little different in that it addresses place, as I note below, in terms of the way it figures in a certain path of thinking, although the relation between place and thinking is itself the overarching concern. In this, the volume's various chapters are essays in *philosophical topology*,[4] based in the attempt to articulate, in various domains and in relation to various topics, that single, simple thought that was referred to at the start—a single, simple thought that nevertheless leads into a complex multiplicity. Second, the volume aims to develop further the claim, made in several other works,[5] that the idea and experience of place, and so the project of topology, are central to the work of the German philosopher Martin Heidegger—a figure who, no matter the complications, failures, and limitations of his thinking, remains arguably the single most important and influential philosopher of the twentieth century. The first chapter is crucial in setting out the overall trajectory of this reading, and the epilogue, to some extent, returns us to it. The volume's two aims are bound together, since Heidegger stands out as the thinker who, more than any other, has taken up place as a key philosophical idea—the very idea of topology being taken from the way Heidegger characterizes his thinking in terms of a topology of being (*Topologie des Seyns*).[6] The topological exploration that is undertaken in the pages that follow is thus an exploration of the way topological thinking appears *in* Heidegger, as well as an exploration of the way topological thinking appears beyond or *after* Heidegger.

Where one ends is often the same as the place one begins, and my contention has always been that Heidegger's thinking has its own end and beginning in one and the same place, no matter whether we call it the *Da* (there/here), the *Augenblick* (moment), the *Lichtung* (clearing), the *Ereignis* (event), or the *Geviert* (fourfold), and regardless of whether we read the elaboration of this place as it occurs in Richardson, Dreyfus, Sheehan, Capabianco, or Figal. Perhaps surprisingly, however, what unites many of Heidegger's contemporary readers, despite their differences over terms and modes of analysis, is a peculiar inattention to, even dismissal of, this most obvious and straightforward of points; namely, that Heidegger's thinking does indeed begin *in this one place*, and that this place is not a metaphorical origin, nor is its appearance a mere accident of language, even though it may seem obscure and enigmatic. Heidegger's thinking is thus *topological* in character in a fundamental and essential sense. Thinking is always placed, and the thinking that Heidegger enacts is not only a thinking that therefore begins *in its place* but also a thinking that attempts to thematize its own *being-placed*—which is, it should be added, the being-placed of all thinking and all presencing—and so too *the very place* of such thinking and such presencing.

The point at issue here is a simple one, even though its elaboration can become complex and sometimes difficult. It is a point already suggested earlier and one that ought to be evident as soon as we begin to reflect on the placed character of our own thinking. Thinking arises, not in some ideal realm removed from the world, but here, in the only place given to us, the place of the world in which our lives are embedded, the place in which we encounter the very things, events, and processes that provoke us to think in the first place. Our thinking may well open up to possibilities that take us far beyond what is immediately present to us, but that does not mean that our thinking in thereby untethered or dislocated from the place in which our thinking begins. In much recent and contemporary thinking, something of this idea has been evident in the work of those many theorists, from Gaston Bachelard to Paul Virilio, who have argued from, and often provided close elaborations of, the way specific modes of thought, themselves bound to activities and practices, are tied to specific circumstances and situations.

Although Heidegger is a key figure throughout the discussions that follow, this book is not a work that belongs primarily to the field of what has become known as "Heidegger studies." What that field might be is perhaps somewhat obscure. Thomas Sheehan seems to present it as if it were a well-defined area of intellectual inquiry, such that a new "paradigm" can be advanced in relation to it.[7] But it is not at all clear what justifies such talk beyond the bounds of a relatively small circle of largely North American scholars whose work is focused on a certain sort of close exegetical and critical engagement with Heidegger's texts. This field, if it is to be called such, is a relatively enclosed and highly self-referential one that makes little or no connection with the larger philosophical landscape of recent and contemporary thought. Although the claim may be too provocative, I am tempted to say that Heidegger studies, in this respect, has become largely disconnected from any broader domain of contemporary intellectual inquiry even within philosophy—and whether it remains true to the sort of fundamental thinking to which Heidegger was so committed seems at least questionable.

As I am less concerned to fit within the framework of contemporary Heidegger studies, so I am also less concerned to remain strictly bound by what might be thought of as the authority of the Heideggerian text. In his preface to *Heidegger and Sartre*—a pioneering work in the topological approach to Heidegger—Joseph Fell comments: "I take seriously Heidegger's notion of the value of 'violence' in interpretation and translation, and I have often turned this dangerous technique back upon Heidegger himself . . . "[8] Such a strategy is one that I would acknowledge as an essential part of my own reading of Heidegger. It follows from a concern with the problems at issue rather than textual exegesis or historical interpretation alone. It means that the reading that results must be seen as a critical one, and not tied to the affirmation of every element that may appear in Heidegger's writings. This approach to Heidegger also has the important corollary that my engagement is not primarily with Heidegger the person, nor with the details of his life, and I would also reject the claim that there is any straightforward path from the biographical to the philosophical.

This certainly does not mean that I would, in any way, endorse Heidegger's actions in supporting Hitler, for instance, or that I would defend his anti-Semitic comments from the late 1930s and 1940s. *Both Nazism and anti-Semitism deserve an unqualified condemnation and rejection.* However, I am not convinced that the pro-Nazi and anti-Semitic comments that appear in some of Heidegger's writings represent core elements in his thinking (though they may well have been tied to aspects of his own person and character), nor do I think that those comments are tied, in any significant way, to the key questions that concern me here, or that they bear, in any crucial way, on the reading of Heidegger's response to those questions. In fact, I take Heidegger's Nazi sympathies and his anti-Semitism, both of which are also tied up with his problematic nationalism and Germano-centrism, to be indicative of the extent to which he fails adequately to follow the real direction of his own thought—fails adequately to address the topological dimensions that are there from the beginning but often remain implicit and only partially articulated. Whether I am right in this cannot, of course, be decided in advance of the actual engagement with the thinking and the questions at issue. Whatever one's prior views on this matter, there is no way around the task of working through the actual ideas and arguments along with the work itself.

This volume is an exercise in topological thinking at the same time as it also takes topological thinking as its focus. While the various chapters that follow do indeed take up a range of different topics, what nevertheless unites them is a common concern with the elaboration of a different kind of thinking—what Heidegger variously refers to as poetic or mediative thinking and, in the 1966 *der Spiegel* interview, simply as the "other thinking."[9] Heidegger often presents this thinking as standing completely apart from traditional philosophy and so as also standing apart from any concern with notions that belong to that tradition, most notably the transcendental and the ontological. Certainly, the terms "transcendental," "ontology," and "ontological" all largely disappear from Heidegger's later writing other than as they arise as a focus for critical comment.

Heidegger cannot, however, completely sever his connection to the previous tradition, and he does not attempt to do so, but neither, for that very reason, is it possible entirely to abandon the language of that tradition. This is especially obvious when it comes to Heidegger's talk of "being." It is the persistence of the term in his thinking, even while he aims to decouple the term from its metaphysical connotations, that leads him to the technique of letting the term "being" appear but as struck through (*durchstreichen*)—what has become known as "writing under erasure," thus: ~~being~~.[10] But this technique merely highlights the problem rather than providing a solution to it. Similarly, the disavowal of certain terms, although sometimes justified, can also lead to a neglect of what was genuinely at issue in the discourse in which those terms operated, and even of the underlying insight those terms were supposed to play a part in elaborating. Moreover, in Heidegger's case, it can all too readily contribute, despite his claims about the inextricability of thinking from the tradition out of which it comes, to what sometimes appears as a form of intellectual exceptionalism, as if Heidegger's thinking were indeed unique and unprecedented.

Such exceptionalism seems to me a form of philosophical hubris. But it also neglects the way in which thinking is never about some form of pure innovation—as if it were a matter of stepping into some place that we have never before encountered. The very character of thinking as topological means that it is always a turning back to the place in which we already are, and that means that thinking is always recuperative, always involves, to some extent, a task of retrieval. Again, this is only to emphasize something already present in Heidegger (as will be seen in the chapters that follow), but I also take this to imply the impossibility of any complete disavowal or abandonment of the terms of previous thinking. The real task is one of rethinking what might have been thought before, and that may well include rethinking the language that has gone before in an effort to allow what was genuinely at issue in that language to emerge. Consequently, unlike Heidegger (in at least some of his moods), I remain committed to the idea that many of the notions that figure so prominently in the philosophical tradition—especially the transcendental and the ontological—remain important and deserve to be rethought rather than abandoned. As they appear here, as well as elsewhere in my work, the aim is to rethink those notions as *topological* and, in so doing, also to show how the topological is already embedded in the philosophical tradition (and is therefore not peculiar to Heidegger alone), even if it is not always acknowledged by it.

One

Out of History to Topology

Over a period of at least forty years, Heidegger maintained a practice of writing down his thoughts in black oilcloth-bound notebooks, now referred to as the *Black Notebooks* in virtue of the color of their binding. The first of these notebooks, from 1931–1941, were published in three volumes in 2014 (further notebooks have been published as additional volumes since),[1] and their appearance gave rise to an immediate uproar, and a continuing debate, concerning, in particular, the pro-Nazi and anti-Semitic comments they contained.

Yet for all the sound and fury surrounding them, it remains unclear what genuinely new insights into Heidegger's thinking the *Notebooks* provide. This may seem a provocative claim, and yet it follows directly from the lack of attention, within much of the debate so far, as to how the *Notebooks* should even be read. Are they to be viewed as giving insight into the "inner" workings of Heidegger's life and thought? And, if so, then on what basis would such a reading be founded? Within what stylistic framing should the *Notebooks* be situated? Is there only one such framing that is relevant (the Nietzschean *Nachlass* is an obvious model, and yet it seems not to be operative as such throughout the *Notebooks* in their entirety)? To what extent might some of the entries be intended ironically or sarcastically?[2] To what extent might they be expressions more of a personal state of mind than of any considered philosophical views? More generally, to what extent is the person of the philosopher determinative of the content of the philosophy?

To take what should be a familiar, but related, example: the interpretation of works of art (certainly works of any complexity or significance) cannot be dealt with simply by referring such interpretation either to the life of the artist or to any artistic intention. Artistic interpretation, including the interpretation of works of literary art, is always a matter of addressing the work rather than the artist, and it is hard to see how it could be any different when it comes to philosophical works. The case of the artwork reflects the case of interpretation more generally. Even the interpretation of ordinary utterances cannot be decided simply by reference to the speaker's intention (or supposed intention), all the more so given that intention does not, in any case, stand outside of interpretive engagement. In that case, there is no easy way to address the nature of Heidegger's work, including the political import of that work, other than by working through the thinking itself. And if the overtly political actions and commitments are taken as part of the philosophy, then that only raises the question of how those political actions and commitments should be read. The question of interpretation cannot properly be evaded, even though it may be ignored.

Few of the basic interpretive questions at issue here have arisen in the critical reception of the *Notebooks* so far.[3] For the most part, the assumption seems to have been that they can be read more or less "naively"—that is, without attention to any questions of interpretive methodology or approach—and even that they can be read in a way that prescinds from their historical situatedness. Heidegger is thus read as if he were writing now with his words having the same meaning and significance as they would in our own contemporary context. Moreover, for many commentators, the interest seems to have been less the direct import of the *Notebooks* for the understanding of Heidegger's philosophy than the use of the *Notebooks* to demonstrate Heidegger's personal political culpability in relation to Nazism and anti-Semitism, and for the philosophical relevance of the *Notebooks* to be taken to follow from this. Here, too, however, the real interpretive work—that required to make a genuine connection between any supposed personal culpability (assuming that the allocation of such responsibility is indeed a genuine philosophical task) and its implications for Heidegger's thought—remains to be done, despite the quantity of words that have so far been expended on the issue.

It is likely to be some time before we arrive at a more sober and balanced assessment of Heidegger's *Notebooks* as they relate to Heidegger's philosophy[4]—and especially as they concern Heidegger's involvement with Nazism and his anti-Semitism. In the meantime, however, in the midst of the hubbub that has come to surround the works, there are some points on which the *Notebooks* do appear to provide illumination, most especially on the development of Heidegger's critique of technology, on the thinking that surrounds the *Contributions*, on his views regarding the radical potential of philosophy, and also, I would argue, on the shift to a more explicitly topological mode of thinking in the late 1940s, but which Heidegger himself connects with the thinking undertaken in the *Contributions* (although the topology that emerges in 1947 is itself distinct from that of the *Contributions* in very significant ways). It is the latter point—the way the *Notebooks* shed light on Heidegger's topology and the development of that topology—that is the focus of this first chapter.

Space, Place, and Time

The topology that becomes explicit in Heidegger's work in the later 1940s is not a feature of the late thinking alone—it is already present in *Being and Time*. Yet just as the topological character of Heidegger's thinking is often ignored by contemporary Heidegger commentary and discussion, so does Heidegger come explicitly to recognize the topology that characterizes his thinking relatively late, even though that topology was present all along. Indeed, in *Being and Time*, it almost looks as if Heidegger shies away from such a topology, at one point appearing to suggest that the prominence of place, whether in his own thinking or elsewhere, is itself a secondary phenomenon. In §70 of *Being and Time*, Heidegger writes:

> Dasein's interpretation of itself and the whole stock of significations which belong to language in general are dominated through and through by "spatial representations." This priority of the spatial in the Articulation of concepts and significations has its basis not in some specific power which space possesses, but in Dasein's kind of Being. Temporality is essentially falling, and it loses itself in making present; not only does it understand itself circumspectively in terms of objects of concern which are ready-at-hand, but from those spatial relationships which making-present is constantly meeting in the ready-to-hand as having presence, it takes its clues for Articulating that which has been understood and can be interpreted in the understanding in general.[5]

The language Heidegger uses here is that of "space" and "spatiality" (*Raum, Räumlichkeit*) rather than explicitly of "place" (whether in the form of *Ort, Ortschaft*, or *Stätte*). It is, however, a language that is all too readily taken, both by Heidegger's readers, and perhaps, at least in *Being and Time*, even by Heidegger, to encompass place as if it were something *spatial*—all the more so since place is not clearly distinguished from space in the early work. The claim that Heidegger makes in the above passage is that the seeming priority of spatialized terms and concepts is a consequence of temporality's own constant tendency to understand itself in terms of the present, and so in terms of the merely present, that is, in terms of the spatial and so also, one might suppose, in terms connected with place. The claim (which we shall encounter again in chapter 9) is in keeping with the overall argumentative direction of *Being and Time* in its movement from the analysis of Dasein's everyday being as it is given in the worldly engagement with tasks and activities—a reengagement that is indeed *spatially* organized and oriented—to the uncovering of its fundamentally *temporal* determination.

That "Dasein's interpretation of itself and the whole stock of significations which belong to language in general . . . are dominated by spatial representations" is not a claim that, in its general character, is peculiar to Heidegger alone. Most notably, Kant, in the first *Critique*, notes that all representation, including the representation even of time, depends on spatiality.[6] As Heidegger employs it, however, the claim figures as part of an argument for what looks to be the secondary character of spatiality and the spatial in relation to temporality.[7] Heidegger's assertion is that the apparent primacy of language is a consequence of Dasein's tendency constantly to understand itself in terms that prioritize the merely "present," and the fact that time itself is understood in this way is an inevitable consequence. Of course, within the framework of *Being and Time*, it is temporality and the temporal that has ontological primacy, not spatiality, and so the seeming primacy of spatial representation must be explained as arising from a mode of understanding that is itself a misunderstanding—the dominance of the spatial covering over the real character of Dasein's being.

Yet the argument that Heidegger attempts here is made problematic by some of the same considerations on which it also depends. Heidegger's argument aims at a separation of temporality from spatiality, since it aims at asserting the priority of one over the other, at the same time as it also relies upon the inextricability of each with the other—and not merely representationally but also ontologically. It is the inextricability of the spatial and the temporal that opens the possibility of treating spatiality as potentially able to be, in some way, "founded" in temporality, and yet there is nothing in this inextricability as such that implies that it should support such a founding relation in one direction alone. Indeed, it seems no less questionable to suppose that one could remove all traces of the "spatial" from the temporal than that one could remove all traces of the "temporal" from the spatial. Heidegger privileges the move from the spatial as founded to the temporal as founding, but without offering any real argument to support that privileging. Indeed, one might go so far as to say that the argument he does offer depends for its plausibility on an implicit equivocation between two senses of spatiality—between what Heidegger himself calls "existential spatiality," *existentiale Räumlichkeit*, and Cartesian spatiality. The first already brings with it a topological connotation, whereas the second is the spatiality of the leveled-out world of unbounded "extension" within which place has no real place at all. Cartesian spatiality can indeed be viewed as a secondary notion, but it is secondary to *existential* spatiality no less than it is secondary to temporality (or at least to that specific mode of temporality that is at issue for Heidegger).[8] Although there is a clear distinction between these two forms of spatiality in the argument of *Being and Time*, that distinction is not referred to in the discussion in §70, so if spatiality is said to be a "founded" mode, then that would appear to include existential spatiality.[9]

Although Heidegger never offers any similar diagnosis of the difficulty that afflicts the attempt to assert the absolute primacy of temporality, he nevertheless comes to recognize that his attempt, in *Being and Time*, to assert the primacy of temporality is indeed mistaken; as he seems implicitly to acknowledge in the lectures on Kant from 1935[10] and explicitly in the 1962 lecture (published in 1969) "On Time and Being."[11] Moreover, Heidegger also comes effectively to abandon the idea that the dominance of the spatial, as presented in *Being and Time*, itself involves a misunderstanding. Although Heidegger never makes this clear, the "spatial," as it is employed in *Being and Time*, is not, as I pointed out earlier, entirely separable from the topological. Cartesian spatiality aside, the spatiality that concerns Heidegger, in *Being and Time*, already includes that which pertains to *place* (existential spatiality is explicitly associated with that mode of being-in-the-world that, already in *Being and Time*, Heidegger calls *Wohnen*, or, as the conventional translation has it, "dwelling"[12]). In this respect, Heidegger's later insistence on the significance of the language of place (for instance, in his comments, in the "Letter on 'Humanism,'" regarding language as the "house of being"[13]), can be seen as something of a repudiation of his earlier denigration of the language of the "spatial" (or at least of the "spatial" as it operates topologically). Moreover, this rejection can be seen as already present in Heidegger's refusal of any metaphorical reading of the language he employs—a language that is indeed frequently topological in character—in his readings of Hölderlin in the early 1940s (an issue to which I shall return in chapters 5 and 6).[14]

One of the difficulties that *Being and Time* presents is a lack of clarity with respect to space, time, and place, and the relations and distinctions between them. This is partly due to the absence of a developed understanding of place in Heidegger's early work. That work draws on topological ideas and images, especially in its accounts of existential spatiality and temporality but without explicitly addressing their specifically topological character. *Being and Time* is thus a deeply topological work even though it does not recognize that topology—even though it is, one might say, confused in terms of its own topological structure.[15] The dominance of a topological mode of thinking, and so of topological and even *spatial* terms and ideas, is a feature of Heidegger's work almost from beginning to end. Heidegger comments, in the *Notebooks*, on his use of "figurative" (*bildlich*) language[16] (which should not be assumed to be the same as a language of *metaphor* but is rather a language of *image*—see chapter 6), and the figurative language at issue here must be understood as a language that almost always involves spatial, bodily, and so also *topological* images (see, once again, the discussion in chapter 6, and also chapter 5). It is a style of language that is clearly evident in *Being and Time*, and it is for this very reason that Heidegger is forced, there, to offer an explanation of the seeming pre-eminence of such topological ways of speaking and understanding.

In Heidegger's earlier *Notebooks*, the primacy of the topological appears most obviously in Heidegger's constant invocation, across many of the entries from the mid-1930s, of the notion of *Da-sein*. The term is regularly hyphenated in the *Notebooks* from around 1932–33 onwards,[17] and the hyphenation draws attention to the *Da*; that is, to the there/here as it is in ordinary German. This leaves open the question as how the *Da* itself is to be understood—the translation should not be assumed to have already done the philosophical work that is at issue in understanding the term. The *Da* can certainly be taken to stand in a close relation to the clearing—to the *Lichtung*—but this is not to say very much and hardly offers much in the way of additional elucidation, doing little more than shifting the semantic focus. The relation between the there/here and the clearing is indeed already suggested by the idea of the clearing itself—the clearing can be said to be a clearing precisely through the way in which it is the opening of a there/here—and the there/here may also be said to be a there/here through the clearing that is established with it. That one might thus give priority to the *Lichtung*—or even to other notions such as the *Ereignis*—over the *Da*, and, in doing so, show place to be a secondary notion, itself depends on ignoring the topology that remains at work in the very terms, *Ereignis* no less than *Lichtung*, that are prioritized in this way.

In the *Notebooks* from 1934, one finds Heidegger interrogating the idea of the *Da* and, specifically, the *Da* as it stands in relation to world (a relation already invoked in an entry from the *Notebooks* from late 1931 in which Heidegger talks of the one task that "matters before everything and for everything"; namely, the opening up of "world-place," or, *Welt-ortes*[18]). "Space!" he exclaims, " '*Where*' is the there [*Da*], such that it is itself the ground of the where?" A few lines further down, Heidegger writes, "World . . . the vibrant middle of the there [*Mitte des Da*] a grounded middle that *stands* in the clutches and joins of time."[19] Yet, if the language of place is indeed evident in the *Notebooks* from relatively early on (not surprisingly given that this language does indeed develop out of the spatial and topological language of Heidegger's earlier thinking), then it is a language that receives even greater elaboration and salience in the *Contributions*. Echoing elements in the just-quoted passage from the 1931 *Notebooks*, Heidegger writes, in the *Contributions*, of *Da-sein* as "the axis in the turning of the event." *Da-sein*, he says, "is the *between* [*das Zwischen*]: between humans (as grounding of history) and the gods (in their history)," and he adds that the between is "not one that simply results from the relation of the gods to humans; rather, one that first grounds the time-space [*Zeit-raum*] for such a relation."[20] The language of the between, of "relation," of "turning," and of time-space that is at issue here, and that receives its first real articulation in Heidegger's thinking in the *Contributions*, is a language that might be said to evoke place in all but name—except, of course, for the prominence it already gives to the "there/here."

Place, Event, and History

The spatial and topological language that appears in the *Contributions*, beginning in 1936, first emerges, along with other key elements, in the *Notebooks* from 1934, and so in the period immediately after Heidegger's resignation as rector of Freiburg University (although it is also a development out of the earlier spatial and topological language that appears, if less explicitly formulated, in *Being and Time*). In the *Contributions*, however, this language is not only given greater elaboration but also seems to pervade the entire work. The very titles of the first four divisions of the *Contributions*—"The Prospect," "The Resonating," "The Interplay," and "The Leap" (the last three are "The Future Ones," "The Last God," and "Beyng"[21])—already indicate a certain sort of orientational setting, a certain sort of *placing*. Moreover, the overall structure of the *Contributions*, in its entirety, is one that Heidegger describes as "a preliminary sketch of the temporal-spatial playing field which the history of the transition first creates as its own realm . . . "[22] These sorts of topological figures recur throughout the work, both in its overall plan and in the exploration and elaboration of the ideas that it aims to address. Thus, to take but one example, Heidegger's discussion of the relation between beyng, the *Ereignis*, and Da-sein proceeds in self-evidently topological terms:

> Beings first arise historically out of the truth of being, and that truth is sheltered in the steadfastness of Da-*sein* . . . Here, out of Da-sein, the complete otherness of the relation to beyng is thought and carried out, and that happens in the time-space [*Zeit-raum*] arising out of the transporting and captivating of truth itself. Time-space itself is a conflictual domain of strife . . . Spacing which is temporalizing)—temporalizing (which is spatializing) (cf. the conflict of the strife) as the most proximate configuring domain for the truth of being, but not a relapse to the common, formal concepts of space and time (!), instead resumption into the *strife*, world and earth—event.[23]

Some of the most important sections in the *Contributions* concern Heidegger's elaboration of the concepts evident in this passage—*Da-sein*, the truth of being, time-space—and almost always the elaboration of these concepts is undertaken, as in the passage above, in ways that are indeed topologically embedded. Time-space is named as the "abyssal ground," as the "structure (joining) of the 'there,' a structure of transport-captivation," as "the site of the moment; the strife of world and earth."[24] One can open the *Contributions* almost anywhere and find topological allusions, images, and concepts. It might be argued, in fact, that part of the problem with the *Contributions* is that its topology is so rampant as to make its character *as* a topology even harder to grasp. The topological language that is used is too various, too differentiated, too intoxicated. Yet a topology it is—so much so that the very idea of the *Ereignis* seems to bring notions of place and placing.

It is no accident, therefore, that Heidegger can say *both* that *Ereignis* is the guiding word of his thinking from 1936 onwards, as he does in the "Letter on 'Humanism'" in 1946,[25] *and*, in the *Notebooks* from around the same time, that it was in 1936 that he found the proper *place* (*Ortschaft*) of thinking for which he had been searching, even in *Being and Time*, and out of which the *Contributions* originated. Moreover, in spite of the "aberrations [*Irrgänge*] and attempts [*Versuche*]" that might seem to lead thinking away from this place, we are always turned back to it, "like a many-turning journey [*Wanderschaft*] within the same place [*in der selben Ortschaft*]."[26] Here, it seems that *Ortschaft* and *Ereignis* are drawn together such that Joseph Fell can claim (as he did already in 1979) that "Heidegger's terms, 'Event' (*Ereignis*) and 'Place' (*Ort*), mean the same,"[27] and, even if this may be thought a little too quick, it is also, especially in the light of what we can now see from the *Notebooks*, very close to the mark. Certainly, the shift in Heidegger's thinking to the *Ereignis* is also the shift to a more direct engagement with place (whether *Ort* or *Ortschaft*)—although it takes Heidegger at least another ten years or so after 1936 to recognize that shift more explicitly for the topological shift that it is. In the *Notebooks* in 1946, Heidegger talks of the way in which the *Contributions* arises out of his finding of the proper place of thinking (*Ortschaft des Denkens*).[28] And, in entries from that same point onwards, he writes of the place of the event (*Ortschaft des Ereignisses*),[29] the place of being (*Ortschaft des Seyns*),[30] and of the topology of being (*Topologie des Seyns*).[31] Yet although the *Ereignis* thus appears to be thought in terms of a topology that Heidegger, from the perspective of 1946, locates in the *Contributions*, that work does not explicitly present itself in such a topological fashion, and there is no mention in the *Contributions* of either topology of being or of the place of being.

The fact that the *Contributions* is not clear as to its own topological character is reflected in the fact that, even for all that its language is so thoroughly topological, there is still no direct thematization of place as such. Indeed, although *Da-sein* and the "there/here" figure prominently, neither *Ortschaft* nor *Ort* has any salience in the *Contributions*.[32] The only term appearing with any frequency that might be translated as place is *Stätte*, more commonly translated (as it is in the English translations of the *Contributions*) as "site."[33] Indeed, one might argue that, for all that Heidegger has abandoned the attempt to tie spatiality back to temporality, a degree of primacy is still accorded to temporality, purely inasmuch as the primary orientation of the *Contributions*, and of many of Heidegger's works from the period of the mid- to late 1930s and into the 1940s, is that of a mode of being-historical (*Seinsgeschichtliche* or *Seynsgeschichtliche*) thinking. Part of the problem here, as in *Being and Time*, is Heidegger's tendency to think time in ways that already treat it in implicitly topological terms (so that the topological is effectively incorporated *into* the temporal), coupled with the fact that, even in the *Contributions*, place is still not directly taken up. The topology that is undoubtedly present in the *Contributions* thus not only does not name itself as a topology in that work, but it also understands itself in terms specifically of the *history* of being rather than the *place* of being.

Already, in the early 1930s, more especially during 1931 and 1932, one can see Heidegger preoccupied with a form of the "history" of being, inasmuch as he sees the National Socialist "revolution" as potentially constituting a pivotal point in that history. Thus, in the *Notebooks* from 1932, for instance, Heidegger refers to:

> The incomparability of the world's current hour, a chamber in which German philosophy should strike up and resound . . . The world-moment of our history: the resoluteness of that moment. We are not able, and do not want, to calculate the future or even to know what is to come. Quite to the contrary, we must and indeed want to create anew our futurity and thereby our entire temporality—the new courage.[34]

Heidegger seems to view philosophy, and so also thinking (provided it is sufficiently courageous and properly oriented), as providing the basis for political action—as having the capacity to lead (*zu fuhren*) and to ordain a future:

> The projection of being qua time overcomes everything hitherto as regards being and thinking; not idea, but mission; not

loosening, but binding. The projection does not break loose to pure spirit but instead first opens and binds blood and soil to a preparedness for action and to a capacity for work and affectivity.[35]

Heidegger soon becomes disillusioned, however, and in 1934, and especially following his resignation from the rectorate in April, his comments in the *Notebooks* start to take on a more critical tone. Whether the cause of his disillusionment is the Nazis' unwillingness to respond positively to Heidegger's philosophical version of what National Socialism might be, or his own seeing-through of the pretensions of Nazi rhetoric to what lay beneath, is irrelevant to the fact of that disillusionment and to the disengagement from Nazism that accompanies it. The last of the entries in the *Notebooks* from 1934 refers to "The Self-Assertion of the German University" (the Rectoral Address) as "the little entr'acte of a great error" (though whether the "error" here refers to Heidegger's own political adventure or to the wider political movement of which it was part, is not made clear), and the entry goes on, in pessimistic fashion, to enumerate various forms of "disintegration" for which the university serves as a "wretched fig-leaf."[36]

With book IV of the *Notebooks* from 1934–35, which carries the subtitle, "Of Da-Sein and Being," Heidegger's comments seem to have moved almost entirely away from matters of politics. Any previous talk of putative new beginnings to which revolutionary politics might lay claim is replaced by the sense that Heidegger seems to attach to the idea of a "second,"[37] or "other," beginning as a beginning *for thinking* (which, although clearly meant to apply to thinking as such, surely also carries something of the connotation of a second beginning for Heidegger himself). What occurs here is a shift away from a particular mode of being-historical thinking, which, in its conviction of the capacity of philosophy to act politically, remained essentially *subjectivist* (despite any disavowals Heidegger himself might have made), and towards a new mode of being-historical (or being-historical) thinking that looks, not to philosophy's capacity for action *in* history, but rather to the engagement of thinking with the primordial phenomenon of both the "there" and history. Heidegger thus writes of "a questioning":

> that pushes itself to its limits, where it experiences itself exposed to what is most question-worthy; where the "there"

> opens up abyssally, where the need of preservational disputation necessitates the "there" (constancy), and history, i.e., a people, becomes itself; history is the venturing | of the gods out of a world and for a world . . . To question the concept of world disclosively = to coground thoughtfully the "there" out of the affiliation to such history.[38]

And a few entries later:

> Philosophy—will not deliver us, will not discover new things (through research), will not (after the fact) raise any worldview to concepts—instead, philosophy will again know the πόλεμος—*the event*—and will fathom the ground and the abyss and the deformed ground and thus will become a plight and the necessity—to seize what has been given as task and to conquer what has been given as endowment—to bring history to a happening—to venture the gods once again.[39]

What is at issue is a mode of being historical-thinking that looks to the way thinking stands in relation to a more primordial occurrence that it neither determines nor directs, but that it can indeed bring to appearance; that looks to the way it stands in essential relation to the *Ereignis*, the event. The shift that occurs here is not only a shift away from a certain form of subjectivism (something evident, for instance, in Heidegger's emphasis on the "abyssal" nature of this thinking) but also a shift away from philosophy as traditionally understood—and so towards a different kind of thinking—which is just what emerges in 1936, privately in the *Contributions* and presaged in the *Notebooks*, as well as publicly in the lectures on "The Origin of the Work of Art" (lectures that are first presented in 1935). In both the *Contributions* and "The Origin," Heidegger begins to formulate a new mode of thinking that is deeply indebted to art and to poetry and that looks to return thinking to its proper place.

Yet even though the thinking that crystalizes in 1936 can indeed be seen to represent a break with the thinking of 1933 and earlier (including, it should be added, with important elements of the thinking of *Being and Time*), and even though it does indeed aim to position itself as against any form of subjectivism, still that thinking takes the form, not of an eschewal of the being-historical, but instead its philosophical clarification and intensification—the thinking that is undertaken in the

Contributions is itself being-historical. Consequently, Heidegger writes that "the event of appropriation [*Ereignis*] is original history itself," and this is because "the essence of being no longer only means presence, but, rather, means the full essential occurrence of the temporal-spatial abyss and thus of truth."[40] It is as if Heidegger's entanglement in the politically active mode of being-historical thinking that dominates his thinking in the early-1930s demands that he rethink the very character of being as historical, and it is this that therefore drives much of the re-oriented thinking in the *Contributions*.

In similar fashion, many of the concepts evident in the *Notebooks* and other writings from the early-1930s—concepts associated with "the people" (*das Volk*) being notable examples—continue into the thinking of the *Notebooks*, from 1934 onwards and into the *Contributions*, but these concepts are rethought and reconceptualized. On the idea of philosophy as "of" a people, for instance, Heidegger writes, in the *Contributions*: "The expression 'philosophy of a people' immediately proves to be most ambiguous and obscure. Quite apart from the indeterminateness involved in talking of a 'people.'" Yet he nevertheless also insists that "[m]editation on what is proper to a people constitutes an essential passageway . . . The philosophy of a people is that which makes people people of a philosophy, grounds them historically in their Da-sein, and destines them to stewardship of the truth of being."[41] The role of the "people," and especially the German people, in Heidegger's thinking during the 1930s and early-1940s, is a key element in the problematic character of the being-historical thinking that occurs in the *Contributions* and elsewhere.[42] History is itself tied to a "people," as is the truth of being, and so the event is also thought in these same terms.

In 1956, Heidegger comments, in regard to "The Origin of the Work of Art," that "the relationship of being to human being . . . is inadequately thought even in this presentation—a distressing difficulty that has been clear to me since *Being and Time*."[43] This is not, however, a difficulty that affects only the understanding of the role of the artist or poet in relation to the artwork as a "setting to work of truth" (which is the focus for Heidegger's comment in 1956), but also the understanding of the role of a "people" in relation to being and to thinking, and perhaps even the understanding of being in its relation to history. The place of thinking that opens up for Heidegger, in 1936, is thus a place that still remains properly to be thought—which is, of course, why he can refer, as he does in the *Notebooks*, to those "aberrations and attempts" that nevertheless accompany his wandering in that place.[44] The shift that occurs in Heidegger's thinking around 1936, radical though it is, does not, then, overcome all of the difficulties that were present in 1933. It is not just that Heidegger retains, for instance, a nationalist proclivity that is part of his personal "affectivity" (Heidegger always remains, to a greater or lesser extent, a German nationalist, even after he has explicitly recognized the problematic character of nationalism), but that the very fact that his thinking in 1936 is so much driven by the need to re-think the terms of his thinking up to 1934, and especially of 1932–33, means that the philosophical thinking of the mid- to late-1930s remains partly entangled with a set of concepts that are, in themselves, problematic—no matter how they are rethought.

What first appears in the *Notebooks* in late 1934, and in the *Contributions* a little later, is a mode of topology that thinks place (or at least place in the guise of the "there/here") being-historically—the *place* of being, even though that place is not yet named as such, is understood as the *history* of being. As such, the thinking that develops from 1934 onwards does not represent the abandonment of a concern with the relation between being and history, but instead turns more directly towards it and towards its philosophical re-conceptualization. It is this more radical turn towards being-historical thinking in the mid-1930s to early-1940s that partly explains why the anti-Semitism that can be seen in the *Notebooks* (and it is perhaps significant that it is directly evident *only* in the *Notebooks*) appears *after* Heidegger's break with Nazism. It was not sympathy with anti-Semitism that drew Heidegger to Hitler. It was rather Heidegger's projection onto National Socialism of his own revolutionary philosophical vision—a vision intimately tied to a conception of the world-historical role of Germany in philosophical and not only political terms. Heidegger's anti-Semitism belongs, therefore, with the more radical being-historical thinking that emerges in 1934–36 and is an artefact of what, I would argue, is Heidegger's misconstrual of the topology of being in terms of the history of being (as well as his misconstrual of history as that which encompasses and is expressed through "peoples" and their destinies). In this respect, Heidegger's anti-Semitism, understood philosophically, is itself tied up with his anti-Nazism. To see this, however, is also to see that the anti-Semitism and the anti-Nazism are both driven by the same mode of *being-historical* "topology," and not the other way around. Moreover, as being-historical, the topology at issue here is already problematic *as a topology* since it puts place, to some extent, under the sway of history (which is not itself properly interrogated), while at the same time leaves place only indirectly thematized.

The Turn (Back) to Place

One of the striking features of Heidegger's thinking of the mid- to late-1930s and early 1940s, compared to that of the mid- to late 1940s and after, is the degree to which the history of being takes on a much more muted character in the later period. Indeed, the history of being largely drops away just as the topology of being comes more explicitly to the fore, and, as it drops away, so too does the language of a "people" also disappear. In 1969, Heidegger is clear on the mistaken character of being-historical thinking, telling his audience at Le Thor: "Thinking *Ereignis* with the concepts of being and the history of being will not be successful; nor will it be with the assistance of the Greeks (which is precisely something 'to go beyond'). With being, the ontological difference also vanishes . . . ."[45] The *Notebooks* suggest, however, that Heidegger's negative assessment of the history of being is not peculiar to 1969. In an entry in the *Notebooks* from 1946–47, he writes: "In a lucid moment, I suddenly recognized that getting over being [*Verwindung des Seyns*], I had also given up philosophy and historiography [*Historie*]. But it still needed some time to understand that with this 'history' [*Geschichte*] had been dropped too."[46] And again, with explicit reference to the *Ereignis* itself: "Nothing happens in the *Ereignis*. There is neither happening nor destiny [*Geschick*] . . . In the *Ereignis*, the essence of history is abandoned. Talk of the history of beings is an embarrassment and a euphemism."[47]

This is not to say that every form of the history of being disappears from Heidegger's late topological thinking. There is still a history that belongs to the attempt to think the place of being, but this history concerns only two elements: the different ways in which the thinking of the place of being has been thought, and the way that thinking, in its metaphysical tendency, is expressed in the rise of technological modernity and the current "plight" of the world. Moreover, the history at issue here is not the history of a "people" but the history *of thinking*—which, as such, provides the place for a thoughtful dialogue that reflects on the very place, of thinking and of being, that is essentially at issue. In the thinking of the mid- to late-1940s and after, one might say that the idea of the "people" has dropped away in favor simply of a new (or perhaps recuperated) thinking of the "human"—a point especially evident in the "Letter on 'Humanism.'" The human, however, is now thought, not from the *history* of being (which is to say, not from "peoples"), but from the *place* of being—from topology.

It is precisely the latter that is, of course, the other striking feature of Heidegger's thinking in the mid- to late-1940s onwards: the more explicitly topological character of that thinking. This is especially so in respect of the entries in the *Notebooks* from this period. One of the simplest ways of demonstrating this is by looking to the occurrences of the term *Ortschaft* in the *Notebooks* from 1942 through 1948, compared to, for instance, the *Contributions*. As I noted above, neither *Ortschaft* nor *Ort* appears in any significant way in the *Contributions*—*Ortschaft* appearing not at all—and yet in the *Notebooks*, *Ortschaft* appears over sixty times (almost all in books II–IV of the 1942–48 volume). The fact that place is implicitly at issue in the *Contributions* and earlier is evident in the centrality of the "there/here," the *Da*. Yet so long as place is approached only or primarily by means of the there/here, it is all too readily interpretable by means of other concepts that can easily obscure the topology at issue. With the appearance of *Ortschaft* as a key term, place is brought directly to the fore. And while *Ortschaft* is a key term in the *Notebooks* of the 1940s, as well as in other late works, *Ort* also emerges as important, all the more so in some of lectures and essays of the 1950s and 1960s. But whichever term is at issue, the same mode of topology seems to be at work. From the mid- to late-1940s onwards, Heidegger's thinking can be understood as focused on the attempt to delineate the place—*topos*, *Ort*, *Ortschaft*—of being. It is thus that Heidegger can designate *Ort*, which he explicitly connects with *topos*, as the term that names the third and most important stage on the path of thinking.[48]

In the thinking after 1946, it is clear that even the event has to be understood in close relation to *place*—whether *Ortschaft* or *Ort*—and it is significant that the *Notebooks* from the 1940s contain many references to "the place of the event" (*Ortschaft der Ereignisses*). The analysis of the event in terms of the fourfold, *das Geviert* (which appears for the first time in the Bremen Lectures in 1949,[49] but which is adumbrated in the *Contributions*,[50] as it is also in "The Origin of the Work of Art"), reinforces this point, since the fourfold is itself an articulation of the structure of place in the gathering of earth and sky, gods and mortals in and through the thing. As gathering and appropriation, both the fourfold and the event belong essentially to the bounded opening that is place—to the "there/here" as well as to the world. One might argue that Heidegger's connecting of the event to the *Es gibt* (literally "it gives")[51] can, in turn, be connected to the "given-ness" that belongs to place and to the way place itself "gives" place. It is not insignificant that the German phrase is normally translated into English by a phrase that calls upon the "there"—*Es gibt* becomes "there is." So often regarded as inadequate, the translation can, in this sense, be seen as offering its own form of illumination. One might even say that the connection between the *Es gibt* and place is already suggested by the Greek understanding of place that is evident in the idea, not merely of *topos*, but also of *chora*. The *chora* is indeed that which supports and sustains, that which allows for appearance by offering its own withdrawal, that which sets free both space and time so as to allow for the lingering of presence.[52]

The dropping away of the emphasis on the history of being and the more topological orientation both appear in Heidegger's postwar thinking along with a more meditative or contemplative stance—one that is often taken to imply a form of "quietism." Certainly, there is a clear difference in tone, as well as in language, when the writing that appears in the *Contributions* and the *Notebooks* of the 1930s and early 1940s is compared with the writings of the late 1940s onwards. Daniela Valega-Neu describes the way in which Heidegger's writing in the *Notebooks* of the 1930s is pervaded by "struggle" (*Kampf*)—"a word," she says, "that abounds in all of Heidegger's *Notebooks*," and she adds that "there are clear indications that for him this struggle is akin to the Heraclitean *polemos*."[53] Along with struggle is an emphasis on endurance, resistance, and refusal, and a style that is declamatory, even, in the Old Testament sense, "prophetic" (perhaps even more so than it is "poetic").[54] In contrast, by the late 1940s, Heidegger's thinking has shed almost all of this and instead takes on a calmer and more questioning tone (even though it remains pessimistic about modernity); rather than a decisive saying, the thinking of the postwar period has the character of an attentive responding—even, as Heidegger sometimes emphasizes, a listening—which is indeed why it is rightly perceived as having a more mediative or contemplative character.[55]

Once again, as with the shift in his thinking that occurs from 1934 through 1936, one might say that this is the outcome of a set of *situational* factors—the end of the war, Germany's defeat, and Heidegger's loss of the right to teach and his subsequent breakdown—but this does not take away from the fact that what is at issue is a philosophical shift that can also be seen as underpinned by a set of *philosophical* considerations. The shift from the history of being to a more direct engagement with the topology of being brings with it a different philosophical comportment that can be understood as coming from a sense of attentiveness to place, a sense of attentiveness that is also tied to a proper responsiveness. This is what Heidegger eventually comes to call, taking the term from the thirteenth century mystic Meister Eckhart, *Gelassenheit*—releasement— which is not to be understood as quietistic, but rather as a different mode of *engagement* (see the discussion in chapter 10).[56] It is as if, in 1936, when Heidegger first finds that "place of thinking" for which he was searching, he is nevertheless not yet able to orient himself in and to that place. It is not until 1946 that he can identify the place at issue as the place it is, and only then can his thinking find its proper orientation in that place—and only then can it speak in a more considered and genuinely reflective fashion.

The Difficulty of Place

As one of the two epigrams to "Art and Space" (the other is from Lichtenburg), Heidegger takes a line from Aristotle's *Physics* IV: "It appears however to be something overwhelming and hard to grasp, the *topos*"[57]—although Heidegger adds, as a gloss on *topos*, "that is, place-space [*Ort-Raum*]."[58] That he does not translate *topos* only as place (*Ort*) is indicative both of the fact that the Greek term does not involve a differentiation between place and space (something also true of the French *espace*), and that Heidegger's own interest is in the way space, *Raum*, belongs with place (*Ort*). Nevertheless, the fact that both space and place may be taken to be at issue in *topos* in no way takes away from the essentially topological character of the inquiry that follows after Heidegger's quoting of this line. In drawing attention to the difficulty of the thinking at issue here, Heidegger draws attention to a difficulty that is not only evident in the history of philosophy, but also to a difficulty evident (and surely experienced) in his own thought. The idea of place is there in Heidegger's thinking from the beginning, and yet the difficulty that it presents means that Heidegger has to find his way back to place—it is the finding of that way back that constitutes his path of thinking. And even when Heidegger seems to have found his way, still place remains obscure and obscured, still there is a tendency for his thinking to wander "in aberration and attempt."

One might say that some of the difficulty for the thinking of place that Heidegger attempts derives from the fact that German has no single term that serves to refer to place in the sort of encompassing way that is true of the English "place"—the latter seeming to capture the idea of both openness and bound without bringing any more specific or technical meaning with it. Both *Ortschaft* and *Ort*, while they share some of the sense that belongs with "place," also tend to have more specific connotations. It is perhaps not surprising, then, that it takes Heidegger some time to come to understand his thinking *as a topology*. German has, one might say, too differentiated a vocabulary when it comes to place: *Ortschaft, Ort, Statte, Platz, Gegend, Bereich*, as well as a range of related terms on which Heidegger draws such as *Da, Zwischen, Offene*. Yet English (which also has its own varied range of topological and spatial terms aside from "place") offers only a partial advantage here, and perhaps no real advantage at all, since the very breadth of the English "place" also means that it is a term all too readily seen as vague, as lacking in real content, as in need of reduction to the more specific notions of "space," and especially of "physical space" (which is what most often occurs in English-language discussions of place). The truth is that every attempt to address place must arise out of and contend with its own place—and that must include the very place that is given in language. Whether we speak Greek, German, English, or any other language, the task of addressing place will always be difficult—as it is always difficult to turn back to that in which we always already are. Moreover, this reflects a more general feature of thinking; namely, that it is opened up to that which is to be thought only through its own being placed, which also means its own boundedness—even, one might say, its own delimitation.

It is because the possibilities of thinking arise out of the bounds of thinking that those possibilities always include the possibility of failure—even that those possibilities must inevitably lead to failure of one sort or another. Heidegger's thinking, as the development of that thinking through the *Notebooks* shows, is no less affected by its place, and so by the bounds and limits that belong to it, than any other thinking, and neither is it any less prone to failure. Thus, in Heidegger's case, one sees not only the possibilities for thinking, but also its failure as one such possibility (a failure that may be more or less problematic)—in 1927, in 1933, in 1936, and even in 1946. Although it is the boundedness of thinking that makes thinking possible, the failures that are inevitable in thinking are never such as to completely determine that thinking—at least not if that thinking is indeed thoughtful (if it is, indeed, *thinking*). Consequently, one does not read a thinker only though their failures, but *despite* them, and what matters is not whether a thinker fails but whether their thinking remains captured by that failure or moves beyond it. Whatever we might say about Heidegger's ability to face up to his personal and philosophical failures publicly, to acknowledge or even to apologize for them, the evidence of the *Notebooks*, and of the course of his thinking over his already published work, demonstrates that he was not entirely captured by those failures but retained the capacity to think and re-think. It is thus the passage of Heidegger's thinking—the path or way along which it moves and the direction of that path—that matters more than any one stage that might be part of it. This is, of course, true of place: it is to be seen, not in any one aspect or picture, but in the movements and directions that are possible both within and from it. Perhaps we should say that part of the real significance of the *Notebooks* is in showing the place of Heidegger's thinking in just this sense—in showing the movements and directions that belong to that place—and in bringing that very place to the fore. It is largely for that reason that this discussion has to come at the very start of this book. Although Heidegger is a thinker of place from the very beginning, it is out of the thinking that emerges into clarity in the late 1940s that the topological character of Heidegger's thinking becomes explicit.

Two

The "Anthropology" of the World

Figure 1. Martin Heidegger and René Char in Provence. Photo by Roger Munier, date unknown (most likely during one of the Le Thor seminars, between 1966 and 1969). Reproduced by kind permission of Jacques Munier.

Martin Heidegger visited Paris for the first time in 1955. To Jean Beaufret, who organized the visit, Heidegger made one key request: "While in France," he wrote, "I would really like to meet Georges Braque and René Char."[1] The meeting with Braque seems to have been pleasant enough, but quite inconsequential.² That with Char, on the other hand, gave rise to a lasting friendship, both personal and intellectual, and to an engagement with the landscape of Provence that, for Heidegger, was deeply affecting. Facilitated by a common relation to Beaufret, their friendship was maintained through correspondence as well as Heidegger's visits to Provence, including to Char's home. On hearing of Heidegger's death in 1976, Char wrote: "Martin Heidegger died this morning. The sun has laid him to rest along with his tools. Only the work remains. The threshold is constant. The night opens itself with love."³ The French edition of *On the Way to Language*—*Acheminement vers la parole*—appeared a few months later. The book contained a dedication by Heidegger to Char. In that dedication, Heidegger asks whether "beloved Provence" might not be "the secretive/invisible bridge from the early thinking/ of Parmenides to the poetry of Hölderlin."⁴ For a thinker whose work comes explicitly to be framed as a "topology of being" (*Topologie des Seyns*), and so as giving a key role to the idea of place (*Ort, Ortschaft*), Heidegger's engagement with Provence is especially significant—all the more so, perhaps, given that it is in Provence, at the seminar in Le Thor in 1969, that Heidegger first draws explicit and public attention to his thinking as just such a topology.⁵

The way place is at issue here—both the specific place, Provence, and place as a fundamental idea in thinking—is directly connected to Heidegger's involvement with Char and the poetical-philosophical concerns that were important, though not exclusively so, in bringing them together. Those concerns encompass the nature of language and of poetry, as well as of the relation between language and being—both of which come to the fore in Heidegger's thinking at the same time as the focus on place becomes more salient. But at issue here, too, is the matter of place itself, its own relation to being, and the way all of this relates to the being of the human. Moreover, what the "human" is here cannot be assumed. The human is both the one who questions *and* the one who is in question. The human thus participates in opening a site for questioning, rather than being the already understood starting point from which such questioning can proceed.

As is already evident from chapter 1, the relation between being, place, and the human is a recurrent theme in Heidegger's thinking, even if not always clearly expressed in the work prior to 1946–47. In Char, the character of human existence is also a central focus. It is present in powerful fashion, for instance, in Char's poems on the cave paintings at Lascaux.⁶ Always, for Char, it is the human relation to *earth* that is foremost. "[M]an," he says, "is only a flower of air held by the earth, cursed by the stars, inhaled by death,"⁷ and, as his close friend, Albert Camus, also writes, "the earth remains our first and last love."⁸ Here, to talk of earth is also to talk of place—place is of the earth, but so too is earth of place (the relationship between place and earth is, however, a complex one that goes well beyond what can be dealt with here). The thinking of the human, and of the human situation, is thus present, in Char and Camus, in a way intimately tied to both earth and place, and so also to landscape, and especially to the landscapes of Provence, and in Camus's case, Algeria. As Camus writes at the end of one of the essays in *Nuptials*, "How can one consecrate the harmony of love and revolt? The earth! In this great temple deserted by the gods, all my idols have feet of clay."⁹ This love of the earth and of place is part of the "Mediterranean humanism" with which Camus and Char are often identified.¹⁰ Such "Mediterraneanism" is evocative of and undoubtedly influenced by, certain topological elements in Nietzsche's thinking.¹¹ It has also been taken, at least by one pair of commentators, to be present in Heidegger.¹² In Provence, then, not only are Heidegger and Char, as well as Camus, drawn together within a single landscape, but so too are a set of key philosophical and poetic concerns—including the question of the human, as well as the relation between philosophy and poetry.

Thinkers and Poets

It is poetry that first brings Heidegger together with Char.¹³ Poetry does not mean merely the making of verse but rather designates a mode of thinking. If Provence is a bridge between Parmenides and Hölderlin, then it is a bridge between two poet-thinkers or thinker-poets. Indeed, in a birthday note to Char from 1971, Heidegger asks whether the work of Cézanne, itself powerfully located in the landscape of Provence and especially of Mont Sainte-Victoire,¹⁴ might point towards just such a joining of poetry and thinking: "In the late work of the painter the twofoldness /of what is present and of presence has become/one, 'realised' and overcome at the same time, / transformed into a mystery-filled identity. / Is a path revealed here, which leads to / a belonging-together of poetry and thought?"¹⁵ These words surely evoke the relation between Heidegger and Char, but no less do they point towards the intimacy of the relation between poetry and thinking in the work of each of them and between poetry and thinking as such. Moreover, when Heidegger talks, as he does in his dedicatory comments to *Acheminement vers la parole*, of Provence as a bridge joining Parmenides and Hölderlin, his choice of names—of just these two thinker-poets (or poet-thinkers)—is enormously significant. Parmenides and Hölderlin each stands in a special relationship, as Heidegger sees it, to the beginnings of thinking (such beginnings being themselves closely bound up with the poetic). Each stands in a relationship to the *first beginning*, which is also the Greek beginning and so the beginning with which Parmenides is closely identified, and to the *other beginning*, which remains before us and of which Hölderlin is named by Heidegger as the prophet. This idea of the two beginnings is something to which I shall return more directly in the epilogue, but it is also relevant to the discussion here, so let me pre-empt a little of what is to come later.

Just as poetry is more than verse, so "thinking," as used here, does not name merely some form of mental activity. Instead, it retains an essential multivocity in which it is impossible completely to separate the several voices that it encompasses. Thus, thinking refers to something thinkers do—a thinking of the sort that Parmenides or Hölderlin enacts. It refers to something that happens historically, that takes the form of an event and activity that belongs to a tradition and a culture, and so to that which can be said to have a historical origin, in a European setting, with the Greeks. In this sense, thinking is something in which the individual thinker is taken up through participation in a tradition of thinking, and this is as true for Parmenides as for Heidegger since both participate in the individual activity of thinking and its historical movement. But "thinking" also refers to something that is the ground for both—to that original opening and orienting that allows any sort of appearance or presence whatsoever—and this is a theme that runs through many of the chapters in this volume.

There is, therefore, an original topology that belongs to thinking in virtue of its own "dimensional" character—a "dimensionality" that precedes time and space, as ordinarily understood, and is the first opening of that free and yet bounded domain in which thought, and that which is thought, emerges. This dimensionality, and so the thinking that belongs with it, is not the dimensionality merely of any ordinary place, yet it only ever comes to pass in the singularity of *this* place—wherever that may be. This dimensionality belongs to the opening of place as it precedes and portends every place in its singular appearance. Poetic thinking is the thinking that moves within this dimensionality at the same time as it also remains in awareness of it. Poetic thinking, which is to say all essential thinking as Heidegger understands it, is thus a form of recollection of place—a constant returning to that in which it is grounded and out of which it emerges—and so, for Heidegger, thinking, *Denken*, does indeed take the form of remembrance, *Andenken*.[16]

Significantly, the way the idea of the beginning figures in Heidegger's talk of both the "first" and the "other" beginning is not simply in terms of a temporal origin or starting point. The beginning is also a place, even a "dwelling-place" (*Aufenthalt*) that gives shelter to thinking, that sustains and nurtures it. At its most basic, it is the oriented situatedness that grounds emergence. In this sense, the idea of a beginning to thinking connects directly with the ideas of place and dimensionality that belong to thinking itself. Inasmuch as thinking is always a recollection or remembrance, then it is so, not in the sense of a recuperation of what is merely past, but rather a recuperation of that wherein we already are. The two beginnings are both turned towards the place of thinking in this way. Yet the two beginnings involve two different forms of recollection or remembrance.

The first beginning is a recollection that, for all that it is indeed a recollection of its own proper place, nevertheless leads towards a covering-over of its character as a recollection, and so an obscuring of its place. Thus, Greek thought is already, as Heidegger sees it, set on the path of metaphysics. But there is the possibility of another beginning to thinking that retains a sense of its own character as a recollecting in the face of forgetting. As Joseph Fell writes:

> The "first beginning" is the "other beginning" disowned or disguised . . . for Heidegger, Being is appearing in place . . . Our history has been sentenced to a dissimulation or displacement of this place and hence of the nature of Being itself . . . The proper future of ontology is not an advance to something essentially new but a remembering of the event of the place in which things have always appeared and can appear.[17]

The path that is opened by the possibility of this other beginning, which is only presaged and not yet realized, is one that moves from Hölderlin, or from that place Hölderlin points toward, *back* towards Parmenides.

(Heidegger says, at Le Thor, that "it is not a question of returning to Parmenides. Nothing more is required than to *turn towards* Parmenides."[18]) It is a genuine reversal in that we are thereby opened, not to any simple *repetition* of the first beginning, but rather to the possibility of the other beginning as it may even be presaged in Parmenides.

The first of the seminars at Le Thor, that from 1966,[19] is significant for the way in which it proceeds almost as a conversation with Char. Almost all of the issues it addresses are issues that emerge in Char no less than in Heidegger—the nature of language, the human relation to world, the idea of presence, including the explicit invoking of Char's notion of "common presence" (*commune présence*), the character of difference and the relation of opposites—and it includes several references to and quotations from Char's poetry.[20] But one of the two figures on whom the seminar is focused is Parmenides (the other being Heraclitus, with whom Char had a close identification). In this respect, even though it might initially seem to take us away from the landscape of Provence, and so might be thought to constitute something of a digression, it is worth paying some closer attention to Parmenides and the Heideggerian reading of Parmenides.

Despite its lack of any explicit thematization of place, Parmenides's thinking exhibits a topological character that is embedded both in its poetic framing and in its key ideas. Parmenides recounts a journey to "the halls of Night," where he is given welcome by a goddess (presumably Night herself—elsewhere in Greek mythology, a counselor to Zeus—or, as Heidegger would have it, *Aletheia*, Truth[21]) who, in that divine setting, then reveals to Parmenides, in a series of almost oracular pronouncements, the ways of truth and of opinion. The topological character and presentation evident here are reinforced when one views the poem as containing echoes of the culminating events in the process of initiation into the mysteries in which would-be initiates were led, often in a state of confusion, disorientation, and even blindness, through a space or series of spaces towards a sudden and dramatic revelation in the presence of the divine—at Eleusis, in the presence of the goddess.[22] As Plutarch describes such initiation:

> In the beginning there is straying and wandering, the weariness of running this way and that, and nervous journeys through darkness that reach no goal, and then immediately before the consummation every possible terror, shivering and trembling

and sweating and amazement. But after this a marvelous light meets the wanderer, and open country and meadow lands welcome him; and in that place there are voices and dancing and the solemn majesty of sacred music and holy visions.[23]

In the poem, as in the initiation (and, as Plutarch also says, in life itself), we are indeed taken on a journey and brought to a place. In that place, we come into the presence of truth—truth in the form of the goddess, in the bestowal of a vision, and in the opening of the place itself.

Heidegger's account of Parmenides is advanced in greatest detail in what were originally the lecture courses that make up *An Introduction to Metaphysics*,[24] from 1935, and *What Is Called Thinking*, from 1951 through 1952 (including, in the latter case, the undelivered part of the lecture that appears in *Early Greek Thinking*[25]). Although the exact path of Heidegger's discussion varies between the two lectures, and despite the seventeen years or so that separates them, a similar view is evident in each (much the same view also appears in the discussion in the first of the LeThor seminars): the elucidation of Parmenides's poem as an attempt at thinking the unfolding of being (*eon*) in its twofold character as the presencing of what is present. This twofold occurs in the form of unconcealment (*aletheia*) in a way that implicates both saying and thinking (*legein* and *noein*), and Heidegger gives special attention to Parmenides's assertion of the belonging together of being and thinking—"the same: to be and to think"[26]—in a way that can be seen to direct us towards exactly the sort of topology already indicated in the discussion above. The human is explicitly implicated in the structure at issue here, since "the question of Being necessarily includes the grounding of Dasein."[27] But, at the same time, the way the human is drawn into what is at issue is not as that which determines or grounds, but instead as indeed that which is itself grounded.

Just as he does elsewhere, the language Heidegger uses in his discussion of Parmenides is itself thoroughly topological—a language of gathering, grounding, opening up, letting-lie-before, bringing-forward-into-view. The very idea of the presencing of what is present is a notion that already brings with it a certain happening of place, a happening of the there/here (the *Da*). Yet, if we turn back to Parmenides's own text, we may also see a mode of topology at work, not only in its framing, but also in its very account of being. Being is understood as one, as unitary, and also as bounded[28]—like "a rounded sphere."[29] It is precisely such bounded unity that is characteristic of place.[30] Parmenides can thus be read, if perhaps somewhat unconventionally, as drawing us back to an understanding of being, not in terms of some unitary "reality" that stands behind or apart from appearances, or into which all beings are submerged, but rather as the presencing of what is present (to use Heidegger's phrase) in its own bounded singularity.

Heidegger's account of Parmenides seems implicitly to move in this latter direction—and not in any merely metaphorical fashion either, since what is at issue here is that original and originary mode of place that underlies any other sense, and of which place, in its more ordinary senses, is derivative. It is thus significant that, in his discussion in *Introduction to Metaphysics*, and in direct relation to his treatment of Parmenides, Heidegger makes a distinction between two senses of appearing or presencing as these relate to space:

> Considered in terms of the essence of space, appearing has two meanings . . . appearing in the first and authentic sense, as the gathered bringing-itself-to-stand, takes space in; it first conquers space; as standing there, it creates space for itself, it brings about everything that belongs to it . . . ; Appearing in the second sense merely steps forth from an already prepared space, and it is viewed by a looking-at within the already fixed dimensions of this space.[31]

Even though Heidegger does not talk of "place" here, the way he characterizes the first sense of appearing draws on what is a necessarily topological set of ideas and images—the "gathered bringing-itself-to-stand" which "standing there . . . creates space for itself."

The difference between these two modes of appearing is based in a difference between the space that arises out of place as the openness granted by the "there" and the space understood as the already present dimension to which every place and every there, and so every appearance, has already been assigned. The first of these is what is at issue in Parmenides and in Heidegger. In his later discussion, as it appears in *Early Greek Thinking*, Heidegger writes explicitly of place in the sense of *topos*: "Ordinary perception . . . never perceives place, τόπος, as an abode [*Aufenthalt*] as what the twofold offers as a home to the presencing of what is present . . . the ordinary opinion of mortals merely follows the 'here and there' . . . of particular 'places.'"[32] Here, Heidegger distinguishes between two modes of place—one is the ordinary everyday mode in which we talk of this or that place, and the other is a more basic but less commonly recognized mode according to which place is the "home" of "presencing and what is present." The latter is surely what is at issue in Heidegger's earlier reference to appearing as it occurs in the "standing-there" that gives rise to space. Yet, though these two modes of place are distinct, and we often give no heed to the more basic mode that Heidegger here invokes, they also make up a twofold of their own: the place that gives "home" to presencing and presence is not some transcendent "idea" that stands outside of the world and things but is rather always and "everywhere" evident in the happening of place in its ordinary and everyday sense. It was especially evident for Heidegger and for Char in the places and landscapes of Provence.

Here, in This Place

At the Le Thor seminar in 1969, Heidegger responded to the opening words of welcome with an expression of his deep attachment to the place in which the meeting was gathered:

> Why am I speaking here in Aix-en-Provence? I love the gentleness of this country and its villages. I love the severity of its mountains. I love the harmony of both. I love Aix, Bibemus, the Sainte-Victoire mountains. I have found the path of Paul Cézanne here, which, from its beginning to its end, corresponds in a way to my own way of thinking. I love this country with its sea-coast because it announces its proximity to Greece. I love all of this because I am convinced that there is no essential work of the mind that is not rooted in an original groundedness [*Bodenständigkeit*].[33]

It is commonplace for the idea of "groundedness," *Bodenständigkeit*, which appears here and recurs throughout Heidegger's work, to be treated as indicative of a conservative nostalgia for the land of one's birth. There are occasions in Heidegger's writings from the 1930s when he does appear to give the term a problematic and nationalistic tone, but those occasions seem to be the exception rather than the rule, and it cannot be assumed that this carries over to the appearances of the term in his later work. Moreover, what is at issue in Heidegger's remarks in 1969 is his attachment to a place in which he was not born, but into which he had been "naturalized," to which he had, in a sense, become "native," a place in which he had found a certain ground. Perhaps all such "groundedness" is like this—not given merely by an accident of birth, but something that one must grow into, something that arises out of an involvement with and participation in.

In Heidegger's case, that "becoming native" was undoubtedly a product of his close identification with and love for Cézanne, whose own work is so deeply embedded in the landscape of Provence, as well as of his friendship with Char, and the active involvement with the countryside and its people that brought with it.[34] But it also seems to have arisen out of a conviction on Heidegger's part that, somehow, there was in Provence—in its mountains, coasts, and towns—a sense of the Greek, even if an imagined sense (though what this means should not be presumed),[35] and so a sense of the place in which Western philosophy, which, despite everything, remained Heidegger's intellectual homeland, had begun. For Char, Provence was the place in which he was born, but not only that. It was also where he worked and lived over much of his life. It was a place in and for which he had fought, a place where friends had died. It was also a place for which he had a deep affection. He writes, more specifically, of L'Isle-sur-la-Sorgue: "I am in love with this tender patch of countryside, with its armrest of solitude, at whose edge storms come gently undone, on whose mast a lost face for an instant lights up and reaches me again."[36]

In Camus, too, one finds a similar expression of this love for a place—and not only as some personal sentiment, but as also encompassing an existential or ontological condition:

> To feel one's ties to a land, one's love for certain men, to know there is always a place where the heart can find rest—these are already many certainties for one man's life. Doubtless they are not enough. But at certain moments everything yearns for this homeland of the soul. "Yes, it is to this we must return." What is strange about finding here on earth the unity Plotinus longed for? Unity expresses itself here in terms of sea and sky. The heart senses it through a certain taste of the flesh that constitutes its bitterness and greatness. I am learning that there is no superhuman happiness, not eternity outside the curve of the days. These ridiculous and essential assets, these relative truths are the only ones that move me.[37]

In Camus, as well as in Char, the felt attachment to a place is tied to a felt sense of human being as inextricably bound to "these ridiculous and essential assets, these relative truths" that are given in earth, in flesh, in sea and sky, in the very places that give shape and substance to our lives. Human being is thus tied to that which is given according to a certain measure and within the bounds of the earth. Significantly, the emphasis here is less on the idea of one's own *identity* as determined by the landscape to which one's life is tied—though this is not absent—as on the way the very *possibility* of that life is grounded in a mode of being-in-place, and so, too, the way the possibility of that life is grounded in that which is singular and transient, which is bounded and subject to "measure" (in respect of the latter, Camus often uses the Greek term *sophrosune*, which also means "moderation").[38] Here, for Camus and Char, is also where one finds beauty, and not in just one place above others but in every place: "In our shadows, there is not one place alone for Beauty. The whole place is for Beauty."[39]

To talk of "groundedness," as Heidegger does, even of our belonging to or our love for a landscape or the "earth," is by no means always to resort to a conservative cliché nor simply to affirm some parochial nationalism.[40] Indeed, in this context, such talk should be read as carrying connotations of the place that belongs to thinking (and to which thinking belongs) that is at issue in the first and other beginnings. Yet even were we to remain suspicious of what Heidegger refers to by such talk of "groundedness," even were we to suppose that there are versions of the attachment to place, no matter how they arise, that are associated with problematic modes of life and thought, still it remains possible to rethink what is at issue here and to reappropriate it to a different use and sense. And that might be especially important inasmuch as we cannot simply shrug off the fundamental matters that are at stake here. Just as what is at issue is not the mere fact of the location that may be recorded on a certificate of birth, neither is it a matter merely of cultural or ethnic identity as these may be expressed in terms of specific places or landscapes. Rather, what is at stake is that prior belonging to the world that is the basis for the very possibility of our having a world—and so for our having of a culture, an identity (however articulated), even a life. For some, it may be preferable to ignore or turn away from that prior belonging-to—perhaps out of a sense of political rectitude, as if ignoring or refusing it would also erase it—but to turn away in this fashion is nothing but a turn into what is essentially a form of bad faith. Whether we like it or not, our being-in-the world is always also a being-in-place—a place that is singular and concrete. Our being here is always a being-here, in *this* place, wherever it may be.[41]

What is at issue here is eloquently expressed in a famous passage from a letter by Hölderlin to his friend Casimir Böhlendorf in 1802. The letter is quoted by Heidegger, in its entirety, in his 1959 essay, "Hölderlin's Heaven and Earth." Speaking of the experience of the natural landscape around his German home, Hölderlin writes:

> Nature in these home regions moves me more powerfully, the more I study it. The thunderstorm, not only in its highest appearance, but precisely in its guise as a power and shape, among the other forms of heaven, light in its effects, nationally and as a principle that fashions a mode of destiny, so that something is holy to us, its urgency in coming and going, what is characteristic of the forests and the convergence in one region of different characters of nature, so that all the holy places are together around one place, and the philosophical light around my window is now my joy; and may I keep in mind how I have come as far as here.[42]

Hölderlin's focus here is not merely the experience of "nature" as it might be understood to be distinct from the "human," but rather of nature as a fundamental mode of appearing—as more akin to what Heidegger understands to be encompassed by the Greek *physis* (something taken up in more detail in chapter 3)—and, together with this, of the experience of such appearing as an experience *of place* in its singularity.[43] Moreover, none of this is reducible, once again, to any simple notion of the "native" or the "national" as it might be tied to spurious notions of exclusionary identity (part of what is striking is indeed the sense of *inclusion*—"all the holy places are together around one place"). Although Hölderlin does indeed invoke a sense of identity—of "destiny" and national character—it is a sense of identity understood in terms of the activity and vibrancy of that specific landscape in which one is already embedded, and with which one is already familiar—an identity determined, shaped, formed, and worked out only in relation to the complexities of one's surroundings, in a dynamic interaction that involves others, as well as oneself, in a complex relationality that encompasses difference as well as sameness, responsiveness as well as activity, listening as well as speech. It is also a sense of identity that is tied, as in Camus, to the way one stands amidst a world that extends beyond one's own horizons and yet is always manifest here, in this place.

In Proximity to Greece

The letter in which the passage quoted by Heidegger appears was written by Hölderlin shortly after his return from France, where he had gone to take up a position as a tutor in Bordeaux. Hölderlin made the entire journey on foot, both to Bordeaux from his family home in Nürtingen (part of what was then the Duchy of Württemberg) and then back again, traveling, first, through Lyon and the Auvergne and, then, on the return, through Paris. Hölderlin never saw Provence, but the "southern" regions through which he passed on his journey left a powerful impression. In a passage immediately before his description of nature in his home region, he writes of how, "in the regions bordering on the Vendée," he encountered "a quality fiercely war-like, and purely masculine, to which the light of life becomes immediate in eye and limb, which experiences the feeling of death like a kind of virtuosity and satisfies its thirst for knowledge." And he goes on to speak of how "the athletic character of the southern people, in the ruins of the spirit of antiquity, made me more familiar with the authentic essence of the Greeks."[44]

The way Hölderlin here invokes the Greeks connects directly with Heidegger's own talk of the "proximity to Greece" that he finds in the landscape of Provence. A similar invocation of the Greek is evident in Camus[45] as well as Char. For both, the idea of Greece, expressed through the experience of a Mediterranean landscape and climate, is directly connected to a certain philosophical-poetic sensibility. As Camus writes:

> The Mediterranean has its solar tragedy which is not that of the mists. There are evenings, at the foot of the mountains by the sea, when night falls on the perfect curve of a little bay, and an anguished fullness rises from the silent waters. Such moments make one realize that if the Greeks knew despair, they experienced it always through beauty and its oppressive quality. In this golden sadness, tragedy reaches its highest point.[46]

"Tragedy" here does not refer to a particular dramatic or literary form, but rather to the same existential or ontological condition that was at issue in the passage from Camus quoted earlier; namely, the character of human being in the world as always lived within the fullness established by limit. Beauty is thus always accompanied by a sense of fragility, transience, and even loss—happiness never comes but without a taste of melancholy (and so "tragedy" here is also associated with a willingness to embrace opposition and difference—evident in Char's avowal of his affinity with Heraclitus).

It is this sense of beauty and of limit, of the exuberance of life and existence as given only within the bounds of the world, that Camus identifies as characteristically Greek, and that he also sees as embodied in, and expressed through, a Mediterranean landscape of sea and sky. In "Hymn in a Quiet Voice," Char writes of Greece in terms that emphasize much the same sensibility:

> The Hellades, the extended shore of an inspired sea, whence at dawn were launched the breath of knowledge and the magnetism of intelligence, swelling with an equal fertility from the powers which seemed perpetual; further off, a globe of strange mountains: a chain of volcanoes smiles at the magic of heroes, at the serpentine tenderness of goddesses, guides the nuptial flight of man, finally free to know himself and perish as a bird; it's the answer to everything, even to the wear and tear of birth, even to the detours of the labyrinth.[47]

One might compare Char's "Hymn" with Hölderlin's rapturous account of the "philosophical light" that he experiences in the landscape of his home. Each describes a similar sense of the gathering together within a single landscape of a complex multiplicity of elements, and each looks to a form of transcendence that is immanent within the concreteness of what lies before.

Although Camus characterizes the sensibility at issue here as characteristically Mediterranean, and as standing in contrast with the Northern sensibility that he identifies with Germany in particular, the fact that he uses such a characterization probably tells us more about Camus, and so also about Char (who shared in this same Mediterraneanism), than it does about the Mediterranean as such. In fact, the emphasis on limit or "measure," Camus acknowledges, "is not peculiar to the Mediterranean."[48] One can find a sensibility, like that evident in Camus and Char, expressed in very different geographical terms elsewhere. Kenneth

White's "Atlanticism,"[49] as it might be called, which is also influenced by Nietzsche (for whom the sea also plays a significant role), is one example, even though it exchanges sun for rain and cloud, and blue seas for dark ocean.[50] The landscape in which Camus and Char orient themselves is indeed a Mediterranean landscape, and their own "proximity to Greece" is thus expressed in terms of that landscape. It could hardly be otherwise. How else is one to speak of the strange mystery of one's engagement in place other than through one's engagement with and experience of those places that one already knows, those places with which one's life is already connected?

The way the relationship to sea and ocean recurs in Camus's and Char's Mediterraneanism, as well as in White's work and elsewhere, is worth some additional comment. The relationship is one that, as noted briefly above, appears in Nietzsche, though primarily as it arises in the context of Nietzsche's focus on Genoa and Venice as places of sea-borne departure out towards the horizon of the world. And images of sea and coast also figure prominently, for instance, in David Casper Friedrich's paintings, in ways directly tied to basic themes relating to human life and experience (see, for example, fig. 2). Part of the reason for the prominence of such maritime ideas and images is surely the way the sea and the ocean are powerfully connected, not only with the experience of that which extends beyond the human alone, and which refuses any subjugation to the human, but also with the liminal—in the sense both of limit and threshold. Of course, one can find such connection elsewhere, too—in mountain, river, field, and forest for example (which is where Heidegger most often looks)—though to which of these one turns will depend on one's circumstances. And although there is no reason why one cannot do this is terms that draw on the character of urban or even interior spaces—the city, the street, the house, the room—there is something about the engagement with the phenomena of nature that makes for a difference here. It is not, however, a difference based simply in the desire to overcome human alienation or separation form the natural order. Rather, in the experience of the urban, the interior, the artifactual, or the "made," what occurs, all too often and for the most part, is an encounter with ourselves rather than anything that marks the limit to ourselves—as if we converse only with ourselves (something Heidegger says is true of modern or "Cartesian" man, in a passage that will be quoted more fully below[51]) instead of being brought to a conversation that takes us beyond ourselves.

Figure 2. David Casper Friedrich, *Die Lebensstufen, Strandszene in Wiek* ("The Stages of Life, Beach-scene in Wiek"), c. 1843. Oil on canvas, Leipzig, Museum der Bildenden Künste.

Part of what Camus and Char have in common is a refusal of the abstract and an insistence on the concrete and singular. In his original essay on "the new Mediterranean culture," Camus spoke of *la patrie*, the "homeland," as consisting not in "the abstraction that precipitates men into massacre," but rather in "a certain taste for life that is common to certain beings,"[52] and he went on:

> It is not the taste for argumentation and abstraction that we lay claim to in the Mediterranean, but its life—courtyards, cypresses, strings of peppers—Aeschylus and not Euripides—Doric Apollos and not the Vatican's copies. It is Spain, its strength and its pessimism, and not the sabre-rattling of Rome—landscapes bursting with sunlight and not the stage-sets where a dictator becomes intoxicated with the sound of his own voice and subjugates crowds. What we want is not the lie that triumphed in Ethiopia, but the truth that is being murdered in Spain.[53]

Camus connects this insistence on concreteness and singularity with a certain political orientation—towards democracy rather than fascism and towards the affirmation of life and humanity rather than power and control. One might argue that it was a tendency towards a similar "abstraction" of the sort Camus refers to here that contributes to the problematic elements of Heidegger's thinking, evident both in Heidegger's enthusiasm for Hitler and his intoxication with the history of being (especially as played out in relation to peoples and cultures), during the 1930s and into the 1940s.[54] It is an abstraction (and enthusiasm and intoxication with it) that also dissipates in his postwar thinking.[55] Indeed, it is hard to see how he could have found the friendship that he did with Char if it had not.

This emphasis on the "concrete" and the singular that is a feature of the attentiveness to place[56] is expressed in Camus's emphasis, shared with Char, on the world and the experience of it as constituted through the unity of opposites (a unity that arises always through the appearing *within bounds*, which is to say, *in place*), and so as also characterized by the constant play of both identity and difference—which is why Heraclitus, along with Nietzsche, is such a central figure for both writers.[57] Camus identifies this as characteristically Greek, writing of how Greek thought, being grounded on the idea of limit, "denied nothing, neither reason nor religion. It gave everything its share, balancing light with shade."[58] Although Heidegger warns against too ready an appeal to the contrast between the "abstract" and the "concrete" (for the conventional connotations associated with these terms can easily lead one astray), the inseparability of identity and difference and the dynamic working together of opposites in the presencing of what is present are also key themes in Heidegger's thinking. They are themes directly taken up in the 1966 Le Thor seminar in connection with the Heraclitean understanding of *logos*, and so as part of Heidegger's engagement with Char. Addressing precisely this issue concerning the unity of opposites, Heidegger tells us that:

> Heraclitus names a belonging to a singular presence of everything that separates itself from another, in order to turn all the more intimately to the other, in the sense that, along the "country path": "Winter's storm encounters harvest's day, the agile excitation of Spring and the serene dying of Autumn meet, the child's game and the elder's wisdom gaze at each

another. And in a unique harmony, whose echo the pathway carries with it silently here and there, everything is made gladsome . . ."[59]

Significantly, the quoted lines here are from Heidegger's short text about the path across the fields near his hometown of Messkirch, *Der Feldweg*.[60] The drawing together of opposites is thus a drawing together that occurs *in place*—and although it thereby occurs within the bounds of place, it nevertheless opens to a boundless depth and richness. This is why Camus's emphasis on limit and measure, and his own critique of the "excess" that he takes to be characteristic of modernity in contrast to the "moderation" of the Greeks, nevertheless also admits an "excess," or intensity *of appearance*, as this does indeed occur within limits. Thus, in a way that also makes direct reference to its embeddedness *in landscape*, Camus describes Char's poetry as carrying with it an opposition of elements that brings about a sudden and extreme form of revelation:

> In the brilliant landscape where Char was born, the sun, as we know, is something dark. At two in the afternoon, when the land is fagged with heat, a black breath blows over it. And so, when Char's poetry appears to be obscure, it is because a furious condensation of imagery, an intensification of light removes it from that degree of absolute transparency which we all too often demand because it makes no demands on us. But at the same time, that point of darkness, as in the sun-soaked landscape, creates around it vast reaches of light in which the human face is laid bare.[61]

And, of poetry, Char writes that it occurs in "that instant when beauty, having kept us waiting for so long, abruptly rises out of common things, cuts across our radiant field of vision, binds together all that can be bound, lights all that must be set alight in our sheaf of shadows."[62] In both of these passages, we see different versions of the same happening of *aletheia*—though presented, in Camus's case, in sudden and dramatic form—that figures so centrally in Heidegger. The way in which such a happening is opened up—in superlative fashion, for Camus and Char and Heidegger, within the Mediterranean landscape of Provence—is precisely what leads all three to find there a certain "proximity to Greece."

Near the beginning of the Le Thor seminars, Heidegger asks why philosophy might have found its first beginning in Greece. He answers:

> The Greeks are those human beings who lived immediately in the openness of phenomena—through the expressly ek-static capacity of letting the phenomena speak to them (modern man, Cartesian man, *se solum alloquendo*, only talks to himself). . . . [H]ow does philosophy arise from the Greek residence in the midst of phenomena? . . . In the relationship of Greek humanity to beings, in the sense of what is unconcealed, is there something that makes philosophy (as investigation into the being of beings) necessary? . . . What occurs in the arising-into-ἀλήθεια? What is at once co-named in the word φύειν? It is the *overabundance*, the *excess* of what presences. . . . In the Greek climate, the human is so overwhelmed by the presencing of what presences, that he is compelled to the question concerning what presences as what presences. The Greeks name the relation to this thrust of presence θαυμάζειν. . . . the dimension of the entirely excessive is that in which philosophy arises. Philosophy is indeed the answer of a humanity that has been struck by the excess of presence.[63]

Provence does not provide a route by which one can simply return to Greece or to the Greeks. But, what Heidegger, Char, and Camus nevertheless find—in Aix, Bibemus, the Sainte-Victoire mountains, L'Isle-sur-la-Sorgue—is the possibility of a turn back towards this "excess of presence." It is an excess that, because it is an excess *of presence*, is also an excess held always within the bounds *of place*.[64] Moreover, this excess, this "superabundance," is not one from which we are held back by language, or at least not by a language that is attuned to the poetic. Char writes that "[t]he flowering hawthorn was my first alphabet,"[65] and, in *Leaves of Hypnos*, he recounts his response, during his years as a resistance leader, to "an officer, up from North Africa," who is astonished that Char's "bougres de maquisands," as the officer calls them ("resistance guys" being the polite translation), "express themselves in a language whose meaning escapes him, his ear rebelling at 'talk in images.' I point out to him that slang is merely picturesque, whereas the language used here springs from the wonder communicated by the beings and things in whose intimacy we live continuously."⁶⁶ Here, language appears, not as something derivative of the human, but as that from which the human itself comes and in which it finds itself. "Poetically man dwells," Heidegger famously affirms, and to dwell poetically is to dwell amidst things and other people, in a landscape, and within a world. To be in "proximity to Greece" is to find oneself opened to the experience of this poetic dwelling, to being affected by and attuned to it, but such proximity is always and only to be found in the bounded opening of one's own placed existence. "What is proper to a place," writes Heidegger, "is contained in the way that each gathers, casts, and attunes the people dwelling there in their deeds and allowances, their poetizing and thinking."⁶⁷ And, in its own way, each place contains the possibility of an opening to that original poetizing that is the opening of place itself.

The World and the Human

The way the human appears in all of this—in Camus's lyrical essays, in Char's poetic invocations, in Heidegger's meditative reflections—suggests that it may be impossible to think the world without recourse to a certain form of "anthropology," which is to say, without recourse to a simultaneous thinking of the human along with the world. In one obvious respect, things could not be otherwise since the thinking of the world necessarily implicates thinking itself and so also a thinking of the thinker (who originally appears, no matter what may come later, only in the guise of the human). Thus, to think the world is to think both the world *and* the human relation to the world—even if the latter appears only implicitly. Yet if an "anthropology" inevitably emerges here, it is an anthropology that must stand apart from "anthropology" in most of its conventional understandings. What comes into view is an anthropology that consists in a bringing forth of the relation of the human (*anthropos*) to that which gathers and lays before (*logos, legein*). Only in this relation does the human ever begin to appear as human, that is, as a distinctive mode of being, rather than as merely another being among beings (whether understood biologically, ethnographically, sociologically, or whatever). Moreover, what is at issue here is not, therefore, an anthropology that concerns the human taken alone, but instead one that specifically addresses the human in relation to the world and might even be termed an anthropology *of the world*.

The latter phrase is certainly an odd one, and not only because of the oddity of invoking "anthropology" in relation to Heidegger. What the phrase intends to capture, however, is the inextricable entanglement of the human with the world and of the world with the human, even as the world necessarily goes beyond the human. To talk of an anthropology of the world is thus deliberately to confound the usual understandings of anthropology, as well as of the human. At the same time, it aims to refocus attention on the relation between the human and the world while refusing any grounding of the world in the human alone. Such an anthropology does not center on the human but on the world, seeing the human as appearing only in and through its relation to the world as that is articulated in and through place. In Heidegger, this is evident most clearly in the character of the "fouring" or "fourfold" (*das Geviert*) as *including* the human (here understood as the ones who die, the mortals, *die Sterbliche*), alongside the gods (the undying ones, *die Unsterbliche*), as well as earth (*Erde*) and sky (*Himmel*), and also going *beyond* the human. The human participates, necessarily, in the fourfold taken in its entirety, but the human does not determine it, nor is the fourfold dependent on the human taken alone. The human is reciprocally determined in relation to the other elements, and, together, the four are constitutive of the fourfold, and yet the fourfold itself stands over and above any single such element.

Nevertheless, the human stands in relation to the world—to the presencing of what is present, to being—in a way that does stand apart from the other things of the world and from those basic forms that are given in earth and sky, as well as in mountain and sea, coast and plain, sun and wind, cloud and rain. Towards the close of the final of the Le Thor seminars, Heidegger comments that "the human necessarily belongs to, and has his place in, the openness (and currently in the forgetfulness) of being. Being, however, for its opening, needs man as the there of its manifestation."[68] What is the nature of the "need" here, and is it anything beyond the "need" evident in the structure of the fourfold whereby the human is an essential element in that structure? Being, it is said, needs the human specifically as "the there of its manifestation." Notice that this does not mean that the human somehow supplies something *to* being from a position *apart from* being. Rather, the human, or perhaps better, that which is the *essence* of the human, is the site of being's appearing—is the site for the presencing of presence. However, the character of the human as such a "site" is complex, since the human is itself brought into the open in this very "site." Here is evident the intimate nature of the connection between place and the human,[69] at the same time as we see how being, presence, and presencing are also tied to place. In the seminar, this appears in the explicit drawing of the implication that "a finitude of being must accordingly be assumed."[70] The finitude that belongs to the human is therefore also a finitude that belongs to being. It is just this that is brought to salience, in multiple ways, in the landscape of Provence.

Three

On Not Naturalizing Heidegger

How does the thinking of nature relate to the thinking of place? And how might the two be connected, if at all, in Heidegger? Certainly, the specific term "nature"—*Natur*—does not appear with any systematic regularity in Heidegger's thinking, nor is it accorded any central role. Indeed, one might well argue that the very thematization of nature in relation to Heidegger is already indicative of a likely misreading. For the most part (there is an important caveat explored below), Heidegger takes nature to refer to a problematic notion within the history of thought rather than to a concept that he aims to reappropriate for his own thinking. Yet, as there is a persistent tendency to want to assimilate Heidegger to a more conventional mode of thinking—one that fits with the interests of contemporary academic philosophizing—so there is also a tendency to want to find ways of reading Heidegger that do indeed give more significance to nature and the "natural" (although exactly what this means is not always made clear). Such a tendency is evident, if indirectly, in the way some analytic readers of Heidegger, especially those inspired by Hubert Dreyfus,[1] read Heidegger as contributing to a naturalistic as well as pragmatically inclined approach to questions of mind and intentionality. For readers such as these, however, the *idea* of nature remains largely in the background—naturalization need imply no thematization of nature as such. Yet, as naturalism has become an increasingly powerful force within contemporary thinking, including within contemporary phenomenology, so it is not surprising to find readings of Heidegger that are more explicit in advancing the idea of Heidegger as both a naturalizing thinker and a thinker for whom nature occupies a central role.[2]

Nature and the Being of Dasein

In *Being and Time*, the concept of nature figures hardly at all. Even though the index to the Macquarie and Robinson translation lists thirty or more occurrences of the term (the Lexicon in the Stambaugh and Schmidt translation lists around forty), all of them deal with nature in the context of other topics, and none addresses nature as the main or sole focus of attention. Yet there is, in *Being and Time*, one passage concerning nature that is both well-known and important. In a discussion of the way things can appear as either ready-to-hand (*zuhanden*), as tools or resources available for use, or as present-at-hand (*vorhanden*), as occurrent objects to be known, Heidegger writes:

> "Nature" [*Natur*] is not to be understood as that which is just present-at-hand, nor as the *power of Nature*. The wood is a forest of timber, the mountain a quarry of rock; the river is water-power, the wind is wind "in the sails." As the "environment" is discovered, the "Nature" thus discovered is encountered too. If its kind of Being as ready-to-hand is disregarded, this "Nature" itself can be discovered and defined simply in its pure presence-at-hand. But when this happens, the Nature which "stirs and strives," which assails us and enthralls us as landscape, remains hidden. The botanist's plants are not the flowers of the hedgerow; the "source" which the geographer establishes for a river is not the "springhead in the dale"[3] [or, as Stambaugh and Schmidt have it, the "source in the ground"[4]].

Here, Heidegger seems more concerned to tell us what nature is not than what it is, and what it is not is something either present-at-hand or ready-to-hand—even though nature can be encountered in both these modes. The passage is, however, significant independent of any question concerning nature as such since it indicates (as Heidegger will emphasize in *The Fundamental Concepts of Metaphysics*) the partial character of the analysis of worldhood offered in *Being and Time*. The world, like nature itself, is not exhausted by the specification of things in terms of their involvement in practical activity nor as objects of theoretical knowledge. Yet, in this passage, Heidegger also invokes the idea of nature as that which "stirs and strives," which "assails and enthrals us as landscape." It is discovered, so Heidegger implies, in the encounter with the "flowers in the hedgerow" and "the springhead in the dale." These last might be taken to suggest that what is at issue in the idea of nature, as Heidegger sees it, is something in many ways quite familiar: it is nature as poetic, as it appears in a way that affects us emotionally and aesthetically, as it provokes an emotional and aesthetic response. This idea of nature is one that is especially familiar in the context of modernity, and particularly the modernity of the Romantic and post-Romantic—and, in that context, ideas of nature and place seem often to converge. Take, for instance, the invocation of nature, expressed through the engagement with a specific *place*, that appears in Wordsworth's lines from July 13, 1798, "Composed a Few Miles above Tintern Abbey, On Revisiting the Banks of the Wye during a Tour":

> I have learned
> To look on nature, not as in the hour
> Of thoughtless youth; but hearing oftentimes
> The still sad music of humanity,
> Nor harsh nor grating, though of ample power
> To chasten and subdue.—And I have felt
> A presence that disturbs me with the joy
> Of elevated thoughts; a sense sublime
> Of something far more deeply interfused,
> Whose dwelling is the light of setting suns,
> And the round ocean and the living air,
> And the blue sky, and in the mind of man:
> A motion and a spirit, that impels
> All thinking things, all objects of all thought,
> And rolls through all things. Therefore am I still
> A lover of the meadows and the woods
> And mountains; and of all that we behold
> From this green earth; of all the mighty world
> Of eye, and ear,—both what they half create,
> And what perceive; well pleased to recognise
> In nature and the language of the sense
> The anchor of my purest thoughts, the nurse,
> The guide, the guardian of my heart, and soul
> Of all my moral being.[5]

The nature of which Wordsworth speaks here is not to be identified, in any simple fashion, with the nature that powers the water-wheel—one of the early drivers of the English *industrial* revolution—nor is it reducible to the system of physical processes, the understanding of which had been so fundamentally altered by the European *scientific* revolution. What Wordsworth speaks of is nature as affecting but also sustaining. It is nature as origin and principle, as anchor and a guide, nature as that which is, one might say, the governing "spirit" of the world, and nature as evident in the singularity of place and landscape. But it is also a nature obscured, and prone to being forgotten (as is place itself), such that it can indeed be recalled and then vividly attended in an experience such as Wordsworth's on the banks of the Wye.

Here, two aspects to the idea of nature seem evident. The first is of nature as that which underpins our own being, as well as the being of the world. It is this aspect of nature that underpins the affective character of the experience of nature and is most powerfully evident in the experience of place. The second is of nature as, in some sense, contrasted with or perhaps opposed to the world of human activity and engagement, hence its obscuration and forgetting. On the one hand, there is the world of nature as it does indeed belong to the wild or rural landscape, to the countryside, and, on the other hand, the world that belongs to "culture," and so to the city, the street, the building, the factory, the crowd. Nature thus appears as incredibly close, but, as the world of human activity and artifice crowds upon us, also impossibly far. In fact, Wordsworth, like many Romantics, has a more nuanced sense of the human relation to nature than is often assumed (a point that will come up again in chapter 9) or than the notion of a simple contrast between the natural and the human might initially suggest.[6] Nature is not apart from the human. Instead, the human has set itself apart from nature (and not only through urbanization and industrialization), and it is thus that the relation to nature is characterized by misunderstanding and forgetfulness. The sense of nature that appears in Wordsworth, as "Tintern Abbey" so clearly exemplifies, is indeed one that encompasses rather than excludes the human (which is why its forgetting is so significant) and does so in a way that is directly tied to the experience of place and landscape. That connection to landscape, in particular, is echoed in Heidegger's comment regarding nature as that which "assails us and enthralls us as landscape."

Nature and Romanticism

There is an important sense in which Heidegger's brief discussion in *Being and Time* does indeed recall the sense of nature that is such a hallmark of Romantic thinking, and especially of Romantic thinking as expressed in poetry (elsewhere he talks specifically of the "Romantic conception of nature"[7]). Yet it is also true that there is another Romantic conception of nature that is very different from that which is characteristic of Romantic thinking in its Wordsworthian instantiation—a form that might be termed "scientific Romanticism," according to which nature, while still taken to be in some sense determinative of the human and emotionally and aesthetically affective, is nevertheless identified with physical process in its entirety, as such process is described by the empirical sciences. Such "scientific Romanticism," or what Gillian Beer calls "romantic materialism,"[8] seems characteristic of Darwin, as it is of many of the advocates of contemporary scientism (who often go rather further than Darwin did in extolling the almost redemptive power of the modern empirical sciences). In Darwin's case, one might take his own scientific Romanticism to be akin to what Aristotle describes in the first book of the *Metaphysics* as the wonder that drives human curiosity and so gives rise to science and philosophy.[9] But what we see in Darwin is a specific Romanticization of the empirical sciences themselves, and in many of Darwin's successors, a Romanticization to the exclusion of any other form of inquiry.

The Romantic conception of nature found in Wordsworth has an important continuity and connection with the Romanticism to be found in Darwin. But where they differ is in the sense that Wordsworth's focus is on nature as initially given *experientially*, and thence articulated poetically and philosophically, whereas in Darwin, though the experiential is not absent, what becomes more important is nature as articulated *scientifically*. For Darwin, the emphasis on the scientific, over, as one might say, the philosophical, also meant a tendency, even though he did not abandon religious belief, towards an agnosticism on many religious issues as they encountered matters scientific. For both Wordsworth and Darwin, however, the romanticism of their thinking is tied, in each case, to a bringing of the human back into proper connection with nature, even though it is with nature understood differently in each case. So, the bringing of the human back to nature—the re-naturalizing of the human—takes two very different forms. In Darwin, it means understanding the human in continuity with the empirical scientific understanding of other "natural" beings—so Darwin famously emphasizes the continuity of the human with the animal (a point often taken to be captured in Darwin's reiteration of the claim that "Nature makes no leaps"—*Natura non facit saltum*[10]). In Wordsworth, however, it means the re-locating of the human in the world, in the landscape, in place, something accomplished in terms of thought and memory as well as physical locale. Seamus Heaney says of the *landscape,* as it appears in Wordsworth's "Michael," that it is both "humanised and humanising,"[11] and perhaps one could say something similar of *nature* as it appears in Wordsworth, except that nature also has an aspect that puts it beyond the human, even as it is encompassing of it.

Darwin's scientific Romanticism, and the particular form of "naturalizing" tendency that accompanies it, reaches its culmination in Stephen Hawking's claim (and Hawking represents one example of the contemporary scientific Romantic) that "philosophy is dead," since "philosophers have not kept up with modern developments in science . . . particularly physics."[12] It is a claim that probably tells us more about Hawking's own intellectual narrowness than it does about philosophy or physics, but which certainly reflects a widespread view that the only real knowledge is the knowledge delivered by the empirical sciences. If Heidegger stands closer to Wordsworth than to Darwin here, and especially to Wordsworth than to Hawking, this is not because he is properly antinaturalist, and in fact neither is Wordsworth. What we find in Darwin and in Hawking is a specific appropriation of nature and the natural that is also, in Hawking's case more so than Darwin's, assimilated to a form of scientific universalism or even chauvinism. Of course, if naturalism is just scientism, then Wordsworth and Heidegger must be opposed to naturalism, but this seems an unwarranted assumption.

Wordsworth's own concern with nature, while it is certainly strongly connected to the affective and poetic, is not itself remote from the philosophical. E. D. Hirsch has written of the affinities between Wordsworth's account of nature and the world and that to be found in Friedrich Schelling. In both, argues Hirsch, there is an emphasis on the reciprocity of subject and object, the mutuality of the relation between mind and nature.[13] Schelling's thinking is, of course, heavily indebted to that of Immanuel Kant. And although not a reader of the Königsberg philosopher, Wordsworth exhibits a similar commitment to the idea of the world, and of nature with it, as already bound up with the being of the "subject" or the mind. Kant's Copernican Revolution is thus one in which Wordsworth seems unwittingly to participate and to which he might even be said to contribute. It might be argued that this does indeed bring to light the real point of contrast between the sort of account of nature we find in Wordsworth, and to some extent in Heidegger also, and that which is characteristic of Darwin and those more scientifically minded thinkers who follow—a contrast that is often put as one between the "naturalistic" and the "transcendental." Putting the contrast in these terms, however, already prejudices the account in a way that suggests that the "transcendental" is in some sense non-naturalistic or even antinaturalistic—a suggestion that I would argue is mistaken in just the same way that it is mistaken to treat Wordsworth or Heidegger as antinaturalists. The contrast at issue here is really one that operates with respect to two different conceptions of nature, one of which takes a certain empirical scientific approach to be determinative, and the other of which puts the emphasis on a different mode of proceeding that, we might say, is explicitly ontological. It is thus not a contrast between the "naturalistic" and the "transcendental" but is perhaps better captured as one between the "philosophical transcendental" and the "empirical scientific."

Nature and the Transcendental

Here it is worth turning more directly, if briefly, to Kant and to the manner in which nature appears in his thinking—or, at least, in the first *Critique* (specifically in the "Analogies of Experience"). There we find an account of nature "in the empirical sense" (a sense consistent with modern scientific thinking), which Kant puts in terms of "the connection of appearances as regards their existence according to necessary rules, that is, according to laws." But he goes on to point out that there are "transcendental laws of nature," which he characterizes as "a priori propositions that are intellectual and at the same time synthetic," and it is on these that the unity of nature as a system of appearances depends.[14] Kant's account of nature, as it might be grasped scientifically, depends on understanding the unitary structure of knowledge or experience as that is developed in the course of the *Critique of Pure Reason*. It is common to find that transcendental account as one that locates the relevant principles of unity in the structure of subjectivity, but it is important to note that whatever subjectivity might be here, it is not the idea of some substantive entity in whose own being the being of nature—or of the world or of anything else—is somehow founded.

This is one of the key points about, not just Kant, but the subsequent thinking of German idealism (including that of Schelling), and, one might say, of Romanticism also: though it may seem to make the subjective primary, it does so at the same time as it transforms the understanding of the subject. In Kant, the "subject" is understood, not as identical with any subject in the usual sense but rather with the entire structure of appearing as it encompasses both empirical subjects and empirically determined objects. The transcendental is a name for this structure of appearing, but it also names the inquiry into that structure. In Kant, then, the transcendental is not that which stands opposed to the natural. Instead it is that which makes the natural, understood as pertaining to the system of appearances, possible *as a system*, or, as we may also say, *as unitary*. The transcendental may thus be treated as that which is prior to nature, or, keeping in mind Heidegger's introductory comments in *Being and Time*, that which pertains to nature in a more primordial and fundamental sense. In a certain sense, the transcendental is the natural. Certainly, from a Kantian perspective, it is vital that the transcendental is not understood as implying a structure that goes beyond that which is given in and through experience itself—the transcendental is not *transcendent* in any sense that would take it beyond the natural. Consequently, the transcendental structure belongs to the system of appearances that is the system of empirical nature, and it must do so if it is to be that which makes appearances possible.

The transcendental is nonetheless a concept that has generally been poorly understood within contemporary, especially English-language philosophy—it being all too often confused with some form of transcendent subjectivism. What is so radical and ground-breaking about the transcendental in Kant—and to a large extent this is carried on in Heidegger despite his own criticisms of Kant (and his criticisms, in the 1930s and later, of the transcendental itself)—is that it aims to provide an articulation of the unity of the world by reference, not to any structure of principle that lies outside the world, but rather in terms of the very principles that belong to it, that are given within and through it. Indeed, it is this concern with unity (though a unity that underpins both the unity and multiplicity of appearance) that echoes the original sense of the term "transcendental" as that which operates transcategorially and so also as that in which the proper unity of the multiple senses of being is to be found. In Kant, the task at issue here is explicitly understood in terms of the project of determining the proper bounds of reason, which are also the bounds of knowledge, of sense, of experience. Kant's own explication of this task is explicitly one that draws on geographical and topological conceptions.[15] The task is thus one of determining the unity and proper extent of a field or region, which means delimiting the boundaries of that field or region, but it is a task that can only be accomplished from within that same field or region.[16] Kant's project is thus one of delineating a certain place from within that place—the place being the place to which we ourselves belong, within which we ourselves find our own being, even as we also participate in the very formation of that place.

In spite of Wordsworth's own independence from any direct influence by Kant, one can nevertheless see in Wordsworth's thinking something of the same transcendental preoccupation. Heaney's characterization of the Wordsworthian landscape as "humanised and humanising" captures some of this. But it is also there in the sympathy Hirsch identifies between Wordsworth and Schelling, specifically on the point of reciprocity or mutuality: the transcendental structure is constituted as unitary through the reciprocity and mutuality of its elements. The transcendental turn that one finds in Kant, is continued in Schelling, and is perhaps echoed in Wordsworth, is the definitive point of differentiation that marks off much of European thought—as exemplified in the phenomenological, hermeneutic, and idealist traditions—from the great majority of English-language philosophy, as well as from those forms of scientistic thinking that dominate so much contemporary discourse.

In this respect, the transcendental is no less absent from Heidegger, even though his own relation to Kant, and to the language of the transcendental, is problematic. In *Being and Time*, Heidegger seems willing to draw on the idea of the transcendental as a way of characterizing his own project, asserting that *"being is the transcendens pure and simple"* and that "[e]very disclosure of being as the *transcendens* is *transcendental* knowledge. *Phenomenological* truth (disclosedness of being) is *veritas transcendentalis*."[17] By the 1930s, however, Heidegger adopts a much more critical attitude towards the idea of the transcendental, associating it with a notion of transcendence (in the sense of projection),[18] that he takes as prone to a subjectivist reading. In this respect, however, Heidegger also sees the transcendental as associated with that mode of thinking that takes the question of world essentially to concern the objectivity of the object.[19] One can indeed be critical of the idea of the transcendental on the grounds Heidegger advances. But there is also a more generous reading that looks to understand the underlying mode of thinking at work in the transcendental as oriented towards just this idea of a unity constituted through the mutual relation of the elements within it. It is a unity not too far removed from that dynamic unity of difference that Heidegger addresses in "The Principle of Identity" and that he associates with the *Ereignis*.[20] This unity is itself topological, and, as such, it stands in an important relation to the topological unity that is at the heart of the transcendental as it is appears in Kant.

It is because the notion of the transcendental is so foundational to post-Kantian European, or "Continental," thought that the clarification of the transcendental in terms of the topological is so significant, since it enables us to arrive at a clearer understanding of what is at issue in the Kantian project itself, as well as to see how that project might also find its continuation in Heidegger. What is at issue in the transcendental is not some epistemological foundation to thinking. It is rather the ontological ground for the possibility of appearing itself—appearing not of what lies apart from or behind such appearing, but of that self-appearing that is presencing, that is being. For Heidegger, this self-appearing does not occur through the operation of something that lies apart from what appears, or through some principle, entity, or structure that is additional to and apart from the world. Presencing occurs through the movement, the happening, that belongs to presencing itself and that is itself the ground for both identity and differentiation, which occurs as both a concealing and an unconcealing.

In Heidegger, this idea is captured, among other ways, in the emphasis on prescencing, and so also on being, as unconcealing, *aletheia*, which he also connects to *physis*. Inasmuch as we might understand nature in terms of *physis* (and there are problems about too close an identification here), then nature—or that which is grasped as "naturalness"—can also be understood as the play of absencing and presencing, as self-emergence, as unconcealing:

> The naturaless of nature is essentially, and hence historically as well, far more ancient than nature in the sense of an object of modern natural science. The naturalness of nature never grows directly out of nature itself; rather it is caught sight

of expressly in that to which ancient Greek thinkers once gave the name "physis"; the rising and receding of all that is present in its presencing and absencing.[21]

In Kant, the presencing at issue here occurs only in and through limit or bound, and the same is also true for Heidegger. Presencing and absencing is always a happening tied to *place*—to the *Da*, the *Ereignis*, the *Geviert* (fourfold), the *Lichtung* (clearing). The presencing and absencing that is *physis*—and is also seen in *aletheia*—is precisely the opening of the unbounded within the bounded.

Nature, Limit, and Place

The absolute primacy of limit in making possible presencing (or "appearing") is an idea that reaches far back into philosophical thinking, even though it remains one of the most overlooked notions within the entire history of thought. It is Kant who brings this idea to the forefront of *modern* philosophy, although, even there, it is only in certain appropriations of transcendental thinking that it seems to have become salient. It is a notion already present in Aristotle, for instance, and in an especially significant way for the thinking of nature, since it appears in the *Physics*, specifically in book IV, where it underpins Aristotle's treatment of place or *topos*. *Topos* is defined by Aristotle as "the limit [*peras*] of the surrounding body, at which it is in contact with that which is surrounded."[22] Aristotle's reiteration of the claim that "to be is to be in place"[23] can thus be read as also an iteration of the claim that to be is to be bounded. Interestingly, one might argue that this Aristotelian idea has a faint echo in Quine's famous dictum that "to be is to be the value of a bound variable,"[24] but more important is the way the idea reappears in Kant and also in Heidegger.

According to Heidegger, boundary or limit (*peras*), *in the Greek sense*, "does not block off but, rather, as itself something brought forth, first brings what is present to radiance . . . The boundary which fixes and consolidates is what reposes, reposes in the fullness of movement."[25] The idea is repeated in the Parmenides lecture from 1942: the boundary, *as the Greeks thought it*, is "not that at which something stops, but that in which something originates, precisely by originating therein as being "formed" in this or that way, i.e., allowed to rest in a form and as such to come into presence. Where demarcation is lacking, nothing can come into presence as that which it is."[26] This account of limit, though it explicitly harks back to the Greeks, could as easily be referred back to Kant. In the present context, however, it is its Greek reference that is especially significant. Indeed, almost the same characterization of limit or bound, with the qualification "as thought in the Greek sense," appears in Heidegger's most sustained consideration of nature, an exploration of the notion of *physis* as it appears in Aristotle:

> In Greek thought, what comes to be and passes away is what is sometimes present, sometimes absent—without limit. But πέρας in Greek philosophy is not "limit" in the sense of the outer boundary, the point where something ends. The limit is always what limits, defines, gives footing and stability, that by which and in which something begins and is. Whatever becomes present and absent without limit has of and by itself no presencing, and it devolves into instability.[27]

Limit and nature are tied together, so that in the sense in which the transcendental is an inquiry into the proper limit that belongs to the appearing of things, the transcendental is, as one might expect, given a reading of Kant, an inquiry into nature just inasmuch as it is an inquiry into limit. Moreover, as limit is tied to place, so too is nature tied to place.

This connection between nature and place is articulated in Aristotle in terms of the way the differentiation of things is itself connected with the differentiation of places through the idea of the natural places to which things are drawn according to their own natures. The teleological character of this structure is what allows the understanding of *physis* as it pertains to the structure of the entire world—or, at least, of the world as it is in the terrestrial sphere. *Physis* is thus that bounded emergence in which a thing comes into its place, and in so coming into place, also comes into the movement proper to it. This connection between *physis* and *topos*, between nature and place, is reflected in the etymology of the English terms at issue here (and this is so despite what Heidegger claims about the problematic character of the modern notion of "nature" and its Latin derivation). Just as nature has associations with birth, so to be born is to come from a place (almost literally so, if we attend to the connection between womb or *matrix*[28] and the Greek *chora*, the latter being also a term for place[29]), to belong to a certain origin—hence the "native" (and also "naturalization" as a process of having conferred upon one the status of belonging to a place).

Heidegger emphasizes that *physis* is a form of emergence—a form of *poiesis*, and yet it is not the only such form. "*Physis* also, the arising of something from out of itself, is a bringing-forth, *poiēsis*. *Physis* is indeed *poiēsis* in the highest sense. For what presences by means of *physis* has the bursting open belonging to bringing-forth, e.g., the bursting of a blossom into bloom, in itself (*en heautōi*)." But there is another form of emergence also:

> [W]hat is brought forth by the artisan or the artist, e.g., the silver chalice, has the bursting open belonging to bringing-forth not in itself, but in another (*en alloi*), in the craftsman or artist . . . *technē* is the name not only for the activities and skills of the craftsman, but also for the arts of the mind and the fine arts. *Technē* belongs to bringing-forth, to *poiēsis*; it is something poietic.[30]

Crucially, however, the difference between *physis* and *techne* is not one in which each is set side-by-side—*physis* has an important priority here. Inasmuch as *physis* is movement, then it is a movement on which *techne* depends. Although the point itself is not clear in either Aristotle or Heidegger, one might argue that *techne* operates only through its manipulation of the movement that belongs originally to *physis*. It is thus that the artisan can be said to be the efficient cause of the artefact. Here, Aristotle's tendency to employ artefactual examples in the understanding of the four forms of cause turns out to be instructive. It enables us to see why the helmsman, as in Aristotle's brief comment in *De Anima*,[31] is the proper origin of the movement of the ship, namely, through the way the helmsman makes use, not only of the movement generated by the oarsmen, but also of wind and current, directing and channeling that movement. The example suggests the possibility that *techne* has no movement properly its own but only the movement derived from *physis*.

Although *Physis* and *techne* may both be forms of *poiesis* they do not stand in a correlative position to one another. A key claim in Heidegger's argument concerning technology (to be taken up further in chapter 8), and so also science, is that both understand nature on the basis of *techne* rather than of *physis*, treating nature as if it were artefactual. This is one key reason why the scientific position of a thinker such as Hawking can be viewed as actually antinaturalistic—it treats nature in a way that assimilates nature to what it is not. The way nature appears within the modern empirical sciences is made clearer when one goes back to the way *physis* and limit, and so *physis* and *topos*, might be connected. If the self-emergence that characterizes *topos* is always a movement within the limit proper to it—one might even say is the realization of limit in and through movement—then *physis* cannot be understood other than in relation to *topos*. Nature, in that case, cannot be understood other than in relation to place—it is this idea that must be the foundation for any genuine "environmentalism." Yet what characterizes modern science, and especially modern technology, is its projection of a mode of being of the world that is essentially placeless and so also limitless. The world is thereby understood as determined by a mode of leveled out and essentially mathematicized spatiality. Heidegger himself alludes to this in various discussions of the rise of the idea of *thesis*, or positionality, as central to the development of modern scientific and technological thought and practice.

The notion of *thesis* is discussed at several places in Heidegger's work, but his 1925 lectures on Plato's *Sophist* contain a particularly sustained analysis. In the course of his exposition of Aristotle's understanding of mathematics, Heidegger considers *thesis* in direct relation to *topos*. *Thésis* is distinguished from *topos* in that *topos*, or place, is *absolute*, whereas *thesis*, for the most part, is *relative*. Thus, all things have a place that is proper to them, and there is also an ordering of places within the *kosmos*. These places are absolute and unchanging. Although there is position within the *kosmos*—a form of position that derives from the cosmic places and so is absolute—position as it pertains to moving things and their parts is always relative. Moreover, the abstract objects of geometry are, by their very nature, removed from any place and as such have no place. Yet, as they retain orientation and directionality (with respect to their parts and with respect to those other bodies to which they may be related), so they also retain position. They therefore have *thesis* but not *topos*. In thus being separated from place, position comes to appear as something abstract, but also as something whose very essence is a *positioning*, or is *being posited*, such that *thesis* appears as *posit, projection*, or even *proposition*, and so also as something essentially *subjective* (since it derives from that which posits or is positioned). The idea of *thesis*, or position, already carries within it, then, the very possibility of the distinction between the place and position, the possibility of a subjective understanding of position and positionality. Moreover, when that is read back into the understanding of place—when any sense of the absolute determination of place is lost—then place becomes no more than mere position, no more than subjective posit or projection. This is just what happens in the history of science, as well as in the shift from the premodern to the modern—*places* become *positions*.[32]

It is this idea of *thesis*, or *position*, that is at work in Heidegger's use of the German terms *Stelle* and *stellen*—and so also in *Gestell* (a connection echoed in the argument for the translation of *Gestell* as just position or positionality). The seeming obliteration of both place and limit, not only within modern scientific thinking, but in the very formation of modernity, is the real source for the modern obliteration of nature. It enables us to see how and why nature might arise as a problem for modernity in a way that is shared across scientific and technological thinking, as well as in forms of political and social organization. The antinaturalistic character of modernity itself, and not only of the scientific or the technological, is thus reinforced—and for Heidegger this means that the essentially subjective character of modernity is reinforced also.

The "Naturalism" of Thinking

At the heart of Wordsworth's thinking, as well as his poetry, is the encounter with something close to that same "nature" to which Heidegger refers when he talks of "the Nature which 'stirs and strives,' which assails us and enthralls us as landscape." This nature is encountered only in the place that is the place for any and every encounter with things and the world—in the place that is the place of the simple emergence of things as the things that they are. Scientific thinking, the thinking of the natural sciences, may be said to emerge out of that same encounter. Yet, in the forms in which it appears in modernity, scientific thinking, and with it the thinking formed in relation to the technological, actually serves to obscure the original and originary sense of nature. The *Seinsvergessenheit*, ("forgetting of being") that belongs to modernity is thus also a *Naturvergessenheit* ("forgetting of nature") as it is also an *Ortsvergessenheit* ("forgetting of place"). Moreover, in this respect, much contemporary "naturalism" is no naturalism at all, since it does indeed forget, overlook, ignore nature in the sense that is at issue here. Moreover, in this same sense, any genuine thinking—certainly thinking of the sort that Heidegger attempts—cannot take any form other than that of "naturalism,"[33] since it cannot be other than a thinking that attends and responds to the emergence of things in just *this* place, which is the place of the world and the place in which thinking already finds itself (and so it will also be a fundamentally *nonreductive* naturalism).

The encounter with nature, understood in the sense elaborated here, whether in relation to Wordsworth or Heidegger, is not an encounter with that which stands over and against the human. It already encompasses the human since the human is itself caught up, and necessarily so, in that same self-presencing or self-emergence. The way the human is implicated here means that the forgetting of nature does not occur because of the assertion of the human against nature but because the human has also been forgotten, neglected, overlooked. The forgetting of nature is a forgetting of the human—a covering over of what both nature and the human properly are. What the human means here, however, is not merely some instance of biological or "natural" being.

Moreover, the place of encounter and of self-presencing (the two being here the same) brings with it a space of indeterminacy, of forgetting and remembering, of listening and questioning. This is only possible in the open space, the clearing, in which language plays an essential role. If the human is just the being who has language (and here a larger question lurks, once again, as to just how the human should be understood), then the human cannot be separated from the question of nature even though nature, like being, is not itself anything human. This is not an instance of anthropocentrism—quite the opposite in fact (it is scientistic naturalism that is properly anthropocentric in the same way that Heidegger claims it is subjectivist). Instead, it is a matter of understanding both nature and the encounter with nature, since it is only through the encounter that nature itself appears. Only when we acknowledge the strange place that the human occupies in the place that belongs to nature can nature even begin to be thought in any adequate fashion. Such thinking, it should be noted, does not imply the overlooking or dismissal of that which is other than human or an unwarranted privileging of the human. Rather, it is only through acknowledging the strange place of the human, by which the human is set apart, that either the human or the animal, the human or that which is other than human, can ever possibly appear. It is indeed only thus that the question of any responsibility to "nature"—which can only be a *human* responsibility and a human *responsiveness*—can ever arise.

Four

Ontology and Hermeneutics

A summary history of modern philosophical hermeneutics has it developing through at least three stages: first, as a methodology of textual interpretation; second, as a methodology for the "human sciences," the *Geisteswissenschaften*, in general; and third, as a mode of fundamental ontological inquiry (the latter also leading to a transformation in the first two). These three stages can be said to be organized around three pairs of thinkers (although others stand in the background): Ast and Schleiermacher, Dilthey and Yorck, and Heidegger and Gadamer. In the work of the last of these, it is the relation between hermeneutics and ontology—a relation that might otherwise be thought to be central to their own appropriation and reconceptualization of the hermeneutical—that nevertheless comes into question. It does so, moreover, in a way that also implicates ideas of place and situation—ideas that are central to twentieth-century hermeneutics, even if not always directly thematized there—and thereby connects directly with the topological thinking that is the main concern of this volume.

That there might be a connection between hermeneutics and ontology that runs throughout Heidegger's work might be thought, however, to be an unlikely claim. Heidegger is critical of ontology in many places, and the abandonment of the ontological difference in his very late thinking might seem to confirm that ontology has indeed been dispensed with.[1] Yet, as was already indicated in the Introduction, there is an important sense in which Heidegger never gives up on ontology—at least not if ontology is understood as a "saying of being"—and a form of ontology remains in the late work no less than the early.[2] In contrast, however, even though hermeneutics is invoked in Heidegger's early work, including *Being and Time*, it is almost entirely absent from the later thinking, despite Heidegger's increasing concern with language. Hermeneutics is, of course, central to Gadamer's work, but he makes few explicit references to ontology. Consequently, one might say that if, in Heidegger, hermeneutics disappears in the face of the persistent inquiry into being (regardless of whether this continues to bear the name "ontology"), in Gadamer it is the thematization of ontology that seems to fall away in favor of the pursuit of the hermeneutical.

The tensions evident here are developed further in the work of others. In Jacques Derrida, Heidegger's thinking is taken as showing the impossibility of any "understanding" of being of the sort envisaged in a hermeneutical ontology—deconstruction thus effectively takes precedence over both ontology and hermeneutics.[3] For Gianni Vattimo, the path from Heidegger and Gadamer onwards, when followed in company with Nietzsche, leads to what might be understood as a hermeneutical abandonment of the ontological—what Vattimo has called "weak thought" (*il pensiero debole*).[4] Yet the original conjunction of ontology with hermeneutics that appears in Heidegger's work, perhaps most notably in the title, as well as the text, of his 1923 lectures, *Ontology—The Hermeneutics of Facticity* (a conjunction Gadamer refers to as like talk of "wooden iron"[5]), and that is also continued in *Being and Time* in 1927, is one that deserves closer scrutiny—especially in the context of the topological issues at stake in the discussions here.[6]

The conjoining of ontology with hermeneutics in the early Heidegger raises questions as to the nature of that which is conjoined. What is ontology as it stands in relation to hermeneutics? What is hermeneutics as it stands in relation to ontology? Why might they be thought to come apart, and why might they be thought properly to belong together? Perhaps the most compelling reason for raising the question concerning the relation between ontology and hermeneutics is that what is surely at issue in this question is the relation between being and language. It is this relation that is already thematized in Heidegger's treatment of ontology as inseparable from logic (and which meant that the title of the 1923 lectures could equally have been either *Logic* or *Ontology*).[7]

In this latter respect, the question of the relation between ontology and hermeneutics concerns the question of the hermeneutical character of philosophy, and this, I would argue, is actually what is already at stake in the late Heidegger's concern with language as the "house of being" (something already touched on in the last chapter, and to which I shall return here as well as in subsequent chapters).[8] Indeed, the connection between ontology and hermeneutics is itself thematized, if sometimes indirectly, in "A Dialogue on Language," from 1950—a work that makes reference directly back to the thinking of the 1920s. Moreover, understanding the intimate relation between ontology and hermeneutics as developed by Heidegger (a relation that is implicit in Gadamer also) entails a transformation in thinking that affects both ontology *and* hermeneutics (as it also affects logic) and that also forces us to attend more carefully to language, world, and place.[9] In short, understanding the relation between ontology and hermeneutics itself moves us in the direction of a topological mode of thinking, but in doing so, it also indicates the manner in which topology itself calls upon the notion of *logos* as well as *topos*.

Place, as we have seen in previous chapters, stands in an essential relation to language. The way place emerges here, however, is particularly instructive since, although it appears, for the most part, by way of what I will refer to later as "hints and beckonings" (*Winke*), it does so, in both the early lectures on facticity and the later dialogue on language, in direct relation to the hermeneutical. Since it is these two works, from 1923 and 1950, that provide Heidegger's two most sustained discussions of hermeneutics, especially as it arises in relation to the question of being, that is, to ontology, so it is on these works that my discussion will focus.

Facticity and Hermeneutics

Let me begin with the early Heidegger—with the Heidegger of 1923. The lectures that make up *Ontology—The Hermeneutics of Facticity* open with a series of comments on the character of both ontology and hermeneutics. In a manner that echoes my passing characterization of ontology, above, as a "saying of being," Heidegger comments:

> Ontology means doctrine of being. If we hear in this term only the indefinite and vague directive that, in the following, being should in some thematic way come to be investigated and come to language, then the word has performed its possible service as a title for this course. However, if ontology is

regarded as designating a discipline, for instance, within the field of inquiry of Neo-Scholasticism or within that of phenomenological Scholasticism and the directions of academic philosophy influenced by it, then the word "ontology" is not a course title fitting for what our theme and manner of treating it will be in the following . . . The terms "ontology" and "ontological" will be used only in the above-mentioned empty sense of nonbinding indications. They refer to a questioning and defining which is directed to being as such. Which sort of being [Sein] is to be questioned after and defined and how this is to be done remain utterly indefinite.[10]

To assume an identification of ontology with any of the various modes of contemporary ontological analysis would already be to predetermine the direction of inquiry when that has still to be established. The idea of ontology as simply the inquiry into the question of being, whatever that might be, remains undetermined as to the exact form ontological analysis might take. The term "ontology" itself is used as a mode of "formal indication" that does not predetermine its subject matter in any problematic fashion. One might well argue that this is just as it should be since the inquiry into being, if it genuinely aims to take up the question of being as a question, can no more assume a prior determination as to the nature of ontology and the ontological than it can assume a prior determination of that into which ontology inquires; namely, being. The questioning *of being* can only take place if pursued in a genuine fashion—which means in a way that is also accompanied by a questioning *of ontology*.

Although it represents a simple and very basic place of departure for Heidegger's analysis, as well as my own, and is not something that Heidegger develops further, the point that appears here is nonetheless a crucial one. So long as we remain focused on being as that which is in question, then ontology also must remain in question. Any decision as to a more determinate conception of ontology necessarily involves a more determinate conception of being. Similarly, the complete abandonment of ontology (which would involve, not merely giving up the term, but the giving up of what is at issue) can only come with the complete abandonment of the question of being (and again, that must involve not merely the giving up of the term, but of what is at issue in that term).[11] Moreover, if the question of being has been forgotten or covered-over, as Heidegger claims, then so too must we say that ontology has been forgotten or covered-over at the same time. We can thus no more make direct appeal to the traditional characterizations of ontology to elucidate what is at issue in ontological inquiry than we can simply refer to the traditional characterizations of being in answer to the question of being.

Just as the question of ontology is raised at the very start of Heidegger's discussion, indeed as preliminary to it, so too is the question of hermeneutics. Heidegger's 1923 lectures provide us, in fact, with one of the longest and most direct disquisitions on hermeneutics that Heidegger offers anywhere in his writings, including even the 1950 "A Dialogue on Language." Heidegger emphasizes that his use of "hermeneutics," in this early work, is not to be construed in the "modern sense" as a *methodology* of interpretation, which he associates particularly with Dilthey (of whose position on hermeneutics, Heidegger says that it is "already quite limited, showing little clarity in regard to fundamental issues, and moving only to a small extent in their direction").[12] Such a conception of hermeneutics as restricted just to a mode of theoretical discourse *about* interpretation is, of course, a common way of understanding hermeneutics—hermeneutics, it is frequently said, is the *theory of interpretation*. As Heidegger understands matters, however, hermeneutics is neither a mode merely *of theory* nor *of methodology*; rather it is to be understood as a fundamental mode *of interpretation* as such.

As is so often the case, Heidegger's account of hermeneutics draws heavily on the Greek origins of the term—on the meaning of the Greek *hermeneuein* and its cognates. A *hermeneus* is an interpreter, "one who communicates, announces and makes known, to someone what another "means," or someone who in turn conveys, reactivates, this communication, this announcement and making known."[13] Referring to Aristotle, Heidegger writes that *hermeneuein* is a form of conversation or discussion, as such it is "the factical mode of the actualizing of λόγος [logos]," and what it accomplishes is "making something accessible as being there out in the open, as public."[14] Hermeneutics is thus itself an interpreting, an announcing, a making known, and as such it is an interpreting that is also self-interpreting. Hermeneutics is "the announcement and making known of the being of a being in its being in relation to . . . (me)."[15] Hermeneutics thus does not and cannot interpret from outside of itself—as if it were neutral, disengaged, unconcerned—but instead always interprets from the perspective of its own being.

What is at issue in hermeneutics is always our own understanding, and so an understanding embedded in our already given interpretive situation. The idea of a "hermeneutics of facticity" is thus not the idea of a mode of interpretation that just happens to take facticity as its object but is, rather, that mode of interpretation that already belongs to facticity as such. Similarly, the facticity to which hermeneutics is directed is not a facticity that stands apart from hermeneutics. What is at issue is the very facticity of the hermeneutical—the factical basis of interpreting.[16] As Heidegger summarizes matters, using terms that prefigure the language of *Being and Time*: "In hermeneutics what is developed for Dasein is a possibility of its becoming and being for itself in the manner of an understanding of itself."[17] The understanding at issue here must, however, already be given, if only implicitly, in Dasein's own mode of being—otherwise, it could never be developed as a possibility *at all*. Hermeneutical understanding thus names both that which is constitutive of Dasein's factical being *and* what develops out of the inquiry into that being.

The theme of facticity is what Heidegger identifies, at the very start of his lectures, as "ontology" (but which can also be referred to as "logic").[18] In its "empty" and "nonbinding" sense, ontology does indeed name "any questioning and defining which is directed to being as such," but, in Heidegger's hands, it is also clear that any entry into the questioning of being can only begin with that original questioning that is already bound up with the being of Dasein—the latter being that "from out of which and for the sake of which philosophy 'is.' "[19] The Heideggerian understanding of the question of being, as arising only in relation to the being of Dasein, is so familiar that it may seem unnecessary to remark on it further. Yet it is easy to overlook what is really at issue here and, in so doing, to miss the full implications of, as well as the proper basis for, Heidegger's manner of proceeding. This is especially so given the character of the inquiry into being that is underway here as, indeed, a *hermeneutics of facticity*.

The two concepts at work in this phrase are closely interrelated— so much so that they appear almost as two aspects of the same unitary phenomenon. The being of Dasein is factical; that is, Dasein is always already given over to its "there/here"—to its being "already-in" the world. Such facticity can be understood as a basic form of situatedness that is also *committed* or *engaged*—a situatedness that calls upon Dasein, that opens up in terms of a set of possibilities, and hence "questions," for Dasein's being (one might say that this is precisely what it is to be genuinely situated, or placed, and so distinguishes "situation" from mere "position"). Yet, understood in this way, facticity is essentially hermeneutical: factical being is being that already interprets itself (that announces itself, makes itself known). Yet this also means that ontology itself, the questioning of being, can only be undertaken from the perspective of facticity and as hermeneutical.

Inasmuch as the question of being is seen as beginning with the inquiry into facticity, and therefore as taking the form of a hermeneutics of facticity (which is also, it should be noted, a hermeneutics of that mode of being that is itself hermeneutical), so the inquiry into being is already transformed into a very different kind of inquiry from that which has traditionally gone under the heading of ontology. The inquiry into being is an inquiry into that which is given in our own facticity. Thus, Heidegger says of philosophy, in general, that it "is a mode of knowing which is in factical life itself and in which factical Dasein is ruthlessly dragged back to itself and relentlessly thrown back upon itself."[20] This aspect of the relation between facticity and philosophical or ontological inquiry reflects the hermeneutical character of the inquiry at issue. Philosophical inquiry always arises out of the hermeneutical, that is, the self-interpreting character of the being of Dasein in which the being of philosophy is itself founded. Moreover, as hermeneutical, philosophy must be understood as a mode of self-interpretation and self-articulation. For this reason, it must always move in the space opened up by the "there/here" of Dasein's being. There can be no other space, no other situation, in which philosophy can emerge, or to which it can make appeal.[21]

Moreover, as the hermeneutical is also discursive, and therefore stands in an essential relation to language ("the factical mode of the actualizing of λόγος"), so the hermeneutical understanding of ontology shifts ontology into the same discursive realm. Whereas Carnap famously announced, in 1931, the "elimination of metaphysics through the logical analysis of language," Heidegger's thinking, even in 1923, presages the transformation of ontology and, with it, a more fundamental appropriation of metaphysics through the hermeneutical understanding of facticity. The course of Heidegger's thinking beyond 1923—and beyond 1927—takes this transformation still further. To see the direction in which this transformation occurs, however, it is necessary to explore, more closely, the idea of the hermeneutical and, especially, the hermeneutical understanding of language that is also at issue. For this, we need to turn from Heidegger's early to his later thinking.

Language, Place, and Hermeneutics

Although, in *Being and Time*, Heidegger is explicit in characterizing his project as aiming at an "Interpretation" (*Auslegung*) of the meaning of being, the only explicit discussion of hermeneutics in that work occurs in a single paragraph in §7, in which Heidegger is at pains to make clear the sense in which the inquiry into the meaning of being can be said to take the form of a "hermeneutics" (his comments summarize some of the points discussed above).[22] It is not until twenty-three years later, in "A Dialogue on Language," from 1950, that hermeneutics reappears as a significant point of focus for Heidegger's thinking, and when it does reappear, it is in a way that, although in some ways less detailed, nevertheless echoes elements of the discussion of the matter in the 1923 lectures on facticity. There is thus significant continuity between the two works, and in his work of the 1950s, Heidegger makes explicit reference back to his thinking in the 1920s.

In the later discussion, Heidegger once again refers the meaning of hermeneutics back to its Greek origins and to the Greek term *hermeneuein*, emphasizing, however, that hermeneutics does not mean merely the interpretation of some message already given: "hermeneutics means not just the interpretation [*das Auslegen*] but, even before it, the bearing of message and tidings [*das Bringen von Botschaft und Kunde*]."[23] The idea of hermeneutics as the bearing of the message, as well as its interpretation, is not entirely absent from the 1923 discussion, even if it is not at all highlighted (and may even appear obscured by some comments). However, not only does Heidegger make the same connection to the god Hermes in the later and earlier discussions, just as he refers to the same passage from Plato's *Ion*,[24] but the references Heidegger draws from Aristotle in the earlier discussion seem to allow for just such a reading as appears in the later: hermeneutics is connected to *discourse* and so to the making manifest of things, to their being unconcealed. Significantly, this aspect of the hermeneutical, as explicated through Aristotle, seems very much to depend on the explication of *hermeneuein* in connection with *logos*, and it is this connection that, as I indicated above, comes to the fore in the later discussion.

In answer to the question as to why he places such emphasis on this original sense of *hermeneuein*, Heidegger refers immediately to the way in which it connects to his approach to the question of being:

It was this original sense which prompted me to use it in defining the phenomenological thinking that opened the way to *Being and Time* for me. What mattered then, and still does, is to bring out [*zum Vorschein zu bringen*] the Being of beings—though no longer in the manner of metaphysics, but such that Being itself will shine out [*dass das Sein selbst zum scheinen kommt*], Being itself—that is to say: the presence of present beings [*Anwesen des Anwesenden*], the two-fold of the two in virtue of their simple oneness [*die Zwiefalt beider aus ihrer Einfalt*]. This is what makes its claim [*den Anspruch*] on man, calling him to its essential being.[25]

If the original sense at work in the term "hermeneutics" is not just the *interpreting*, but also the "bearing of message and tidings," and if this original sense is what opens up the possibility of bringing out the being of beings, "not in the manner of metaphysics, but such that being itself will shine out," then hermeneutics is not merely an "interpretation" of being in any usual sense. Instead, it concerns the bringing forth of the very being of beings—a bringing forth that mirrors the character of being as itself the presencing of what is present (what Heidegger frequently refers to in this discussion as just the "twofold"). The character of hermeneutics as self-interpretation can now be read differently—not as the interpretation of some hidden aspect of the hermeneutical, but rather as the uncovering of the self-showing character of the hermeneutical and of being, as such (thus also drawing the hermeneutical into the domain of the Heideggerian understanding of truth as *aletheia*). Indeed, one might argue that this is already what is at issue in Heidegger's original use of hermeneutics in *The Hermeneutics of Facticity*.

The reading of the character of the hermeneutical in Heidegger's thinking is reinforced when one reflects on the role of facticity in the earlier work. If, as I have argued elsewhere, facticity is understood in terms of Dasein's own essential situatedness (something suggested by Heidegger's own emphasis on the "there/here"), and of hermeneutics as a kind of "wakefulness" to Dasein's factical situation, then the language of "interpretation," as usually understood, seems ill-adapted to what is at issue. Rather than interpretation, perhaps one should understand the hermeneutical as itself essentially concerned with a fundamental mode of *awareness* and *orientation*—as essentially a matter of finding oneself *in one's situatedness*, of finding oneself *in place*. Certainly, it is only *in place* that any form of appearing, of presencing, or of showing can occur, while such presencing can itself be understood as a "placing" and a "taking place." Thus, the later Heidegger talks of his thinking of being as a *topology*—as "a saying" of the place of being (*Ortschaft des Seyns*). One might argue, in fact, that the unity of the twofold—of presence and presencing—is itself encompassed only in and through the unity of place, even as the unity of place is itself worked out only in terms of the twofold of presence and presencing.

The character of the hermeneutical as connected to a fundamental mode of appearing or showing, and the way this might also be tied to the bearing of a message or tidings, clearly brings to the fore the relation between hermeneutics and language, and with it the question of the understanding of language that might be at work here. This is already suggested by the character of Heidegger's treatment of the matters at issue, both in *The Hermeneutics of Facticity* and in other works from around the same time, as one that implicates logic no less than ontology: *hermeneuein* cannot be addressed independently of *logos* any more than it can be dealt with apart from *to on*. Moreover, language itself appears as a mode of bringing to appearance, showing, or making present. This is evident throughout much of Heidegger's earlier thinking. However, the originary character of language in this regard is an even stronger theme in the later works, including "A Dialogue on Language." One of the exchanges in the latter runs as follows:

> I: For long now, I have been loathe to use the word "language" when thinking on its nature . . . J: Which word do you use? I: The word "Saying." It means saying and what is said in it and what is meant to be said. J: What does "say" mean? I: Probably the same as "show" in the sense of: let appear and let shine, but in the manner of hinting [*in der Weise des Winkens*].[26]

Clearly, part of what is at issue here is the intimate connection of language, or "saying," and being—as indicated through the reference to "show," in the sense of "letting appear and let shine." Moreover, given that this exchange appears during a discussion in which the being of hermeneutics is itself at issue, and in which hermeneutics is seen as a the bringing of message or tidings, then so we can see the understanding of language as a "saying" that is also a "showing" to reflect back on the character of hermeneutics as such.

The term *hermeneuein* refers us, not to some secondary act of interpretation, but instead to an original event of showing or letting appear—through an event that also draws us toward it, an event that hints or *beckons*,[27] as connoted by the German *winken* (although *winken* can also carry a sense of greeting—something that cannot be entirely absent here either). This latter term takes on a special significance in Heidegger's discussion. Of *Winke*, or *beckonings*, Heidegger says: "They are enigmatic. They beckon to us [*Sie winken uns zu*]. They beckon away [*Sie winken ab*]. They beckon us toward that from which they unexpectedly bear towards us."[28] The showing that is at issue here, and that belongs to language as well as the hermeneutical, is not some simple presentation of what is already determined but, instead, like the appearances of the gods themselves, both hides and reveals, concealing in its very shining.

The character of hermeneutics, as a "bearing of message and tidings," thus cannot be construed in terms of the delivery of something complete and transparent in content. Indeed, the message that is borne, Heidegger tells us, is the message "which the twofold's unconcealment" speaks to us,[29] and the message that is so spoken can be nothing other than unconcealment itself, including our own prior belonging to such unconcealment. If this is a message that can only take the form of *Winke*, of beckonings, then this is because there is nothing revealed here that does not also carry an essential concealment with it. Hermeneutics is itself concealing as well as disclosive. It is a "bearing of message or tidings" and so also a "saying," but one that indeed beckons and thus directs us to what shows—as it is itself a kind of showing—rather than simply declares. All the terms that operate in Heidegger's thinking, and especially in his late thinking, should be understood in this "hermeneutic" fashion, as *Winke*, as beckonings. As such, they constantly play out within a space in which different senses overlap and in which the same term can carry multiple connotations.[30] The reader who looks for a single univocal interpretation of Heidegger's text will thus always be disappointed, but such a reader is also likely to be one who has assumed exactly the reading of the hermeneutical that Heidegger warns us against—one who has assumed a mode of interpretation that remains *merely* interpretive ("*in the manner of metaphysics*") and so fails to attend to the more fundamental disclosure, the shining appearance, that is at issue here.

Heidegger's talk of *Winke* also serves, once again, to beckon us back towards the character of showing—whether the unconcealment of the twofold or the showing of the hermeneutical itself—as always "taking place" in the place opened up by the "there/here" to which human being is already given over. *Winke*, as Heidegger characterizes them, always involve a situatedness and directedness, a movement towards or away. Not only Heidegger's use of terms but also his very thinking takes the form of such a beckoning—a drawing-into a certain place of thinking, a calling-back towards the place in which thinking is already situated. Such beckoning, or hinting, is topological in its own character, as is the idea of the "bearing of message or tidings" that Heidegger sees at work in the hermeneutical. The bearing of a message is always a matter of a certain "journey"—a carrying from one "place" to another (even if those two places are but two aspects of the same)—while its speaking, or "saying," also invokes a circumstance and an occasion. The topological connotations that are evident here run throughout "A Dialogue on Language," in which there is constant reference to modes of movement and stillness, distance and nearness, trail and direction. They are evident in the very presentation of the piece as a "dialogue"—as a placed conversation *between* speakers (even if the exact place of that conversation remains largely unspoken) that allows for an openness in which something can emerge into unconcealment.

The character of dialogue, as occurring within an open space "between," is itself significant. Such a between arises only in the space opened up in place since it is only within place that there appears the necessary boundedness on which such a between-space depends. Space can be understood to emerge out of just such a between, and the idea of space itself seems to be tied to the idea of the interval or *diastema*. Contrary to the way the history of space and place has so often played out, space cannot properly be understood as independent of place any more than the unbounded can be understood as independent of the bounded, the open understood apart from the closed, the unconcealed apart from the hidden. In attending to the showing, or letting shine, that is at the heart of the hermeneutical, what is also attended to is this very between—a between that is evident in the idea of the twofold, as well as in the figure of the dialogue; that appears in the hermeneutical "relation" itself,[31] as well as in the very character of language. The

Ontology and Hermeneutics | 77

dimensional character of language will be an important theme in this chapter as in the next (something already hinted at in chapter 2). In the exploration of that dimensionality, both ontology and hermeneutics figure as part of a single topology. Language is that within which the presencing presence that is being properly comes to place, and the inquiry into being is thus always an inquiry into the placedness that is opened up only in and through language.

Place and the Hermeneutical

Despite being full of topological hints and indications, "A Dialogue on Language," for the most part, only indirectly thematizes the place that it nevertheless invokes—and this is as true of language as it is true of place itself. Towards the end of the dialogue, however, as the two participants attempt to characterize the common neighborhood in which their thinking seems to move, that neighborhood is itself brought into view in a way that also seems to illuminate the place of dialogue as the place of speaking or saying and of presencing—and in an explicitly topological fashion:

> I: The question of the site [Ort] in which the kinship that you sense comes into play. / J: Your question reaches far. / I How so? / J: The distance is the boundlessness which is shown to us in *Ku*, the sky's emptiness. / I: Then, man, as the message-bearer of the message of the two-fold's unconcealment, would also be he who walks the boundary of the boundless. / J: And on this path he seeks the boundary's mystery . . . / I: which cannot be hidden in anything other than the voice [Stimme] that determines and tunes his nature [die sein Wesen be-stimmt].[32]

This is a dense passage and one that is rich in implications. Not only is the question of place (*Ort*) brought directly into view, but it appears in a way that connects it with one of the elements in Heidegger's own "fourfold,"—*Sky* [*Himmel*]—but here characterized in terms of distance, emptiness, and boundlessness. Yet, immediately, the connection is made to "man," to the human, as "he who walks the boundary of the boundless."

Place is precisely that bounded opening into the boundlessness of world that is exemplified in the emptiness of sky as it is "shown to us," as it opens above us, as it appears within the horizon of our own being there. Moreover, this place—and the mystery that belongs to it as the boundary itself belongs—is hidden and therefore also revealed in the voice, the saying, which is surely nothing other than the voice (*Stimme*) that sounds in language. It is this same voice that determines and tunes (*bestimmen*) the nature of the human. The human is the one who is attuned to, and tuned by, that voice, just as it is also attuned to, and tuned by, the place that sounds in the voice and in which the voice sounds. Here, the cleared place that belongs to being appears as "cleared" in a way that invokes the spatiality of sound no less than of light. As Heidegger comments elsewhere:

> *Hellen* [to clear], along with *hell* [clear], mean the same as *Hallen* [to resound] in the sense of "resounding." In the sense of the [primordial] event of the self-manifestation of being, *Hellen* [to clear] occurs originally as *Hallen* [sounding], as tone. All other beings fall short of this fundamental tone [*Grundton*].[33]

The intimate connection between sound and place (and between sound and space) is sometimes overlooked.[34] Yet, in Heidegger, the essential connection between the two means that the idea of place as clearing always carries more than just a visual connotation: the clearing is a saying, as it is a beckoning, as it is an opening. The clearing is a place, and a place that sounds in language, just as language sounds in place.

The sounding that Heidegger takes to occur within the clearing is the same sounding that occurs in the voice and so in the Saying that is language. It is a sounding that belongs to the clearing as much as to language and the voice. The clearing sounds. In his essay on the poet Hebel, Heidegger writes of both the sounding of voice and the shining of script:

> A word of language sounds and resounds in the voice, is clear and bright in the typeface. Voice and script are indeed sensuous, yet always within them a meaning (Sinn) is told and appears. As sensuous meaning, the word traverses the expanse of the leeway between earth and sky. Language holds

open the realm in which man, upon the earth and beneath the sky, inhabits the house of the world.[35]

As it is a bounded and yet open domain, so the clearing is a between—a domain of differentiation as well as identity. This between is given most immediately and directly in the between—the open domain—of earth as it stands in relation to sky.[36]

Earth and sky are the two elements of this between. In one sense, both function as the bounds or limits of the between, but in another sense, it is earth that is the bound, that which the human walks, whereas sky is the open and so, in the terms of "A Dialogue on Language," also the boundless. The between is thus the between of earth and sky, which is also the between of the bounded and the boundless, which is the between of place, which is the between within and from which the world opens-up.

Language holds open this between even as it is made possible by it (without world there is no language, but without language there is no world either[37]). How is it that language can hold open the between in this way? How is it that language can play such a fundamental role in the possibility of world? In the passage just quoted, Heidegger seems to imply that it is the character of the *word*, as the making present of meaning in the sensuous (which is also the making present of that which goes beyond the present), that enables the opening and holding open of the between-space of world. There is much in this idea that deserves further exploration, but what seems most worthy of consideration here is the way this depends upon a between that already belongs to language as such. If language unifies the sensuous with the meaningful, then this is only because it also differentiates them, and it is this very interplay of unity and difference, as it occurs in and through language, that is surely the more fundamental structure. If the between is understood in terms of such an interplay of unity and difference, then language and the between must be inextricably linked—and, more than this, as the between lies at the heart of the topological (for *topos* is the emergence of the open within what is bounded), so place and language must also be intimately connected; hence the significance of the place as it sounds in the voice, and of the voice as that which resounds in the clearing.

In language—in Saying—there resides the possibility of a sameness that is also a difference. In mundane terms, this appears not only in the way in which what is said belongs with what it speaks about, even while it is also distinct from it, but also in the very rhythm of language, which may become song, in which repetition enables articulation, and in which differentiation of sound and script makes possible a unity of sense. It is this possibility of identity in difference and of difference in identity, given in the idea of the between, that is the very essence of language, of Saying, and so also of showing, or of letting-appear.[38] It is this unifying-differentiating that is operative in Heidegger's original deployment of the so-called "ontological difference," but which the language of the "difference" (along with, perhaps, the usual understanding of the "ontological") threatens to obscure. It is the same unifying-differentiating that is also evident, less problematically, in the concealing-unconcealing that is *aletheia*, in the onefold/twofold of presencing and presence and in the bounded boundlessness of *topos*, of place. The between that holds language and place apart is thus also what unites them, and it is this between to which the hermeneutical also belongs and to which it draws us. For all that Heidegger makes only occasional appeal to the language of the hermeneutical and is often seen to have abandoned it altogether in his late thought, it is nevertheless hermeneutics that opens up the Heideggerian transformation in thinking. It is hermeneutics that allows phenomenology to become a way into the question of being, understood as focused specifically on the "there/here" of being as it opens into world. It is hermeneutics that enables the understanding of language as that which holds open the differentiated unity of world.

The very idea of such a hermeneutics as applied to ontology, and especially of ontology as itself taking the form of a "hermeneutics of facticity," must indeed appear as an impossibility ("wooden iron" in Gadamer's phrase) if it is understood in *conventional* terms—that is, if it is understood apart from the transformation that this mode of thinking also brings about, if it is understood merely as an *interpretation*, in the usual sense, of factical existence. Facticity will always be resistant to such an "interpretation," just as the presencing of what is present will always resist the attempt to think such presencing in the terms of "metaphysics." Yet the Heideggerian transformation of thinking, while it may be said to be brought about through Heidegger's appropriation of the hermeneutical, is also a transformation in the hermeneutical as such. That transformation occurs partly through the very turning of hermeneutics in the direction of ontology, but also, and more importantly, through the topological reorientation that becomes an increasingly central element in Heidegger's thinking and that is already present even in the 1920s. The place of thinking that is opened up through this transformation and reorientation is the place that thinking never leaves. It is the *topos* of being, the *topos* of the *hermeneuein*, the *topos* that also belongs to *logos*.

The place of thinking that appears here is one in which both language and the hermeneutical are shown as belonging together, as standing in an essential relation to being and so to the unconcealment of the twofold, to the presencing of presence. This place of thinking, which opens in the between-space made possible by language, is not a place that allows for any movement behind or beyond. It is a place that can only be explored in and through language, although the manner of that exploration is one that demands that we remain with both the place that appears and the language that allows that appearance. The transformation that opens-up through the way language comes to the fore in this way is thus not one that leads in the direction of more formalized analysis (Carnap's "logical analysis" of language has no place here[39]). Instead, it takes us back to the "essential simplicity" that language already possesses,[40] requiring that we attend to language in its own Saying/Showing. Similarly, the hermeneutical engagement in and with place is not an engagement directed at making transparent what is otherwise obscure, of eliminating all traces of what is hidden in favor of some unsullied disclosure but, rather, is a matter of letting stand forth the emergence into openness that is the presencing of presence.

In "A Dialogue on Language," we find the following exchange:

> J: I believe that now I see more clearly the full import of the fact that hermeneutics and language belong together. / I: The full import in what direction? / J: Toward a transformation of thinking . . . / I: The transformation occurs as a passage . . . / J: . . . In which one side is left behind in favor of another . . . / I: . . . and that requires that the sites be placed in discussion. / J: One site is metaphysics. / I: And the other? We leave it without a name—[41]

It is this topological-hermeneutical engagement that appears as opening a place of thinking, which, if we are to employ such terms, stands apart from the place that belongs to metaphysics (although even metaphysics stands apart here only inasmuch as it already misapprehends its own place). If this engagement is given the name of ontology (as Heidegger refrains from doing, but surely remains a possibility), this is not because it fulfills some prior designation of the nature of the ontological, but because ontology, if genuinely understood as a saying and, presumably, also a showing—a disclosing—of being, must always remain an "empty" name. It refers to nothing more than that original place in which being, always enigmatically, is brought to appearance—to place as the between-space that is opened by language and towards which language beckons.

Five

Language and Place

One of the characteristic features of Heidegger's later thinking, as the last chapter showed, is its concern with language. Indeed, one might say that the centrality of this concern is a clear marker of the more strongly hermeneutical character of the later thinking (the thinking of the postwar years especially) compared to the earlier—a character that is present despite Heidegger's seeming disavowal of hermeneutics (or, at least, of the language of hermeneutics) in the later work.[1] However, the concern with language in the later Heidegger also develops alongside the more explicit turn towards the topological—towards *topos*, or place (*Ort/Ortschaft*)—that is the hallmark of the later thinking. The topological and the hermeneutical directions in Heidegger are thus convergent, as we saw in the previous chapter, but Heidegger's topological "turn" (which is really a *return* to something that is present throughout his thinking) develops out of his increasing engagement with language and poetry, especially as this is mediated through the work of Hölderlin.[2]

That language and poetry are indeed tied together with place in the later Heidegger is especially evident in the 1947 "Letter on 'Humanism,'" where language is spoken of as that which gives "home" to being and in which human being "dwells [wohnt]."[3] The themes that appear here connect directly back to Hölderlin.[4] Moreover, they do so in a way that is continuous with the engagement with the poet that had been underway in Heidegger's thinking for at least the previous fifteen years (from the early Hölderlin lectures beginning in 1934 to the Ister lectures of 1943[5]) and that would continue long after (including in the 1959 volume, *Unterwegs zur Sprache* [*On the Way to Language*][6]). Heidegger's discussions of language and poetry, and especially his relation to Hölderlin so far as these matters are concerned, have often taken the attention of commentators, but the way language, poetry, *and place* come together in late Heidegger, and especially the place of language within the topology of being, is seldom remarked upon—perhaps unsurprisingly, given the lack of real attention that is accorded to place generally. It is the connection between language, poetry, and place, and so between topology and poetry, to which this chapter will more closely attend. This was, of course, already a theme in chapter 2, but it will be approached here in a somewhat different way with the emphasis being much more directly on the topology that belongs to language and poetry as such.

Language and Dimensionality

The topology that is at work here—and with it, the connection between dwelling, the event, and language—recurs throughout many of Heidegger's later essays, including, of course, the "Letter on 'Humanism,'" in which it is language that provides a dwelling place for human being, just as language is also the house of being. Within this topology, the possibility of appearing, the possibility that beings can come to presence in their being, is seen as dependent upon or occurring within a certain mode of dimensionality that, in Heidegger's earlier thinking, is most often referred to as the open or the between, sometimes in terms of nearness (*Nähe*), but, in the later thinking, is sometimes also referred to simply in terms of the dimension [*Dimension*] or dimensionality. In the "Letter on 'Humanism,'" Heidegger talks of being as this very dimension, writing that "in the determination of the humanity of the human being as ek-sistence what is essential is not the human being but being—as the dimension of the ek-stasis [*als die Dimension des Ekstatischen der Eksistenz*]."[7] The talk of being as dimensionality occurs together with the assertion of language as the house of being. The dimension that appears is not, as Heidegger is at pains to stress here and in similar passages, anything spatial in the usual sense, although it is a dimensionality that frequently appears in contexts in which it might be thought to have spatial connotations, in some sense or other. It is a dimensionality that appears most clearly perhaps in the dimension that is opened up between earth and sky—the dimensionality that belongs, one might say, to world, and also to place—on which Heidegger elaborates in "'. . . Poetically Man Dwells . . .'" (1951):

The upward glance passes aloft toward the sky, and yet it remains below on the earth. The upward glance spans the between of earth and sky. This between is measured out for the dwelling of man [*dem Wohnen des Menschen zugemessen*]. We now call the span thus meted out the dimension [*die Dimension*]. This dimension does not arise from the fact that earth and sky are turned toward one another. Rather, their facing each other depends on the dimension. Nor is the dimension a stretch of space as ordinarily understood; for everything spatial, as something for which space is made, is already in need of the dimension, that is, into which it is admitted. The nature of the dimension is the meting out—which is lightened and so can be spanned—of the between: the upward to the sky and the downward to the earth. We leave the nature of the dimension without a name.[8]

Significantly, Heidegger once again refers to the dimension that is invoked here as that which allows for *dwelling*. Dwelling depends, Heidegger tells us a few lines later, "on an upward-looking measure-taking of the dimension, in which sky belongs just as much as earth."[9] The "measure-taking" is also a spanning of the dimension between earth and sky, and, as such, it depends on a taking measure of that dimension into which human being is gathered and in which it belongs (in and to which it is "appropriated").[10]

If Heidegger does not refer directly to language at the same time as he talks of "measure-taking," this is not because language and measure-taking stand apart from one another. The measure-taking on which dwelling depends is *poetry* (poetry is that which *builds* dwelling and it does so by *taking-measure*[11]), and the essence of language is, as we have already seen, to be found in poetry. Consequently, if poetry is a measure-taking, then such measure-taking must also belong to language—or perhaps we should say that the measure-taking in which poetry consists stands in an essential relation to the character of language as precisely that which allows us into the dimension of being—that "beckons" us towards that dimension.

In "The Nature of Language" (1957–58), Heidegger is explicit in drawing attention to the way that the being of language, "saying" [*Sagen*], and "nearness" belong together—nearness, however, is given specifically in the encounter between the regions of world (earth and sky, gods and mortals) that occurs in the fourfold:

Anticipating, we defined Saying. To say means to show, to make appear, the lighting-concealing-releasing offer of world. Now, nearness manifests itself as the motion in which the world's regions face each other. There arises the possibility of seeing how Saying, as the being of language, swings back into the presence of nearness. Quiet consideration makes possible an insight into how nearness and Saying, being of the persisting nature of language, are the Same. Language, then, is not a mere human faculty. Its character belongs to the very character of the movement of the face-to face encounter of the world's four regions. There arises the possibility that we undergo an experience with language, that we enter into something which bowls us over, that is, transmutes our relation to language. How so? Language, Saying of the world's fourfold, is no longer only such that we speaking human beings are related to it in the sense of a nexus existing between man and language. Language is, as world-moving Saying, the relation of all relations. It relates, maintains, proffers, and enriches the face-to-face encounter of the world's regions, holds and keeps them, in that it holds itself-Saying-in reserve.[12]

In his essay on Hebel, as we saw earlier, Heidegger writes of how the word "sounds and resounds" in the voice, showing as "clear and bright" in the script. Meaning appears as sensuous, says Heidegger, and, as such, language "holds open the realm in which man, upon the earth and beneath the sky, inhabits the house of the world."[13] Here, language appears explicitly as that which grants openness—which lets things into their proper relation with one another—but this occurs in relation to the elements of the fourfold itself, especially in relation to earth and sky, and so "holds open" the realm of human dwelling. Moreover, this relating and opening, which, as we saw earlier, encompasses both sameness and difference, does indeed seem to imply a dimensionality that belongs to relating and opening as such—a dimensionality that is surely the same as that to which Heidegger refers in the "Letter on 'Humanism'" and in "'. . . Poetically Man Dwells . . .'" It is the role of language as that which grants the openness for such dimensionality—which can be understood as itself a form of dimensionality—that grounds Heidegger's characterization of language as the house of being.

The way language and dimensionality are brought together in the later Heidegger, in these passages and others, is directly connected with the character of language as both opening and relating. Opening is an opening of the dimensional—it is a clearing, a making-room, one might even say a *spacing*. Relationality requires such dimensionality since relationality only arises between what appears together and yet also apart.[14] Dimensionality, in turn, also requires relationality. There is no opening up into an unlimited, horizonless realm, but always and only into the realm of the between. The dimensional is this very realm—as is the relational also. For this reason, one might say here that the dimensional and the relational are not separate but, rather, are two aspects of what is essentially the same. Both arise out of the between or, as one might also say, out of the bounded open that is place (as open, it can also be said to be boundless, but as such, it is a boundlessness that belongs always and only together with the bounded), which is why the language of the house, and the home, recur so often in Heidegger's discussions of these matters.[15] What the house provides is a delimited realm that, through its delimitation, gives room to things, allows them leeway, grants them a place. The house provides a dimension within which things come into their own, which also means come into the world, and this is why language can be said to be the house of being. Language is thus dimensional and relational. And if language is, as Heidegger claims, "the relation of all relations,"[16] then perhaps it should also be said to be the "dimension of all dimensions."

As language belongs together with the event, so what is said of language can be said of the event too: as appropriative, and so as letting things into their proper relation as both different and the same, the event is both relational and dimensional. What the connection to the event also shows, however, is that the neither the relationality nor the dimensionality at issue here can be a matter of the simple standing of one thing over against and apart from another.[17] Heidegger talks of the glance as "spanning" the between, of the "turning" of the regions of world, of saying as "world-moving," of the word as "traversing" the leeway between earth and sky. The relationality and dimensionality that concerns Heidegger is thus the relationality and dimensionality that is also tied inextricably to activity and to movement. The event draws together this sense of the active and mobile with the relational and dimensional; hence the description of the event, in *Identity and Difference*, as the "self-vibrating realm" and of language as "the most delicate and thus the most suspended vibration holding everything within" the realm that is the event.[18] The event is itself the happening of dimensionality and of relationality—and this happening is the happening of language. In the "Letter on 'Humanism,'" Heidegger comments: "The one thing thinking would like to attain and for the first time tries to articulate in *Being and Time* is something simple. As such, being remains mysterious, the simple nearness of an unobtrusive prevailing. The nearness occurs essentially as language itself."[19] One might add that language, in its own turn, occurs as this same nearness—and it is thus that it is the very house of being, that in whose home human beings dwell. In this way, Language appears as a *place*, a *topos*, and as that which grants such a place, which is why topology can indeed be understood as a "saying" of the place of being. Moreover, topology here names both *the saying of place that occurs in thought and in poetry* (in "the poetry that thinks") and *the giving of place to being that occurs in and through the belonging together of saying and being as such*.

The Saying of Place

When Heidegger asserts, as he does in the familiar phrase from the "Letter on 'Humanism,'" that "language is the house of being," the idea of language is brought into question, as well as of being, but so too is the idea of the "house" and what it is "to house." The house, which here does not refer merely to some contingent physical structure, is itself a topological concept—a mode of place and placing that is, perhaps, one of the most basic. It is that within which one dwells, in which one is given a place, afforded shelter, and allowed rest as well activity. Through its delimitation of space, the house grants space, room, dimension.

To house is to grant place—and here place is said to be granted to being and to human being. This granting of place to human being, its being "at home," holds regardless of the emphasis on the homelessness of our contemporary condition, or even of the critique of home as a site of oppression, subjugation, or violence. Once again this does not mean that in being "at home" one finds oneself secured against all uncertainty or questionability, but rather that one first finds oneself placed in the world, and in being so placed, one's own being appears as an issue. In this fashion, only the one who is already at home can be "homeless";

only the one who is already housed can be in need of "housing." Gaston Bachelard writes that "on whatever theoretical horizon we examine it, the house image would appear to have become the topography of our intimate being,"[20] and, although this claim plays out in several different ways in Bachelard's work, it nevertheless indicates something of the fundamental nature of the house, and so also of home, *as topological*, and thus *as ontological*. Once again, then, we are brought back to the connection between topology and ontology.

In claiming language as the house of being, as that in which human beings dwell, Heidegger claims this very nature *for language*. Language is thus that within which one dwells, which gives place, affords shelter, and allows rest and activity. One may even be led to say that, if language is the house of being, then there must also be a sense in which language itself grants space, room, and dimension precisely through its delimitation of space, room, and dimension. Part of the task before us is to understand how and why this might be so—*What does it mean for language to have such a nature?*—but equally significant, the task is also to understand the topology that is at work here. How can we speak of the house—and so of place or dimension—as belonging to the character of language or of being? What does it mean to speak of them in this way?

In the "Letter on "Humanism,'" Heidegger comments that "one day we will, by thinking the essence of being in a way appropriate to its matter, more readily be able to think what 'house' and 'dwelling' are"[21]—suggesting that we think less readily in such a way now. The comment comes in the context of a warning against reading the phrase "the house of being" as if it were merely an "adornment of language" or involved "the transfer of the image 'house' onto being."[22] It is at this point that the question of poetry comes directly into view, not only in terms of the way it sheds light on the questions of being or of language, but also in terms of its own nature and the nature of poetic language, including its own relation to the topological (something touched upon in chapter 2, and to which I will return in chapter 6). Moreover, although the poetic and the topological are indeed brought together here, it is not poetry alone nor even poetry as tied to language that is fundamentally at issue. The inquiry into the place of language within the topology of being, with which the question of poetry is implicated, includes within it the question of topology itself. What, we may ask, is the nature of topology that language and poetry are so closely bound to it? Or, to put a familiar Heideggerian remark and phrase into an interrogative form:

What is the character of the saying of place that is involved in the topology of being, and what is the topology of being that it takes the form of a "poetry that thinks"?[23]

A mode of topological thinking, even if not made explicit, is indeed present in Heidegger's thinking almost from the start. Yet, although this means that Heidegger's thinking can be construed as fundamentally an attempt to think the essentially placed character of being, the nature of the placedness at issue here, and of place itself, cannot simply be taken for granted. The famous "question of being" is thus inseparable from the question of place—the response to both questions takes exactly the form of a *topology*—and yet the question of place brings with it further questions about the thinking that place demands, and about those concepts with which place is most immediately associated: notably, time and space. If the focus of Heidegger's early work often leads in the direction of the thinking of place through the thinking (and rethinking) of time, then much of the later work leads towards a rethinking of space or, perhaps better, of "dimensionality" within a more direct and explicit thinking of place itself. Such a rethinking is especially important given the way in which the Western philosophical tradition, increasingly so within modernity, has tended to prioritize space over place, as it has also tended to prioritize the spatial over other concepts, including time, which is why the critique of the "Cartesian ontology of the world," essentially an ontology based in the idea of a homogenous and leveled-out mode of spatiality, is such an important element in the argument of *Being and Time*.[24]

The centrality of both place and space as themselves sites for questioning is brought to particular clarity with the increasing focus in Heidegger's work, in the period after *Being and Time*, on truth as *aletheia*—unconcealment (*Unverborgenheit*)—and with this, on the associated concepts of the "clearing" (*Lichtung*), the "open" (*Offene*), and the "between" (*Zwischen*), as well as on time-space (*Zeit-Raum*), and directly on place or locality itself (*Ort/Ortschaft*). Although the idea of language as the house of being occurs quite late, a topological conception of language is nevertheless present, even if sometimes equivocally, from relatively early on in Heidegger's thinking—in the way, for instance, in which the character of language and, more fundamentally, of *logos* is understood as a "pointing out" of things in their being. Understood thus, language already depends on a certain sort of placing, even as it is itself a form of placing or bringing-near. So, any sort of speaking opens into a space in which that speaking takes place, even while such speaking itself depends on being already "placed" as a condition of its possibility.

One might argue that all of these concepts, including the topological conception of language, the idea of truth as unconcealment,[25] and even the notion of the "event" that is so central to Heidegger's later thinking,[26] can be seen as aspects of the "there/here" (*Da*) that looms so large in *Being and Time* and that remains in the later work, even if its occurrences there are less frequent. One might argue, in fact, that the reason the term *Da* appears less often in the later thinking is that the idea is effectively taken up into the various forms of *topos* that appear there. Moreover, Heidegger's emerging concern, particularly under the influence of Hölderlin, with *earth* (*Boden, Erde*) and later, sky (*Himmel*), a concern that reaches its full realization in the idea of the fourfold, not only powerfully reinforces the topological orientation of Heidegger's thinking in general but also does so in way that is focused directly on the question of the poetic and, perhaps more immediately, the question of language.

Language as Topological

As Heidegger so often emphasizes (and Gadamer frequently reiterates), language is not to be understood as merely something that human beings "possess." Human being is linguistic—which is to say that it is pervaded by language, it is a being *in* language (and already a topological inflection is evident in this "in"). As human being is tied to language, so language is also intimately tied to the possibility of world:

> Language is not merely a tool which man possesses alongside many others; language first grants the possibility of standing in the midst of the openness of beings. Only where there is language, is there world, that is, the constantly changing cycle of decision and work, of action and responsibility, but also of arbitrariness and turmoil, decay and confusion. Only where world holds sway is there history. . . . Language is . . . the primal event [*Ereignis*] which disposes of the highest possibility of man's being.[27]

The openness of beings that is granted through language is not a matter of language creating or producing either an open domain for appearance or what comes to appearance within that domain. In this sense, not only is language not something "possessed," but neither is language something that "produces." There is thus no sense, in Heidegger, of any form of linguistic "constructionism" (or of any form of social constructionism either). Language grants openness, and in so doing, language may also be said to be a form of "freeing" or "clearing" that allows beings to come forth *in their being*—that is, as the things they already are.

That language lets beings appear in their being does not mean that beings thereby come to presence in a way that is somehow "complete" or "transparent." This would, in fact, be to misunderstand the very nature and possibility of what it is for something to come to presence. It would also be to forget Heidegger's constant insistence on the character of every revealing, every appearing, as belonging within the play of concealing/unconcealing that is truth as *aletheia*. The appearing of beings is therefore always such that they appear always with a certain cast or "look." This is the very nature of what it is to appear or to come to presence and can be understood as tied to the character of any appearing as always situated or placed. Yet, even though beings come to presence in particular ways, and so in different ways, they nevertheless come to presence as the beings they are. That we speak of things in different languages does not mean that there must be different things of which each language speaks. Indeed, the very nature of things is that they can indeed be spoken of differently—across utterances and across languages. In letting beings appear in their being, language thus lets beings appear, and yet it does so in a way that does not curtail the inexhaustible possibilities of which the being of beings consists. For this reason, Heidegger can say of language, as we saw in chapter 4, that it "beckons us [*winkt uns*], at first and then again at the end, towards a thing's nature [*das Wesen einer Sache zu*]."[28] It draws us into nearness to beings without determining beings in that nearness.

So long as we remain with a conception of language that takes language as merely another "natural" phenomenon that occurs within the world—as part of the "natural history," as it were, of the human species (and so also as a phenomenon continuous with forms of animal communication)—then we will fail to penetrate the essence of language that is at issue. What concerns us is not language as a natural or biological phenomenon, but language *as ontological*. If we often fail to recognize this, the reason is partly to be found in the very nature of language. Language is so pervasive and so fundamental that it tends to withdraw in the face of that which it lets come to presence. It is thus easy to overlook the linguisticality of human being and instead to see the human as more fundamentally grounded in what is pre- or nonlinguistic—in the "pragmatic" engagement with things, for instance, or in the bodily or "experiential." In this way we seem to see "through" language,[29] not in the sense that it is the means by which we see (for that would be to treat it as some medium between us and the world, which it assuredly is not), but in the sense that we do *not* see it and are indeed given to disregard it or to reduce it to its ordinary and specific instances, whether as speech or text or as formalized semantic and syntactic structure.

As it is a letting of beings appear in their being, so the granting of the openness of beings in and through language is a letting of beings into their "own," into what is proper to them, but, as such, it is also a letting of beings into their proper "relation" with one another—both as together and apart. The granting of openness is thus a granting of both difference *and* sameness. This is the real character of the openness that is at issue here and why it is indeed *a freeing* and *a clearing*—and why it also implicates things and world, as well as human beings (in their singularity and communality) and things. In the last of the passages quoted above, language is said to be "the primal event [*Ereignis*] which disposes of the highest possibility of man's being." The German term *Ereignis*—the event—carries within it a sense of "what is proper to," or what is often rendered into English as "appropriation" (occasionally giving rise to the translation of *Ereignis* as "event of appropriation").[30]

The idea of language as that which lets beings appear in their being, and so in terms of that which is indeed proper to them in their difference and their sameness, thus already indicates a connection between language and the notion of the event as "appropriative," as that which lets beings into what is proper to them. Consequently, in a passage from which I quoted earlier, Heidegger writes:

> The event of appropriation is that realm [*Bereich*], vibrating within itself, through which man and being reach each other in their nature . . . [T]o think of the event as the event of appropriation [*Das Ereignis als Er-eignis denken*] means to shape the structure of the event as this self-vibrating realm. Thinking receives the materials for this self-suspended structure

from language. For language is the most delicate and thus the most suspended vibration holding everything within the suspended structure of the appropriation. We dwell in the event inasmuch as our active nature is given over to language [translation modified].[31]

The topological characterization of the event that is evident in this passage (the event as "realm," as that "through which man and being reach"), and that is also evident elsewhere in Heidegger's thinking on the matter, should not be overlooked, yet just as important is the way in which the topology at work here also encompasses language. Language and the event are once again seen as belonging together, but in two different ways. Not only does language "hold everything within . . . the event," but we are said to "dwell in" (*wohnen . . . im*) the event inasmuch as we are given over to language. Here, one might say that it is the event that appears as "that which gives home to human being" (to use the language of the "Letter on 'Humanism'") rather than to language, except that the very distinction between language, or the essence of language, and the event seems not to be such as to allow one to exclude the other. To use a form of words Heidegger uses elsewhere, language, or the being of language, and the event now appear as "the same."

The Spatiality of Language

If language is dimensional, if it is relational, then why is it not also *spatial*? That certainly seems to be the implicit direction in which much of this discussion leads. As we saw earlier, however, although Heidegger recognizes that a sense of spatiality seems to be invoked in talk, for instance, of the dimension, he also insists that what is at issue is nothing spatial or, at least, nothing spatial "as ordinarily understood."[32] In the passage in which this is addressed in the "Letter on 'Humanism,'" Heidegger comments that "the dimension is not something spatial in the familiar sense. Rather, everything spatial and all time-space occur essentially in the dimensionality [*im Dimensionalen*] that being itself is."[33] Dimensionality and spatiality are here distinguished in a way that, on the face of it, seems peculiar. After all, what is dimensionality if it is not spatial? One cannot answer that the dimensionality at issue is temporal rather than spatial. Such a response only leads to a further question as to whether this would entail the implicit spatiality of the temporal itself (the problem, after all, is that dimensionality seems to bring spatiality with it). Even more fundamentally, it seems to ignore the fact that what is surely indicated by Heidegger's comment, even if not made explicit, is that it is not only the spatial that occurs in the dimension but also the temporal (thus one might say, analogously, that the event character of the event is "not something temporal in the familiar sense"), and so it is the relation of both spatiality and temporality to the dimension that is in question. Moreover, if it is indeed the case that dimension is not to be construed as spatial "in the familiar sense," then the same ought to be said of the dimension *as dimensional*, especially since "in its familiar sense," the dimension *is* spatial. Indeed, one might argue that to claim that the dimension is not spatial "in the familiar sense" is thereby also to claim that it is not dimensional "in the familiar sense."

What almost certainly lies behind Heidegger's refusal of a spatial understanding of the dimension is, first and foremost, the desire to rule out any notion of the dimension as associated with space "construed physically-technologically"—with the idea of space "that was first determined by Galileo and Newton" and that consists in the idea of a "homogenous separation that is not distinct in any of its possible places, that is equivalent in all directions, but not sensibly perceptible."[34] The passage from the "Letter on 'Humanism,'" however, might be thought to make for complications here since although Heidegger there refers to the dimension as "not something spatial in the familiar sense," he also says that "everything spatial and all time-space" occur in the dimensionality of being. And in a note, appended to the phrase "everything spatial," he adds: "Space neither alongside time, nor dissolved into time, nor deduced from time."[35] His comments in the "Letter on 'Humanism'" are echoed in the discussion of the dimension in "'. . . Poetically Man Dwells . . .'": "everything spatial, as something for which space is made, is already in need of the dimension, that is, into which it is admitted."[36] This might be taken to imply that it is not only spatiality "in the familiar sense" from which the dimensionality at issue is marked off, but from all and every sense of spatiality.

Whether or not, in the passages in question, it is Heidegger's intention to exclude every sense of spatiality from the dimension, such an attempt to exclude the spatial completely would itself raise problems in those passages (since it seems at odds with the qualifications "as ordinarily understood" and "in the familiar sense"), but it would also be at odds with the way Heidegger later treats spatiality as amenable to a reading that does indeed seem to be very close to the way he also treats dimensionality. Immediately prior to his assertion of the belonging-together of saying and nearness, in "The Nature of Language," Heidegger considers the character of nearness itself and, in doing so is led directly to consider the nature of space and, with it, time. Heidegger distinguishes between time and space "conceived as parameters" (presumably what underpins the "ordinary" or "familiar" sense of both terms) and the "timing and spacing" that "moves the encounter of the four world regions" and to which the character of language is itself bound.[37]

In "Art and Space," from 1969 (the source for the characterization of space in its Galilean-Newtonian sense quoted above),[38] the focus is primarily on space (time does not appear in this discussion except inasmuch as there is an emphasis on activity), but the movement of thought is very similar. Heidegger first identifies what we may think of as the ordinary or familiar sense of space in its "physical-technological" construal, but then he asks whether this must count as "the only true space" and, more importantly, how we can find "what is peculiar to space." In response to the latter question, Heidegger writes:

> There is an emergency bridge, one that is narrow and swaying. We attempt to listen to language. Whereof does it speak in the word "space" [*Raum*]? Clearing-away [*Räumen*] speaks in it. This means: to clear out [*roden*], to make the wilderness open. Clearing-away brings forth what is free, the open for humans' settling and dwelling.[39]

Here, and in the discussion that follows, Heidegger follows the clues given by language toward a thinking of space that is more fundamental than that given in space as "physical-technological," and that does indeed seem to converge with his thinking of nearness and of the dimension.

Perhaps significantly, the language of the dimension is absent from "Art and Space," as it is also absent from "The Nature of Language." In the latter, it seems to have been replaced by the talk of nearness and the "face-to face encounter" of the fourfold. In the former, it appears to have given way to a rethought conception of the spatial as grounded in clearing-away, which is itself understood in terms of "making-space" [*Einräumen*] and then again as "granting and arranging" [*Einrichtens*]:

On the one hand, making-space admits something. It lets what is open hold sway, which among other things grants the appearance of present things to which human dwelling sees itself consigned. On the other hand, making-space prepares for things the possibility of belonging to their respective whither, and out of this, to each other.[40]

The way in which Heidegger here talks of making-space as at the heart of space and the spatial (and which he also goes on to connect directly to place in a way that is highly significant)[41] seems to parallel the way in which he elsewhere talks of language or of saying. Indeed, in thinking of language as the house of being, we are already thinking of language as a making-room in the sense Heidegger employs in "Art and Space."

Understanding each in terms, not of what is "usual" or "familiar," but rather of what is proper to it—in terms of the essential and originary—then language and space appear as belonging closely together. Language, or saying, is indeed making-space—*spacing*—but so, too, perhaps, must space, or making-space, be understood *as saying*. Although the latter idea is not explored in "Art and Space," it nevertheless seems to be a conclusion to which we are inevitably drawn. It is precisely what seems to emerge from out of Heidegger's previous reflections on language, in which space is already at issue, even if sometimes obscurely so. To think language topologically, then, is not only to allow the relation between language and place to emerge but also to attend to the very spatiality of language itself—a spatiality that is nevertheless always bound to place.

Six

The Refusal of Metaphor

It is commonplace, especially among English-speaking readers, to treat the later Heidegger as having moved away from philosophy towards poetry, and his topological approach to language, as well as the vocabulary and style of that approach, may be thought to confirm this. What is the talk of language as "the house of being," or as "nearness," if it is not poetic or an attempt to engage in a form of poetic expression? Moreover, if such thinking does indeed move in the direction of the poetic, then surely this also means that what is at work here is a mode of thinking that operates, as surely poetry does itself (or so it is assumed), primarily within the realm of the metaphorical. The reaction of many readers of Heidegger's later thinking, for whom the "poetic" character of that thinking is seen as a barrier to any properly philosophical engagement, is undoubtedly based in just such a reading.

Commonplace though this reaction is, it nevertheless represents a serious misreading of the later thought and of the development of Heidegger's thinking overall. There can be no doubt that Heidegger is critical of traditional philosophy, that he can be said to have abandoned it and even to have proclaimed that philosophy has, in some sense, come to an end. Yet what is abandoned is indeed a *traditional* mode of philosophizing, not necessarily philosophy as such. It might even be said that, on one possible reading, what Heidegger intends, in his very focus on the *end* of philosophy, is a move back towards philosophy—towards that which lies at the origin of philosophy since the end is also the beginning[1]—rather than a move away from it. The question of philosophy aside, however, it should be clear that the poetic shift in Heidegger's thinking is no mere accident, nor is it only stylistic. It arises, instead, out of the very nature of that thinking and is integral to it. Moreover, it is also not a shift towards a metaphorical mode of expression, in any usual sense, but is, rather, an attempt to return to a more primordial mode of speaking, one that is attuned to the very place of speaking, of thinking, of being. Here, the consideration of space and dimensionality that was embarked upon in previous chapters is especially instructive for the way it illuminates the character of space and dimensionality in their relation to language, and of all three in relation to place. In addition, however, it brings directly into view the issue of the meaning of the terms that are at work here, the nature of the thinking in which Heidegger is engaged, and the role of metaphor, of image, and of the poetic.

Metaphysics and Metaphor

In the previous chapter, I noted how, in the "Letter on 'Humanism,'" Heidegger warns explicitly against certain readings of terms such as "house" and "dwelling," suggesting that we are too quick to assume that we already know what such terms mean. The passage was quoted in part earlier but is worth quoting here in its entirety:

> Thinking builds upon the house of being, the house in which the jointure of being, in its destinal unfolding, enjoins the essence of the human being in each case to dwell in the truth of being. This dwelling is the essence of "being-in-the-world." The reference in *Being and Time* (H54) to "being-in" as "dwelling" is no mere etymological play. The same reference in the 1936 essay on Hölderlin's word, "Full of merit, yet poetically, man dwells upon this earth," is not the adornment of a thinking that rescues itself from science by means of poetry. The talk about the house of being is not the transfer [*Übertragung*] of the image "house" onto being. But one day we will, by thinking the essence of being in a way appropriate to its matter, more readily be able to think what "house" and "dwelling" are.[2]

That part of what Heidegger has in mind here is indeed to rule out any merely metaphoric reading is suggested by his specific rejection of the idea of any sort of image "transfer" (the Greek *metaphora* or *metaphero* meaning precisely to "transfer" or "carry across"). Elsewhere, Heidegger explicitly attacks the metaphorical itself. It serves, he says, "as a handy crutch in the interpretation of works of poetry and of artistic production in general . . . [that] . . . exists only within metaphysics," urging us to be wary "that we don't precipitously take the talk of thinking as a listening and a bringing into view to be mere metaphors and thus take them too lightly."[3] Yet, although it is quite clear that Heidegger refuses or rejects metaphor, it is equally clear that this involves no rejection of poetry. Indeed, Heidegger's refusal of metaphor occurs in just those passages in which the issue of poetic language, and Heidegger's own use of such language, is to the fore. It occurs, one might say, as part of Heidegger's defense of poetry.[4] The obvious conclusion to be drawn is that, as Heidegger sees it, poetic language, and so too, the language of genuine thinking, is not to be construed as based in the metaphoric.[5]

If we take this conclusion seriously, then it has important implications for our reading of the topological in Heidegger.[6] The language of place (and of space as well)—which means the language of the dimension, nearness, the open, the between, house, dwelling, earth, sky, even of the event—cannot be treated, if it ever was, as merely metaphoric. To do so would allow us effectively to ignore the genuine topology at issue in that language—whether because the supposed metaphor is seen as philosophically irrelevant (the metaphorical becoming a marker for what we can ignore) or because the metaphor is philosophically essential *as metaphor* (and so in its character as always a carrying across or a pointing beyond). Instead, we must attend to place as it is in its own character, which is to say, *in its own being*. This is the very point that is contained in the remark, in the "Letter on 'Humanism,'" that "one day we will, by thinking the essence of being in a way appropriate to its matter, more readily be able to think what 'house' and 'dwelling' are."[7] Heidegger's claim is that it is by thinking *being* that we will come to understand *house* and *dwelling*—which might be thought strange, as if we have to think through being in order to get to the thinking of house and dwelling, except that it simply restates Heidegger's familiar claim that all genuine thinking is a thinking *of being*—a claim that can now be seen to carry with it the refusal of metaphor, since metaphor is construed as something precisely other than this.

Here we see why metaphor and metaphysics are so much bound together. Both are forms, perhaps the *same* form, of *forgetting*. Not only is metaphor metaphysical, then, but one might say that metaphysics is itself metaphorical. It is, in the language of the ontological difference, a crossing over of the ontological difference in which that difference is also effaced. It is a movement away from being towards beings. It is also, in the language of the topological, a movement away from place that is essentially displacing and disorienting. In this latter sense, one might say that, in both the metaphor and in metaphysics, we lose sight of the place in which we nevertheless always remain.

Metaphor and Literality

If Heidegger's language, and especially the language of topology, is not to be construed metaphorically, then one might suppose that such language must instead be understood, in some sense, *literally*. Not only is the literal that which is not metaphorical, but what is at issue in, for instance, Heidegger's talk of "house" and "dwelling" is the question of what dwelling and house themselves *are*, and this is surely just the question of the literal meaning of the terms at issue here, their "first" meaning, as it were[8] (although once the notion of the literal is deployed in this manner, the question then arises as to just how the literal itself should be understood—a question that is, however, all too seldom even raised). Such an approach might be taken to involve a significant reversal of the usual understanding of the idea of the poetic. Rather than being given over to the metaphoric and the "nonliteral," it may well be taken as more properly literal, and so more properly "first," than language in any of its other forms (including, for instance, that of the "scientific").

Talk of the "literal" might be construed, in a way that does not put too much theoretical weight on the notion, as emphasizing simply the need to take seriously the language that is used—and so as guarding against taking language, to use the comment quoted earlier, "too lightly" (as the resort to a metaphoric reading might encourage). Such a weak sense of the literal is perhaps unobjectionable, yet it might also be thought that any stronger notion of literality will be problematic in this context (even if it can be applied elsewhere) no less than is the metaphorical. The literal is surely the prosaic, the ordinary, the familiar, yet the mode of speaking that is at issue here is quite other than prosaic, other than ordinary, other than familiar. The literal is often taken to bring with it a sense of speech as constrained and univocal—as determinate and without ambiguity (which is, one might say, part of what seems to be at issue in the contrast with the metaphoric—the latter being taken as a form of polysemy or equivocity and the former of monosemy or univocity), whereas poetic speaking, the speaking in which Heidegger is engaged, while not lacking in lucidity, surely brings with it an excess that goes beyond any strict or determinate delimitation of meaning.[9] Moreover, it might well be argued that what is at issue here is a mode of speaking that is the origin for all and any speaking whatsoever and so comes before any possible distinction between the metaphorical and the literal.[10]

There is something right about all of this but also something mistaken. The originary saying of being, which is an event given to human beings and to which they are already given over, is indeed neither literal nor metaphorical, and Heidegger makes no claims about either metaphoricity or literality in relation to that event. Such speaking is a form of poetic speaking—poetic speaking in its most original form as *poiesis*—but it is the speaking *of language*, which can be heard in poetry (and indeed in all language), even though it is not a speaking accomplished merely through the use of language by the poet or the thinker. In speaking, language speaks the human, not the human that speaks language. What is at issue in the discussion of metaphor in Heidegger is the character of the poetic speaking that is undertaken by the poet and thinker—the form of speaking exemplified in Hölderlin's poetry, as well as in that of René Char, in Heidegger's own thinking, and in any genuine attempt to address the question of being, of language, or of place. It is here, *and only here*, that the issue of metaphoricity arises—or can arise even as a question (it cannot be a question for the speaking that belongs to language as such)—and so also here, and only here, that any question of literality arises.

In general, the distinction between the metaphoric and the literal is probably best seen as a purely correlative one—what appears as literal in one context may be metaphorical in another (the same is true of the distinction between "dead" and "live" metaphor)—and so concerns two different ways of understanding language, two different interpretative approaches, rather than two substantively different modes of meaning or of linguistic being.[11] Such a correlative sense is of little help, however, in thinking about the issues at stake in Heidegger. As already noted, Heidegger does not himself draw on any distinction between the literal and the metaphoric, nor does he offer any substantive theory of the working of metaphor or of the relation between metaphor and literality.

Heidegger's rejection of any metaphorical reading of the poetic does not imply that the poetic is therefore given over to a simple univocity or determinacy—which also means that if Heidegger's language were to be construed "literally," rather than metaphorically, then the sense of literality at stake could not be such as to imply univocity or determinacy either. Here, we should understand any sense of literality that might be applied as consisting simply in the demand that we attend to language itself—thereby understanding the literal in something like its original sense, as that which concerns the letter or the word. Such a focus on literality, which would stand outside of the usual contrast with the metaphoric, could thereby be understood as a way of remaining true to Heidegger's insistence, for example, in "Art and Space," that we must listen *to language*,[12] and that we must do so even in our own speaking.

The Image and the Poetic

What comes to the fore here is indeed a mode of speaking that is not metaphorical and yet retains that essential vibrancy—what I have referred to elsewhere as an *iridescence*[13]—that belongs to language as such (to language, one might say, as that "most delicate and . . . most suspended vibration"). Such vibrancy is not the same as mere ambiguity, nor does it stand as a mode of equivocity that remains merely within the contrast established by the pairing of equivocity with univocity. In the lectures on Hölderlin's "Remembrance," Heidegger remarks: "So long as we remain within the language of 'univocity' [*Eindeutigkeit*] and 'equivocity' [*Vieldeutigkeit*] we grasp the word after the standards of 'logic.' But in truth any real word has its hidden and wide spaces of vibration."[14] Clearly, the vibrancy that Heidegger asserts as belonging to every word can be viewed as a form of equivocity or polysemy—of *Vieldeutigkeit*—and so this comment does not represent a rejection of the equivocal or polysemous as such. Rather, it can be seen as an assertion of its primacy, and such a reading is confirmed by Heidegger's treatment of *Vieldeutigkeit*, elsewhere in the later thinking.[15] Heidegger's rejection of metaphor thus goes together with his assertion of the essential vibrancy of language.[16]

Yet this vibrancy, as is evident from Heidegger's characterization of the event, does not belong only to language. It is a vibrancy that belongs to the event and to being, to nearness and the dimension—a vibrancy that belongs to the word *and to thing*. "It is enough here to consider just this," Heidegger says in the lectures on Hölderlin's "Remembrance," "'things themselves' before any so-called 'symbols,' are already poetized."[17] This is why the metaphorical has no role here, and also why we may decide to draw on a certain conception of the literal[18]—because poetry is already given in the thing itself, as it is given in the event, in being, in the original and originary saying of language, by which the thing is called forth, by which it is let into the open, by which it is placed.[19] We may thus recall Char's remark, from the discussion in chapter 2, that "[t]he flowering hawthorn was my first alphabet"—both language and the poetic arise in and from out of the *placed* being of things (which is also why language and the poetic, taken in their most basic sense, must be understood as given *to* the human rather than imposed *by* the human).

Heidegger's rejection of metaphor might also appear to involve the rejection of the image. Certainly, image and metaphor are themselves often viewed as belonging together.[20] Yet there is surely a sense in which the image extends more widely than the metaphor alone. When Heidegger presents us with the phrase "the house of being," even if he does not present us with a metaphor, what he seems to present us with is an image, even if the nature and status of that image can be put in question. Moreover, the vibrancy that Heidegger speaks of as belonging to language might well be thought to be precisely a vibrancy also shared by the image—not the image as determinate representation, but the image in the indeterminacy and richness of its concrete presence. In the brief passage quoted near the beginning of this discussion, Bachelard speaks of the "house image," and his own investigation of the house is framed within an inquiry into poetry and the poetic image—poetry being essentially concerned with the image.[21] The image as Bachelard uses it here, however, appears not to be merely a representation but something much more—something that does indeed bear investigation, and whose character is not immediately apparent despite the immediacy with it may present itself. The relation between metaphor and image, and between image and poetry, is thus one that remains to be clarified.

It may be thought, however, that the matter is clear enough already. In the "Letter on 'Humanism,'" for instance, Heidegger denies that there is any transfer of the image "house" onto being.[22] In "The Ister" lectures, he insists that "the rivers in Hölderlin's poetry are . . . in no way symbolic images that are merely more difficult to interpret in terms of degree," since "if that were the case, they would still remain essentially 'symbolic images.' Yet this is precisely what they are not."[23] Similarly, in the lectures on Hölderlin's "Remembrance," Heidegger comments that "the master-key of all poetics, the doctrine of image and metaphor, in the realm of Hölderlin's hymnal poetry, opens not a single door and brings us in no way into the open."[24] It would be easy to suppose that Heidegger does indeed treat the metaphor and the image together, rejecting both. Yet the passages, like these, in which Heidegger is critical of images and the language of images (which is what we might suppose poetic language to consist in), typically involve the image only under a particular construal. So, in "The Ister" passage, it is the *symbolic* image that is rejected; in the "Remembrance" discussion, it is the image as tied to metaphor, but also, once again, to *symbol* (and so to the idea of that which refers to something else; namely, a world beyond or behind—*Hinterwelten*)[25]; and in the "Letter on 'Humanism,'" to the *transfer* of the image (which may be thought already to be implied in the idea of the symbolic).

What is at issue here, so far as the image is concerned, is thus the image as tied to a movement beyond and away from the thing—and so precisely to the image construed as symbolic.[26] It is thus that in the "Remembrance" lectures, Heidegger concludes his discussion of image, symbol, and metaphor with the remark, already quoted above, that "it is enough here to consider just this: 'things themselves,' before any so-called 'symbols,' are already poetized."[27] What then of the image construed, not as symbol, but *as* thing or as belonging *with* the thing? The association of the poetic with the image ought to provoke a question concerning the image in the poetic, and, in fact, Heidegger himself raises such a question and does so in a way that does not imply the rejection of the image as such. In "The Nature of Language," he asks:

> What, really, does "figurative talk" [*bildliche Redewiese*] mean? We are quick to give the answer here, never giving it a thought that we cannot claim to have a reliable formulation so long as it remains unclear what is talk and what is imagery [*was Rede ist und was Bild*], and in what way language speaks in images, if indeed language does speak so at all.[28]

The figurative, which in the German is quite explicitly "of the image" (*bildlich*) or, as we might say, "imagistic," is itself usually taken to stand in contrast with the literal, but here that contrast also appears to be questionable—at least inasmuch as figurative talk is indeed imagistic, and inasmuch as it remains unclear to what extent the image is indeed distinct from the symbol or may, instead, be said to belong with the thing.

In "'. . . Poetically Man Dwells . . . ,'" Heidegger takes up the idea of the image, not as something symbolic or as transferred, but as connected to the very possibility of appearing—appearing as the coming into the realm of the visible:

> Our current name for the sight and appearance of something is "image." The nature of the image is to let something be seen. By contrast, copies and imitations are already mere variations on the genuine image which, as a sight or spectacle, lets the invisible be seen and so imagines the invisible in something alien to it. Because poetry takes that mysterious measure, to wit, in the face of the sky, therefore, it speaks in "images." This is why poetic images are imaginings in a distinctive sense: not mere fancies and illusions but imaginings that are visible inclusions of the alien in the sight of the familiar. The poetic saying of images gathers the brightness and sound of the heavenly appearances into one with the darkness and silence of what is alien. By such sights the god surprises us. In this strangeness he proclaims his unfaltering nearness.[29]

Poetry, Heidegger says, speaks *in images*, but, presumably, this does not mean that it necessarily speaks *in metaphors*. The image and the metaphor appear, on this account, to be distinct. The metaphorical is figurative, and yet the figurative is not always metaphorical, nor is it straightforwardly to be opposed to the literal. If one conceived of the metaphor differently—not as essentially a transfer or symbol, but as an image understood as a genuine appearance—then the way would be open for a rethinking of the connection between the metaphorical and the figurative, between metaphor and poetry, and between metaphor and thinking.[30] Whether one can argue that there is such a possibility implicit in Heidegger's approach,[31] it is nevertheless not the path Heidegger himself adopts. Metaphor is thus rejected. Yet the image as distinct from the symbol, and the character of the poetic as oriented to such images, seems to be affirmed.

Although the discussion of the image may initially seem like something of a detour, it nevertheless turns us back to what is central. Indeed, one might argue that the entire mode of thinking that is instantiated in Heidegger's later work is essentially oriented to the image—even that it occurs *in images*.[32] Yet this focus on the image means something very specific: it is a mode of *seeing* that remains with things, allows things to appear, allows them to come into the open. The image that is at issue here is thus not the image as representation (which means that the thinking at issue must be distinguished from the "representational thinking"—*vorstellendes Denken*—of which Heidegger is elsewhere so critical);[33] it is not the image as symbol; it is not the image as it might be thought to operate in the metaphor, understood as a form of transference; and it is not the image as somehow contrasted with that which is literal. Instead, what is at issue is the image as that which gathers and shows, and, if we take note of the way such gathering and showing can be said to house and to place, perhaps we might even say that what is at issue is the way the image can be said to house thinking—to be a home for thinking.

Something of this is surely at work in Bachelard, for whom the investigation of the house is indeed an investigation of the image (the latter being a central focus for much of his later work), and in whose work the image houses as much as does the house itself. As noted earlier, the image as it appears in Bachelard is not merely a representation, and it also has nothing of the character of the metaphoric as that appears in Heidegger. Bachelard claims that, in the engagement with poetry, "[we] are asked to consider an image not as an object and even less as the substitute for an object, but to seize its specific reality."[34] Moreover, it is precisely in virtue of its relation to the image that Bachelard declares poetry to be the origin of language.[35] The image possesses a dynamic and active character—it "reverberates"—like that which Heidegger attributes to language, and it is through the sonority of the image that the poet is said to speak "on the threshold of being."[36]

Heidegger says that the reason poetry speaks in images is "because poetry takes that mysterious measure, to wit, in the face of the sky." The taking of measure is, as we have already seen, directly tied to the dimension, to the opening of the fourfold. It is a spacing and a placing—or, perhaps better, an entering into that spacing and placing, a gathering and a saying. The taking of measure does not address itself to what lies beyond, even though it does gather what is alien and what is familiar. But the place of this gathering is the very place of our own being, as well as of the things that are gathered around us and in which the fourfold is itself gathered. The character of Heidegger's thinking, of poetic thinking as a thinking in images, also returns us to the character of that thinking as a thinking of place. Thus, the poetry that thinks can indeed be said to be the saying of the place of being, to be, in truth, the topology of being.

Placing and Saying

Gadamer draws attention to the way in which Heidegger pushed against the constraints of traditional philosophical language in trying to find a vocabulary adequate to the direction in which his thinking was headed—and he also draws attention to Hölderlin as playing a crucial role in the attempt to find such a vocabulary. Referring to the essays contained in his book *Heidegger's Ways*, Gadamer remarks that, there, his aim is "to make it clear that the use of language in the later Heidegger does not represent a drifting off into poetry, but rather is situated completely in tune with the thinking which led him into a whole new line of questioning."[37] Here, Gadamer is not concerned to deny the poetic character of the later thinking but rather to argue against its treatment as merely a contingent affectation and to emphasize instead its character as a direct and necessary outcome of the radicalization of Heidegger's thinking in the period after *Being and Time*. The aim of the inquiry undertaken here has been to show that this radicalization is directly bound up with the turn towards topology—towards the saying of the place of being.

The turn towards place not only requires a different use of language—one that both draws upon and converges with the poetic—but it also brings language itself directly into question. To think the being of language is to think the being of place. Thus, saying *is placing* just as placing *is saying*. It is the necessity and intimacy of this relation that forces thinking towards poetic saying. It does so, not because poetry involves some rhapsodic movement beyond, but because of the way it remains *here*, with things, in the very openness of the world. Heidegger writes: "Poetry does not fly above and surmount the earth in order to escape it and hover over it. Poetry is what first brings man onto the earth, making him belong to it, and thus brings him into dwelling."[38] Poetry, one might say, has its own being in the saying of the place of being—both in the saying and in the saying that responds to that saying. It is thus no surprise that the thinking of place has so often been concentrated among poets—and we need not look only to Hölderlin or even to Char in this regard. In English, in fact, it might seem as if the thinking of place has been the almost exclusive preserve of poets, of whom John Clare and William Wordsworth are only two of the best-known examples.[39] Poetry is place-disclosing, not only of individual places, but of place itself, and so of our own place, which is the place of being.

Yet what is also disclosed in poetry is language—poetry is indeed that which first makes language possible[40]—and in poetry, the question of place and the question of language are shown as belonging together. The region of their belonging is topology, and what poetry both reveals and instantiates is the nature of language *and* the nature of language *in its belonging to such a topology*. Significantly, however, and in contrast to the language to which philosophy is often taken to aspire, the language at issue here is not the language of completion or finality. Poetry exhibits no such completion, nor can it ever properly aspire to it. This might already be thought to follow from its inevitable polysemy—its iridescence, and the iridescence of things, as explored above—but it does not follow from this alone. Because poetry is *a saying*, it is irreducible simply to *something said*. As such, it does not consist in something that, in being said, is thereby completed or finalized, and so set behind us. The saying of the place of being that is "the poetry that thinks" is, as saying, something towards which we are constantly turned, something that always remains *before us*. Here we remain always "on the way," just as we remain always "on the way" to language (the two "ways" are, in fact, one). What this means, however, is that the "difficulty" of language—which Gadamer identifies as leading Heidegger towards the language of poetry and into the engagement with Hölderlin—is not a difficulty that poetry, or Hölderlin, could ever enable Heidegger to overcome. The "difficulty" is one that belongs to language as such.

As language is the house of being, so language is the place of being. Thus, the topology of being, which is the saying of the place of being, is also the saying of language. Moreover, saying and placing here appear as the same—one may say that this is partly what is captured in Heidegger's use of the term *Erörterung*, which can now be understood as the placing that occurs in and through language, in and through which language is itself placed, exemplified in Heidegger's approach in "Language in the Poem," in which *Erörterung* is directly thematized.[41] In being "on the way" to language, we are also, therefore, "on the way" to the place that language is, which is to say that we are on the way *to place*. Indeed, in being "on the way," we already find ourselves given over to place, for to be "on the way" is already to be turned towards place. And, more than this, to be turned towards place, even to be placed, is itself to be "on the way." Heidegger comments that "the place, the gathering power, gathers in and preserves all it has gathered, not like an encapsulating shell, but rather by penetrating with its light all it has gathered, and only thus releasing it into its own nature."[42]

Placing—and place itself—is not some simple "remaining within" that holds what is gathered in an already determined locatedness. Instead, it is a gathering and a turning, a constant movement towards, rather than a final coming to rest. The "difficulty" of language that leads Heidegger towards poetry is thus not a difficulty that belongs to language alone but is rather a "difficulty" that belongs to language as placing, a "difficulty" that belongs *to place*. As such, however, it is not a difficulty to be overcome. Instead, it is a difficulty that marks the continuing questionability of language and of place. It is this questionability that is opened up in the thinking of poetry and to which poetic thinking also responds. In doing so, such thinking directs attention to its own place—to the place of saying and the saying of place—at the same time as it also heeds that place and the saying that belongs to it.

Seven

Finding Ourselves in the World

"Nothing is more usual in philosophy, and even in common life," declared David Hume, "than to talk of the combat of passion and reason, to give the preference to reason, and to declare that men are only so far virtuous as they conform themselves to its dictates."[1] It is no less usual today than it was in Hume's time, although it is more often expressed nowadays by reference to *emotion* than to passion. To take one prominent contemporary example, Peter Singer argues that the reliance on intuitions in ethical decision making is problematic on the grounds that intuitions are essentially driven by emotional responses that are poor guides to the moral decisions at issue.[2] In a slightly different context, Paul Bloom provides another instance of the same general tendency, arguing against the role of empathy in ethical thinking. Here, too, the emotional content of empathic responses often misleads us, according to Bloom, giving rise, once again, to questionable ethical judgments.[3] Not only in Singer and Bloom, but also more widely, emotion is frequently taken to be both a poor guide to ethical conduct and to be subversive of such conduct—the latter being more properly based in a purely rational and "objective" assessment of decision and action, with emotion being thereby relegated to the domain of the merely "subjective" and so also of the variable and the untrustworthy. Significantly, this contrast between emotion and reason is often accompanied by a particular conception of reason, according to which reason tends to be viewed as essentially *calculative*—as involving a certain sort of linear processing of values of the sort exemplified in formal logic and mathematical calculation.

The "Combat" of Reason and Emotion

The approaches of Singer and Bloom exemplify the tendency identified by Hume—a tendency so basic and widespread as often to go unremarked—to treat emotion (or "passion") and reason as distinct and often opposed elements. This is a powerful idea within ethical thinking, especially the sort of consequentialist and utilitarian thinking to which those such as Singer and Bloom are committed, but it is not restricted to ethics alone. That the traditional contrast between emotion and reason remains at work in contemporary philosophy, outside of ethics as well as within, is noted by Matthew Ratcliffe. Referring to the way emotion has itself been addressed in much recent discussion, Ratcliffe comments that "the structure of the debate still presupposes that theoretical, detached cognition epitomises the nature of our most basic relationship with the world. Emotions are either evaluative constituents of propositional attitudes or they are distinct from such attitudes and thus peripheral to the way we relate to the world."[4]

Ratcliffe's work is especially noteworthy, not only for the way it contests the contrast between reason and emotion that is at stake, but also because it does so in a way that draws directly on Heidegger's thought.[5] In this, Ratcliffe exemplifies something of the contemporary influence of Heidegger's work (most famously, perhaps, through the appropriations of Heidegger by Hubert Dreyfus and also by John Haugland[6]) in philosophy of mind, philosophical psychology, and cognitive science. Part of what marks out Ratcliffe's approach, however, is that it is in many ways more attentive to the details of Heidegger's thinking than is often the case elsewhere. Ratcliffe's development of that thinking, as it applies to the understanding of the emotions and of reason and rationality, is an important source for the discussion to be undertaken in this chapter. Yet it is not just the potential contribution of Heidegger's thinking to the understanding of emotion, or the relation between emotion and reason, that is at issue here, but also the way such considerations shed light on Heidegger's own thinking, and especially the way they connect with the topological dimension in that thinking.

The contrast between emotion and reason often lies beneath other forms of philosophical controversy and critique. It seems to be an important element (even if not the only element), for instance, in the frequent criticism of Heidegger, particularly in English-language thought, as an "irrationalist"—as supposedly a thinker who both promotes the emotional over the rational, and whose thinking is characterized by the way it gives primacy to emotional or affective considerations over properly rational ones. The criticism is perhaps most strongly apparent in readings of Heidegger's later thinking and especially in the idea (remarked upon several times in previous chapters) that it is characterized by a turn to poetry and mysticism. This does not seem merely to be a claim to the effect that there is a lack of *argument* in the later work (a claim sometimes applied to the earlier work as well), but that the argument is of the *wrong sort*—that it does indeed depend on emotional affect rather than logical or rational evaluation. Moreover, as the criticism is more strongly evident in regard to the later thinking, it also seems more strongly directed against the topological elements in Heidegger. In this respect, then, the question concerning the "combat" referred to by Hume is a question that also concerns the style and orientation of the sort of philosophical thinking to be found in Heidegger—and, of course, in other thinkers who follow a similar path.

Hume notes that this combat does not belong only to philosophy—whether in ethics or elsewhere—but is no less usual "in common life." It is indeed so widespread that it is a readily apparent theme in popular culture, where it is often played out, though in a way that runs counter to the common philosophical prioritization of rationality, through the assimilation of the contrast between emotion and reason to that between the human and the nonhuman (the contrast has also frequently been presented, and continues to be so in some quarters, in gendered terms, through the paring of the rational male with the emotional or "intuitive" female[7]). For instance, in the iconic 1960s TV series *Star Trek*, the contrast was a recurrent theme, being exemplified in two of the series' main characters: the science officer, Spock, and the ship's captain, James Kirk. The latter's "human" emotions were often shown to win out over Spock's pure "rationality"—a rationality derived from his nonhuman "Vulcan" ancestry.[8] The contrast is often presented in the form of duos like that of Spock and Kirk or, to take another example, Conan Doyle's pairing of Watson and Holmes.

The contrast is as readily apparent in contemporary popular culture (if often complicated in various ways) as in the 1960s, and yet the contrast does not only appear in terms of popular cultural representations. It is often embedded in modes of organization, in styles of leadership, in political ideology and rhetoric, and in activities and processes. In this respect, one might say, with Heidegger, that the combat of emotion and reason has taken on a "metaphysical" form, shaping the very way in which the world is presented and with which it is interacted. In many areas of contemporary life and society, there is thus an increasing focus (one that was presaged in the past but not so fully realized) on the primacy of what are often represented as purely rational modes of engagement. Whether we look to algorithmic decision making, more generalized forms of artificial intelligence, various modes of economic thinking—especially those that privilege the "market"—or even some of what is termed "evidence-based" or "evidence-led" decision-making,[9] there is a similar emphasis, in different ways, on the purely "rational" and "objective." There is a widespread assumption, not only that reason and emotion are distinct, such that reason can operate independently of emotion (or of anything else for that matter), but that, as Ratcliffe emphasizes, our primary engagement with the world ought indeed to be (even if it not always is) by means of reason alone, and that the primary mechanisms that should order our lives ought to stand apart from any emotional dispositions or tendencies. Given the narrowed-down conception of reason and rationality that is often assumed here—essentially that of the sort of calculative thinking noted earlier—the model for our mode of engagement with things becomes that of a detached intellect operating on things as if they were both apart from us and yet also completely subject to our control.

For the most part, the separation of reason from emotion, and even the idea of emotion itself, is something modern (the term coming into English only in the sixteenth century).[10] In Plato, for instance, where one also finds a distinction between different parts of the soul or *psyche*, the contrast is between the appetites (*epithumia*), spiritedness (*thymos*), and intellect or rational insight (*nous*).[11] And although it is commonplace to find the modern contrast between reason and emotion being read back into the Platonic account, to do so is significantly to simplify and thereby also to obscure the nature of that account. Even the Greek emphasis on the importance of intellection—that which pertains especially to *nous*—cannot simply be equated with the modern emphasis on rationality (especially on rationality as calculation). Given the modern origins of the terms at issue, it is not surprising to find the neuro-psychologist Antonio Damasio referring to reason's prioritization over and separation from emotion as "Descartes' error"—thereby also identifying this view with the seventeenth-century philosopher René Descartes.[12] One might well take issue with the historical accuracy of

Damasio's invocation of Descartes here—the error is surely not Descartes's alone, even if it does not go back to Plato either.

Yet although it may well have earlier (if arguable) precedents and has sometimes been contested by movements within modernity (including Romanticism and idealism), the idea of the prioritization and separation of reason in relation to emotion does indeed appear as something characteristically modern. One might even say that this idea has become part of a certain *mythos* of modernity, such that to be modern is to extricate oneself from the control of what is often taken to be a more primitive set of drivers, including emotions, and to give oneself over to the "superior" power of reason and intellect, understood in terms of a certain sort of capacity for abstraction and calculation. The betterment of human being is thus typically associated with the escape from emotional attachments and constraints through the liberating power of calculative rationality alone—our engagement with the world being like that of a purely abstracted intelligence. Even the presence, within modernity, of a strand that emphasizes individual self-expression—often in the form of emotion—and that is associated with the idea of "authenticity" (discussed in chapter 9), sees it typically operating within the same duality of emotion and reason that is at work in the modern emphasis on rationality over emotion.

There is, of course, considerable ambiguity around the idea of "emotion" that is at issue here. Not only is this suggested by the example of the rather different division of the soul to be found in Plato, but it is also a point that becomes evident when we ask whether, for instance, curiosity and surprise are to be counted as emotions. It certainly cannot be assumed that they are not—or that they are somehow purely "rational" modes of affectivity or responsiveness. Whether they are emotions and how we ought to differentiate emotions from simple attitudes, from moods, appetites, affects, passions, or even "feelings," are perhaps best treated as questions to which there are no absolute and determinate answers—despite the philosophical heat some have generated.[13] The history of emotions—which includes the inquiry both into the past understanding and experience of emotion and the emotional content of historical events and experience[14]—shows that the way in which emotions are classified, and even what is taken to be an emotion, is not fixed but changes with other social and cultural circumstances, just as the manner in which certain emotions are portrayed also shows a degree of variation. And although Darwin famously argues for the universality of emotional expression across both human and other animals, his account still leaves room for a degree of variation—the thesis of universality being, in any case, restricted primarily to *facial* expressions.[15]

To treat emotion in broad fashion, as it might encompass a range of states and dispositions, does not itself make much difference to the idea of the contrast between emotion and reason that is so commonly assumed (the contrast is seldom expressed in precise terms). Moreover, the fact of such breadth in how emotion might be understood does not mean that emotions are themselves somehow arbitrary or completely determined by convention, such that there is no underlying truth to our emotions and the judgments we make about them, but rather that the reality of emotional life is such as to support many different understandings and interpretations of it. Our emotional lives, like our lives generally, form complex landscapes that always allow for many different descriptions and depictions that are no less true for the fact that they are many. Precisely because of the breadth, as well as the indeterminacy, that attaches to emotions and emotional life, "emotion" will be employed in my discussion in this chapter in a wide rather than narrow sense—which means that it will be used in a way that does indeed include affects, moods, passions, and the full range of felt states and attitudes by which, as the term "emotion" itself implies, we are *moved*. That idea of "movement" (or agitation or excitation, which the etymology of "emotion" also suggests; the term coming, *via* the French, from the Latin *emovere*, meaning "to move out from")[16] is an important one—to which I will return—since it brings with it the idea of emotions as what give force and direction to our lives.

The latter idea of emotion as *motivating* and *orienting* stands in sharp contrast to those approaches that seem to underlie the ethical thinking of those such as Singer and Bloom, even if never spelled out, according to which it is possible and preferable to live one's life in a way given over to reason alone—to live in a way that sets emotion to one side. So deep-seated is this idea of the primacy of reason that it can be hard even to make plausible the suggestion that it might be erroneous. Yet erroneous it surely is, and it is the nature of the error, as well as an alternative way of thinking, that I want to explore. Not only is reason not the master (though whether it is, as Hume claimed, the slave is another question), but our very access to the world is possible only on the basis of our prior emotional engagement with things and of the fact that reason is already bound up within this structure rather than being apart from it.[17] Heidegger's work turns out to be important here, not only because of the way it eschews the idea of philosophical thinking as based only in the narrowly "logical" or "objective" (which does not mean it eschews reason or rationality), but because Heidegger also suggests a different way of thinking about emotion, and a different role for it, in the structure of human being-in-the-world, than has traditionally been assumed.

Reason, Emotion, and the World

One of the problems with a purely "rational" approach to the world—were such a thing possible—is that it offers no indication of how we should engage with things or even what it might be with which we should engage. Understood in the manner in which it is set against emotion, reason is not *substantive* but almost entirely *formal*. This is one way of understanding Hume's famous claim that reason is the "slave of the passions," in other words, that *reason has no motivating power*.[18] Reason must therefore serve that which does motivate, namely, the passions, and it must do so by, among other things, enabling the identification of the means to those ends towards which we are indeed motivated. But in doing this, it concerns only the relations between ends and means, and between different objects, as those ends and objects are already picked out in certain ways by the passions, that is to say, by our own prior emotional stances towards the world.

In this respect, one might argue that a purely rational approach to the world would not, in itself, offer any means by which the self could attach to things. It would remove us from the source of that which motivates and engages us, and it would do so because of the way rationality seems to require abstraction or distance—the more rational, the more removed from the concreteness of our situation, but also the more removed from any impetus towards action. This is what underlies the supposition that is sometimes encountered to the effect that the attitude of pure calculative rationality has an inevitable tendency towards indifference or even a form of boredom—something that is suggested, for instance, by Georg Simmel's analysis of the effect of that form of rationalization that belongs with monetization.[19] It is such tendency towards indifference that may even be said to underlie the idea that pure rationality tends inevitably towards a form of inhumanity since it no longer has any sense of the true value of things. On such a basis, if we really were to take the form of a purely rational mode of being-in-the-world, we would also, by that very fact, be removed both from objects and from ourselves, having nothing to motivate us towards objects or even in relation to ourselves. Put simply, we would not *care* about anything and, as such, would have no interest in anything either. In this respect, it is not only that reason does not motivate, as Hume argues, but that reason, as traditionally conceived, does not *orient* either.

When we first encounter things, it is typically not in some abstract or neutral fashion. Instead, we find ourselves in the world in ways that already position or place us in relation to things in certain ways. In the most general sense, we may say that we always find ourselves in the world in a way shaped by prior cares and concerns. Sometimes those prior cares and concerns are themselves directly shaped by powerfully felt emotions, but they are also shaped by more moderate feelings or complexes of feeling that we may not even notice, such that we separate them out as distinct feelings. In those everyday cases, our engagement derives from more long-standing and settled emotional attachments and dispositions that provide the basic frame within which our actions and decisions are situated. Emotion orients in a way that reason does not. This emotional engagement with the world, which is also an evaluative engagement, does not only involve those general modes of comportment towards and responses to the world, such as boredom, excitement, curiosity, or wonder, but many, more specifically focused emotions and attitudes that are at work in our everyday involvement with things. Emotion is thus an integral part of the felt experience of finding oneself in the world (although this need not imply that all such felt experience is emotional[20])—something echoed in one of the German terms that Heidegger uses to refer to mood or emotional disposition, *Befindlichkeit* or, most literally, "finding-oneself-ness."[21] In the Macquarie and Robinson edition of *Being and Time*, the term is awkwardly translated into English as "state of mind," but in the Stambaugh and Schmidt translation as "attunement," with the latter translation carrying a sense of "being connected to," inasmuch as it implies being tuned, or attuned, *to* something.

It might be argued that there is no real discussion of emotion as such in Heidegger—and certainly not in *Being and Time*. Heidegger's focus in the latter work is surely on moods, *Stimmungen* ("attunement" can also be used to translate *Stimmung*, since the term derives from *stimmen*, one of whose meanings is "to tune"[22]), with the term *Befindlichkeit* being used to refer to moods in their ontological character: "What we indicate *ontologically* with the term *attunement* [*die Befindlichkeit*] is *ontically* what is most familiar and an everyday kind of thing: mood [*Stimmung*], being in a mood [*das Gestimmtsein*]."[23] Yet if we accept, as argued earlier, that the language of "emotion," "mood," "affect," and even "feeling" is not susceptible to any precise differentiation and determination, so that "emotion" can be used in a broad sense that encompasses "mood," then such an objection will be hard to sustain in the absence of any explicit clarification on Heidegger's part. In fact, *Being and Time* provides no evidence that what is at issue in the discussion of *Stimmung* and *Befindlichkeit* concerns mood as clearly distinct from emotion.[24] Moreover, the way in which the same topic is discussed elsewhere confirms the lack of any such clear differentiation in Heidegger's approach.

In *The Fundamental Concepts of Metaphysics*, Heidegger addresses the question of what he terms the "fundamental attunement" (*Grundstimmung*) that belongs to philosophy and, in doing so, also returns to the topic of mood or attunement (*Stimmung*) more generally. Although the term *Befindlichkeit* does not appear in this discussion, it is nevertheless clear that moods or attunements are understood in much the same fashion as in *Being and Time*, and so as "the fundamental ways in which we *find* ourselves *disposed* in such and such a way."[25] Heidegger makes mention of a wide variety of states including joy, contentment, bliss, sadness, melancholy, anger, grief, good humor, liveliness, depressiveness, apprehensiveness, and boredom (the latter being a major focus for discussion). He also refers to moods, or attunements, as "feelings" ("Stimmungen sind Gefühle").[26] Feeling (*Gefühl*) reappears as an issue for Heidegger in a much later series of lectures—those on Nietzsche from 1936 through 1937—along with passion (*Leidenschaft*) and affect (*Affekt*).[27] With these three terms, "each an arbitrary substitute for the others," says Heidegger, "we depict the supposedly irrational side of psychic life."[28] Moods, whether as *Stimmungen* or *Befindlichkeiten*, are not specifically taken up, but since Heidegger notes in *Being and Time* that they "have long been familiar ontically under the terms of affects and feelings,"[29] they can be presumed to be implicitly at issue.

While Heidegger notes various ways in which feeling, passion, and affect might be distinguished (and discusses the difference between specific instances, notably anger and hate, love and joy), he does not argue for any simple or absolute differentiation between them. In fact, he asserts that the real matter at issue, which is not just a question of the meanings of terms, concerns "whether . . . the essence of affect and of passion exhibits an original, essential connection . . . and . . . whether this original connection can truly be understood if only we grasp the essence of what we call 'feeling.'"[30] As Heidegger pursues this "original connection" in the Nietzsche lectures, and so in relation to Nietzsche's own thinking, it leads directly to the will: "[W]illing is feeling," says Heidegger, and feeling is "a state of attunement [*Zustand als Gestimmtheit*]."[31]

What concerns Heidegger, in both the earlier and later discussions, is a broad range of emotional or affective states, including but certainly not restricted to moods—as if they were some subclass of these—all of which he describes using a similar language of finding oneself, of being open to and in relation with, of being *situated*. In the Nietzsche lectures, this language is evident in Heidegger's characterization of the essence of *feeling* [*Gefühl*]:

> A feeling is the way we find ourselves in relationship to beings, and thereby at the same time to ourselves. It is the way we find ourselves particularly attuned to beings which we are not and to the being we ourselves are. In feeling, a state opens up, and stays open, in which we stand related to things, to ourselves, and to the people around us, always simultaneously. Feeling is the very state, open to itself, in which Dasein hovers. [32]

Feeling, one might say, is the opening up of a certain situatedness; it is the finding of oneself as standing in a certain relation, and so in a certain way, to things and to oneself. In asserting the connection of will and willing to feeling ("willing is feeling"), Heidegger is therefore also asserting the character of will and willing as just such an opening up of situatedness, so that "it is will itself that has the character of opening up and keeping open,"[33] and although Heidegger is elsewhere critical of the idea that willing is the *primary* mode of relatedness to the world, this does not mean that he denies that it can be a mode of such relatedness. The language that is here used in relation to will and feeling is much the same language used in *Being and Time*, as well as *The Fundamental Concepts of Metaphysics*, in connection with mood or "attunement." Thus, in *Being and Time*, Heidegger writes:

> Mood makes manifest "how one is and how one is coming along." In this "how one is" being in a mood brings being to its "there" . . . In attunement, Dasein is always already brought before itself, it has always already found itself . . . The moodedness of attunement constitutes existentially the openness to the world of Dasein . . . Attunement is an existential, fundamental way in which Dasein is its there.[34]

And in *The Fundamental Concepts of Metaphysics*:

> Attunement is not some being that appears in the soul as an experience, but the way of our being there with one another . . . Attunements . . . are precisely a fundamental manner and fundamental way of being, indeed of being-there [Da-sein] . . . Attunements are the fundamental ways in which we *find* ourselves *disposed* in such and such a way.[35]

Both mood and feeling are presented by Heidegger, throughout his work, as essentially *disclosive*. In the language of *Being and Time*, they are "fundamental existential" modes of the "*equiprimordial disclosedness* of world."[36] As such, they belong to that larger structure, by and through which the world and the things in it show themselves. This applies no less to emotion, in the broad sense used here, than it does to mood or feeling. Emotion is that which moves us in and towards the world and, so, in relation to things, others, and ourselves, such that aspects of the world stand out for us and give direction to what we think, decide, and do.[37]

Empirical and Ontological Approaches

Heidegger is undoubtedly the key figure in the articulation of this "disclosive" account of the emotions (hence his prominence in Ratcliffe's work), and yet such an account is not peculiar to Heidegger alone. Something similar appears explicitly in the work of Otto Bollnow (to whom I will return below), as well as being present, even if often left implicit, in the work of Merleau-Ponty, Bachelard, and others. Part of what draws these thinkers together is a commitment to the idea that our primary engagement with the world is not that which belongs with a merely "rational" attitude to things (as this is usually understood) but is, instead, an engagement that belongs with emotion and affect. Moreover, as these thinkers share a broadly phenomenological—and *ontological*—approach to the issues at stake, so they also tend to treat those issues as extending beyond the realms of the biological or psychological alone. This is obviously so in the case of Heidegger, for whom what is at issue are certain basic structures of human being-in-the-world—structures that are indeed existentially fundamental. Thus, in the Nietzsche lectures, Heidegger comments that, when it comes to a genuine understanding of affects, passions, and feelings, "it is not a matter for psychology, nor even for a psychology undergirded by physiology and biology. It is a matter of the basic modes that constitute Dasein, a matter of the ways man confronts the Da, the openness and concealment of beings, in which he stands."[38] It is a matter, one might say, of the way human being finds itself already *placed* in the world in a fundamental way.

To be sure, one cannot be *in* the world at all, responding and acting in relation to things, without also being emotionally engaged *with* the world, since it is emotion, broadly understood, that orients us in a way that makes response and action possible. If we are to understand ourselves as genuinely acting in and responding to the world, then we cannot take ourselves as emotionally inert. On this basis, emotions cannot be construed as *contingent* properties, capacities, or affects that belong to subjects *in addition to* their other capacities as acting and responding beings[39]—as would be the case on a purely empirical (i.e., psychological or biological) approach. Instead, emotion refers us to a basic feature of subjectivity (hence the emphasis on the ontological); namely, to the way subjectivity is always *oriented* in relation to its environment and the objects around it. It is precisely this orientation that, as it is also felt, is experienced *as emotion*—so that one might almost go so far as to say that emotion or, more accurately, the experience of emotion is a matter of just such felt *orientation* (or, in some cases, of *dis*orientation).

Emotion (and so also mood, feeling, passion, and affect) belongs to the necessary structure of being-in-the-world. To be in the world is to be emotionally affected, although how affectedness plays out in any individual case will, of course, vary enormously. It is thus important to note that emotional affectedness is not to be measured simply by the overt display of such affectedness, nor is it a matter only of certain types or levels of affectedness. Even individuals who seem to be emotionally apathetic (as in autism or, more rarely, alexithymia) are not emotionally inert but, rather, have difficulty in recognizing emotion in others or themselves, or have only a limited range or level of emotion. To be genuinely and completely apathetic or emotionally inert would be to have utterly lost the capacity to engage with oneself, with others, and with the world—to have lost the very capacity to respond and to act.

The sort of approach to the emotions that is present in Heidegger's work is quite distinct from the more empirical type of inquiry that appears in the work of neuropsychologists and cognitive scientists—including scientists such as Damasio. Yet as Mathew Ratcliffe points out, Heidegger's approach can be seen as convergent with, and indeed supported by, much contemporary work on the emotions in their relation to cognition and behavior.[40] In a review article in *Science*, for instance, the neuropsychologist Ray Dolan writes, in quite general terms, of emotion as tied to the capacity to find value in the world—which is, one might say, another way of describing what I have referred to as the capacity for orientation. Dolan writes:

> An ability to ascribe value to events in the world, a product of evolutionary selective processes, is evident across phylogeny. Value in this sense refers to an organism's facility to sense whether events in its environment are more or less desirable . . . emotions represent complex psychological and physiological states that, to a greater or lesser degree, index occurrences of value . . . the range of emotions to which an organism is susceptible will, to a high degree, reflect on the complexity of its adaptive niche. In higher order primates, in particular humans, this involves adaptive demands of physical, socio-cultural, and interpersonal contexts.[41]

It is worth noting, too, the way many contemporary neuroscientists contest the supposed separation of emotion and cognition—a separation that phenomenology also rejects as untenable. In his discussion, Ratcliffe cites Damasio's work, but he also considers other aspects of the way emotional responses, or the lack of them, directly affect the capacity to engage with the world. He cites certain breakdowns in cognition—Capgras's syndrome and anosognosia—that are linked to damage to particular neural pathways in the brain also associated with emotional response.[42] Both involve a deficit in relation to what can be referred to as *cognitive* emotions—in particular, doubt—and therefore involve a failure in the ability to recognize the possible falsity of beliefs and need for their revision, as well as appropriate behavioral adjustment.

Contemporary neurophysiological accounts of emotion, and of the underlying mechanisms of emotional response that connect them with specific parts of the brain, provide important insight into the contingent physiological basis of emotion. But such insight does not, in itself, provide any basis on which one could arrive at specific ontological conclusions, even though it may well be useful in informing ontological reflection on the phenomena at issue. Empirical neurophysiological and ontological accounts operate at different levels of analysis and explanation. They may well be complementary but cannot properly be in competition (the idea that the neurophysiological is inconsistent with the ontological depends on having already assumed an ontological construal of the neurophysiological). Moreover, a phenomenological-ontological approach to the emotions can also reveal aspects of the emotions that may not be so immediately evident from a neuropsychological perspective alone.

This is especially true of Heidegger, whose thinking on the emotions is indeed characterized by a sense of the way the emotions relate to orientation, with placedness, and thus bring the understanding of the emotions directly into the sphere of the topological. This is made especially salient with Heidegger's use of the term *Befindlichkeit* but is evident, too, in Heidegger's talk, in the Nietzsche lectures, of what is at issue as concerning "the ways man confronts the Da, the openness and concealment of beings, in which he stands." The language here, as in so much of Heidegger's thinking, is strongly topological in the way it connects to and invokes ideas and images of place and situation, and a similarly topological emphasis, although variously articulated, can be found in much of the phenomenological and hermeneutic literature in which the emotions are addressed.

In this latter respect, the work of Otto Bollnow deserves attention, even though it is arguably less philosophically interesting or important, overall, than is Heidegger's, for the way in which it attends directly to the connection between emotion and world—although again, like Heidegger, Bollnow's focus is specifically on mood or, in German, *Stimmung*. Bollnow's early work, *The Nature of Moods* (*Das Wesen der Stimmungen*), focused specifically on moods,[43] but his later writings, notably *Mensch und Raum* (appearing in English as *Human Space*), addressed the issue of lived space (a notion of space close to what might be termed *topological spatiality*). However, Bollnow also drew the two themes of mood and space together. In *Mensch und Raum*, he emphasizes the importance of mood in the understanding of space, but he also stresses the way mood is not a property merely of the subject nor of the object:

> Mood is a characteristic of just about every space . . . Mood is itself not something subjective "in" an individual and not something objective that could be found "outside" in his surroundings . . . Mood . . . concerns the individual in his still undivided unity with his surroundings . . . One speaks of a mood of the human temperament as well as of the mood of a landscape.[44]

Together with Hermann Schmitz, in whom one also finds a connection between emotion, or mood, and the spatial,[45] Bollnow has been influential in the development of recent thinking around the notion of *atmosphere*—a notion that has been particularly influential in architecture and the arts and is developed further in the work of writers such as Gernot Böhme[46] and Peter Zumthor.[47] The atmosphere of a space is the felt quality that belongs to that space, as that is determined by the physical and, more specifically, the sensory qualities of the space. In the work of many of these writers, however, and sometimes in Bollnow, too, it can be ambiguous as to whether the idea of atmosphere, or of the mood of a space, refers to a quality of any and every space or only of some spaces. If one follows the argument that I have sketched, however, then every space or, better, every *place* (since space in this sense is always the space of a place) is always infused with mood and atmosphere. Atmosphere, or emotional affect, is part of the orienting and oriented character of a place, so that to be in it is already to be affected, to some degree or other, by its atmosphere. The atmosphere of a place is thus tied to the character of a place as having its own oriented and orienting character.

The Topology of the Emotions

The topology that is evident here is taken up only infrequently, however, and often the focus on topology is effectively lost as other notions—like that of atmosphere—come to the fore. Moreover, this is true of many phenomenological discussions, more generally, as well as of the discussion of Heidegger, in particular. Nowhere in any of Ratcliffe's analysis of mood in Heidegger, for instance, is the topology that seems at work in Heidegger's thinking, as it relates to mood and emotion, taken up in any direct fashion. Indeed, at one point, Ratcliffe might almost be thought to be explicitly ruling out a topological reading, remarking that "in maintaining that moods constitute a sense of belonging to the world, Heidegger does not mean that one has a subjective state called a mood and that this somehow contributes to perception of one's spatiotemporal location in relation to other entities."[48] Ratcliffe immediately expands on the comment, however, by adding that "to find oneself in a world is not, first and foremost, to occupy the perspective of an impartial spectator, neutrally gazing upon things from a particular space–time location."[49] In other words, the sense of "finding oneself in the world" that is at issue here is not to be construed on the model of any form of abstracted spatial or temporal *positioning,* and this would be true even on a topological account. Ratcliffe, however, offers no such account.

Given that there is indeed a topological as well as more broadly spatial set of notions at work in relation to mood and emotion, especially in Heidegger, it is a little surprising that Ratcliffe's comments remain so brief and so narrowly focused only on ruling out one particular interpretation.[50] Of course, the absence of any direct attention to the topological in Ratcliffe's treatment—the failure to develop or even to consider, in any explicit fashion, the possibility of a topological understanding of mood and the emotions—merely reflects the more widespread neglect of the topological that has been noted elsewhere. This absence may be partly explained by the fact that the considerations that otherwise lead in the direction of a topological account seem, instead, to lead Ratcliffe towards the thematization of the body and, so, inasmuch as spatiality is seen to be at issue, to bodily spatiality. Ratcliffe is not unusual in this. It is commonplace, in many cognitive scientific as well as phenomenological accounts (including, for instance, Schmitz's work, noted earlier, and, most notably perhaps, in that of Merleau-Ponty[51]), to find the topological effectively taken up into the bodily—the turn towards place being thus displaced and redirected into a turn towards the body.

This being so, it should immediately be added that there can be no question but that the body is important in the issues under consideration. Orientation and situation always, even in the case of states that may otherwise be regarded as "inner," involves the body. This is not merely because orientation relates to action and bodily affect, but also because orientation depends on differentiation in oneself that can be related to differentiation in the surrounding world. This is a point famously made by Kant,[52] but one can readily see it for oneself, once one reflects on the way one's acquaintance with the different parts of a space are intimately tied to the way those parts of space relate to the different parts of one's body—as the spaces before, behind, above and below, to the right and to the left are grasped through the front and back, top and bottom, left and right of one's body. Without differentiation in one's body, one would be unable to grasp differentiation in space, in much the same way that a map is meaningless and useless unless it can be related back to one's own bodily position. The same point applies to those more complex forms of orientation that are associated with emotion. As modes of orientation, they already predispose the body in certain ways and are thereby evident in certain bodily states including bodily postures, comportments, and directions.[53]

The orientational character of emotion, together with its bodily character, means that emotion must be closely connected with bodily states and dispositions. However, the way the body is implicated here—along with the orientation and situational character of emotion generally—does not entail (as should already be evident) that emotion is therefore noncognitive in character. This is not only because the contrast between the cognitive and the bodily or orientational involves a false dichotomy, nor because of the existence of what I referred to earlier as cognitive emotions, but also because the very orientational character of emotion already brings cognitive content with it (even if it is not always exhaustively characterized in any simple propositional specification).[54]

Notwithstanding the importance of the bodily in relation to emotion—and to orientation and situation—the body cannot occupy any foundational role in this regard, so cannot be regarded as central in the way that is often assumed. There are two reasons for this: first, what the body is, and so the mode of being proper to it, cannot be taken for granted; and second, the body can provide no independent basis on which orientation and situation can themselves be understood. Heidegger does not ignore the body. Yet what makes Heidegger's thinking of the body obscure for most readers is that it is not a thinking of the body that remains with the body as usually understood. The body is itself questionable in Heidegger's thinking—hiding a problematic of its own, as he puts it.[55]

Yet it is commonplace to find the body taken, even if implicitly, as though it were itself an underlying entity or principle in which all else could be taken to inhere——the body is thus effectively treated as a *subiectum* (a ground or *hypokeimenon*) and thereby gives rise to its own corporeal ontology. Moreover, if we try to investigate what the body might be, apart from some such assumed notion of the corporeal, we find that we are inevitably led to notions of the *lived* and the *active* body, and thereby to a structure in which space and place are necessarily also implicated. In this respect, one may say that Heidegger holds an "extended" view of the body no less than he may also be said to hold an "extended" view of the mind (inasmuch as either term is applicable in a Heideggerian context) since both body and mind are understood in a way that is inextricably tied to the understanding of the way Dasein is always already *in* the world. "Body" and "mind" name two aspects of that "being in."

Thus, even though Heidegger avoids offering an account of the body as such, *Being and Time* is not, as Peg Birmingham points out, without an account of embodiment. The structure of embodiment is given through the structure of existential spatiality,[56] which is itself an essential part of the analysis of the "being in" that belongs to "being there/here."[57] More generally, one can say that the embodied character of human being is embedded in a more fundamental topology (which includes but is not restricted to human being alone) and that becomes clearer in the later thinking. That embodied character of human being thus follows from the placed character of human being rather than the other way around (which means that it is also a consequence of the essential finitude with which such placedness is directly connected).[58]

Giving proper recognition to the role of embodiment in emotion requires giving proper recognition to the topological structure with which both emotion and embodiment are necessarily implicated. Heidegger's account of the topological structure at issue here is not fully articulated. So far as the analysis of mood or emotion is concerned, the early work lacks clarity on the topological structures at issue, while the later work is not concerned with emotions or mood as objects of analysis. Nevertheless, Heidegger's account is significant because of the way it shows how mood and emotion are not to be construed as merely "subjective" or "psychological" phenomena but, rather, are to be understood as part of a topological structure that encompasses both the externality of the world and the internality of the self (a theme that will emerge in the discussion of "authenticity" in chapter 9).

Moreover, if to be capable of thinking and acting requires the sort of placed disposed-ness—the prior relatedness to place—that is at issue in mood and emotion, as is evident in Heidegger's analysis, then what this also shows is the way cognition and action, and so also rationality as such, depend upon place and placedness. The contrast between the rational and cognitive and the emotional is thus a false one—dependent upon a false and narrowed-down conception of reason and cognition, no less than of the emotions themselves. Reason and emotion are not opposed. Instead, they form part of a single topological structure—the structure of being-in-the-world, of being there/here, of being-in-place.

Two important points follow from consideration of the way emotion and reason are tied to place in this way. The first point follows from the refusal, evident in Bollnow as well as in Heidegger (although differently expressed), of the identification of emotion as subjective and reason as objective. Both emotion and reason are best understood as founded in the interrelation of agents with the world that occurs in and through place and placedness. What this brings with it, in ontological terms, is a relational understanding (one that has recurred throughout the discussions in this volume) of the nature of the self and the world. Neither stands entirely apart from the other, and both are to be understood only in their mutual interrelation. This topological relationality (and, as topological, it is a relationality constituted around multiple localities or regions) involves a tripartite relationality of and to the self, of and to others, and of and to things.

Such relationality entails that the usual dichotomies that are so often employed, including that of subjective and objective, but also of mental and physical, can no longer function in any absolute fashion. Those dichotomies, if they are to be retained, must be understood as themselves operating within a similarly relational ontology—one that can be understood as entailing a form of "nonreductive naturalism" or, as I referred to it in chapter 2, a "romantic materialism." According to the latter (and to reiterate the account given earlier), the material is to be understood as material only inasmuch as it stands in an essential relation to the felt, the thought, the imagined, and the remembered.[59] And, inasmuch as it is suffused with these, in their own turn, the felt, the thought, the imagined, and the remembered are shaped and formed through being embodied in the material—not only the materiality of the body, in its movement and its rest, in its activity and affectivity, but also in the materiality of things, whether made or unmade, and in the materiality of land, water, and air, of earth and of sky. It is only amidst such a "romantic materiality" that we are able to find ourselves in a place (and so in space and time) and thereby in the world.

Emotion, Truth, and Thinking

This chapter began with the way in which the "combat" between reason and emotion remains an element in contemporary ethical thinking. In this respect, however, the sort of topological account of emotion, and of the relation between emotion and reason, that has been sketched here ought to lead towards a more nuanced, and more complex, understanding of the nature of ethics, and of ethical decision and action. Part of the problem with the sorts of accounts of ethics and morality that one finds in writers such as Singer and Bloom is their tendency to treat ethics as founded in a sort of desituated view of the world—exactly the sort of purely abstracted and "objectified" view that has been part of the traditional understanding of reason. But it should now be evident that, just as this involves a mistaken understanding of reason, so it also involves a mistaken understanding of the ethical.

Ethics arises only on the basis of our embodied, oriented being in the world, and this means that ethics will only be understood—and ethical decision and action will only be possible—to the extent that the emotional is addressed as well as the rational. It is always possible that our emotions can mislead, that we can be misoriented (and this is how we might understand some of the problematic elements that Bloom identifies in relation to empathy). Yet we do not rectify such misorientation by looking to remove ourselves from the very possibility of being oriented or being placed. A properly topological ethics would be one that encompasses the emotional and rational as both are embedded in our situated engagement in the world. The detailed exploration of such an ethics remains a significant task that is yet to be accomplished. There may well be elements in the tradition exemplified by Hume that will be relevant to such a task, and one might also look to some of Emmanuel Levinas's thinking in this regard (although Levinas also presents some problems from a topological perspective[60]). The idea of a *topological ethics*, which appears here, and which is adumbrated in Heidegger's comments concerning the connection between *ethos* and abode *(Aufenthalt)* or "dwelling-place" in the "Letter on 'Humanism,'"[61] nevertheless remains something that demands much more consideration and elaboration.

A large part of what is at issue in the thinking of the emotions is the thinking of our relation to the world, and so also our relation to place. And for the most part, the way that relation is currently thought, if it is genuinely thought at all, is in terms of the privileging of a certain sort of abstracted and displaced stance that we can now say is not a real privileging of the rational as such but, rather, the privileging of only a certain abstracted—and so disembodied and displaced—mode of rationality. Moreover, this seems currently to hold across much of contemporary society and culture (certainly as it is oriented towards the "Western" or "European"), and not only within academic philosophy or ethics. In this privileging of abstract or displaced rationality, what also occurs, however—in addition to a loss of the proper understanding of both reason and emotion, as well as of their interrelation—is a loss of any proper sense of our place in the world, and so of any proper orientation to things or to ourselves. Here the question of orientation brings with it the question of truth.

To be disoriented is to lose a sense of place, but when this is construed in epistemic terms (and knowledge is no less shaped by place than is reason), it also means to lose hold of truth or of any standard of truth. This is indeed where we find ourselves today. Curiously, our "post-truth" world is one that is often characterized in terms of the privileging of emotion over reason—so *The Economist* could say of the world epitomized by the previous US president, Donald Trump, that, in this world, "feelings, not facts, are what matter."[62] Yet the loss of any sense of truth is not about the triumph of emotion, not if what I have so far said here is correct. The loss of any sense of, or respect for, truth is indeed a form of disorientation at the most general level, but that disorientation is as much a disturbance that pertains to the emotions as it is does to reason. This disturbance affects both emotion *and* reason. It involves their seeming separation and the taking of both to extremity. Ours is a time of extremity, in which both emotion and reason have been ripped from their proper places, so that both are now disoriented and disorienting.[63] Regaining a sense of their proper place, finding again our own place in the world, is the most pressing task for the future. It is a task that is fundamental to our capacity to address all the challenges that face us, both the sociopolitical and the environmental, which are intimately bound up together.

Earlier in this chapter, I noted the way in which the assumed contrast between emotion and reason often underlies other forms of philosophical controversy and critique, including the charge of "irrationalism" commonly leveled against Heidegger. Heidegger is himself critical of the "customary" mode of thinking that is referred to, in the Nietzsche lectures and elsewhere, as "representing" or "conceptualizing" (*gewohnte Vorstellen*), and that is distinct from the "poetic" or "meditative" thinking that was discussed in chapter 2.[64] Aligning closely with the commonplace idea of reason and rationality as operating in terms of a sort of linear "calculation,"[65] such "representational thinking" (*vorstellendes Denken*)[66] is characterized in *What Is Called Thinking?* as "one-track" thinking (*eingleisige Denken*), since it assumes a univocal direction and character in what is at issue in thought and in its own character as thinking.[67] It takes "concepts" as its objects—as that on which it operates—treating those concepts as completely under the control of the thinking process. Since concepts or representations can also be understood as pictures or images (*Bilder*), Heidegger argues that this mode of thinking is one oriented to the picture or image.[68]

The idea of the image as it appears in connection with this notion of representation is to be distinguished, however, from the idea of the *poetic* image that Heidegger takes up elsewhere and that was discussed in chapter 6 (and that is also important in relation to Char in chapter 2). The poetic image is essentially indeterminate, having a depth and inexhaustibility that partly derives from its concreteness and immediacy, whereas the representational or conceptual image is taken to be determinate or, at least, determinable. The poetic image is also fundamentally tied to a mode of *placed thinking*—and this is directly tied to the character of such thinking, and of the image that figures as belonging to it—as indeed *poetic* thinking.

In his critique of representational thinking, Heidegger takes as his target the conventional view of thinking that is itself part of the contrast of reason with emotion. Heidegger does not deny a role for thinking that is indeed representational or conceptual, and even that operates in a linear and calculative fashion.[69] What he rejects is that thinking can be exclusively understood in this way or that it is the primary way in which thinking is to be understood. One reason for supposing that it cannot be primary is the fundamental role played by mood or emotion—specifically, attunement or *Stimmung*—in the opening of the world. We find ourselves in the world through being in place, and that being-in-place is given in and through the disposedness towards things that belongs with mood and emotion. On this basis, all thinking, even that thinking which already distances itself from things (at the very least, in terms of the sort of cognitive emotions noted earlier), will remain emotionally disposed in some fashion or other.[70]

What is at issue in the poetic or meditative thinking that Heidegger, in his later work, distinguishes from representational thinking is a thinking that proceeds, knowingly, on the basis of its own prior disposedness towards things—its own fundamental attunement. But in addition to this, poetic or meditative thinking is a thinking that already attends to its own placedness, as thinking that attends to its place (and so to the indeterminacy and inexhaustibility that belongs with it) and that is already oriented towards the thinking of that place in the very act of thinking. It is also, one might add, a thinking that attends to things and so releases things to their own being. Heidegger thus ties thinking, understood in this way, to releasement, *Gelassenheit* (a topic discussed in more detail in chapter 9)—[71]and this is surely a mode of attunement, disposedness, affectedness, even though it is not *only* that.

As poetic or meditative, Heidegger's thinking is not irrational or antirational, although it may well be dense and often demanding.[72] It remains bound to reason and to thought (or better, to *logos* and to *nous*, to *legein* and *noein*),[73] but to a different and more fundamental sense of reason—to reason as it may be realized in releasement, or *Gelassenheit* but thereby also to reason as itself *topological*. Such a topological reason, and the poetic or meditative thinking in which it is expressed, is a theme that has hovered over the discussion throughout the preceding chapters (it has also come to ground as a key issue at various points so far) and will continue to do so in the chapters to come. It is a mode of thinking connected to the poetic, as Heidegger understands it, but also, I would argue, to the hermeneutical—already implicitly at issue, therefore, in the discussion in chapter 4. As it is connected to the hermeneutical, so it also embodies something of the so-called "circularity" of the hermeneutical—where that circularity is to be understood in terms of the way thinking and understanding always move, whether it acknowledges it or not, within the place already opened up to it. Indeed, both the distance and nearness that are evident in thinking, and so in reason itself, are impossible without the prior opening of the place in which thinking moves and to which thinking must already be disposed and attuned. Rather than a combat, there is an essential interdependence, even a reciprocity, at work between reason and emotion. What we might think of as mindfulness and heartfulness[74] belong together as essential elements of the same thoughtful engagement in place.

Eight

Technology and Spatialization

Commitment to an optimistic progressivism has long been characteristic of mainstream politics, on both the left and the right. Thus, whether one is socialist or social democratic, liberal or conservative, neoliberal, or even neoconservative, the tendency is to assume that we can shape the world according to our interests and desires—we can make the world "better"—and that this is possible through our increasing mastery of various technologies. The improvement of the world is thus seen essentially to be a technological promise. Technology is progressive, even utopian, and progress is technological. Although commonplace, this general view is given particularly clear exemplification in Stephen Pinker's *Enlightenment Now: The Case for Reason, Science, Humanism, and Progress*.[1] Pinker does not make the connection between technology and progress as directly as I have here, instead placing the emphasis on science and reason. Yet it is quite clear that the argument of *Enlightenment Now* depends heavily on the idea that the application of scientific knowledge is the means by which human life has and will be improved, and so, even though technology may not be named as such, the close connection between technology and science means that technology is indeed at issue.

Despite the scientific and technological evangelism exemplified by Pinker and others like him, there is reason to suppose that the progressivism associated with technological modernism is, to some extent at least, misplaced, and that, regardless of the various instantiations of modernity with which technology is associated, regardless of whether technology is associated with an egalitarian or neoliberal agenda, and regardless, too, of the many benefits of specific technological advances and devices, the essential structure of technology nevertheless also conceals a danger within it. This was certainly Heidegger's position,[2] and the aim of this chapter is to explore the reason for Heidegger's questioning attitude towards technology (he rejects the idea that it is a form of pessimism[3]), and the way in which it is connected to the topological character of his thinking.

Modernity and the Critique of Technology

Heidegger's critical approach to technology is neither unusual nor idiosyncratic. It stands, in fact, within a long tradition of European questioning of technological modernity in general—a tradition exemplified by Rousseau, notably in his first *Discourse*;[4] by the critiques of both Nietzsche and Kierkegaard on the destructive character of the present age; by Weber's exploration of the "iron-cage" of rationality; and by the arguments of a range of twentieth-century thinkers from Arendt and Marcuse to Adorno and Camus.[5] For all of these thinkers—including Heidegger—the concern is not with any specific technological device or set of such devices, but with technology in a more generalized contemporary form, which is one reason why the critique of technology so often tends to take the form of a critique of modernity.

It is notable that such criticism or skepticism is generally less evident in English-language culture, which has remained more straightforwardly (one is tempted to say, naïvely) "progressivist" and optimistic about technology and its promise. Thus, when Stephen Hawking and others raise concerns about modern AI technology, it is not technology as such that concerns them but, rather, a specific technological domain and direction.[6] Indeed, much of the contemporary English-language concern with technology, over the last hundred years or so, has focused on the possible dangers of forms of artificial intelligence—and so the focus has often been on the "machine"—or even artificial forms of human life. Mary Shelley's *Frankenstein* is notable as one of the most significant English-language explorations of both the promise and the peril that technology presents,[7] but it also exemplifies this very tendency.

Moreover, technological skepticism has frequently been viewed, especially in English-language circles, as associated with conservative and even regressive forms of political thought. Heidegger's involvement with National Socialism is typically taken to confirm this connection (notwithstanding the fact that Heidegger came to view Nazism as part of the very technological modernity of which he is critical), as has the nostalgic and backwards-looking Romanticism that is viewed by many as characterizing his thought in general (Romanticism typically being seen as the great countermovement to the rational progressivism that Pinker identifies with the Enlightenment.)[8] Such perceptions have been reinforced by the way in which the critique of technology has so often been coupled with the critique of liberalism (or of certain forms of liberalism)—something evident in Nietzsche and, to some extent, in Heidegger, as well as in writers such as Ernst Jünger. The fact that the critique of technology is also associated with thinkers—like Arendt and Camus—who are explicit in affirming many broadly liberal and progressivist ideals (even if they remain critical of much mainstream politics) is often, on such an account, ignored or overlooked.

Although it can be situated within this larger European tradition, and it is important that it be so situated, Heidegger's critique of technology nevertheless stands out—and not only because of its singular impact and influence. Heidegger is explicit in connecting technological modernity with certain modes of spatiality and spatialization in a way that has no real parallel elsewhere. Perhaps the only other thinker who makes a similar connection is Paul Virilio, but, in Virilio's case, space and spatiality are less directly taken up, being either tied to more specific contexts (as in the work on architecture and territory) or secondary to the focus on movement, speed, and acceleration.[9]

Yet most commentators give little or no attention to the way spatiality and spatialization, and so the sort of topological analysis in which the analysis of spatialization must indeed be embedded, enter into the Heideggerian critique. The language of "nearness" that appears in Heidegger's discussions of technology is often noted,[10] and with it the claim that *"all distances in time and space are shrinking,"*[11] but beyond this, there is little or no inquiry into the ideas of space and place that might be implicated by such language. It is as if these phenomena are *consequences* of technology rather than part of its essence. A recent volume, which proclaims itself to be "the first comprehensive and definitive account of Martin Heidegger's philosophy of technology," contains in its index not a single entry for space, spatiality, place, or topology—nor is there any significant discussion or analysis of these in its chapters.[12] Similarly, Andrew Mitchell's translation of the term that Heidegger uses for the essence of technology—*Gestell*—as "positionality," immediately suggests a direct connection to spatiality, yet Mitchell nowhere pursues the connection in any sustained fashion, neither in his introductory comments to the translation nor in his monograph-length investigation of Heidegger's fourfold.[13]

In some ways, the neglect of the way place and space figure in Heidegger's critique of technology merely reflects the treatment of Heidegger's thought more generally: the topological character of his thinking is largely ignored. Yet such neglect is especially striking given the way in which spatial and topological themes have been so central to the discussion of modernity and its interconnection with technology that are commonplace in the literature outside of philosophy. David Harvey's *The Condition of Postmodernity*, for example, takes the phenomenon of "time-space compression" as central to his analysis.[14] The idea of such "compression," if not always expressed in just that form, has a widespread currency in observations concerning the experience of modernity,[15] but it also has a more specific origin in both Marx's claim concerning the way capital strives towards "the annihilation of space by time"[16] and Heidegger's observation, already noted above, concerning the "shrinking" of distance. Indeed, wherever one looks outside of philosophy, it is almost impossible to find any analysis of modernity or its technological character that does not draw upon some aspect of spatial or topological (or topographic) analysis.[17]

Inasmuch as the critique of technology follows directly from Heidegger's analysis of the character of world—and especially of the human mode of being-in-the-world—and place and space have central roles in that analysis (particularly in the later thinking), so the Heideggerian critique of technology cannot be other than topological in its basic character. Admittedly, Heidegger does not always draw explicit attention to the topological character of his approach, and those discussions that most directly address technology, most notably "The Question Concerning Technology," tend not to thematize space and place in any explicit way. Nevertheless, one has only to attend to the language at work in Heidegger's critique of technology to see how the spatial and topological are indeed centrally at issue there, even if often only implicit. Heidegger speaks, as noted already, of nearness and distance, of position and positionality (both as it can be heard in *Gestell* and in the Greek *thesis*), of *Bestand* (which like *Gestell* relates back to *stellen*, "to stand"), of the fourfold or *Geviert* (a term that connects to the four cardinal points[18]), of dwelling or *Wohnen*, and of releasement or *Gelassenheit* (the German terms in each case carrying their own topological connotations[19]).

Technology is not a specifically modern phenomenon, and yet technology and modernity are indeed closely linked—which is why one might well talk of what is at issue here as a phenomenon that conjoins modernity and technology, hence "technological modernity." As already noted, Heidegger's critique of technology, like that of other European thinkers from Rousseau to Virilio, is inevitably also a critique of modernity—although this does not mean it can automatically be viewed as "antimodern" in the sense of expressing a desire to go back to some premodern form of life. Heidegger is certainly attentive to the fact that technology predates modernity, but he nevertheless argues that technology takes on a distinctive character in modernity.

"Technology" is a somewhat equivocal term: it refers both to something old and something new. For this reason, clarifying what is genuinely new about technology in modernity is an important task. Heidegger talks of how modern technology involves a "challenging" (*Herausforderung*) that previous technologies did not, but the nature of such challenging also requires further elucidation. Indeed, as with so much of Heidegger's thinking, it is not enough simply to remain within the orbit of the terms he already employs. What is required instead is to find ways of thinking what is at issue that reveals the underlying structure of Heidegger's thinking and that is appropriate to our contemporary situation. The aim of this chapter is thus not to repeat Heidegger's own analysis but, instead, to clarify that in which the analysis is grounded, in which it has its own origins, and thereby to arrive at a better understanding (one more suited to where we are now) of Heidegger's thinking, as well as of the phenomena and the questions such thinking aims to take up.

Technology, Modernity, and Reason

Part of what ties modernity and technology together—apart from their interconnection with the structure of historical process—is the very idea of both as tied to progress. To reiterate the point made at the start: progress is technological, and technology is progressive—and one might say the same about modernity. As it appears here, "modernity" does not refer only to the historical period that is the present (or to that historical period that leads up to and includes the present) or even to the way in which the world happens currently to be configured, socially, politically, culturally, or economically. "Modernity" also names a *project*—a specifically progressive project. That project is not only a project of modernity but is typically identified, historically, with the Enlightenment (as is modernity itself) or with a certain version of the Enlightenment[20]—hence the title of Pinker's *Enlightenment Now*. Pinker takes the Enlightenment to be characterized by the commitment to reason, to humanism, and to science.[21] But one can also see both the Enlightenment and the project of modernity as configured around the twin ideas of reason and freedom—with reason encompassing science and freedom encompassing, to a large extent, the humanistic. Indeed, within the framework of much Enlightenment thinking, reason and freedom are themselves taken to be closely intertwined: reason is understood as the purest form of freedom and freedom is that in which reason finds its realization.[22] The emphasis on freedom and reason frequently (though not always) brings with it a commitment to the unbounded nature of human possibility and the seemingly unlimited power of reason. Having freed itself from the shackles of tradition and superstitious belief, human being, which is to say human reason, is free to realize itself in a way that has no a priori bounds, and that realization, of course, is one that, for the most part, is seen to proceed via the scientific and the technological (the latter often being viewed as more or less identical).

The twentieth century, along with the unfolding twenty-first, provides a significant body of evidence that casts doubt on exactly the rational progressivism that underpins the idea of modernity at work here. Yet the rational, progressivist ideal, and the notion of freedom that goes with it, nevertheless remains a powerful element in contemporary culture and society—one that may even be said to be reinforced by the "enemies" that appear ranged against it. The appearance of extremist religious movements, of which the Islamic State (ISIL or DAESH) is the most notable recent example, have thus typically been seen as throwbacks to a premodern past—as intrusions, into modernity, of a medievalism that cannot have any long-term viability. A similar attitude is often taken towards extremist forms of political conservatism—among which German National Socialism is often taken as the primary instantiation. From the perspective of the project of modernity, such phenomena do not represent a breakdown in the forward momentum of that project but are temporary interruptions to be overcome. They may even be viewed as disruptions to which the movement of modernity itself gives rise—a product of the friction that its movement creates.

Yet the treatment of modernity, in terms of an inexorable movement towards the realization of freedom and reason in the world, elides the fact that modernity is not instantiated only by those social and political forms that fit the "progressivist" model. National Socialism, for instance, was not a purely antimodern phenomenon but incorporated strongly modernist elements within it, and can even be seen as instantiating a form of modernism.[23] The ISIL, in spite of its oppressive and violent character, has been a movement enmeshed with, and thoroughly reliant upon, modern technological systems—including weaponry, communication, organization, finance, and especially the use of digital and web-based systems to disseminate its message and promote its cause. Similarly, the contemporary rise of authoritarian populism is based in the deployment of technologies for mass communication and control. The latter, of course, was already evident in the case of German National Socialism in the 1930s. Under Josef Goebbels as propaganda minister, the Nazi regime pioneered the use of radio for mass communication and indoctrination.[24] The supposedly antimodern often turns out to be part of the modern, while even the modern includes elements of the "antimodern" within it.

At this point, one might be tempted to distinguish between the "project" of modernity on the one hand (a project that is progressivist and emancipatory) and modernity as it names a particular time of historical development on the other (a time that encompasses elements that are both progressive and regressive, emancipatory, and oppressive). The trouble with such a distinction, simple and straightforward though it may seem, is that the project of modernity cannot be so easily disentangled from modernity as a temporal or historical phenomenon, since to attempt to do so is to make obscure any sense in which the project of modernity can be said to be "of" modernity in the first place. Perhaps part of the mistake here is to suppose that modernity is indeed something abstractly "rational" rather than concretely "material"—as if reason were operative in history while nevertheless being apart from it, as if the project of modernity stood outside of the actual occurrence of the modern.

The event of modernity is not the gradual realization of a rational ideal in the world but, rather, the unfolding of a set of material processes and structures that are increasingly mediated through globalized technological systems. These systems contain tendencies that go beyond any specific instrumental or rational end that may be served by specific devices and systems, and so beyond any capacity for rational prediction or control in the ordinary sense—a point that is central, in fact, to Heidegger's own account of technology. This material unfolding may still be viewed as the unfolding of something rational, but to use reason in this way is simply to assume an identification of the rational and the technological in a way that already shifts the very idea of reason itself. Moreover, the very idea that one might question technological progress becomes, almost by definition, a mark of irrationality. It is thus that critics of technological progressivism are so often characterized as "Luddites"—Luddism being seen as a form of irrational and nostalgic conservatism rather than the expression of working-class activism that it originally was.[25]

The Question of the "Essential"

The technological construal of reason that appears here was already a focus of discussion in the previous chapter. There, the opposition of reason and emotion was seen to be entangled with a conception of reason that is tied to the instrumental and the calculative and thereby closely bound up with technological modernity as Heidegger understands it. Heidegger's supposed "irrationalism" is not a rejection of reason, as such, but a rejection of the exclusive construal of reason in this very fashion. It leads Heidegger to be critical also of the dominance, in philosophy especially, of what, as we saw earlier, he terms "representational" or "conceptual" thinking (*Vorstellen* or *vorstellendes Denken*), which might also be construed as a form of "technological" thinking, since what is at issue is essentially the attempt to exercise mastery or control over that which is thought.

Although Heidegger is frequently criticized for his "essentialism"—a charge often made with respect to his account of technology[26]—his refusal of representational thinking is tied up with his rejection of that mode of traditional philosophical inquiry that proceeds by looking to identify the being of things through an analysis of the properties or essential features of things (*quidditas* in Latin).[27] Consequently, when Heidegger takes up the question of essence in his own work, as he does in *Being and Time*, for instance, in relation to the question of the essence of Dasein, it is not a matter of finding some definitional specification of what Dasein is as that might be given in a concept or as a representation. Instead of the identification of some set of "present 'attributes' of an objectively present being which has such and such an 'outward appearance,'"[28] the inquiry into the essence of Dasein is an inquiry into "possible ways for it to be, and only this."[29] To use the language of the later thinking, one might say that the inquiry into essence (*Wesen*) is an inquiry into ways of appearing or presencing (*Anwesen*). Moreover, since the inquiry into being that is at issue here—whether the inquiry into Dasein or of technology—is never an inquiry into the being of some one thing apart from others (presencing is always a presencing *in the world*), so the inquiry into essence is invariably an inquiry into a mode of being *in relation*.

Although "relation" is commonly treated as an abstract notion, and the term's French and Latin etymology reinforces this (especially in the idea of relating as "reporting"), "relation," like "connection," has its origin in the concrete sense in which what is separate is nevertheless brought together (to re-late is literally to "bring back"), and so brought together across distance. Relation is, to use a common Heideggerian term, a form of nearness, and so also of placedness or being-placed. The topological connotation here is invariably overlooked, just as it is overlooked with so many terms and ideas. The tendency is always to abstract from the concrete topology in which thinking is embedded, yet that does not mean that the topology ceases to be significant. The idea that the inquiry into essence is not a matter of determining the properties that belong to a thing as it is independent and self-sufficient but rather of coming to understand the way in which that thing stands *in relation to* other things leads precisely towards what can be termed a *topological* understanding of essence. To inquire into the essence of a thing is thus to inquire into the place of that thing, which is to inquire into that which bounds the thing, as well as that from which it comes and by which it is sustained and supported.[30]

Even though the exact ways in which Heidegger addresses the question of essence shift through the course of his thinking (just as the way he addresses the question of metaphysics also shifts), and the specifically *topological* understanding of essence that is at issue here remains largely implicit, still this basically relational approach remains consistent. Whenever Heidegger talks of "the essential" ("essential" sometimes translates *wesentlich*, but sometimes also, in the later essays, *eigentlich*, the term that appears in English translations of *Being and Time*, somewhat problematically, as "authentic"[31]), he means what pertains to the being of what is in question and so to the way what is in question comes to presence—and therefore also the way it comes to place (presencing being always a placing). And, in contrast to the conventional understanding, essence as it appears thus is not something determinate or completely determinable. The essential, as Heidegger understands it, retains an ineliminable *indeterminacy*—it is indeed a way of presencing, rather than being identical with some already existing and delimited presence.

Although it might seem initially outlandish, Heidegger's way of approaching the question of essence bears comparison with Donald Davidson's critique of the traditional philosophical style of "what is . . ." questioning. As a result, it is worth taking a brief detour through this aspect of Davidson's thinking as a way of better illuminating what may be at issue in Heidegger's thinking of the "essence" of technology. As usually understood, "what is . . ." questioning aims at the definitional clarification of notions, such as truth and knowledge, by reducing them to clearer and more basic terms. Davidson argues, however, that this is seldom, if ever, productive, and he takes the inquiries into notions of "beauty, courage, virtue, friendship, love, temperance," in certain of the Platonic *Dialogues*, as illustrative of this.[32] The general point is seen by Davidson to apply to the inquiry into truth no less than it does elsewhere. Consequently, he views the attempt to provide any precise or reductive specification of truth as doomed to failure from the start. This does not mean, however, that Davidson abandons the attempt to understand what is fundamentally, or "essentially," at issue. Instead, Davidson argues that the task must be to understand how the idea or phenomenon at issue connects with the larger structure in which it is embedded, and, as in Heidegger, the elucidation of that structure is never a matter of some complete specification but always remains, to some extent, indeterminate. In the case of truth, Davidson's approach is to look to how truth connects with meaning, belief, error, and so forth,[33] and it is an approach that can be seen to characterize his approach, not only to truth, but also to almost all the key notions with which he engages.

Davidson would not himself characterize his inquiry into the question of truth—or any other question—as focused on uncovering the "essence" or the "way of being" of truth. And although this reflects an important difference in vocabulary between Davidson and Heidegger (a difference that is connected to the fact that Davidson operates within a much more conventional *analytic* framework—or what readily appears as such), it does not exclude the possibility of a real convergence in terms of their respective approaches. Moreover, even the fact that Davidson couches his discussion in terms of an inquiry into "concepts" (which he commonly does) need not undermine such convergence. Davidson's talk of concepts needs to be read in the context of his thinking in its entirety, and it is on that basis, and only on that basis, that any comparison with Heidegger becomes possible. In fact, "concept," like many of the other terms that Davidson employs, does not operate in Davidson's work in quite the same way as is conventionally assumed. If concepts are taken as determinate "ideas," then there are no concepts in Davidson. Instead, the inquiry into concepts (the latter term bringing an essential sense of *connection* with it) provides Davidson with a way of thinking though the relational structure to which certain phenomena belong—of coming to a sense of the *region* or *landscape* in which they are embedded and to which they also contribute.[34]

What Davidson's inquiry into truth aims to uncover is perhaps best characterized in terms of an attempt to show how truth is *situated* within a larger structure—which is why talk of a region or landscape is not inappropriate here. The topological language that thus comes into view is no mere "ornament" but reflects the underlying structure of the Davidsonian approach. It is indeed a matter of looking to the *place* of the ideas or phenomena at issue and of mapping out a *region*. Davidson's own use of topological ideas and images (including that of "triangulation") reinforces this.[35] In Davidson, this topological approach is not restricted to a single question, that of truth, but is characteristic of Davidson's overall *methodology* and is closely tied to the holistic element in Davidson's thinking (which is partly why the approach does have to extend to encompass more than just the question of truth). In the case of Heidegger's inquiry into the essence of technology, the topological approach he adopts also means that there is no attempt to provide some sort of definition of technology or to reduce technology to some set of basic properties as might be specified in such a definition. Instead, Heidegger looks to understand the way technology connects with a structure that includes human action but that is not based in human action alone (and so is not based simply in human intentionality either[36]). Technology, as Heidegger understands it, is thus part of a larger ordering of the world with which human being in the world is necessarily entangled, but which shapes human action even as it is also, in part, shaped by human action, and that is entangled with other structures and phenomena.

It is common to treat technology as simply an adjunct and outcome of human activity—as that by means of which human beings extend their abilities to act in the world so as to realize their interests and desires. Such a construal of technology, which Heidegger characterizes as both instrumentalist and anthropological,[37] is implicit in Pinker's account of human progress. One might argue that, in its view of reason as the instrument by which freedom, and so the betterment of human life and existence, is to be achieved, the Enlightenment takes reason as offering a certain "technology" of freedom. This becomes even more apparent when the Enlightenment is understood in relation to both a set of social, economic, and political developments that occur in the seventeenth and eighteenth centuries and to the developments in scientific knowledge that take place at the same time (developments that all serve to interact with and to reinforce one another). Reason is taken to be exemplified in the new knowledge emerging from the sixteenth century onwards, across the natural sciences, and to which the human sciences also aspire.

The project of modernity is thus also a project of technology. It is a project not merely of abstract knowledge or contemplation but of knowledge as connected with concrete forms of action and change. On this basis, technology comes to be seen as instrumental, as serving the end of freedom (or, more generally, of the amelioration of human life and existence), but in the sense both as that which enables freedom and, in many cases, as that which embodies freedom. Freedom itself tends to be construed increasingly in instrumental terms, both as the means by which other goods are realized and as itself realized through the proliferation and multiplication of instrumental capacities. The contemporary infatuation with technological novelty and the "gadget" is partly driven by such an idea, and by the idea of technology as offering just such an increase in possibilities and freedoms—even possibilities and opportunities we had not realized we desired or needed (the freedom, for instance, to photograph the meal that one has just been served and immediately communicate the image to one's friends). Notice too that here freedom becomes identical with an increase in *both* the instrumental structure that is available *and* the ends that instrumental structure enables.

Part of the problem with the instrumental construal at work here is that it leaves out the manner in which technology modifies human action, even in ways that are not directly connected to human interests and desires. Certainly, one might say that the very character of human being is technological (as does José Ortega y Gasset[38]). Yet although this expresses the inextricable intermeshing of the human and the technological (something with which Heidegger would not disagree), it tells us little, on its own, about the nature of technology as such and certainly cannot be taken to imply that technology is therefore merely a means to human ends. The identification of the technological with the humanly instrumental is itself closely tied to the optimistic progressivism of contemporary modernity, even if it is nevertheless consistent with a critical view of *specific* devices or techniques. It is also a feature of those many contemporary approaches to technology that, even though they may emphasize its supposed multiplicity of form and type, nevertheless continue to understand technology as nothing over and above a multiplicity of devices, techniques, and processes geared to differing ends, as embodied in different social and political forms and structures—approaches that thereby offer no insight into technology as anything other than such a multiplicity.

Heidegger argues that the instrumental and anthropological way of understanding technology is inadequate, in that it effectively assumes technology as something already given. Technological devices, processes, and structures are simply the means to the achievement of certain ends, but as such, their character as means is not questioned and neither is the idea of the instrumental—which means that the possibility of a genuinely critical engagement with technology is severely restricted. In the discussion of *physis* and *techne* in chapter 3, I pointed out how, for Heidegger, *technē* cannot be understood as independent of *physis*—*techne* operates through *physis* and on the basis of it—but both are modes of *poeisis*, of emergence or bringing-forth, of appearing or presencing. In his discussion of technology, particularly as developed in "The Question Concerning Technology," Heidegger emphasizes the relation between *physis* and *techne* so as to bring out the character of technology as a mode of presencing, and so also as a mode of unconcealing or revealing—*aletheia*. Understood in this way, the essence of technology cannot be found in the instrumental alone since the idea of the instrumental is the idea of that which operates within what is already given, already present, already revealed. Moreover, the instrumental construal, because it does not acknowledge the character of technology as a mode of revealing, cannot engage with the character of that mode of revealing, and so cannot engage in any thinking that would address its limits in any fundamental fashion. On an instrumental construal, the only critique possible—the only potential *limit*—concerns the extent to which the means is adequate to the end.

Understood as instrumental, technology is essentially a secondary phenomenon, derivative of human activity and interests, and so, at least in principle, subject to human direction and control. Since the technological is thereby effectively reduced to the instrumental (technology is itself a means to some human end or ends), the understanding of the technological that appears here is one that takes technology to have no essence other than the instrumental, which is to say, the technological itself—and so the very idea of the technological dissipates in the multiplicity of technologies and of instrumental, or means-end, connections. In pressing on the question of technology as a question concerning technology's *essence*, Heidegger is forcing attention onto the character of human engagement in the world, as that is shaped by the forms in which that engagement is enacted. In doing this, Heidegger is also forcing attention onto the way the world and all that comes to presence within it, including human being, is shaped by that same engagement.

Inasmuch as we give the name "technology" to the mode of engagement at issue here, then what technology refers to is the structure of human engagement in the world in modernity and to that structure as it encompasses the way of revealing or coming to presence of the human and the world in modernity. "Technology," says Heidegger, "is . . . no mere means. Technology is a way of revealing,"[39] and as such, technology is something fundamental and ontological. This way of understanding technology clearly goes far beyond the usual way in which technology is understood or addressed, which remains overwhelmingly oriented to a view of technology as instrumental, and so to a view of technology as something already given and as secondary to human action and interest—on which basis the investigation of technology is largely a matter of various forms of empirical social, political, or economic analysis. The standard objections to Heidegger's approach, to the effect that it is "essentialist" or "reificatory," often depend on ignoring Heidegger's own critique of the notions of the essential and the real. More fundamentally, they amount to a simple rejection of the ontological dimension to the question of technology, as Heidegger puts it. The issue of the being of technology, and so of its essence, is not shown to be mistaken, but simply refused or dismissed.

Space, Place, and Modernity

The essence of technology, Heidegger tells us, is nothing technological. It is not instrumental, nor is it to be found in any particular form of technology or in any instrument or device.[40] Heidegger's own account of the essence of technology, which, as we have already seen, does not depend merely on identifying some set of defining or essential features, is bound up with his account of the character of modernity and, especially, with his understanding of the development of Western science and philosophy since the Greeks. It is thus not separable from the critique of metaphysical and representational thinking that runs through so much of Heidegger's writing, nor, indeed, from his attempt to elucidate a different kind of thinking that is attuned to being and to place. It might be thought that Heidegger's critique of technology is, in this sense, a *consequence* of his critique of science and philosophy and of the metaphysical and representational—despite the fact that Heidegger asserts the priority of the technological over, especially, the scientific.[41] Yet precisely because Heidegger is committed to something like the romantic materialism or nonreductive naturalism referred to in chapter 3, so he is also committed to the idea that thinking, including scientific and philosophical thinking, is always embedded in the world and in worldly events, structures, and processes. The "metaphysical" and "representational" are not mere attitudes or forms of intellection but take concrete form in the way the world is configured. The character of technology as an ordering of the world, and so as a way of revealing and presencing, is thus evident in those forms of scientific and philosophical thinking with which it is also inextricably entangled, even in those cases where its character as such an ordering may still be in the process of unfolding.

Central to Heidegger's account of what is at issue here is his critique of the dominance of spatialized modes of thought and practice—modes of thought and practice that, as they are spatial, are also tied to the mathematical, to the numerical, and to the quantitative. However, space, as was emphasized earlier, is an equivocal notion. Understood as tied to place, space can be taken to name the openness of place—the cleared "room" that is given in and through place—an openness that is bounded and heterogenous, so that one can talk of different spaces that belong with different places. On this basis, space is something like a dimension of place, and so is also coupled with time—space being place in its openness and time being place in its character as a dynamic opening, such that place is thereby understood as encompassing the play of time and space (*Zeit-raum*, or as Heidegger sometimes has it, *Zeit-Spiel-Raum*[42]). But space can also name that which seems to stand apart from place, inasmuch as it stands apart from any notion of that which is intrinsically bounded and, in this sense, space is almost identical with pure extendedness—an extendedness that is, for the most part, homogenous, anisotropic (without directionality), and unbounded—and it is also measurable and quantifiable in a way that place is not. Indeed, in this latter respect, the very ideas of measure and quantity (and even of number) themselves appear intrinsically bound up with the spatial,[43] even though the connection is not always self-evident. Set against such a background, place, if it appears at all, can only be subsidiary to space, reduced to mere location or position within a larger extended field, and, as such, reduced to little more than something conventionally or arbitrarily designated.

Understood in this way, space is something *modern*. One might well argue that modernity has its origins, in fact, in the rise of space (and so its dominance over place[44]), both as a *sui generis* idea within science and philosophy and as a basic organizing principle in new forms of organization and practice within society at large. The rise of the modern state, for instance, is closely tied up, not only with the development of new forms of spatial organization and ordering in relation to territory and territorial sovereignty, but also with new modes of administration and governance based around what are essentially spatialized techniques of surveillance and control.[45] In this respect, the spatialized ontology that Heidegger identifies in Descartes—and against which Heidegger sets his own account in *Being and Time*—is merely the philosophical counterpart to the social and political spatialization that was taking place in Europe in the sixteenth and seventeenth centuries.[46]

What is at issue in modern philosophy and science, and in modern forms of planning and organization (as well as modern technology generally), is the dominance of the representational and the calculative, and indeed, there is little to choose between the dominance of the latter and the dominance of the technological. Thus, Heidegger can speak almost as if they were one and the same phenomenon: "[T]he world now appears as an object open to the attacks of calculative thought, attacks that nothing is believed able any longer to resist. Nature becomes a gigantic gasoline station, an energy source for technology and industry."[47] What is crucial to understand, however, is that what unites all of these is the essential tendency towards a spatialized mode of understanding and ordering of the world—the spatial being closely tied to the calculative, the numerical, and the quantitative.[48] It is such spatialization that is fundamentally at issue in that which Heidegger identifies as the essence of technology—namely, *Gestell*.

Both *Gestell* and the other term that plays a key role here, *Bestand*, carry, as was noted earlier, spatial or topological connotations. That this is so can be seen, though seldom if ever acknowledged, in the usual translations of *Gestell* as "enframing" and "positionality," and of *Bestand* as "standing reserve," "stock," or "resource." *Bestand* comes from *stehen*, meaning to stand, so that *Bestand* is that which "stands ready"—and to stand ready is always to stand somewhere, in a certain position, for something. *Gestell* comes from *stellen*, meaning to set or to position, and *Stelle*, also from *stellen*, means a position or location. *Stellen* is at work in the term translated as representation, *Vorstellen/vorstellen*, as well as in *herstellen* (to produce), *bestellen* (to order) and *verstellen* (to block, obscure, reset, or misplace). In ordinary German, *Gestell* refers to a framework for holding things in a certain arrangement of positions—as does a bookcase.[49] However, as Heidegger uses the term in relation to the essence of technology, it refers not to something apart from that which is framed but, rather, to a framing that consists simply in the interrelating of things as part of a single network or structure.[50] Looking to the way other terms using the "Ge-" prefix (*Gebirg*, a mountain range, and *Gemüt*, an overall disposition or set of mind) operate to indicate a form of "gathering" (of mountains or dispositions), *Gestell* is intended, by Heidegger, to mean something like a system of positions or positionings—but in a way such that *Gestell* might be understood as a *positioning* in the same way that *Gebirg* might be understood as a *mountaining* or *Gemüt* as an overall *disposing*.

As a positioning, *Gestell* is also a spatializing—the positioning at issue here is just the pure positioning that arises within the pure extendedness of the spatial. Since the spatial—when understood as apart from, and prior to, the topological—lacks any limit that belongs to it, and since this means that the spatial also lacks any qualitative differentiation that is its own, so the spatialization of the world that is at work in modern technology tends to efface any real differentiation between things, just as it affects any difference between places, drawing everything into a single all-encompassing spatiality. In Heidegger's account, this is evident in the way he describes the reduction of everything to *Bestand*, and thereby made available to and incorporated into the larger system. As he says, in respect of the technological appropriation of nature, "the energy concealed in nature is unlocked, what is unlocked is transformed, what is transformed is stored up, what is stored up is, in turn, distributed, and what is distributed is switched about ever anew."[51] Unlocking, transforming, storing, distributing, and switching about are, as Heidegger says, ways of revealing. They are also ways of revealing that depend on the idea of an expansive and unbounded space within which such unlocking, transforming, storing, and distributing can proceed in a seamless and unobstructed fashion. The space of technology is a space of connectivity, but it is therefore also a space of uniform, unbounded, extendedness. In many contemporary discussions of modernity, and especially of the world of digital information and communication, a language very similar to that which Heidegger employs is used to describe the way in which everything is nowadays transformed into a network of unbounded connectivity and flow—a network of pure spatialization. Indeed, the self-evident character of the contemporary world, as given over to such a spatialized ordering, is one of the reasons behind the so-called "spatial turn" that is so salient within contemporary theory.

In his discussion of Heidegger on technology, Andrew Feenberg considers Heidegger's account of the way the fourfold—earth, sky, divinities, and mortals—are gathered and brought to focus in the thing, which, in Heidegger's example (from the essay "The Thing"), is an ordinary jug. Feenberg asks whether Heidegger can be read, on the basis of this account, as intending to "move us from a substance metaphysics to a network metaphysics, a sort of field theory of things."[52] Feenberg is critical, however, of what he sees as the lack of detail in Heidegger's account, and he also argues that Heidegger's account of the thing, as it stands in relation to the fourfold, appears arbitrary in the way it treats, for instance, the jug in contrast to technological devices. "Devices are things too," writes Feenberg. "Modern and technological though they may be, they too focus gathering practices that bring people together with each other and with 'earth and sky,' joining them in a world."[53] Feenberg's comments echo Hubert Dreyfus's reading (which in turn draws on Albert Borgmann's work) according to which modern technological devices are capable of gathering in exactly the same way as Heidegger's jug.[54]

There is a superficial similarity between the sort of relationality that is evident in Heidegger's account of the way the world is gathered in the thing and the connectivity, itself tied up with the representational and calculative, that is so central to contemporary technology. After all, spaces and numbers can connect things too, and the spatialized system of technological modernity is surely also one that reveals a world. That technology is a mode of revealing, and that it does indeed reveal the world, in a certain way, is not disputed—neither here nor in

Heidegger's thinking—and as it reveals, so too does modern technology also "gather." But there is a crucial difference between the relationality that is at work in Heidegger's account of the thing and the fourfold as against the connectivity that is at work in modern technology: one is topological, whereas the other is purely spatial; one is tied to place, and the other, to mere position. Place does indeed *gather*, and it does so, as we have seen in discussions in earlier chapters, through the way it also *bounds*. Space, on the other hand, since it lacks any bound of its own, tends towards dispersal, and the connectivity that belongs to it is what Heidegger describes in terms of a transforming, storing, distributing, and switching about. It is a connectivity in which the device appears largely as a nodal point that enables the connectivity of the system to operate through it rather than as a thing in and around which other things, events, and persons are gathered within a place.

The spatialized connectivity that is at work in modern technology, and the inexorable drive towards an increase in such connectivity, appears both in relation to specific technologies—in the increasing complexity and capacity of those technologies and the devices associated with them—and to technology as a larger system. What one sees in the development of technology, in general, is an increase in the complexity and capacity of specific technologies and devices, as well as the increasing interconnection between technologies and devices. Technological systems become more expansive and encompassing and increasingly connected to one another. As those connections multiply, so the devices and systems that function as points of intersection or *convergence* within the system of connectivity—the nodal or "switching" points as they were referred to earlier—become increasingly complex as more and more connections are routed through them. To take a particularly salient and familiar example, the mobile phone is increasingly integrated as part of a wider and more encompassing system of communication, information, and action, at the same time as the phone itself encompasses more and more activities and capacities.[55] The phone is thus no longer just a device for contacting other individuals by voice but becomes a text messenger, a camera, a credit card, a means of identification, a GPS locator, a tracking device, a document reader, a news source, a photo album, and so on. Moreover, this tendency towards connectivity and convergence occurs not only with respect to single technological systems or devices but also with respect to the entire field of such systems and devices. The successive improvement of particular devices that is part of technological development thus always occurs as part of the improvement across whole ranges of devices and systems—which also means that one never encounters, except as technological remnants or repressions, advanced technologies that operate only with respect to a narrow range of devices or in narrowly circumscribed domains. Technologies are systematic, not discrete, so the development of technology is always the development of a system that expands across the entirety of a society's activities—a systematizing movement that operates upon both systems and devices.

The *convergent connectivity* that is evident here, and the fact of *ever-increasing* convergence and connectivity, is central to the way technology constitutes itself (and the manner by which technology "does" this is no different from that by which other systems also "act" in ways that exceed the intentions and the control of individuals). Moreover, this is apparent not only in the self-formation of technology but also in the way modern technology, or, more accurately, the extreme spatialization that is central to it, forms the world in which it operates. Modern technology organizes the world in certain ways (in ways, once again, that exceed individual intention and control), establishing certain pathways and relationships as salient over others. To some extent, this is true even of the simplest technologies, so that one can even argue for a continuity, though Heidegger pays no attention to it, between the technology of the earliest hominids and our own digital technologies. All technologies organize the world in certain ways, but not all technologies organize the world in the extreme and encompassing fashion that is true of modern technology, and this is partly because premodern technologies operate in ways that remain configured around more localized devices and systems. Put simply, they remain oriented to place rather than to space. Although continuous with previous technologies, modern technology represents a break within the history of technology through the way in which it achieves a radical shift away from the device, away from localities of activity and organization, towards the spatialized "system."

One can say of modern technology, as does Heidegger,[56] that it is no longer oriented around "things," or "objects," but around systems of consumption and production, in which what is produced is only material for further consumption, further production, and from which any real sense of the differences between things has been eliminated. The character of technological modernity, as drawing everything into a single such system of pure connectivity, is a large part of what underlies the disquiet Heidegger famously expressed in the *Der Spiegel* interview (originally given in September 1966, but not published until after Heidegger's death

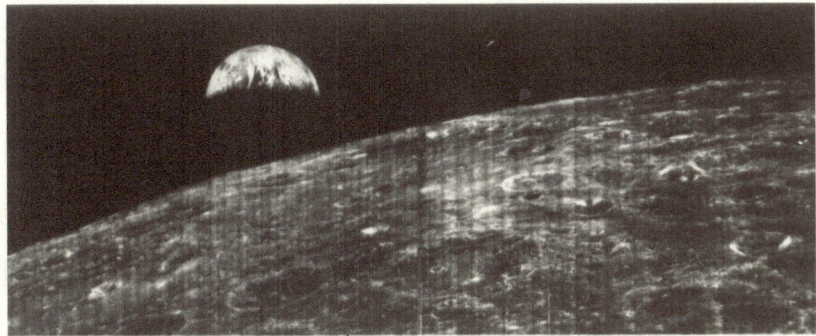

Figure 3. The first view of Earth taken by a spacecraft from the vicinity of the Moon. The photo was transmitted to Earth by the Lunar Orbiter I and received at the NASA tracking station at Robledo De Chavela, near Madrid, Spain. The image was taken during the spacecraft's sixteenth orbit, on August 23, 1966. NASA.

in 1976) at seeing the first images of the earth from space, showing the earth in its entirety (see fig. 3, a photo taken by *Lunar Orbiter I*, in August 1966, just a month before the interview).[57] Here even the earth appears as taken up into the same system of technological, spatialized connection, symbolized by the framing of the photograph—the world is itself reduced to a picture.

Technology, Limit, and Failure

It is commonplace to talk of the radical changes wrought by technological modernity—and that there is indeed a radicalism about it that derives from its *spatializing* character must not be overlooked. Yet the idea of radical change is part of the discourse by which technological modernity elaborates itself, being one version of the progressivist story of modernity (although it is only part of that story, within which there are multiple and sometimes incompatible narratives). Technological modernity does not change—because it does itself depend upon—the more basic ontology of the world, of human being, and of revealing and presencing. Nowhere is this clearer than in the operation of connected digital technology, which, for all that it proclaims the freeing of human activity from the constraint of physical location, still works, and can only work, through our own embodied and located engagement with specific systems and devices. In its spatializing character, technology effaces the very placedness on which it nevertheless depends. As a result, technology misunderstands its own place, its own limit (it is strictly unrepresentable within the spatialized frame of modern technology), and, in so doing, it misleads as to its own character as technology, even as it also obscures the human relation to the technological. Thus, modern technology appears as a "signless cloud," to use a term from the Parmenides lectures of 1942–43, a "withdrawing concealment in the midst of its very obtrusiveness."[58]

Technology's own self-representation, which appears in the many ways in which technological capitalism proliferates itself (including but not limited to advertising and entertainment, as well as politics), not only hides the placed character of technological functioning but also tends towards its continued re-presentation in instrumental terms. This is as true of the technological system that is modern capitalism as of any more particular technological device, whether it be the mobile phone, the computer, or the drone-based weapon systems that are now beginning to dominate modern warfare. These devices and systems are extremely powerful, and their power derives from their spatialized and connected modes of operation, yet their very encompassing nature, and the increasingly complex connectivity on which they depend, is also a source of fragility.

Modern technological systems are prone to breakdown in a way that older, simpler technologies were not, and protecting against their propensity to breakdown itself requires the development of further technological systems that have this as their primary aim (thus, many modern technologies become technologies whose main aim is the prevention of technological failure).[59] Paul Virilio argues that technology arises in a way that is intimately tied to its own breakdown, such that every technology brings with it the concept of its own failure, the concept of the "accident."[60] This becomes something for technology constantly to try to overcome, even though such attempts do not eliminate but only shift the character of the failure at issue. Technological modernity's difficulty in grasping its own limit, its own breakdown, its own failure, is not merely indicative of an instrumental or prudential problem for technology but, rather, shows something much deeper. What is at issue here is technology's own tendency to obscure, not only its own character, but also the very appearing of things as the things they are—which means the obscuring of the bounds within which things appear, the obscuring of the place that belongs to their appearing *as things*.

The obscure and obscuring character of technological modernity stands as an ironic counterpoint to the idea of "enlightenment" that is so much at the heart of the project of modernity. But there is more than just irony here. The inability of technological modernity to understand itself other than instrumentally, and even to elaborate itself in ways that cover over the very boundaries and limits that make it what it is, means that technological modernity carries within itself an inevitable tendency to breakdown and failure that it cannot adequately represent and to which it can only respond in technological terms—which means in ways that often exacerbate rather than ameliorate. Thus, technological modernity, which promises the utopic, so often seems to end in one or another form of the dystopic.

So-called "neoliberal" economics (along with various other forms of "economism") provides a particularly salient example of the technological transformation of everything into number and quantity—a transformation brought about through the specific form of spatialization associated with monetization, managerialization, and marketization. Yet the evident failure of neoliberalism as an effective technique of governance and management should, in this respect, be unsurprising—not only the fact of its failure, but the way that failure seems not to have hampered its continued operation (its *economic* failure has, in other words, been no obstacle to its *political* success).[61] As an especially salient example, the case of neoliberalism reinforces Heidegger's point that, although technology may look to justification in instrumental terms, it is not and cannot be primarily instrumental. The inner rationale of technology, in its encompassing and systematic character, is *not* based on instrumental success but, rather, on its character, as Heidegger emphasizes, as a mode of revealing, which can be understood, put more mundanely, in terms of the way technology remains always committed to its own globalizing and spatializing imperative (an imperative that, in any case, overrides any specific realization of it).[62]

Technology and Its Danger

The sort of optimistic progressivism that Pinker exemplifies is not without some foundation—the last few hundred years have seen enormous improvements in the quality of human life. But the amelioration of the human condition has also come at a huge environmental cost. As the benefits to human life have increased, rates of extinction and the destruction of habitats mean that almost all other forms of life on the planet have been diminished. And in the longer term, this diminishment presents a significant human threat, as food chains are disrupted, weather systems become unstable, and even such basic requirements as the availability of clean air and water can no longer be relied upon. Heidegger's critique of technology does not depend on ignoring the benefits that technology brings. Neither does it consist merely in setting those benefits against other dangers, of which the most obvious is indeed the danger to planetary environmental well-being. Indeed, while Heidegger recognizes the environmental threat that technology presents, he sees that threat as founded in something more fundamental.

What the questioning of technology shows is the way the essence of technology resides not simply in the power that technology brings or in the way that it seems to give mastery of nature (though a limited mastery to be sure) to human beings. The essence of technology is to be found in the globalizing, systematizing, *spatializing* that is *Gestell.* The danger of technology, which becomes a danger only with the radical form of spatialization that emerges with *modern* technological development, lies in its obscuring of place—in its obscuring of that bounded but open realm that gives room to the simple presencing of self, others, and world. When that placedness is covered over through the rendering of place as mere position, through the effective obliteration of difference, through the transformation of the human, the nonhuman, the instrument, and the thing into elements within a system of consumption and production, of transfer and accumulation, of benefit and risk, then what remains is a world of alienation, displacement, and disorientation. Technology does not abolish place, but rather forgets and obscures it. The task is to find ways of remembering and of recuperating—and, in doing so, to perhaps recover what Heidegger calls a "free" relation to technology, which may also require a freeing of technology itself, if that is indeed possible, a recovery of technology's own being-placed, technology's own essential limit and ground.

It may be argued that the topological analysis of technology, sketched here, goes beyond anything explicitly "authorized" by the Heideggerian texts. Yet to reiterate what was said in the introduction to this volume, such authorization is not my sole or primary concern, and that is especially so here. The question of technology is indeed more important than any question that might pertain to Heidegger alone. But in any case, the analysis advanced in this chapter does not seem to me to exceed, in an unwarranted fashion, what is evident in Heidegger's own discussions, even if there are some elements that it omits. As I argued earlier, if one takes seriously the fundamentally topological character of Heidegger's thinking, then it is hard to see why one would (or how one could) ignore the topological elements that are clearly at work in his thinking of technology. One can allow that Heidegger does not fully develop those topological elements, yet that does not mean that they are absent, and it also makes the task of their elaboration and development even more important. This is especially true if one takes the view, as I think one should, that such a topological analysis enables insight into the character of technology and so into our contemporary situation. Without such insight, we will remain blind to the reality of where we are and incapable of any genuine response.

Nine

From Extremity to Releasement

The concluding poem in volume 2 of the *Lyrical Ballads*, Wordsworth's "Michael," is a tale of misplaced trust, betrayed love, lost hope, and grief. Quite apart from its significance in other respects—and it is one of Wordsworth's best-known works—the poem articulates a strong sense of the interconnection of human life with the place or places in which that life is lived. Indeed, it is a poem that has played a central role in some of my own discussions of the relation between place and human being,[1] just as it also figures centrally in Seamus Heaney's elaboration of the idea of a "sense of place" in English poetry.[2] The poem's protagonist, the shepherd Michael, is a man bound to his own stretch of country—the landscape of Grasmere Vale in Westmoreland. Of the fields and hills that belong to that landscape, Wordsworth writes that they were, to Michael, "his living Being, even more/Than his own Blood—what could they less?"[3] Wordsworth's poem is notable for its position within Wordsworth's own literary *oeuvre* and for its significance as a poem of place, however the poem is also a key work in the thinking of "authenticity," as this term is applied to persons and to human life and existence.

Although the term has a wide currency in English (with direct correlates in other European languages, including *authenticité*, in French, and *Authentität*, in German), "authenticity" has become commonplace in the English language discourse around Heidegger's work, largely as a result of its early use to translate the Heideggerian term *Eigentlichkeit* from *Being and Time*, otherwise most directly translated as "ownness." "Authenticity" is thus read as a key Heideggerian notion, such that Charles Guignon writes of Heidegger as "the philosopher whose writings brought the term 'authenticity' into common parlance."[4] Yet this way of approaching Heidegger, and the drawing of Heidegger's thinking into the domain of the thinking of authenticity—which, as we shall see, has its own particular character, especially in English—gives rise to significant difficulties. Part of the aim of this chapter is to explore those difficulties, but also to consider the notion of authenticity as it stands in relation to the thinking of place and the possibility that a genuinely topological approach might lead in a rather different direction than that associated with authenticity in its historically distinctive, and also popularly assumed, sense. However, the path to be followed here is somewhat indirect. It begins, not with Heidegger, but with the way authenticity has been taken up in the reading of Wordsworth's "Michael" as well as the connection of authenticity to ideas of the self, before engaging with the way the term stands in relation to Heidegger's thinking and then returning to Wordsworth and to Grasmere Vale.

Authenticity as Idea and Ideal

Authenticity, as it applies to human life and existence, is a distinctively modern notion, and its historical origins and development are crucial in any attempt to understand the issues that surround it. Lionel Trilling's *Sincerity and Authenticity* is undoubtedly the key work on which any historically attentive discussion of authenticity must draw, and it takes Wordsworth's "Michael" as one of its main textual sources for the emergence of an ideal of authenticity in the eighteenth and nineteenth centuries. Trilling's treatment of "Michael" has little to do with the poem's topological orientation or significance. Instead, the figure of Michael appears in Trilling's discussion at just that point at which Trilling moves from the concept of sincerity to focus squarely on the idea of authenticity as such. Trilling writes:

> Michael says nothing; he expresses nothing. It is not the case with him as it is with Hamlet that he has "that within which passeth show." There is no within and without: he and his grief are one. We may not, then, speak of sincerity. But our sense of Michael's being, of—so to speak—his being-in-grief, comes to us as a surprise, as if it were exceptional in its actuality, and valuable. And we are impelled to use some word

which denotes the nature of this being and which accounts for the high value we put upon it. The word we employ for this purpose is "authenticity."[5]

As Trilling presents matters, the concern with authenticity arises in the context of what he refers to as an "ontological concern . . . [a] preoccupation with the sentiment of being."[6] It is primarily a matter of a certain mode of the self in which the self is entirely encompassed by the passion, feeling, or commitment that belongs to it. In Michael's case, this "being authentic" takes the form, extreme though it may seem, of his own being as a "being-in-grief." Trilling's focus is thus on authenticity as an *exceptional* mode of being of the self—singular and extreme—in which the self is completely and utterly given over to that which it is, and as which it also appears. It is this that Trilling finds exemplified in an especially clear form in Wordsworth's "Michael."

Contrasting the sense of authenticity that appears in Wordsworth with that in Rousseau, Trilling writes that "our sense of what authenticity means involves a degree of rough concreteness or of extremity which Rousseau, with his abiding commitment to an ideal of patrician civility, does not give us but which Wordsworth does. Michael is as actual, as hard, as dense, weighty, perdurable as any stone he lifts up or lets lie."[7] Here, authenticity seems to mean an actuality of being that may be so exceptional and extreme as even to offend against our normal sensibilities. As a result, Trilling concludes that authenticity is "a polemical concept, fulfilling its nature by dealing aggressively with received and habitual opinion."[8] But even more than this (and, for some contemporary readers of "Michael," this may seem surprising), the authenticity that Trilling takes to be present in Wordsworth's poem, and that is given concrete form in the figure of the old and grieving shepherd, is so extreme as to carry a potential violence within it. According to Trilling, it is the same violence that is given explicit and paradigmatic expression in Joseph Conrad's *Heart of Darkness* (a work that stands, along with the poem "Michael," as one of the key texts in Trilling's account).

It is this violence that appears in terms of the aggressive and, in Trilling's terms, "polemical" assertion of the individual self and its autonomy against the existing social order and its settled conventionalities—an assertion, even, should it come to it, against the very order of nature and of the world. Trilling takes this to be characteristic of the modern notion of authenticity. What drives this assertion is the demand for a reality, an actuality, a truth that goes beyond the ordinary truths of everyday life and appearance. And, if this demand should be such as to result in the destruction of that which is less than real in this sense, or that stands in the way of such real, authentic being, then so be it. Thus, Trilling reminds us of the Greek origins from which "authentic" and "authenticity" derive—"*Authenteo*: to have full power over; also, to commit a murder. *Authentes*: not only a master and a doer, but also a perpetrator, a murderer, even a self-murderer, a suicide."[9] Here, Conrad's character, Mr. Kurtz, who is indeed master, doer, perpetrator, murderer (perhaps even, in a sense, a self-murderer, certainly a self-destroyer) appears as the authentic hero (the hero *in extremis*) facing up to the reality of his own self and those around him—reality that also turns out to be a horror. It is a long way from Westmoreland to the Congo, and yet it would seem, if we follow Trilling's account, that the gap between Kurtz and the old shepherd Michael, unlikely companions though they may be, is not so great. Although differing in manner of expression and mode of realization, both are seemingly joined by the ideal of authenticity, and by the extremity of being and of the self that the commitment to authenticity apparently brings with it. Some might see the figure of Martin Heidegger, with his own supposed emphasis on the "authentic" set out in *Being and Time*, as an obvious companion to these two—Heidegger's enthusiastic support for National Socialism, in the early 1930s, providing an indication of the violence and extremity that authenticity carries with it.

Although authenticity is frequently appealed to in a wide range of discussions,[10] it is a notion seldom critically analyzed. One of the few works to attempt to do so, philosophically, is Charles Guignon's *On Being Authentic*. Guignon devotes considerable attention to a critical examination of the way in which the ideal of authenticity has developed and the ideas with which it seems to be associated. However, a significant part of Guignon's account, most notably the final chapter, "Authenticity in Context," is given over to a re-visioning of authenticity in terms of the social context in which the self is located and defined. Authenticity becomes, on this account, "essentially a social virtue."[11] In this, Guignon draws heavily on Charles Taylor, who argues in similar fashion, as well as on Bernard Williams.[12]

What Guignon offers is thus not a rejection of the idea of authenticity as such—an idea about which he claims "there is obviously something clearly right"[13]—but, rather, a rejection of a certain conception of authenticity and an argument in favor of an expanded version of what authenticity might mean. "What is problematic," he writes, "is not the goal of being authentic, but the predominance of any one perspective on the rich and dense weave of undertaking and responsibilities that make up our lives."[14] In expanding the notion in this way, Guignon brings authenticity into connection with a notion to which it might otherwise seem to be opposed, *releasement* or *Gelassenheit*.[15] Guignon's use of the term draws on the work of Hans-Georg Gadamer as well as Heidegger, and his characterization of what it involves is immediately suggestive of a topological dimension—though not one that Guignon explicitly takes up. Releasement is, he says, "a heightened sensitivity to what is called for by the entire situation . . . a kind of situational awareness of what should be done."[16] Characterized in this fashion, releasement appears as a giving of oneself over to a world of shared involvement with others—a form of *self-release*, in contrast to the more usual emphasis in authenticity on *self-possession* and independent self-realization.

Authenticity, Romanticism, and the Self

Like Trilling, Guignon also draws on Wordsworth as an important reference point in charting the development of the modern idea of authenticity. Unlike Trilling, however (whose examination of authenticity is often mentioned but seldom addressed in any detail in philosophical discussions of the notion), Guignon looks not to the early poems—not to "Michael" or any of the poems that make up the *Lyrical Ballads*—but, rather, to the later works and, especially, the *Prelude* (a work begun in 1798, though worked on continuously by Wordsworth throughout his life and published just after his death in 1850[17]). Adopting elements from the reading of Wordsworth advanced by Geoffrey Hartmann (a reading that itself seems, as Jonathan Bate points out, to derive from the work of Paul de Man),[18] Guignon treats Wordsworth as holding to a set of views that Guignon takes as characteristic of Romanticism: namely, that there is a need "to recover a sense of oneness and wholeness that appears to have been lost with the rise of modernity"; that this can only be done through "a total immersion in one's own deepest and most intense feelings"; and that "the self is the highest and most all-encompassing of all that is found in reality."[19]

The ideas at issue here are seen by Guignon to underpin the focus on the self that is also a characteristic feature of authenticity and that sees the recovery of the real as a matter of the recovery of the self, understood as requiring a turn inward, and, in Guignon's account, a turn away from the world or, at least, towards an internalization of the world:

> Romanticism, far from providing an alternative to scientific objectification, simply turns reality over to the sciences once and for all and rests content with creating its own reality in imagination. Romanticism's final story is that we can let science have reality, because *we* have another reality—a special reality that is in here, within the self. Given this view of things, however, the self is not just the centre of the universe. It *is* the universe. For the sort of Romanticism found in *The Prelude*, there is simply no place for anything outside the self.[20]

As a picture of Romanticism or, indeed, of the German idealist tradition with which it is connected, this account is a little too simple. Romanticism contains various strands within it, not all of which are consistent with the account Guignon offers here.[21] Moreover, one can as much argue that Romanticism proposes a rethought understanding of the self that, in contemporary parlance, is *externalized* or *extended*, as one can view it as tending towards an internalized conception of the world. Whatever one might say about *The Prelude*, however, if one turns back to that earlier poem set in Grasmere Vale that is the focus for Trilling's account (the second volume of *Lyrical Ballads*, in which "Michael" appeared, being published in 1800), then the latter work is most definitely *not* one that sets the self *against* nature or the world, but that does exactly the opposite. "Michael" is, as we have seen, a poem that has its origins in a sense of the deep interconnection between place and self, and between place and the human.[22]

There can be no doubt that the ideal of authenticity does develop in tandem with the modern preoccupation with the individual self. But if we follow Trilling's account, then the real problem with authenticity is not merely the focus on the individual self alone but, rather, the tendency towards the exceptional and the extreme—a tendency that is expressed in terms of the desire for a reality that, to rework Trilling's words, will be "as actual, as hard, as dense, weighty, perdurable as . . . stone." Understood in relation to the self, authenticity thus names something *metaphysical*—an exceptional or superlative quality of being. It names a mode of the being of the self in which the self appears as more true, more real, more actual—more *being*—than anything that might lie outside of it. Often, such exceptionality will take the form of an extremity, if not an *excess*, of feeling, of willing, of acting—even of *power*. It is authenticity in this form that takes center stage in Trilling. Indeed, one might argue that it is what founds the contrast Trilling draws between authenticity and *sincerity*. Thus, Trilling writes of "authenticity" that it suggests "a more strenuous moral experience than 'sincerity' does, a more exigent conception of the self and of what being true to it consists in, a wider reference to the universe and man's place in it, and a less acceptant and genial view of the social circumstances of life."[23] Sincerity belongs with the idea of a settled and civilized life, whereas authenticity, on this view, holds the possibility of its overthrow and even its destruction.

Guignon does not give much attention to rebutting Trilling's claims about the extremity and exceptionality associated with authenticity, insisting that what is crucial about authenticity "is not just the intensity or fervour of the expression it carries with it,"[24] and that the problem with Trilling's contrasting of authenticity with sincerity is that it "makes authenticity look like a purely personal matter."[25] The extremity and exceptionality that Trilling identifies, which is not a matter of mere *expression* but an extremity of *being*, is thereby effectively brushed aside in Guignon's account in favor of authenticity as essentially social—in line with the readings of authenticity to be found in the work of Taylor, Williams, and others. Moreover, Guignon also argues that the idea of authenticity that he takes to be the focus for much of Trilling's analysis—which Guignon takes to be characterized by an emphasis on the individual self as apart from the social—is itself incoherent. It is so, claims Guignon, just in virtue of the fact that it supposedly gives an incomplete picture of authenticity by leaving out its essentially social character.[26] Here, however, Guignon seems simply to beg the question at issue, assuming from the first that authenticity is indeed a valuable and coherent notion, that the idea of authenticity found in Trilling must be inadequate, and that authenticity must therefore be understood differently.

Guignon's assumption that there is a positive sense to authenticity is shared by a great many of those who propound theories of authenticity within the contemporary philosophical and psychological literature. And few would contest the ethical significance or relevance of the ideals of integrity and sincerity that are typically at work in such theories. Yet the issue is not whether one can *assert* a positive sense of authenticity, but whether the historical development of the idea and even its contemporary popular associations provide *grounds for* such an assertion. Trilling's analysis of the historical development of authenticity, and especially the way authenticity arises as something distinctive and so as apart from sincerity alone, strongly suggest a negative answer here—the positive sense of authenticity does indeed seem to be severed from the historical development of the idea. Moreover, even were it to be the case that the idea of authenticity as Trilling identifies it—authenticity as tied to an extreme and exceptionalism view of the self as self-determining and self-possessed—was incoherent, this need not imply that Trilling's account is itself mistaken but might well be indicative of an incoherence in the very idea of authenticity. And that is surely one of the conclusions that can readily be drawn from Trilling's own account.

In support of his analysis, Guignon asks us to imagine individuals who are genuinely and deeply committed to ideals that are empty, trivial, or lacking in worth. Guignon's claim is that, no matter the fervor or intensity of their commitment,[27] we would not regard these individuals as living authentic lives. Authenticity is thus supposed, according to Guignon, to carry a content that goes beyond just the requirement of self-possession—being understood to require not only the living of a life that is *one's own* but the living of a life that is *worthwhile* and that satisfies a criterion of worth that is socially oriented. But once again, as a defense of authenticity, this assumes what it aims to show. One might well grant that a life committed to empty superficialities would be unlikely to be authentic—but one might well claim that this is because such a life would involve no real commitment to anything. What it shows, in other words, is that the supposedly authentic life requires content, but it tells us nothing about exactly what that content ought to be. And so there remains the possibility that a life, such as that exemplified by Conrad's Kurtz, could be an authentic life even though it is an ethically problematic life.

One cannot defend authenticity by stipulating its ethically worthy character—which is more or less what Guignon and so many others appear to do. And this is all the more so in the face of Trilling's argument concerning the way authenticity seems bound to forms of extremity and exceptionality—as exemplified by Kurtz—since such extremity and exceptionality are what make authenticity problematic. Trilling shows how this arises through the historical development of authenticity as something different from sincerity. However, one can see this same idea of authenticity at work even in many popular appropriations of authenticity. It is evident, for instance, in the positive evaluation of contemporary political leaders, even though they may be manifestly dishonest, as nevertheless "authentic," because of their seeming lack of concern for conventional opinion, because they "are what they are," and because what such individuals often project is a sense of their own self-confident assertion, self-possession, authority, and power. In this way the sociopathic individual can often appear as the model for the authentic individual—which is exactly what Kurtz shows. Such individuals are the ones who are willing to realize their desires come what may, to exercise the power they have acquired no matter the consequences, and who are determined to stamp their own mark on the world, and the people, around them.

Authenticity and Truthfulness

Perhaps the most common characterization of authenticity, as it applies to human life and existence, is that which is captured in the injunction from Shakespeare's *Hamlet*, spoken by Polonius to Laertes, "to thine own self be true."[28] Trilling treats this line in terms of sincerity rather than authenticity, although he nevertheless sees it as standing within the history of the development of the latter—our reading of the line assimilating it to the contemporary idea of authenticity that is, strictly speaking, anachronistic in relation to Shakespeare's text. Both sincerity and authenticity can indeed be said to involve a basic notion of *truthfulness*,[29] and of truthfulness *to self*, and it is this that enables the seeming treatment of authenticity and sincerity as more or less interchangeable notions that one finds in authors like Guignon, as well as Williams, and many others. But the truthfulness at issue is not identical in these two cases, even though this is frequently overlooked. One might say that the difference between these two forms of truthfulness is that sincerity is a matter of being true to oneself in one's interactions with others, and so is social in character, whereas authenticity involves truthfulness to oneself irrespective of others, and so, notwithstanding Guignon's contrary claim, is personal, perhaps even antisocial. Yet although this is, to a large extent, correct, it does not capture all that is at issue.

The modern notion of authenticity does not have its beginnings in discourse about the personal and the social, or, indeed, about the self. Instead, as Trilling points out, the origins of the notion lie "in the museum, where persons expert in such matters test whether objects of art are what they appear to be or are claimed to be."[30] One can see how a notion of truthfulness is at work here and also how it operates in many ordinary uses of the notion of the "authentic," as, for instance, when we say of a meal that it was "authentically" Italian, of a hand-woven carpet that it is an "authentic" Persian rug, of a painting purported to be by Rembrandt that it is an "authentic" work by the Dutch master, or of a building that looks like it is six hundred years old that is an "authentic" Tudor structure. Significantly, however, the particular sense of truthfulness at issue here is one very much tied to the idea of a *determining origin* or *authority* that gives that whose authenticity is in question its character as authentic.[31] Thus, the authenticity of the meal, the carpet, the painting, or the building is typically ascertained by going back to something that determines the character of each in just that respect that is at issue. In the museum case, cited by Trilling, this process of going back to some original and authoritative determination is clearly evident in his reference to the idea of the expert who can "test whether objects of art are what they appear to be or are claimed to be."

The process of "authentication" that Trilling invokes is one in which the aim is indeed to establish a link back to a specific determining origin, whether in a historical period, a geographical location, or an individual artist, craftsman, or workshop. Not a matter of truthfulness to self alone (a notion that, in any case, probably only applies here in terms of the congruence between what the thing is and what it presents itself as being), authenticity is that particular form of truthfulness that looks to a connection back to a determining origin or authority. Moreover, it is this that underpins any distinction between sincerity and authenticity in terms of a social or personal orientation. As should also be clear, it is the connection back to a determining authority or origin that grounds Trilling's association between authenticity and exceptionality. In the case of Wordsworth's "Michael," and following Trilling's account of the poem, that determining origin or ground is the self-evident character of Michael's grief as belonging to his very being.

If we take authenticity just in terms of some general notion of truthfulness to self, then we will find it difficult, not only to distinguish authenticity from sincerity, but also to dispel the ambiguity that allows that notion of truthfulness to self to slide over into the stronger notion of a grounding in some determining origin—in some exceptional or superlative mode of the self or of existence—in which it is independent of sincerity or from any other "social" virtue. This is part of what makes discussion of authenticity so awkward. On the one hand, authenticity calls up a set of notions, especially that of truthfulness, that seem to be part of our normal ethical discourse and as such can be seen to belong with notions of moderation and civility. On the other hand, the character of authenticity, when applied to the self and as connected with the idea of truthfulness as tied to a determining authority, tends us towards a form of truthfulness that is antagonistic to truthfulness in its more usual forms, and towards an extremity and exceptionality that is sometimes antisocial, if not also violent and dangerous. The result is a potential oscillation or instability within the very concept of authenticity, and because one of the poles of that oscillation is that of exceptionality and extremity, so the oscillation is a dangerous one.

The danger that attaches to authenticity is made all the greater in virtue of the fact that, when intended in relation to the self, the very constraints that normally obtain in other ordinary uses of authenticity no longer apply. The self is a contested concept, and the domain that belongs to it has no clear or definable boundaries—unlike, for instance, the domains of regional cuisine, handicraft production, or art collecting (or, one might add, the social practices that provide the usual setting for truthfulness in the sense associated with sincerity). This is another aspect of the ambiguity, or instability, that seems to be part of the problem of authenticity and attaches to the notion as such, quite apart from any ambiguity that may arise in particular representations of it. Indeed, it is an instability that one might argue is already present in Shakespeare's use, in *Hamlet*, of the idea of "truthfulness to self." What is at issue here may well belong, in its original literary and historical content, more to sincerity than to authenticity, and yet part of what Shakespeare seems to be doing is playing with, and perhaps even casting doubt upon, the very idea of such truthfulness.

As is often pointed out, the line in *Hamlet* that expresses this idea of truthfulness to self is put in the mouth of a character who himself exhibits little in the way of the commitment he impresses on his son. Polonius is presented as something of a scheming, pompous, self-interested windbag. And so, despite the tender and sincere tones in which it is expressed and by which the audience is surely intended to be affected, Polonius's exhortation to Laertes to be true to himself carries with it a degree of ambiguity, even tension, that does not derive only from the lack of truthfulness evident in Polonius's own character.

Part of the focus of Shakespeare's play is Hamlet's own uncertain sense of self, his uncertainty about what is true in the world around him, as well as in his own soul. In a context in which the self is thereby put into question, what is to be made of the injunction to be true to oneself—especially when that injunction is put by a schemer and a fool? The ambiguity surrounding Polonius's advice to Laertes becomes all the greater when we realize that Laertes is the one who, at the end of the play, is so consumed by grief, animosity, and the desire for revenge that he is open to the manipulative wiles of Claudius, precipitating the final duel that brings the whole sequence of events to its bloody and extreme conclusion. Put in the context of the concern with authenticity, *Hamlet* may be seen as indicating a new uncertainty about the self that puts into question the very ideal of truthfulness to self, even when understood in terms of sincerity, and that can also be seen to carry something of a foreshadowing of the horror and extremity that is to come.

Shakespeare aside, one may well ask what the self can be, anyway, such that one can indeed be true to it? How does authenticity operate here? What are the criteria to which one would look to determine whether a self is authentic *as a self*? Such questions, which arise in critical discussions of authenticity elsewhere,[32] are not answered by interrogating authenticity understood merely in some sense of truthfulness—and even the reference to the self is of no help here, just as abandoning talk of the self is of no help either. Understood just as truthfulness, authenticity carries no real content beyond the idea of a distinction between the truthful and the false, the real and fake—and it no more tells us what is to count as authentic than the related concept of truth as applied to sentences provides us with a list of truths or with a rule for identifying the true as opposed to the false. Moreover, the need to identify a real content and distinctive to authenticity is just what sets up the problematic tendency within the language of authenticity that leads towards the sort of extremity and exceptionality, the actuality and reality, that Trilling identifies. It is thus that authenticity has marked itself out historically as indeed a significant and substantive idea, even as having a degree of power and authority of its own.

There are not the resources within the notion of authenticity to bound or limit its application to the self, but neither can one look to an account of the self, whether socialized or not, to try to fill out the notion of authenticity. Although such an account will tell us about the self, it will shed little light on *authenticity* as such (at best, filling out the context in which the idea of the authentic might be applied). Moreover, there is always the possibility that even if the self is understood as social, as Guignon argues, then authenticity might re-emerge as an extreme and exceptionalist form of socialized self, and this, one might argue, is precisely what one finds in some forms of nationalism and totalitarianism in which authenticity is gained through submersion of the self in the nation or state or through giving oneself over to the relation to the leader. George Orwell's *Nineteen-Eighty-Four* can thus be read as a portrayal of that mode of authenticity that is part of the ideology and practice of the totalitarian state—of the authenticity that comes with the recognition that the collectivity of the state, not the individual self, is the only reality, "as actual, as hard, as dense, weighty, perdurable as any stone."

That there is a distinction between authenticity and ideas of sincerity and truthfulness is evident, not only from Trilling's historical analysis, but from a widespread contemporary usage in which authenticity has exactly the sense of something more perduring and more real than the self—or life—as ordinarily experienced or understood. It is this that is partly evident in some of the contemporary uses of authenticity, Trilling aside, of which Guignon is himself critical (uses he associates, as I note below, with the "self-help movement"). Consequently, one does not need to affirm authenticity to affirm the importance of sincerity or truthfulness. And rather than try to assert a revised form authenticity somehow purified of its extreme and exceptionalist connotations, it seems better to abandon the notion, at least as applied to human life and existence, admitting its irretrievably problematic character.[33]

Authenticity and Releasement

Given the problems that attach to authenticity, it is perhaps significant that Guignon's account concludes, not with authenticity as such, but rather with *releasement* or *Gelassenheit*. And Guignon writes that he intends the notion of releasement as a counter to "the dangerous one-sidedness built into the concentration on authenticity in certain areas of the self-help movement."[34] Releasement certainly stands in stark contrast to the sort of exceptionality and extremity that is evident in Trilling's account of authenticity. As I noted earlier, Guignon's characterization of releasement treats it in terms of "a heightened sensitivity to what is called for by the entire situation . . . a kind of situational awareness of what should be done."[35] This does not mean, however, that releasement involves a complete turn away from the self—the very idea of situation presupposes a self, whether understood as body, agent, or "subject," that is situated, and to be aware of the situation in its entirety is to be aware of both that which is situated as well as that within which it is situated. The point is well illustrated by a familiar example used in relation to the understanding of spatiality: to grasp one's spatial situation one must be able to relate the parts of space to the parts of one's own body.[36] Analogously, in order to grasp one's situation, one must be able to relate aspects of that wherein one is situated to aspects of oneself. If releasement is indeed a form of *self-release*, it is so, not in the sense that it involves a complete abandonment of the self, but rather inasmuch as it means a releasing of the self *into the situation*, and so also a releasing *of the situation* in the direction of the self.

Guignon's own explication of releasement draws on Gadamer's model of conversation, in which we are indeed given over *to the conversation* and so allow the conversation *to take us along within it*,[37] as well as on Heidegger's explicit use of releasement as an alternative way of relating to modern technology.[38] Releasement, in the latter context, is specifically a matter of "letting be" as well as of "letting go,"[39] and so of taking an attitude to technology, and to the world, that refuses the attempt at control or mastery. Moreover, Heidegger's own account of technology is one that sees technology, not as something wielded by human beings, but rather as an all-encompassing ordering of things that extends even to the human (a point central to the discussion in chapter 8). Releasement, in the Heideggerian context, must therefore mean a refusal also of those forms of dominating control or mastery that are directed at the self—forms of control or mastery that one might argue are paradigmatically at work in many contemporary versions of the ideal of authenticity. It means recognition of the self as characterized not by its exceptionality or extremity—and certainly not in the sense of mastery or self-assertion—but by its openness to the world, by its dependence on the world, by its vulnerability to the world.

Heidegger's discussion of releasement may arise most explicitly in relation to the question of technology and the response to it. But it nevertheless permeates much of his later thinking, coming to the fore alongside the increasingly explicit shift in Heidegger's thinking towards place and topology.[40] If one were to accept the standard reading of Heidegger's early work, in *Being and Time*, as indeed giving a central role to the notion of authenticity and the authentic, then the emphasis on releasement in the later work could be seen as a direct counter to the earlier, and Heidegger's work as a whole could then be seen as describing a movement from the extremity and exceptionality of authenticity to the very different mode of comportment that belongs with releasement. Certainly, there is an extremity and exceptionality evident in Heidegger's thinking and writing in the 1930s and early 1940s, especially in association with his emphasis on the history of being during that period (something briefly referred to in chapter 1).[41] However, that there is a specific notion of *authenticity*, certainly in the sense identified by Trilling, that is at work as a central element in Heidegger's thinking seems demonstrably false.

The terms "authenticity" and "authentic" do not, of course, appear in Heidegger's work at all, not even in the form of the German *Authentizität*. Instead, as noted earlier, the term translated as "authenticity" in *Being and Time* is *Eigentlichkeit*.[42] The latter derives from *eigen*, meaning "own," and is also related to *Ereignis*, which is such an important term in Heidegger's later thinking but which, in ordinary German, means "event." Recognizing the sense of "own" at work here, Heidegger's use of *Eigentlichkeit* seems closest to something like "ownness" or even "propriety" or "appropriateness" (remembering that the English "proper" carries the sense of that which belongs to, or is one's own, hence "property," with much the same connection holding in German, where property is *Eigentum*). Variations on the language of "own," *eigen*, also appear elsewhere in German philosophical writing—to take one notable example, in *Cartesian Meditations* (more or less contemporaneous with *Being and Time*), Edmund Husserl talks of *eigen* and *eigentlich*, of *Eigenheit*, also translated as "ownness," and *Eigenheitssphäre*, "sphere of ownness."[43] It is thus that Theodore Adorno's *Jargon der Eigentlichkeit*, translated into English as *The Jargon of Authenticity*, is not directed at Heidegger alone. As its German subtitle suggests—*Zur deutschen Ideologie* [On German ideology]—its real target is a larger tradition of *ontological* inquiry encompassing the work of Søren Kierkegaard, of the German idealist, and of phenomenology, including that of Husserl, that has little to do with authenticity in the sense at work in Trilling.[44]

Even though one might well say that what is authentic is indeed that which is true, real, or genuine, and that this can be further elucidated in terms of that which is "proper" or is "owned," still authenticity in the sense at issue here means something more than what is at work in any of these alone. Authenticity carries a particular focus on the individual self, no matter how it is articulated, as that which is the touchstone for the real and the true, that to which all sense of the proper and the owned must be referred, and as the autonomous source of its own being—hence the emphasis on an excess of feeling or passion with which authenticity is often associated. Similarly, while Heidegger's use of *Eigentlichkeit* overlaps with elements also present in the idea of authenticity—perhaps most notably the importance of Dasein not losing itself completely in the world of the everyday, or of the anonymous "One" (*das Man*)—still *Eigentlichkeit* does not carry the same emphasis on the individual self, individual feeling, or individual *being* as apart from everything else. Moreover, as Heidegger emphasizes, *Eigentlichkeit* is not an extreme condition of the self standing apart from the world: "A*uthentic being a self* is not based on an exceptional state of the subject, detached from the they, *but is an existentiell modification of the they as an essential existential.*"[45]

So far as the ideas of the self and self-relatedness are concerned, the language of *Eigentlichkeit* refers to what is largely a *formal* structure. It is, Heidegger says elsewhere, "not moral, but fundamental-ontological [nicht moralisch, sondern fundamentalonologisch]."[46] What is at issue is thus a very different sense of self, and of truthfulness to self, than is at work in the "polemical" sense of authenticity that Trilling identifies in "Michael" and so in the emphasis on the authentic self as an extreme form of being or reality. *Eigentlichkeit* is not about authenticity in this sense. Instead, it concerns an attentiveness to an ontological structure that makes possible the very being of the self as usually understood, which is to say that it makes possible the being of any and every such self—and as that structure is *ontological,* so it is also *topological*. This attentiveness sits alongside ideas that also connect to the idea of releasement, *Gelassenheit*—which does not appear in a completely unprecedented way in Heidegger's later thinking alone. Ian Alexander Moore points out that there are over a hundred references to *Gelassenheit* throughout Heidegger's work.[47] And in a later annotation to *Being and Time*, Heidegger refers to the idea of "letting go" as a way of understanding the notion, used specifically in relation to *Eigentlichkeit,* that one must "become what you are" (a line taken from Friedrich Nietzsche and ultimately from Pindar).[48] Heidegger asks: "But who are 'you'?" and immediately answers, "The one who lets *go*—and *becomes!*"[49] Not only does this connect with the letting-go of releasement, but it also indicates that far from being an assertion of an already given self, *Eigentlichkeit* requires that one be open to a fundamental *change* in the self—open to the self as something that one *becomes* rather than a locus of assertion or prior actuality.[50]

Guignon's own characterization of releasement as "a kind of situational awareness" stands in opposition to ideas of authenticity of which Guignon is critical. However, it also brings into view the notion of *situation*, and so too the idea of being in *place*—after all, what is it to be situated but to be placed (*situ*, in the original Latin, meaning "site" or "place")? As noted earlier, Guignon does not attend to the topological dimension that is indicated here (his account of releasement is, in any case, somewhat curtailed), but it is an important dimension that is developed further in Heidegger's account.[51] Releasement is the freeing-up that occurs through a proper relation to the bounds that are one's own—to one's own place. As such, releasement involves a freeing of one's attitude towards the self no less than a freeing of one's relation towards the world. In this respect, releasement involves a different mode of understanding of the self and the world, and of the relation between them, and so also brings with it a different mode of relating.

There is no detailed elaboration, in Guignon's discussion, of the relation between the idea of releasement and the "dialogical" conception of the self that he also explores and that plays an important role in the argument he advances for authenticity as a "social virtue." The most that he offers is a relatively brief reference to Gadamer on conversation. Yet such a dialogical account of the self, which does indeed connect in more detailed ways with ideas in Gadamer and in Heidegger, involves a different *ontology* of the self, one that treats the self as essentially relational and dynamic and also as embedded in and shaped by its situation, by its being in place. It is no accident, then, that Heidegger's elaborations of releasement not only occur in the course of those discussions in which the idea of relationality is to the fore (an idea itself bound up with the notion of the event, the *Ereignis*, as was evident in chapter 5),[52] but also in those discussions in which he is directly concerned with the elucidation of topological ideas and themes.[53] Understanding the self, topologically, means understanding the self as it is given in relation to its bounds—as it is released to them and as they also release the self into the world. And this idea is already present, even if not always explicitly apprehended or expressed in topological terms, in *Being and Time*.

Place, Releasement, and World

Let us come back from Heidegger to Wordsworth and so to the figure of the shepherd Michael and that "straggling heap of unhewn stones" in Grasmere Vale. Trilling takes "Michael," as we have seen, to be a poem that provides a picture of authenticity as exceptionality and extremity. There can be no doubt that it does that. Yet, as we have also seen, it does something more than that. When Trilling tells us that, for Michael, "there is no within and without," he echoes Wordsworth's own description of the way the seeming externality of the Westmoreland landscape has become internalized in Michael—it is his "living Being"—even as his grief is given material embodiment in the heaped stones before us. Although it exemplifies a mode of authenticity, as well as telling a story of individual grief and loss, "Michael" is primarily a poem about *place*—as is made clear by Wordsworth when he writes of the tale of Michael:

> It was the first,
> The earliest of those tales that spake to me
> Of Shepherds, dwellers in the vallies, men
> Whom I already lov'd, not verily
> For their own sakes, but for the fields and hills
> Where was their occupation and abode.[54]

The tale of Michael is a tale etched into a landscape. It is the tale *both* of an individual man and of a certain place in Westmoreland—the one being inseparable from the other. Moreover, as a landscape bears the marks of human stories—stories that belong to that landscape, even though the landscape also goes beyond those stories—so every landscape always bears the marks of what is lost, of what is past, of remembrance and forgetting. Place and loss—and with it, sadness, mourning, even grief—are always linked. This is perhaps the real meaning of *nostalgia*, understood not in terms of the desire for the return of a past time (as is so often assumed) but in terms of the experience of place as also, and inevitably, an experience of loss and the pain of loss.[55]

Set against the background of the inquiry into authenticity, "Michael" presents a complex set of ideas, since it can be seen as encompassing notions of both extremity and releasement—or at least of that "released" conception of the self that understands it as standing in an essential relation to its situatedness, to its being-in-place. One might object, of course, that the situation, the place, that appears in Wordsworth is simply the situation as physical location, As such, it may be thought to lack the sense of social situatedness that is actually at issue in Guignon's discussion—whether as implied in his idea of releasement or in the dialogical conception of the self that he takes from Williams, Taylor, and others. There is a longer argument that could be put here, but, in brief, there can be no social situation that is not also physically embedded and embodied, and even the physical landscape carries with it a depth of social significance. The social is itself etched into the materiality of physical situation, into the materiality of place, just as the materiality of place is itself saturated with the structures and significations of the social.

The sense of releasement towards place, or interdependence with it, that is evident in Wordsworth's "Michael" is also not restricted to that poem alone. Although it is true that Wordsworth's poetry increasingly comes under the influence of ideas from the German idealist tradition that gives particular emphasis to the self, it is also true that Wordsworth retains a clear focus on the connection to nature and landscape as central to his work (something demonstrated, as Jonathan Bate emphasizes, by the fact that it is *The Excursion*, a work in which nature and landscape are no less important than in "Michael," that was considered the "summation" of his work by Wordsworth himself, as well as by his nineteenth-century readers[56]). Yet, although Wordsworth does not forsake a commitment to the idea of the intimacy of the relation between self and place, and so to the idea that it is indeed only *in the world* that we can find ourselves, there is nevertheless also a tendency in Wordsworth towards a thinking of authenticity that is tied to place.

Trilling identifies the figure of Michael as exemplifying an ideal of authenticity as exceptionality. One might suppose that such authenticity belongs to Michael alone, yet, if we take into account the way Wordsworth's poem also emphasizes the interdependence of Michael with the place in which his life is embedded, then we surely cannot but see the authenticity at issue here as attaching both to Michael *and* to the landscape to which he belongs. Moreover, there seems no doubt that there is, in Wordsworth, a clear sense in which authenticity can attach to places, and that part of what is at issue in a poem like "Michael" is actually the extolling of certain places as sometimes morally more valuable or significant than others. Thus, the pastoral landscape of Grasmere is set in contrast, in the course of two lines toward the end of the poem, to "the dissolute city" in which Luke gives himself "to evil courses."[57] Grasmere Vale is a place that Wordsworth loves, and his love for that place does indeed take on an almost metaphysical character, so that the place, and the broader countryside of which it is a part, appears as exceptional—as making possible a mode of being-in-place that is to be found perhaps nowhere else.[58] In that case, we would have to say that Wordsworth presents a curious mixture that combines a sense of authenticity, and the exceptionality and extremity that goes with it, as well as a sense of releasement, and both of these are tied closely to the Wordsworthian concern with place and the interdependence of self with place. There is an instability here that reflects the instability in the concept of authenticity itself. It is an instability that seems to lie at the heart of Wordsworth's thinking but that may also be part of the very attempt to think place in terms of authenticity.

There is certainly a common tendency for authenticity to be applied to place no less than to the self. Sometimes this is in a mundane sense that is more or less the same as the museum sense identified by Trilling and is most obviously at work in heritage contexts. Yet it is also used in ways that seem to carry a stronger moral connotation—much as seems to be implicit in Wordsworth. In such cases, the idea of authentic place often connotes something almost *utopic*—a realization of the enchanted garden, to use Guignon's phrase, from which modernity seems otherwise to have barred us; a place that will ground and secure our existence; a place that will allow us to be what we essentially are. The architect Christian Norberg-Schulz, who was largely responsible for making the Heideggerian concept of "dwelling" well-known in architectural circles, is sometimes read in a way that suggests his commitment to such an idea of authentic place.[59] Within environmental thinking, one can argue that there is also a tendency, even stronger than in Norberg-Schulz, to think of certain places, most often wilderness places, as "authentic" and also as exceptional—sometimes so much so that their exceptionality is taken to warrant the exclusion of humanity from those places.[60]

There can be no doubt that there is an ethical dimension that properly belongs to the thinking of place, and also to the human intervention in place—whether in relation to architecture, the environment, urban planning, or elsewhere. Moreover, that ethical dimension may well be seen to be critically determined by the interdependence between place and self, as much as by the interdependence that obtains between self and other (indeed, I would argue that these two sets of dependencies are themselves interdependent). Yet, if place is thought through the notion of authenticity, then it is likely to give rise to the same instability as arises when authenticity is deployed as a way of thinking about the self—and to the same exceptionality and extremity. Moreover, just as there is no need to appeal to authenticity in thinking ethically about the self, neither is there any such need in thinking about place. In every case, as I argued above, the ethical content that is supposedly taken up in the idea of authenticity is derived from, and articulated by means of, concepts that are not themselves dependent upon that idea.

Place, along with the self, must be thought through the concept of releasement rather than by means of authenticity. Moreover, the very idea of place should already lead us in that direction. There are no exceptional or superlative places, at least *not* in the sense demanded by authenticity. Additionally, and perhaps more importantly, place is never encountered as some determinate, immediately present entity or structure. Although we may often imagine places as if they were identical with what is presented on the travel poster or postcard, places always resist any such reduction or encapsulation. Even the place of Wordsworth's "Michael"—Grasmere Vale—is not exhausted by any *romantic* image of rocky hillside and quaint cottage. Places entangle other places, are entangled in those places, and entangle us within them. Places draw us in, allowing a releasing of the self into the place and a releasing of the place into the self (so much so that we may find our own identities inseparably bound up with the places we inhabit). Moreover, although we may come, individually, to view some places as more important to us than others, this is merely a function, not of any exceptionality that pertains to just those places, but of our own very placedness—which means only that we find ourselves *here* rather than there, in *this place* rather than some other. Our being given over to place—our being released to it—is not a being given over to the exceptional, to the utopic, to the secret, or to the subterranean, but to the ordinary and everyday world that is, as Wordsworth puts it, "the world / Of all of us."[61]

For all that "Michael" also contains within it an expression of the problematic idea of authentic exceptionality, I would argue that, even there, one can discern this ordinary world and our releasement into it. Releasement is present in Wordsworth's poem both in Michael's intimate connectedness to the landscape in which he lives and in the fact that it is *in grief* that his being is taken up. Although that grief is indeed exceptional and extreme, it is also, as grief, indicative of the dependent and vulnerable character of the self—of the self as incapable of any complete self-sufficiency or self-determination. It is thus, as I noted above, that grief and place—and so, now, perhaps grief and releasement also—can be seen as themselves linked. Michael's grief is exceptional, as it is authentic and also extreme, but, at the same time, it runs counter to some of the key elements in the ideal of authenticity, directing *us* as readers (even though it does not and cannot direct Michael himself), not in towards a separate and enclosed self, but out towards a more encompassing place, towards a more encompassing world.

Ten

Where Are We When We Think?

The first volume of Hannah Arendt's *The Life of the Mind*, titled *Thinking*, takes as its presiding epigraph a translation from the German of a set of lines from Heidegger's 1951–52 Freiburg lecture series on thinking, which appear in English as *What Is Called Thinking?*:

> Thinking does not bring knowledge as do the sciences./ Thinking does not produce usable practical wisdom./Thinking does not solve the riddles of the universe./Thinking does not endow us directly with the power to act.[1]

In setting Heidegger at the head of the volume, Arendt indicates how much Heidegger's influence is at work in its pages, even though much of what Arendt argues runs against aspects of Heidegger's thought. At the end of the volume, Arendt takes up a question that seems to echo, though it makes no explicit reference to it, Heidegger's talk of a "place" (*Ortschaft* or *Aufenthalt*) for thinking. She puts her question in the following form: "Where are we when we think?" Her answer, advanced within a few pages, seems to be: "nowhere."[2]

Yet having asserted the placelessness of thinking, Arendt goes on to claim that thinking nevertheless has a location in relation to time; namely, in the gap "between" past and future. Thinking is thus seen as fundamentally temporal rather than spatial, and this, one might argue, is tied to a certain prioritization of time over place or space. In this apparent prioritization of time, Arendt's account mirrors aspects of Heidegger's analysis in *Being and Time*, since there, as we saw in chapter 1, Heidegger also argues in a way that seems to give priority to temporality over spatiality, and thereby to time over both space and place. Yet the way time appears here directs attention—in both Heidegger and Arendt—to the problematic character of such prioritization. The inquiry into the place of thinking, even when it is supposed to lead to time, seems, in the end, to lead us back, if not to space, then certainly to place.

At the outset, however, and especially given the initial directness of her claim that the place of thinking is nowhere, it looks as if Arendt's account in *The Life of the Mind* presents a challenge to the sort of topological approach championed here—and inasmuch as such an approach is to be found in Heidegger (even if not always consistently), then Arendt's account is also a challenge to Heidegger. But Arendt's position is challenging quite aside from the way the idea of the place of thinking might be developed in some existing body of thought. The notion that thinking is placeless brings with it a very different conception of what thinking is, especially when compared to a mode of thinking that insists on thinking's essential placedness. At the same time, the question of the place of thinking (and the way *place* figures or does not figure in that question) is tied to some of the core issues in Arendt's own thinking.

Strikingly evident in Arendt's treatment of the place of thinking is the way in which her apparent privileging of time draws upon ideas that are nevertheless essentially bound to place—time itself, one might say, comes to be understood in terms of place. Thus, despite what one might think of as the "temporalism" to which she seems committed, Arendt nevertheless develops an account of the temporality of thinking, in *The Life of the Mind* and elsewhere, that is fundamentally *topological*. The movement in Arendt's discussion of the place of thinking is thus actually a movement that takes us back to place, despite having apparently set it aside, through the implication of place in the understanding of time. In this respect, the way the question "Where are we when we think?" appears in Arendt's work, and the manner in which it is addressed, actually opens up a path, though a rather complex one, towards understanding the way time and place (and space, too) belong together. It is the belonging together of place and time that is a large part of the focus of this chapter. Yet also at issue is the way that belonging together is routinely overlooked—even for a thinker whom we might otherwise think of as less susceptible to philosophical habit or convention. Indeed, what Arendt demonstrates, as does Heidegger, too, on occasion, is how fundamental and ubiquitous is the topological in thinking, and yet also prone to being overlooked, neglected, or ignored.

The "Placelessness" of Thinking

Almost from the outset, there is an oddity in Arendt's approach to the question of the place of thinking as she presents it. It is an oddity that relates both to the speed with which she moves to an answer and her seeming disregard for alternative responses to her question—in particular, for an obvious sense in which thinking does indeed have a place. Thus, to the question, "Where are we when we think?" one might well respond, most immediately and intuitively, by saying that where we are when we think is just *where we are*—where we are ourselves placed—and that the act of thinking does not change our place in the world, even though it may well provide us with a different perspective on that place. One might add, furthermore, that thinking always arises, can only arise, out of the place in which we already find ourselves—so not only does thinking *have a place*, but, in many respects, it can be understood as a response *to our place*.

The placed character of thinking is surely no less evident—perhaps even more so—in the case of philosophical thinking. Does not Heidegger have his hut at Todtnauberg? And what of Thoreau and Wittgenstein with their own secluded cabins? Nietzsche certainly has his Sils Maria and explicitly acknowledges the direct connection between his thought and the places in which it arose.[3] Even in Arendt's case, one might argue that her own thinking was embedded in the library and the classroom—in her own library especially (a quite extensive one)—and it is surely no accident that she writes so eloquently of Walter Benjamin's relation to the library and bookroom.[4] Here, it seems hard to believe that there is not some element of self-revelation on Arendt's part. In fact, no matter what else we say about the relation between thinking and place, it should be clear that thinking is always placed and that where it takes place is not accidental to thinking—that the place of thinking is essential in grounding, sustaining, and giving rise to thinking. Whether we look to Heidegger or Nietzsche or Wittgenstein or Thoreau—or even to Quine or Rawls (to cite representatives of a very different tradition)—we find thinkers whose thought bears the marks, even if unconsciously presented, of the places in which it originates.

On the face of it, then, there seems something counterintuitive about Arendt's claim that thinking has no place, that it occurs nowhere. It might be said that this is, nevertheless, to misunderstand Arendt's question—to take it too literally and to miss its fundamental character. What concerns her is not the place of the *thinker*, one might say, but the place of the *thinking* in the thinker (although at one point she approvingly quotes an Epicurean saying, "live in hiding," as providing a "negatively exact description" of the *topos* of the man who thinks[5]), and this is not reducible merely to where the thinker is. Indeed, when one looks to this aspect of the matter, one might even claim that Arendt's position has something intuitively right about it. After all, although the thinker will always be somewhere when they are thinking, thinking itself surely occurs *in a place* only incidentally, as it were, through occurring *in* the thinker. Moreover, the very experience of thinking might seem to suggest a view of thinking as always involving a certain withdrawal or retreat from things—most dramatically exemplified in the case of Socrates[6]—and so also a certain removal or remoteness from the places in which we find ourselves. Such removal might be thought to be tied to the universality and generality that appears essential to thinking.

Arendt's assertion of the placelessness of thinking, and of the associated primacy of time, is undoubtedly tied to this idea of thinking as involving withdrawal or removal. Indeed, Arendt herself calls attention to just these features of thinking in the analysis that makes up the first volume of *The Life of the Mind*. It is this analysis that appears to provide the basis for Arendt's assertion of the placelessness of thinking, as that is set out in *The Life of the Mind*—an analysis that is summarized at the beginning of the discussion of the place of thinking in terms of three main points: (1) "thinking is always out of order, interrupts all ordinary activities and is interrupted by them";[7] (2) "the manifestations of the thinking ego's authentic experiences are manifold,"[8] which seems to mean that thinking serves not only to render uncertain what may otherwise be assumed, but also to establish differences and oppositions; and (3) "thinking always deals with absences and removes itself from what is present and close at hand."[9]

This is not the end of the matter, however, since the fact that thinking has these features—even the fact that it involves withdrawal or removal from the ordinary places in which we find ourselves—does not, of itself, show that thinking is therefore placeless. To infer the placelessness of thinking on this basis is already to construe the question of the place of thinking as a question that concerns the relation between thinking and the "ordinary" places of our lives. It is on the basis of that assumption, together with the idea that thinking stands somewhat apart from those "ordinary" places, that the conclusion that thinking has no place follows—or seems to follow. Of course, put more carefully, what follows is only that thinking has no *ordinary* place, not that it is placeless.

Indeed, when one reflects on the experience of thinking as an experience of withdrawal or removal, recognizing also the character of withdrawal or removal as topological in character, then one is easily led to the idea, not that thinking is a withdrawal or removal *from place*, but that it involves a withdrawal or removal from one place towards another—that it actually involves a movement *to a different place*. One might also say that the experience of thinking, as a withdrawal or removal, is actually an experience of thinking as the opening up of a "gap" between thinker and world—so, thinking can be said, as it often is, to involve a certain form of alienation, estrangement, or *displacement*.

The way place emerges here, as potentially ambiguous between different places or senses of place (whatever they may be), serves to render place uncertain, to bring the idea into question, and yet place is not thereby set aside. What do we mean when we ask after the place of thinking—or when we contrast the supposed placelessness of thinking with the placed character of our ordinary activities? What sense of "place" is at issue in ordinary talk of the "sense" of place? In asking after the place of thinking, then, not only are we led to consider whether thinking has a place, but in the very asking of that question we ought also be led to question place as such, and so to question the "place" in which we ordinarily live and act. Of course, on the face of it, this is not the direction in which Arendt's own discussion seems to lead. She makes no attempt to engage explicitly with the question as to what place might be, even though she herself raises the question of place in the question of the place of thinking. Inasmuch as the notion of place does indeed remain ambiguous, however, so the issue of place remains alive in Arendt's thinking and is not necessarily closed off.

Thinking as Something "Inner"

Even so, the idea that place might remain at issue here seems initially belied by the character of Arendt's own discussion. Having raised the question of the place of thinking, she then seems, almost immediately, to put the issue of place behind her, suggesting that the way in which the question is framed—the way it asks after the *place* or *topos* of thinking—is misguided or mistaken:

> Perhaps our question—Where are we when we think?—was wrong because by asking for the *topos* of this activity we were

exclusively spatially oriented—as though we had forgotten Kant's famous insight that "time is nothing but the form of inner sense, that is, of the intuition of ourselves and of our inner state." For Kant that meant that time had nothing to do with appearances as such—"neither with shape nor position" as given to our senses—but only with appearances as affecting our "inner state" in which time determines the "relation of representations."[10]

There are two crucial assumptions in this passage that deserve attention: first, that in talking of the *place* of thinking, we treat thinking as if it were "exclusively spatially oriented," and, second, that thinking is something essentially *inner* and, therefore, something essentially temporal.

The first of these assumptions—the treatment of place and space as more or less interchangeable—is not uncommon, but it is highly questionable. Place and space are certainly related notions (just as place and time are related also), and yet, as has been emphasized in various points in the previous chapters, they are not identical or at least cannot be assumed to be so. Moreover, the distinction between the two has not gone unnoticed, even in recent philosophy. There is an implicit distinction between place and space in Kant, even as the two are also related,[11] and the distinction is especially important in Heidegger's later thinking, where there is a clear insistence on the difference between place (*Ort/Ortschaft*) and space (*Raum*), as well as a questioning of the conventional view of space itself.[12] One can even argue, despite the lack of any developed conception of place in the earlier work (and the fact that the specific terms *Ort/Orstschaft* do not figure there at all), that there is an implicit distinction between space and place in *Being and Time*—something suggested by the different character of existential spatiality (*existenziale Räumlichkeit*) in contrast to the homogenous spatiality of physical extension to be found in Cartesianism.[13] The significance of this distinction in later Heidegger may be thought to make Arendt's lack of attention to it all the more surprising.

The second assumption—that thinking belongs to what is inner *and non-spatial*—seems to beg the original question, especially given Arendt's ready assimilation of place to space. If one already takes space and place to belong to what is outer, and time to what is inner, then to say that thinking is not something outer is just to say that it is not spatial or placed; while to say that thinking is something inner is already to associate it, on this account, with temporality rather than with spatiality or place. If the claim regarding the inner character of thinking is to carry any argumentative weight, we need some independent account of the inner and the outer as these are related to thinking, and of the supposed association of the one with time and the other with space (and so with place). Arendt does not offer any such account, instead seeming to do little more than invoke the supposed authority of Kant on the matter—although the idea of thinking as inner might also be thought to be implied in Arendt's conception of thinking as "the soundless dialogue we carry on with ourselves,"[14] such a dialogue being construed as internal to myself.

Yet the distinction between the inner and the outer as applied to thinking may well be viewed, regardless of its Kantian origins, with some suspicion. There are good reasons for rejecting a view of thinking, or of mental activity generally, as existing only in some internal, private realm—and this is surely one of the key lessons of the anti-Cartesian tendency that has been such a central thread in much of the philosophical thinking of the latter half of the twentieth century, from Heidegger to Wittgenstein, and that is evident in contemporary ideas of situated or extended cognition.[15] Heidegger contests the legitimacy of the distinction directly when, in his "Conversation on a Country Path," he quotes approvingly from Goethe: "Nothing is inside, nothing outside/For what is inner, that is outer."[16] Heidegger's refusal of any simple version of the distinction is not restricted to this discussion alone but runs throughout his thought. It is a refusal tied to a view of thinking, and of the life of the mind generally, as taking place, not in some private "inner" realm, but as always externalized in the world. The very being of thinking as it is so intimately related to language is indicative of the way in which we are always drawn into a domain that is "outside," just as much as it is "within" us. We thus encounter ourselves in thinking (as Arendt's idea of thinking as the "soundless dialogue of me with myself" suggests), and yet this encounter is not one that has to be understood as therefore "inner" in some sense that sets it outside of or apart from space or place. Moreover, even if there is *some* sense to be attached to the notion of the "inner" and of interiority as applied to thinking, there is no reason to suppose that this implies any abstraction of thinking from the spatial or topological, nor a view of thinking (or the mind) as belonging *only* to such an inner realm.

The very language of the "inner" and "outer," as Kant himself was aware, is a language drawn from spatiality or, better, from the topological (which makes problematic the very idea of the "inner" as involving something non-spatial). Yet even though talk of an inner and outer is to invoke the spatial, space does not itself have an inner or an outer. Only place allows for such a distinction, since only place brings the required sense of boundedness. The experience of the inner is, one might say, just the experience of placedness—of *being-in-place* (more specifically, it is tied to a certain experience of *being-within-bounds*). Not only does Arendt seem to ignore the topological dimension at work in the distinction between the inner and the outer, but, in her appeal to Kant, she also seems actually to overlook Kant's insistence on the interconnection of the inner and the outer, and of the spatial and the temporal, as essential to the very possibility that thought can be contentful. This is a point that can be seen already to be presaged by Kant's insistence on the necessary connection between subjectivity and objectivity and, connected with this, on the necessity of spatiality to the possibility of differentiation that is essential to content.[17] Arendt's assumption of the inner-outer distinction and its correspondence to a distinction between the spatial and temporal is thus problematic even on the Kantian grounds that Arendt herself seems to invoke. The appeal to that distinction as the basis for the claim concerning the placelessness of thinking already begs the question. It ignores the complications within the Kantian framework and depends upon an untenable, or at least highly questionable, view of the key concepts at issue.

Thinking and the "Moment"

The move to the idea of thinking as something inner hardly seems to offer any independent basis for the notion that thinking has no place. Indeed, the way Arendt seems to give priority to temporality in her discussion of thinking has less the appearance of a developed *argument*, whether Kantian or otherwise, and more the character of a presumption. In fact, the real focus of Arendt's discussion of the place of thinking is not place or space, but time, and the question concerning the place of thinking seems to function as little more than an expository device to introduce the task, in Arendt's words, "of finding out where the thinking ego is located in time and whether its relentless activity can be temporally determined."[18] Not only, then, does the discussion move from the *place* of thinking to the *time* of thinking quite abruptly, with little real consideration given to the question of place that seems briefly to be invoked, but the issue of the time of thinking seems to be what underpins the discussion all along.

Central to Arendt's discussion of the matter is a parable she takes from Franz Kafka's *Notes from the Year 1920*, in which Kafka describes a figure, "He," on a path beset by two antagonists. One presses him forward from behind, while the other blocks the path ahead pushing him back. He gives battle to both, at the same time dreaming he could be lifted out of the fight and stand, instead, as adjudicator over the battle between the two.[19] Arendt's use of this parable is not peculiar to her discussion in *The Life of the Mind*—she also deploys it in the preface to *Between Past and Future*.[20] Moreover, the title of the latter volume describes exactly the situation of Kafka's "He," as Arendt interprets it, and Arendt makes clear that she regards the essays that make up the volume as "exercises" in thinking that are explicitly oriented to this temporal "between."[21] Although the discussion in *Between Past and Future* adumbrates the discussion in *The Life of the Mind*—with much of the discussion in one more or less repeated in the other—the former does not begin with the question, "Where are we when we think?" nor is the question of the place of thinking even alluded to in the earlier work. Instead, Arendt's discussion begins with a line from René Char's *Leaves of Hypnos*—"Our inheritance was left to us by no testament"[22]—that expresses the seemingly new situation of the world, and especially Europe, following the end of the Second World War in particular (but also a problem for modernity more generally), in which the gap between past and present can no longer be bridged by tradition. The gap between past and future appears as a problem, and yet also as a kind of solution, since it is in that gap that Arendt sees the proper exercise of thinking as located.

The problem that both *The Life of the Mind* and *Between Past and Future* address is thus already understood as a problem about the temporality of thinking and, one might add, about the temporality of the human condition. Time is typically understood as linear—as a constant succession of moments from the past to the future through the present—but the insertion of the human into time, by which such linearity can be recognized, also breaks that linearity, producing the discontinuity and conflict that appear in Kafka's parable. Time is thus brought both to appearance and into conflict at the point of human insertion into time. The conflict that Kafka describes is, however, not merely a conflict *within time*, between two aspects of temporality, but a conflict *within the human condition, a conflict that afflicts thinking itself.* Thinking can only occur in relation to time. Without time, without past and future, thought has nothing to concern it, nothing that is demanded of it. Without time, thought cannot even arise, yet time also seems to curtail the possibility of thinking, leaving it caught between the incessant demands of past and future. This is expressed, in Kafka's parable, in terms of the conflict between being caught up in the struggle of past against future and in what Kafka describes as the dream of stepping outside of that struggle.

Remaining within a conception of time as linear, and so seeming to have no option but to respond immediately to the demand of the future by the mere repetition of the past or, as one might also say, to respond to the demand of the past by its repetition in the face of the future, thinking loses any sense of its own possibility, is given over to entrapment, exhaustion, and loss. It is because it does disrupt the linearity of time, however, that the insertion of thinking—of the human—into time brings with it the chance for thinking to grasp its own temporality in a way that stands outside of that linearity. Arendt talks of the insertion of the human (Kafka's "He") as deflecting the two forces at play here, producing a third angle of force diagonal to the original two—a third force that does not merely return us to the past or to the future, since its direction is diagonal to both, even though it has its origin in the present, but rather opens up as a gap in time ("this small non-time space in the very heart of time")[23] that allows a respite from the struggle and, therefore, opens up the possibility of going beyond that struggle. Here, it is precisely the *finitude* of the human, its being *in time*, that also *disrupts* time and that allows the finitude of human being into the expansiveness of the world.

One might say that this disruption in time, this "gap" between past and future, makes thinking itself possible, except that it is also what is made possible by thinking—"Only insofar as he thinks . . . does man in the full actuality of his conscious being live in this gap of time between past and future."[24] Thinking is the opening up of this gap (or the opening up of the gap *for* human being). It is the disrupting of the usual linearity of time as this arises out of the experience of that linearity. The parable to be found in Kafka does indeed describe the situation of a particular historical moment, whether of the immediate postwar world or of modernity more generally, in which the gap between past and future has been revealed by the loss of tradition. But as Peg Birmingham argues, it also describes the temporality of the human condition, which is the temporality of *natality*[25]—the temporality that belongs with the having of a beginning, as well as the capacity to begin anew, and with the capacity genuinely to judge and to act. Here, natality is not merely a fact of physical birth but is tied to the generative capacity of thought—to thinking as event and initiation. As it happens, this conception of thinking, as it stands in relation to natality (and so also to a particular temporal conception), is itself suggestive of a direction in Arendt's own thought that appears to go against her initial characterization, at least in *The Life of the Mind*, concerning the question of the place of thinking, and that instead opens towards a topology that is embedded within Arendt's own thinking.

In *The Life of the Mind*, although not in *Between Past and Present*, Arendt follows her account of the parable from Kafka with another story (an "allegory" as Arendt refers to it) taken from Friedrich Nietzsche's *Thus Spoke Zarathustra*,[26] that might appear, on the face of it, to reinforce the temporal focus of her discussion. The story concerns Zarathustra's arrival before a gateway at which two pathways meet—each stretching to an eternity before and behind—and whose name is inscribed above it: *Augenblick*, the "moment," the "now."[27] The image that Nietzsche presents here is strikingly close to that which appears in Kafka's parable. Even though it lacks Kafka's dramatization of the situation as one of conflict, it nevertheless presents much the same idea of two counterposed paths meeting at a single place. Moreover, that place—in Nietzsche's story the gateway that is the *Augenblick*—appears only for the one who stands before it and who is no mere onlooker but is engaged in that place. Without him, without Kafka's "He" or Nietzsche's Zarathustra, there is no meeting place, no gateway, no point of conflict, but only one road stretching interminably.

In Nietzsche, the story that is told is related directly to the doctrine of the eternal recurrence—the idea that time is a constant repetition of the same, in the face of which we can either react with revulsion or with joyful affirmation. Knowledge of the eternal recurrence forcibly brings us back to the now as that in which we find ourselves and the world. In affirming the eternal recurrence, we thus affirm the now, the *Augenblick*, in all its open, if bounded, expansiveness (and not merely as an element in the procession of past, present, and future), and we say "yes" to the world, overcoming the "revenge against time" (the desire to escape from time), whose expression is metaphysics. Arendt quotes Heidegger, from his 1937 lectures on Nietzsche: "This is the authentic content of the Doctrine of Eternal Recurrence, that Eternity *is* in the Now, and that the Moment [*Augenblick*] is not the futile Now which it is only for the onlooker, but the clash of Past and Future."[28]

The moment or now that appears here, and that is identical with the gap that Arendt identifies in Kafka's parable, is also connected, by Arendt, with the idea of the *nunc stans*, the "standing present," that appears in the work of Augustine and Duns Scotus. Arendt is careful to note that, in its original form, the idea of the *nunc stans* appeared as a "model and metaphor for divine eternity,"[29] whereas the gap between past and future, the *Augenblick* as it appears in Nietzsche and Heidegger, is defined in direct relation to human finitude (it arises, after all, through human placedness "in" time). The *nunc stans* appears, however, much earlier in the first volume of *The Life of the Mind* than does the discussion of Kafka. It occurs in the context of Arendt's discussion of thinking as always withdrawn from the world, even to the extent of being beyond any notion of spatial or temporal distance. There, she writes:

> Since space and time in ordinary experience cannot even be thought of without a continuum that stretches from the nearby into the distant, from the now into past or future, from here to any point in the compass, left or right, forward and backward, above and below, I could with some justification say that not only distances but also space and time themselves are abolished in the thinking process. As far as space is concerned I know of no plausible philosophical or metaphysical concept that could plausibly be related to this experience; but I am rather certain that the *nunc stans*, the "standing now," became the symbol of eternity—the "*nunc aeternitas*" (Duns Scotus)—for medieval philosophy because it was a plausible description of experiences that took place in mediation as well as in contemplation, the two modes of thought known to Christianity.[30]

What matters for Arendt in regard to the *nunc stans* is its origin in the experience of thinking, or the experience of a certain kind of thinking, and the way this experience is itself seen as standing in relation *to time* (something expressed in the idea of the *nunc stans* as a model of eternity yet need not be taken to depend on any commitment to the latter notion). In this respect, the connection between thinking *and time*, rather than place or space, might be thought to be confirmed—and this seems to be reinforced by Arendt's use of the stories from Kafka and Nietzsche.

It is significant, and perhaps a little curious, that Arendt's discussion of the question at issue here should make mention of Heidegger, but that it does so only in relation to Heidegger's commentary on the *Augenblick* in Nietzsche. Arendt's position, as set out at the end of the first volume of *The Life of the Mind*, looks almost to be a summary reprise of elements of Heidegger's account of "ownmost" or (to use the conventional translation) "authentic" temporality (*eigentliche Zeitlichkeit*) as set out in *Being and Time*—an account in which the idea of the *Augenblick* also figures, and in which there is, *contra* Arendt,[31] direct reference to Nietzsche's thinking (though without the sort of detailed engagement that occurs in the later lectures). Yet despite its seeming echoes in *The Life of the Mind*, Arendt makes no explicit reference to the discussion of temporality in the earlier work.[32] Moreover, this remains so despite Arendt's lengthy and often insightful discussion of Heidegger, which focuses on the turning from the early to the later work as that involves the questions of thinking and willing (the title of the section is "Heidegger's will-not-to-will"), that is contained in volume 2 of *The Life of the Mind*.[33]

In division 2 of part 1 of *Being and Time*, Heidegger presents an account of ownmost temporality (*eigentliche Zeitlichkeit*) as the ecstatic unity of future, past, and present, realized in the *Augenblick*, in and through which the disclosedness of the world, and so the being of Dasein, is grounded.[34] Heidegger does not employ the idea that appears in Arendt of a "gap" between past and future, but he does present both ownmost temporality and the *Augenblick* as having a similarly open and generative character to that which also figures in Arendt's account. Heidegger explicitly distinguishes the *Augenblick* from the idea of the *nunc stans*, which he treats as merely an extrapolation of the idea of ordinary time,[35] whereas Arendt treats the *nunc stans* more in line with Heidegger's understanding of the *Augenblick* and so with his account of ownmost temporality. Yet, regardless of their views of the *nunc stans*, Arendt and Heidegger share a focus on the finitude of human being, which they also take to be determined primarily in relation to *time* (although to time understood as something other than mere succession). As Heidegger puts it: "[T]ime is that from which Dasein tacitly understands and interprets something like being at all. Time . . . [is] the horizon of all understanding of being and every interpretation of being."[36] In this respect, and notwithstanding the significant role played by existential spatiality in Heidegger's account, both Heidegger and Arendt give a priority to time, including, so it would seem, to time over space. Moreover, since neither the early Heidegger nor Arendt clearly distinguishes space from place, the prioritization of time over space also appears as a prioritization of time over place (an issue already addressed, so far as Heidegger is concerned, in chapter 1).

Such seeming "temporalism" or "temporocentrism"[37] notwithstanding, one of the remarkable features of Heidegger's discussion in *Being and Time* (already mentioned in chapter 1), and of Arendt's in *The Life of the Mind*, is the constant resort to spatial ideas and images—to a topology, in fact—so that at the same time as the focus is supposedly on temporality, temporality is itself presented spatially and topologically. The very character of Heidegger's analysis in *Being and Time*, as oriented to that mode of being that is Dasein, ought to indicate the way place, as given in the *Da*, the "there/here," is already at issue (even though this is sometimes denied by commentators). Moreover, Heidegger's articulation of the *Augenblick*, in that early work, is inextricably tied to the notion of *situation* [*Situation*], while the idea of the *ek-stasis* at work in ownmost temporality also carries a topological connotation through its character as a "standing out." In *The Life of the Mind*, having established the temporal "location" of thinking (which is not strictly "in time" at all), Arendt talks of that "location" in spatial and topological terms: it is indeed a "gap," and so a "space between"[38]; it is said to be a "non-time space"; and it is described as identical with Kant's "land of pure intellect."[39] Even the language of Kafka's parable, on which Arendt focuses, is spatial and topological, as is that of Nietzsche's story (in both cases, one is placed on a pathway, in a gateway), while Arendt's geometrical development of the Kafka parable is also essentially spatial. Similarly, the idea of the *nunc stans*, the "standing moment," invokes a sense of place or placedness through the very idea of that which stands (*stans* coming from the Latin word *stare*, meaning "to stand") and so could perhaps be said even to return us to something of what is at issue in the Heideggerian *ek-stasis*, as a "standing out from."

One might be tempted to reply, on Arendt's part at least, that, since she explicitly presents much of her discussion of the place and time of thinking as *metaphorical*, her use of spatial and topological ideas should be construed as metaphorical also, and thus need not be construed as in tension with her commitment to the primacy of temporality. Such a response does nothing, however, to resolve the apparent difficulty

Arendt faces here, since the problem concerns the seeming inescapabilty of recourse to spatial and topological terms, regardless of whether those terms are employed metaphorically or "literally." That such terms cannot be eliminated even from the thinking of time is itself is acknowledged, as we saw in chapter 1, by Heidegger in §70 of *Being and Time*. There, Heidegger argues that the ineliminability of spatial and topological language (which he treats under the heading of the *spatial*) nevertheless does not undermine the priority of temporality over spatiality, on the grounds that it is a consequence of the tendency for Dasein to give itself over to the categories of the everyday. Much the same claim reappears in Arendt:

> [T]he time continuum depends on the continuity of our everyday life, and the business of everyday life, in contrast to the activity of the thinking ego—always independent of the spatial circumstances surrounding it—is always spatially determined and conditioned. It is due to this thoroughgoing spatiality of our ordinary life that we can speak plausibly of time in spatial categories, that the past can appear to us as something lying "behind" us and the future as lying "ahead."[40]

Elsewhere, Arendt reiterates the point with reference to Bergson's claim that, in the thinking of time, we inevitably draw on space, transforming time into space. On this basis, the task is to maintain a sense of the distinct character of time, even in the face of such a tendency.

Temporality and the Topological

It is curious that both the early Heidegger and Arendt appear to resist the spatial and topological elements that nevertheless surface constantly in their thinking. Part of the reason for this resistance is undoubtedly the lack of a clear and explicit articulation of the concepts of place and space themselves (despite the implicit distinction between space and place, and certainly between different modes of spatiality, already at work in *Being and Time*), together with the fact that part of what both Heidegger and Arendt are concerned to reject is a narrowly spatialized mode of thinking, of the sort typically associated with Descartes and the dominance of physical theory. Arendt's position is especially peculiar, however, not only because of the ambiguity of its stance in relation to the topological, or even its apparent and unacknowledged reprise of the Heideggerian position in which those same ambiguities are present, but also because, by the time Arendt wrote, Heidegger had significantly adjusted his position with respect to the understanding of time, space, and place, and the topological framework of his thinking (which was always present even if not always explicit) was so much more to the fore.

Heidegger's 1951–52 lectures, *What Is Called Thinking?*—the lectures that provide those lines that stand at the head of the first volume of *The Life of the Mind*—do not end with an affirmation of the primarily temporal character of thinking but, rather, through consideration of the relation between thinking and questioning, thinking and memory, thinking and thanking, thinking and being, they end with an affirmation of the way thinking is called as a response to what is to be thought:

> "What is called thinking?" At the end we return to the question we asked at first when we found out what our word "thinking" [Denken] originally means. *Thanc* means memory [Andenken], thinking that recalls, thanks [Danken]. But in the meantime, we have learned to see that the essential nature of thinking is determined by what there is to be thought about: the presence of what is present, the being of beings.[41]

This return to "the presence of what is present" is not a return to some purely temporal phenomenon. Instead, it implicitly evokes the idea of *topos* that is such a strong element in the later thinking and that is adumbrated in the earlier. "The presence of what is present" takes the form of a "coming close," a "being here/there." As presence is itself always a happening within certain bounds, so "the presence of what is present" is a happening within and of a place, and in this way the topological character, even of time, begins to appear. The topological direction of Heidegger's thinking in *What Is Called Thinking?* can be discerned in his very account of thinking as remembrance—of *Denken* as *Andenken*—since not only does this play upon the character of thinking as a gathering that mirrors the gathering of place, but it also implicitly invokes the topological character of memory itself (memory is both placed and placing). Indeed, elsewhere Heidegger talks of remembrance as itself "placement into being."[42]

To repeat a point that runs throughout my discussion in this volume: the topological shift that is evident in *What Is Called Thinking?*, and that is explicit in Heidegger's other writing from the same postwar period, is not a shift to an entirely new perspective. It draws out elements already present, even in *Being and Time*. It does, however, involve a shift away from the early and apparent claim concerning the priority of the temporal, as originally asserted, and towards a recognition of the topology that also belongs to time. The prioritization of temporality that one seems to find in Arendt's discussion in *The Life of the Mind* and, along with it, the apparent de-emphasis on spatiality is thus something that Heidegger had already explicitly abandoned (if it was ever a key element to begin with) in the rethinking of *Being and Time* that occurred in the period following its publication. This shift in thinking is not some idiosyncratic aspect of Heidegger's intellectual development but arises as a response to problems immediately present within the attempt to think the relation of being to time, as well as to space, and of being to the human. These problems are evident in Arendt's account no less than in Heidegger's. Part of the difficulty is that the concept of temporality to which early Heidegger and Arendt appeal, whether as given in the idea of the "now," the *Augenblick*, in the modified version of the *nunc stans*, or in the temporal "gap" between past and present, cannot simply be assumed to be a more primordial form of temporality. This is something that would have to be shown, and it is obscure how this could possibly be done. In fact, neither early Heidegger nor Arendt offers any attempt to do so. Moreover, what lies at the heart of the putative notion of temporality that is at issue here is precisely the idea of a "time" that is characterized by its expansiveness and openness—by what might otherwise be associated specifically with the idea of place.

If Heidegger does not immediately acknowledge the way place is implicated here (at least not in *Being and Time*), it is, as I noted above, partly a result of the lack of a sufficiently developed and explicit vocabulary of place and space in his early work, something that he comes to address largely through his engagement, through the 1930s and into the 1940s, with poetry and, especially, with Hölderlin. Despite her closeness to Heidegger (and also to Kant—who is more subtle in his appreciation of these matters than is sometimes recognized), the turn toward an explicit recognition of the problems relating to place and space, and also time, and towards a clarification of what is at issue there, never seems clearly to have emerged in Arendt's work. There is thus no turn towards an explicit topology. As a result, Arendt does indeed seem often to assert a rather simple distinction between space and time and to resort to an ambiguous conception of place. Nevertheless, there is a topology that seems to run through much of Arendt's thinking—and not merely in the sense that is implied by her seemingly unanalyzed reliance on spatial and topological ideas and images. Instead, there is a sense of *topos* at work that does indeed connect with some of the ideas we find given explicit attention in the later Heidegger, even though Arendt does not draw attention to them, in quite the same way, or explicitly acknowledge their topological character.

Thinking is, on Arendt's account, an event, but even its character as event—as a "taking place"—does not imply that it is temporal alone. What is crucial to the "event-character" of thinking is not its temporality in the conventional sense (the sense associated with the linear progression of past, present, and future) but, rather, its character as an opening and an emergence. This understanding of the event, however, draws it precisely into the domain of the topological—into the domain of an understanding of place as that which, through its very boundedness, allows the opening that makes for appearance, including the appearance that occurs in thinking. And this is, of course, precisely the understanding of the event that is already present in Heidegger—and present, in his later thinking, in a quite explicit fashion. It is, indeed, already present in the idea of the *Ereignis* as a bounded yet open realm that gathers and releases, that is temporalizing and spatializing. Indeed, while the *Ereignis* harks back to the *Augenblick* (the two are, in fact, etymologically linked[43]), it also connects more directly with the topological character of Heidegger's later thought. Joseph Fell puts the point directly: "Heidegger's terms 'Event' (*Ereignis*) and 'Place' (*Ort*) mean 'the same.'"[44] The event, whether understood in the terms used by Heidegger or Arendt, is essentially a happening of place.

What underpins much of Arendt's inquiry in *The Life of the Mind* is the *same* question that she tells us emerged for her out of the Eichmann trial: What might be the connection between the absence of thinking and evil?[45] Arendt returns to this question in the pages immediately prior to her discussion of the place of thinking.[46] There, Arendt provides what is perhaps her most succinct account of the nature of thinking, and, although continuing to use language that is ambiguous as to the placed character of thinking (describing thinking as, for instance, "the dematerialized quintessence of being alive"[47]), she also explicates thinking in terms that are themselves suggestive of its placed character. This is especially so when one considers her emphasis on thinking, which she characterizes here, as elsewhere, in terms of the "two-in-one" dialogue with one's self, as essentially tied to plurality—a plurality present in thinking in the form of the difference that arises within one's own self.

> [T]he specifically human actualization of consciousness in the thinking dialogue between me and myself suggests that difference and otherness, which are such outstanding characteristics of the world of appearances as it is given to man for his habitat among a plurality of things, are the very conditions for the existence of man's mental ego as well, for this ego actually exists only in duality. And this ego—this I-am-I—experiences difference in identity precisely when it is not related to the things that appear but only related to itself.[48]

There are some additional oddities about the discussion in which this passage appears (including in some of the brief references to Heidegger that occur here). If we focus on just this issue of difference and identity, however, then not only does it connect directly to the way the later Heidegger talks about the *Ereignis* (which both gathers and differentiates), but it also implies a certain topology that belongs to it. The interplay of difference and unity—including the very possibility of a standing out of the self in relation to itself and to the world—can only occur within the openness of place. Indeed, the very displacement that might be thought to be required by the possibility of thinking as a separation within the unity of the self is nonetheless a particular mode of placement. The way place—and so also space—appears here, even though seemingly unrecognized by Arendt, is evident elsewhere. It can be found in Heidegger, in Kant, where it underpins the idea that representation is always spatial, and perhaps even in Levinas, where otherness is itself understood in terms of an essential exteriority.[49]

In fact, not only the two-in-one character of thinking, but also the characteristic features of thinking to which Arendt draws attention elsewhere, can all be derived from the topological—the event-like—character of thinking. The disruptive character of thinking is a consequence of the rupture that occurs in the very opening of the world that is the happening of place. The manifold experiences in which thinking is manifest arises out of the essential plurality that is opened up in place—place being itself both a differing and a gathering. The withdrawal of thinking results from the way in which the opening of place is also a separating out—a standing out—at the same time as it is a relating to. Thinking is a mode of being-in-place, in which the placed character of that being, and the bounded openness that therefore belongs essentially to it, is brought into view and so brought potentially into question. In thinking, we come to recognize our own place, as we come to recognize ourselves, and in "coming out of hiding," as Arendt puts it, we also come into the space of thinking.

Place, Space, and Natality

In Arendt, as Peg Birmingham points out, the event-character of thinking, which we can now see entails its placed character, is tied to natality—to having the character of being born, of having a beginning (an idea that, Birmingham notes, is not absent from Heidegger). In this way the *generative* character of thinking is brought to the fore. Natality, which is no merely temporal concept (any more than is the *Augenblick* or the *nunc stans*), already brings its own connection to place, since to be born is to come into the world in a certain way. It is to come into a place in the world and so to belong to a place (which, in one important sense, is precisely to be *native* to it). Moreover, although the comparison is certainly not Arendt's, such a conception, both of thinking and of the "time" that belongs to thinking (the *now*, the *gap*, the *moment*, the *standing present*, the *event*)—and in which it is also located—is suggestive of the Platonic *chora*, the "womb," "matrix," or "receptacle," which is itself a mode of place, understood as that which gives room to, and so supports and sustains, the emergence of thing into being.[50] Such a connection reinforces the topological character of Arendt's account of thinking. However, it is also indicative of a topology that belongs to natality—a topology of natality that is brought out precisely through ideas at issue in Arendt's focus on the now.

Although directing attention to the connection between Arendt's account of thinking and the idea of natality, Birmingham notes that Arendt does not herself make any connection between natality and the idea of the now or *Augenblick*—at least not as that appears in Heidegger (and this reflects the fact that, as noted earlier, Arendt makes no reference to Heidegger's discussion of the *Augenblick* or of temporality, as given in *Being and Time*).[51] In explicating this connection, Birmingham looks particularly to Heidegger and also to the way in which natality is understood in Arendt as involving both the fact of physical birth—our first birth—and a second birth in language. Birmingham's argument is that these two births are inseparably tied together, despite Arendt's tendency often to insist on their separation. In arguing thus, Birmingham advances a view of natality according to which being born is a matter both of one's physical and linguistic entry into the world—"to be born, to be a mortal, is to have been welcomed, to have been given a name . . . the 'second birth' is never simply laid over the first. Instead, both births happen at once."[52] As Birmingham sees it, the temporality of the now, the gap between past and future in which thinking is located, is also tied to natality in a way that implicates language. As the capacity for articulation, language is always grounded in what already is, and yet it also retains the potential for radically new forms of articulation—for saying what has not been said before. Thus, Birmingham claims that "the temporality of the *Augenblick* is the moment in which a speech without prior authorization nevertheless can assume authority in the course of its saying."[53]

The way language figures here—in Arendt's own account, as well as Birmingham's development of it—is especially significant for the inquiry into the topology of thinking. Language has a topology, and a spatiality, that belongs essentially to it. One might even argue that the connection evident in the very word "topology" is expressive of a fundamental connection between place and language. This is especially clear in Heidegger, for whom language is also tied to the *Ereignis*, to the event that is the happening of place. Language is that by means of which, Heidegger tells us, we are able to find our place in relation to the *Ereignis*—one might even say, using a typically Heideggerian locution, that the event and language are the "same" (*die Selbe*). Relating this directly to the notion of the now in Arendt, one might say that the "gap" that is at issue here is a gap that is held open by language itself—much as Heidegger claims, as we have seen previously, that it is language that "holds open the realm in which man, upon the earth and beneath the sky, inhabits the house of the world."[54] The topology of thinking is thus also a topology that belongs to language, and it is reflected in the character of language as that which sustains the possibility of any and every "between," in which the openness of world first emerges. As a mode of *topos*, language is given first and foremost in its concrete instantiations—in speech and text—which although always given in their own singular situatedness are nevertheless not restricted to that situation alone. The event of speaking and writing is one in which meaning is opened, and new horizons of understanding emerge—language is itself generative, initiatory, liminal. Here, the natality that is tied to language is evident as a natality that is also tied to the very character of *topos*—for it is indeed only in and out of place, a place held open by language in the same way as language takes form in place, that anything can come forth, can appear, can emerge as new.

In arguing for the close entanglement of physical and linguistic natality, Birmingham argues against Arendt's sometime tendency, noted earlier, to treat the two as separable; the birth in language as a more abstract and disembodied version of the birth of the body. Birmingham's emphasis on the two as one—that we can be given over to birth or to death, and that they can be salient elements in the very structure of our life and being—is dependent on our emergence into language. It is language that opens the space of human being in its boundedness by birth and death; language that gives access to the place of human being and that allows the human entry into the world. Birmingham's argument, and the tendency in Arendt that she aims to counter, runs analogously to my own, if from a different direction. In both cases, we are concerned to argue for a much closer relationship between what otherwise appear in Arendt as the situated and the displaced, the concrete and the abstract.

The Place of Thinking

One might suggest that, in arguing for the topological character of thinking, I have merely shown that thinking has a place, and even a space, that belongs to it, but that this does not show that there is any place that belongs specifically *to thinking*—consequently that Arendt's claims that thinking has no place, and that where we are when we think is nowhere, has not been shown to be false. Yet it is only on the basis of our concrete situatedness in the world, our being-placed—which also means our facticity and our finitude (appearing in Kafka's parable and Nietzsche's allegory as the concrete placement of the protagonist on the path and before the doorway)—that allows for the possibility of thinking and so also for the experience of the moment that Arendt takes as essential to thinking.

The situatedness at issue here is both temporal and spatial—but, as such, it is essentially topological, a placing into place that allows the genuine entry into world and the engagement with self and with other. The place, the *topos*, in which thinking finds itself is nowhere other than in the world in which we already find ourselves. It is thus that we seek places that allow us the silence and solitude for contemplation, and even when, like Socrates, we find ourselves an "inner" space in which we can distance ourselves from our immediate surroundings, where we do this is nowhere apart from the place in which we already stand. The place of thinking and the spaces in which thinking finds room for itself are not places separated from the world in which we are already present. Those places and spaces are always given within the place of our prior being in the world and never entirely remove us from it. Indeed, that they do not is itself a condition for the very possibility of thought. It is not thinking that is nowhere, in fact, but the lack of thinking. The thoughtlessness that is evident in Eichmann's case—the thoughtlessness that Arendt argues makes for the possibility of evil—remains oblivious to its place, and, as such, it never finds the space that is necessary to confront itself, to recognize others, or even to acknowledge the world. Such lack of thinking, and the possibility of evil that it engenders, arise precisely out of a failure to attend to the place of thinking.

Rather than being nowhere when we think, we are always somewhere. Yet that somewhere cannot be understood as if it were some simple location—as if our thinking belonged to some point in a system of coordinates. The "where" of thinking, the proper place of thinking, is the original place in which the world opens to us. To think is to come back to that place—indeed, to return and to remember—and so to attend and respond to what lies before us. Not to think is to fail to attend and respond to what calls us to think, to fail to turn back to the place of thinking. It is to forget, although in such a way that the forgetting and, with it, the possibility of remembrance is also forgotten. Eichmann represents just such a failure of thinking of the most extreme kind, and yet Eichmann's failure is not unique. In the contemporary world, the failure of thinking, even if manifest in more mundane ways than in Eichmann's case, appears as the rule rather than the exception. It is evident in the meaningless sloganizing that dominates current political discourse; in the empty hyperbole of advertising and entertainment; in the hollowed-out language of management and bureaucracy (a language that subverts the very language of the ethical to which it so often makes appeal). "Most thought-provoking in our thought-provoking time," says Heidegger, "is that we are still not thinking."[55] Yet, in a world that is indeed characterized by displacement and the effacement of place, such a lack of thinking is surely an inevitable consequence of that very displacement. Thinking is a form of placing, and of attending to place. It is also a returning to and a finding of oneself—though never a finding of oneself alone. To think is to come back to the place in which thinking itself begins, which is also the place in which we find our own beginning—the place in which, it might be said, we are born into the world.

Epilogue

To the Other Beginning

For Joe Fell

The idea of philosophy's—or thinking's—"other beginning" (*der andere Anfang*) appears in Heidegger's work in the 1930s, especially in the *Contributions*. It is also present in the *Notebooks*, as well as being echoed in some later works. Exactly what the other beginning may be, Heidegger leaves indeterminate. What it certainly is not, however, is simply a beginning that has yet to be realized, and, for this reason, it is not to be understood as an event in some linear history. Instead, it is a beginning towards which thinking is underway, and thus a beginning that is also *an end*—not in the sense of a terminus, but rather as that which gives thinking its proper shape and unity.[1] For Heidegger, the "other" beginning always stands in a relation to the "first" beginning (*der erste Anfang*), which he typically locates in Greek thought, consisting in the original understanding of being as primordial emergence, *physis*, and as unconcealment, *aletheia*. This first beginning, however, is already prone to a forgetting and so to a turn away from the understanding that is granted there. Thus, the first beginning itself gives rise to the necessity for an "other" beginning. Heidegger later refers to the shift from the first to the other beginning as "the turning" (*die Kehre*) of thinking, and as this turning is also a *re-turning* or *turning back*, so the shift from the first to the other beginning is a turn back towards the first beginning, though not a simple repetition of it.

Heidegger's Turnings

References to "the turning" occur throughout Heidegger's work—and not only in relation to thinking—so the turning, as referred to here, is not the only sense of the term as Heidegger employs it, nor is it the only turning that belongs to thinking. That Heidegger's talk of "turning" should encompass a range of senses is not surprising—there are various senses of "turning" and "returning" at work in my own discussions in this volume, quite apart from Heidegger's use of such terms—and the fact that there is a range of senses associated with such terms is itself connected to their relatively commonplace character.

Thomas Sheehan has attempted to provide a systematic analysis of Heidegger's uses of the original German term *die Kehre* and its cognates,[2] but it is arguable that such an enterprise overlooks the fact that Heidegger's talk of "turn" and "turning" probably ought not to be construed as part of any special technical vocabulary, despite its sometimes unusual character. The eschewal of technical language is part of what marks Heidegger's later thinking as different from the earlier.[3] However, the very idea that Heidegger's thinking, whether early or late, is amenable to a strict and systematic structuring is to misunderstand Heidegger's own resistance to such systematicity. It also goes against the "iridescent" character of almost all of Heidegger's key terms. Those terms carry an ineliminable equivocity that means that each carries a multiplicity of senses and connotations—different terms often shading into and overlapping with one another. And while such iridescence, as I noted in chapter 6, belongs to the very essence of language, it is also a characteristic feature of Heidegger's own use of language.

From a topological perspective, the lack of strict systematicity is only to be expected. Who would suppose that one could systematize a place without losing sight of the place itself? The situation is no different when what is at issue is the place, the *topos*, of thinking. Moreover, Heidegger's talk of turn and turning is itself topological in character, reflecting the topological orientation (even when it remains implicit) of his thinking as a whole. To be in a place is to be turned to that place and to the elements that belong within it and, sometimes, even to be turned to one's own situatedness in the place. Moreover, places have a movement, a turning, that also belongs to them (a movement that might be said to reflect and be reflected in the movement that belongs to iridescence), while orientation is itself accomplished through the turning of one's body. Turn and turning belong to place in an essential and fundamental way, and the turning that is the turning to the other beginning is not the only turning that is in play here, even though it may be the most salient from the perspective of the present discussion.

Ever since William Richardson's monumental early work on Heidegger's thinking,[4] it has been commonplace to think of the turning as referring specifically to that "concrete autobiographical event" (to use Arendt's phrase)[5] that separates early from late Heidegger and that is usually dated to the early or mid-1930s. It is the focus on the turning, as referring to just this "event," that is part (though certainly not all) of what Sheehan contests. That this is not the only sense in which the idea of the turning can be applied to Heidegger's thinking should be self-evident, however, and it seems doubtful that Richardson or, indeed, Arendt would have been much troubled by the idea that there are various turnings at work in Heidegger—and not only in relation to his intellectual biography. As was noted in chapter 1, the shift that occurs in the mid- to late 1940s is also a significant turn towards a more explicit mode of topology, and its timing matches the shift that, Arendt also argues, occurs around the same time and is exemplified in the "Anaximander Fragment" from 1946—although Arendt interprets this turning differently (at least, on the face of it) from the way it is interpreted here.[6]

Sheehan's own expressed desire, to uncover "what [Heidegger] 'really' was driving at throughout those 102 volumes of his Collected Works,"[7] is undoubtedly what underlies his own tendency to try to find a single and consistent line (most clearly exemplified, it seems, in the Heidegger of *Being and Time*) that unifies Heidegger's thinking from beginning to end and that effectively reduces the various turnings to superficial shifts within a single line of movement. In this respect, Sheehan's approach is strikingly *unhermeneutical*—especially so where Heidegger is concerned—but it is no less *atopological*, and for similar reasons. Just as no ordinary place allows any single view to determine it in its entirety (the place is not the view—not *any* view), so the primacy of place in any and all thinking implies that thinking, like place itself, is always iridescent, always multivalent, always *indeterminate* (which means if there is one way of characterizing thinking, then there are many ways).[8] This is not to deny that there may well be a "single thought" that guided the course of Heidegger's work. Yet any such thought, in its very singularity, will always contain a multiplicity within it. Thinking, even of what is singular, is always something to be worked out, is always subject to interpretation and reinterpretation. It is a path to be followed, and yet a path from which one can stray, a path that includes detours and deviations and a path whose final destination cannot always be foreseen.

Whatever the details of any specific reading of the turning, however, it should be clear that Heidegger not only uses the language of turning and return (and of "reversal," this being another of the ways in which *Kehre* is sometimes translated) in many different ways, but that he also talks of the turning as it occurs in thinking as a "world-historical" phenomenon *and* as it occurs in the thinking of an individual thinker. The two are not disconnected, and yet they are not identical. Indeed, there must be some degree of separation between them, since there would otherwise be no possibility of any thinker being able to see beyond the limits of their own thinking as determined world-historically. Moreover, in such a case, Heidegger could not even offer the sort of analysis of the turning, the clearing, the place of being, the *Ereignis*, and so forth, that he presents in his many writings, let alone any critique of the contemporary world or its history. That there is any possibility of freedom in thinking, notwithstanding the degree to which it is also always constrained, depends on thinking *not* being completely determined by its world-historical context. And this, of course, is necessarily so: the boundedness that belongs to place (including to the place *of thinking*) is precisely such as to ground both limit and the overcoming of limit. This is not a point that Heidegger anywhere makes, and yet it is essential if there is to be any possibility, even for a thinker such as Heidegger, to grasp the character of the other beginning as such. One might say that all genuine thinking must be a thinking that is constantly turning back to the other beginning, even though that turning may never be accomplished or completed.

The Relatedness of the Two Beginnings

The movement from the first to the other beginning, whether in the thinking of a historical epoch, a society, or an individual, is a movement that is predicated upon the essential relatedness of the two beginnings, even as it is also impelled by the difference that obtains between them. That difference arises out of the loss, the forgetting, the dissimulation that is already at work in the movement from the first beginning. Thinking is prone to losing itself almost from the very start. Thus, the history of thinking, of philosophy, *of being*, becomes a history of forgetting and dissimulation. This takes on a special character in our own time, in the era of technological modernity (as we saw in chapter 8) since ours is a time in which place itself seems almost to have disappeared in the face of an all-encompassing system of technologically mediated connection, management, and surveillance—of perpetual movement, transformation, and flow.

Heidegger often tends, especially in the 1930s, to inscribe this *history of forgetting* within a *history of being* (*Seinsgeschichte*), which is itself enfolded within a world-historical perspective encompassing peoples and nations, including the Germans and Greeks, and also the Jews. In the latter case, this history of being has been associated with a form of anti-Semitism that is briefly evident in some lectures from the early-1930s but also emerges occasionally in the *Notebooks*, most notably in the 1940s. Such anti-Semitism, and the nationalism with which it is closely connected, is tied to Heidegger's obsession during the 1930s and 1940s with a narrative of the history of being that is centered on Europe and Germany.[9] Yet such a narrative has no essential connection to the sort of topological account that can also be found at the core of Heidegger's thinking. Indeed, the topology that is evident in Heidegger's work is itself antagonistic to the anti-Semitic and nationalist sentiments that Heidegger seems to espouse, and probably also antagonistic to his world-historical account of being. On this basis, there is a deep inconsistency that runs through Heidegger's work of the 1930s and 1940s, and that arises because of the inadequacy of his own thinking in the face of the topology it also points towards. Here, it is important to recall the comment from Joesph Fell to which I referred in the introduction: "I take seriously Heidegger's notion of the value of 'violence' in interpretation and translation interpretation, and I have often turned this dangerous technique back upon Heidegger himself."[10] Such a strategy is one that seems to me essential to any serious engagement with Heidegger, and it is certainly a part of my own reading. It follows from a concern with the problems at issue rather than textual exegesis or historical interpretation alone. It means that the reading that is advanced has to be viewed as a critical one and as certainly not tied to the affirmation of every element in Heidegger's texts.

With this in mind, the history that is at issue in Heidegger's "history of being" can be understood, and is almost certainly *better* understood, in much less grandiose terms than those that Heidegger tends to employ. It is a history that has two forms. In its first form, the history of forgetting is part of any and every attempt at thinking—part of the story or narrative that all thinking instantiates. Thinking is always threatened by, and so is prone to, a forgetting or even a hiding of its own place—of its own beginning and end. The forgetting at issue here is exactly analogous to the "forgetting" that occurs in all action (all the more so if one accepts that thinking is itself an action of sorts). When we act, we focus on what is before us and not on the oriented locatedness that makes the action possible (indeed, when we try to focus on that oriented locatedness, we often lose the capacity effectively to act). In its second form, the history of forgetting is evident, not in the sort of Spengler-esque world-history of nations and peoples to which Heidegger seems prone in the 1930s and 1940s, but in those "genealogies" of modernity that are present in the work of a range of thinkers from Foucault to Weber. Such a genealogical analysis is also present in Heidegger, sometimes alongside the world-historical, and it allows the identification of certain broad shifts that seem to be characteristic of the development of European thought and society, broadly conceived, up to the present.

These shifts should be familiar to anyone who has any reasonable sense of the history of Western philosophy from the Greeks to the present day, and they include a shift, though not always consistent or uniform, towards the primacy of natural science (and so a generalized prioritization of natural scientific over other forms of explanation), an increased concern with epistemology (and so a focus on knowledge as well as on the separation of knowledge from the world), and an increasing tendency to give priority to the quantitative over the qualitative in almost every domain. In social and political terms, these shifts come together in contemporary forms of globalization, corporatization, bureaucratization, monetarization, and even militarization. As they relate to a history of forgetting, these shifts are all exemplary of the tendency, within the history of thought as such, to think less and less about the broader context in which thinking is already embedded and, instead, to take as at issue only that which appears from within the structure of our existing knowledge and practices (that is "positioned" within an existing system). In other words, the place of thinking, and so the beginning and end of thinking, is taken for granted or ignored, and the real questions are taken to concern particular modes of practices of thinking, what arises within them, and the assumed objects of those modes or practices.

The history of forgetting that underpins the contrast between Heidegger's two beginnings is, in topological terms, a history of the forgetting of the place of thinking as that arises, as already noted above, in the "history" that belongs to any instance of thinking, no matter its historical context, and in the history of thinking, at least in European terms, from the historical origins of thinking to thinking in its modern form or forms. The two beginnings thus mark out the historical movement of thought from the Greeks to an as yet unknown future, and they also direct attention to the character of thinking as always *between* two beginnings—between that from which thinking comes and that to which thinking turns back in order to find itself again—even though that other beginning (and the first beginning with it) may be refused or ignored. In *Being and Time*, the ordinary and ever-present tendency towards forgetfulness was what Heidegger called "falling" and a characteristic of everydayness.[11] The task for *Dasein* was to recover itself through a recovery of its own futurity and so also its own historicality. From this perspective, the two beginnings are already implicit in the structure that *Being and Time* delineates—in the relation between historicality (our first beginning) and futurity (our "other" beginning), which includes our being towards death. Falling, like the forgetfulness that underpins the relation between the two beginnings, underpins the relation between historicality and futurity, just as forgetting underpins the relation between the first and other beginning. Understood in broader historical terms, the relation between the two beginnings is thus a version of the relation between historicality and futurity writ large.

The relation between the two beginnings is an issue to which Joseph Fell also directs attention. The first beginning, he says, is "the 'other beginning' disowned or disguised." It is disguised by the very fact of the forgetting that bridges the connection between the first and other beginning. The other beginning could therefore not consist simply in a reversion to the first beginning, since, as Fell points out, the other beginning is "a remembering of what is forgotten in the first beginning," nor could the other beginning be an entirely original or novel beginning in itself (it must be "other" to that which is "first"), since what is forgotten in the first beginning is what "'remains' and 'rules' in spite of that forgetting."[12] Thus there must indeed be two beginnings. Fell's way of reading the two beginnings not only prefigures the reading suggested here, but it also prefigures the topological character of that reading—taking the other beginning as indeed a matter of a return to, or remembering of, place:

> [F]or Heidegger, Being is appearing in place . . . Our history has been sentenced to a dissimulation or displacement of this place and hence of the nature of Being itself . . . The proper future of ontology is not an advance to something essentially new but a remembering of the event of the place in which things have always appeared and can appear.[13]

Fell's analysis of the two beginnings explicitly draws together Heidegger's introduction of the two beginnings in the writings of the 1930s with ideas from the later thinking, thereby connecting the two beginnings directly, not only with Heidegger's analysis of technology, but also with his account of the happening of world and place that occurs in the fourfold. The movement towards the other beginning thus involves, in the terms of Heidegger's thinking, a "step back into where we already are."[14] This step back is the counter to the turn away from the "where" that occurs in the first beginning, and it reaches its extremity in technological modernity. The "where" at issue here "is the Place displaced, the Fourfold's 'time-play-space,'"[15] and the step back, which is also a return towards, is a step back to that place, to the fourfold.

The Centrality of the Topological

Part of what is significant about Fell's approach, both here and elsewhere in his reading of Heidegger, is the way he attends so carefully and closely to the topological character of Heidegger's thinking. Fell is, in fact, the first commentator genuinely to address Heidegger's thinking as a topology and so as a mode of thinking in which place plays a central and ineliminable role. In this respect, Fell's work runs against the widespread tendency, not only to ignore the topological character of Heidegger's language, but also, when it is brought to notice, actively to downplay it or even to deny that the language in question is indeed to be understood topologically. This neglect of the topological in Heidegger is all the more problematic in that it occurs against Heidegger's own refusal of metaphorical interpretations of his language, as well as the iridescence noted earlier,[16] and his persistent call that we attend to what language itself says—to what one might call the "actuality" of language.[17]

This is a topic already discussed at greater length in chapter 6 (and touched on again in chapter 9), but it is worth reiterating some of the key points at issue here. One cannot treat Heidegger's language as metaphorical, just as one cannot reduce it to any simple mode of literality either. When Heidegger uses the phrase "house of being," he both draws upon our already existing familiarity with home and house as dwelling-places, as places of shelter and sustenance (even if our actual houses and homes are sometimes inadequate in this respect), and renders that familiarity uncertain: *What is it to house; what is it to be a home?* Heidegger undertakes the same questioning in "Building Dwelling Thinking"—"Was ist, zu wohnen?" he asks (in the standard translation, "What is it to dwell?"). Yet this "rendering-uncertain" only occurs if we allow language already to place us in relation to our concrete experience of what is at issue here, house and home, *Wohnen*—if we allow language to let us into the space in which such questioning can arise. That space is not a *metaphorical* space, at least not in the usual sense of the metaphorical. It is, perhaps, akin to the space of the image but, again, not in the sense in which this too is often employed. It is not a *literal* space, since the notion of literality has no clear purchase here either.

Heidegger's insistence on taking seriously the language that he uses, and on attending to what is immediately given in that language, is reiterated at many places in his writing and is an explicit feature of his work, at least from the time of his engagement with Hölderlin in the 1930s. Connected with this is the fact that, by the postwar period (although the trend is evident much earlier), Heidegger's writing has also lost almost all of the vestiges of any technical philosophical vocabulary—including that of phenomenology. This is part of what is at issue in the idea that the later Heidegger resorts to poetry, although it is more accurate to say that he abandons philosophical technicality, looking instead to find a way of thinking that remains with language, and with the concrete experience of language, as it occurs together with the happening of place and of world. Inasmuch as Heidegger does move to a mode of poetic speaking, it is because he also moves to a mode of speaking that is grounded in place and in the attentiveness to place—that is fundamentally topological—a point at the heart of the argument throughout the present volume.

Given the self-evident character of the topology at work in Heidegger, it might be thought surprising that it is, for the most part, ignored or overlooked in contemporary scholarship. Again, to take Sheehan as an example, for all that he uses a vocabulary, taken from Heidegger, that is imbued with topological ideas and images, these are never taken up in any direct fashion. Indeed, with respect to the idea of Dasein and its seeming focus on the *Da* (the there/here), Sheehan appropriates Gertrude Stein's quip, originally directed at Oakland, California, to assert that "there is no 'there' there."[18] Yet the neglect of the topological, and the broader tendency to resort to metaphorical and other forms of reading that allow such neglect, is not to be found only in the reading of Heidegger. It is a characteristic feature of philosophy and philosophical thinking more generally. It is a phenomenon that is strikingly evident, for instance, in Arendt's work, as we saw in chapter 10. Philosophy is deeply imbued with topological ideas and images, and yet their topological character is, for the most part, systematically ignored or disregarded. Indeed, the topological character of our own speaking, especially our thinking about thinking, is almost always passed over or, if it is noticed, seen as an irrelevant artefact of etymology (Heidegger's attentiveness to issues of etymology, even if sometimes idiosyncratic, is tied to his concern with the experience given in language). It is as if we do not wish to acknowledge what is before our very eyes: that our thinking is itself placed; cannot occur apart from place; is itself a form *of placing* and *being-placed*. In his *The Fate of Place*, Edward Casey masterfully explores the way place has been increasingly overtaken by space within the history of Western thought.[19] What is yet to be written, however, is the genealogy of philosophy that would uncover philosophy's own topological underpinnings, as well as its neglect and refusal of them—that would uncover the topology that has always been present at the very center of philosophy, as at the center of thinking.

Hegel, Miller, and Relationality

Fell's analysis of Heideggerian topology is not undertaken in relation to Heidegger alone but also addresses the work of Jean-Paul Sartre. The fact that *Heidegger and Sartre* has such a joint focus is not just a quirk of Fell's own particular philosophical sympathies. Instead, it derives from a concern to work through certain issues within the understanding of ontology and phenomenology, and, among other things, to understand the role of Hegel in relation to phenomenology. Fell writes that one of the "provocations" of the approach he takes in *Heidegger and Sartre* is "a very broad definition of the phenomenological movement designed, in part, to point to a positive relation between Hegel and Heidegger."[20] Hegel is thus important in Fell's account, despite being a problematic figure for Heidegger,[21] yet important, too, for a broader understanding of the idea of philosophical topology.

The topological significance of Hegel, and part of the reason for his significance in Fell, can be found, not only in Hegel's interest in geography,[22] but in the Hegelian emphasis on relationality—something that has been taken up in various ways by Hegelians and post-Hegelians, and is especially evident in the theory of recognition that has been so prominent in much recent Hegel scholarship.[23] Although often presented, particularly by contemporary anglo-analytic thinkers, who often treat it as one of the problematic features of idealism, as consisting of the idea that there are no *relata*, only relations,[24] the emphasis on relationality, whether in Hegel or Heidegger, is more to do with the refusal of any form of reductive foundationalism and an emphasis on mutual constitution. The latter is exemplified, not only in Hegel's account of recognition (whereby self-identity always involves the identity of the other—mirrored in Heidegger's account of the relation between identity and difference), but also in the idea of equiprimordiality (*Gleichursprünglichkeit*) in *Being and Time*, and in the structure of the fourfold in the later essays.

The connection to Hegel also brings us closer to one of the other great influences at work in Fell's thinking, John William Miller. It is sometimes forgotten, especially by those outside the immediate circle in which it holds sway, just how indebted American pragmatism is to the tradition of Hegelian idealism, as well as to German idealism more broadly (although it is a connection strongly reaffirmed in Robert Brandom's work)[25]—the idealist influence, and the relationalism that comes with it, being clearly evident in the holist and coherentist elements in pragmatist thinking. Miller was himself influenced by Emerson as well as by Josiah Royce (a key figure in the dissemination of idealist thinking in North America) and C. I. Lewis (whose influence leads on through Quine and on to Donald Davidson).[26] Notwithstanding his exposure to realist strains of thinking, which are also taken up into his philosophy, the idealist influence is central in Miller's work and is evident in his own adoption of an essentially *relational* mode of ontology (although its relationality is not strongly thematized by Miller) that refuses to look to any single, separate entity or principle as its underlying ground. The primacy Miller accords the "act" and "actuality"—and of what he calls the "Midworld" (which is the domain "of symbols and functioning objects,"[27] in which both subjectivity and objectivity are grounded)—is the primacy of that which is the locus or "matrix" out of which elements emerge (and is itself constituted in that very emergence), rather than of any sort of self-subsisting *subiectum*. Like Heidegger, Miller also has something to say about philosophy's beginnings: "Philosophy has no presuppositions," he writes, "the end and the beginning are reciprocal."[28]

At the core of any topology is an emphasis on relationality, and so all topological thinking involves a commitment to some form of relationalism—a point that should already be evident from the preceding discussion. Place is itself fundamentally relational. To be in place is to find oneself implicated within an encompassing locality that is implicated in and with other such localities. Places are themselves not identified with any one thing but with congeries of things and events. They are formed in and through the relations between things, events, and other localities, just as those things, events, and localities find their own formation in and through place. Moreover, any genuine relationalism, as we have seen in the discussion in earlier chapters, is also implicitly topological. Relations do not ramify endlessly but take shape within certain localities or regions, within certain bounds. The notion of "boundary" is itself the idea of that which allows for the establishing and unfolding of relations, and this is part of what is captured in Heidegger's repeated characterization of the boundary (repeated in this volume also) as productive rather than merely restricting: "A boundary is not that at which something stops but, as the Greeks recognized, the boundary is that from which something begins its presencing."[29]

The idea of a relationality without bounds—an idea widespread within contemporary thinking and, especially, the contemporary thinking of technology and globalization—is only possible on the assumption of an infinite spatial extension as that in which such relationality inheres; in other words, on the assumption of a purely spatial, as opposed to a topological, ontology (and this, of course, is what is at issue in the "spatialization of the world" that was the focus of chapter 8). Such an ontology, which is partly what Heidegger attacks in *Being and Time*, is rendered problematic by the fact that space is grounded in the same *place*, the same *topos*, that the assertion of the primacy of an unbounded relationality seeks to deny. Even the relationality of an extended space emerges only in and through the boundedness of place.

Topology and Hermeneutics

Many of the contemporary readings of Hegel that reinforce the significance of relationality through their focus on the Hegelian theory of recognition do so in a way that emphasizes the continuity with Kant, and that thereby also read Hegel hermeneutically.[30] The way both Kant and hermeneutics enter into the discussion here is important because it suggests a slightly different trajectory of thinking from that which appears, at first blush anyway, in Fell's account. Indeed, it is also indicative of a difference between Fell's account and my own. My emphasis tends to be Kantian, more so than Hegelian, at the same time as the tendency in my thinking has been towards hermeneutics, more so than towards phenomenology (this is partly, in fact, what also tends my own thinking towards Camus rather than Sartre).

It is easy, however, to overestimate the differences here, the reality being that they are more differences in emphasis than in substance. So far as the choice between Kant and Hegel is concerned, this partly manifests in my own preference for explicitly retaining the notion of the transcendental (despite Heidegger's own abandonment of the notion), which I take to stand in a direct relation to the topological. Yet one can well argue that something like my notion of the transcendental is also at work in Fell, just differently expressed.[31] Similarly, when it comes to the question of hermeneutics or phenomenology, the difference does indeed seem not to be a major one—all the more so given that Fell himself acknowledges his own very broad construal of the phenomenological movement (partly intended to allow the inclusion of Hegel within it).[32] Nevertheless, this is an issue on which there is a little more that ought to be said, not so much because of the difference between Fell and me, but because of the significance of the relation between topology and hermeneutics.

Although close, hermeneutics and phenomenology each stands in a slightly different relation to topology. The difference is perhaps most succinctly put by saying that, whereas phenomenology *leads in the direction of place* (as Heidegger's work partly shows), hermeneutics *already begins with place* (something that Heidegger's work also demonstrates). The primary focus of hermeneutics is on the *situatedness* of understanding, which implies an essential connection to *finitude*, as well as to *facticity*, and so on the primacy of situation, which is also the primacy of place.

Hermeneutics is an essential thinking of the "between" (a notion to which I shall return),[33] out of which understanding, along with any and every "appearing," arises, and which is identical with the bounded relationality that belongs to place. In its focus on the situation, and on the situation as also an event of encounter in which something appears that makes a demand upon us, hence hermeneutics attends first to that which is to be understood—to the "thing,"[34] so hermeneutics already stands aside from the usual oppositions of subject and object and outside also of any "subjectivism."[35] If I were to point to one of the ways in which the thinking exemplified in this volume aims to take further the ideas that Fell's work pioneers, then it would be in the attempt, not simply to develop further the topology present in Fell's account, but also to try, more clearly, to demonstrate the interrelation of the topological and the hermeneutical. Yet this is perhaps only a matter of drawing out what is implicit in Fell's work, rather than a point of contestation with it. Indeed, it might be said that the core of the difference between my thinking and Fell's is that Fell assumes an already hermeneuticized account of phenomenology (one adumbrated in Miller through his engagement with Royce as well as C. S. Peirce), whereas my approach is one that begins within hermeneutics and, only then, takes up phenomenology.

Not only is place a more directly thematized issue within hermeneutics, but so too is the idea of relationality itself. One might thus argue that one of the ways hermeneutics enters into Fell's account is actually through the way he explicitly draws upon relational conceptions, and since this is done, in part, through Hegel, so one might also argue that Hegel is the means by which a hermeneutical mode of thinking enters into Fell's account, and that Hegel also represents an important source of hermeneutical influence within philosophy more widely, albeit one that derives from a thinker not usually regarded as standing within the core hermeneutical tradition.[36] It is partly on the basis of its relational character that I think it is possible to view Miller as himself a topologically oriented thinker and, on this account, *hermeneutically* oriented as well.

Moreover, so far as the topological character of his thinking is concerned, it is notable that Miller also looks to something like another beginning for philosophy, a beginning that requires we overcome the alienating and subjectivizing tendencies that otherwise seem so prevalent.

The idea of such another beginning is suggested by Miller's own turn towards the Midworld, which is itself a turn back to the body, to act and actuality, and to the thing—or what Miller calls the "functioning object."[37] The Midworld, as its name suggests, is not a world beyond or behind but a world "between" (here the hermeneutical reappears). Yet this between-ness is not the between-ness that arises out of the separation of already existing entities. Instead, it is the between-ness, and so also the unity, out of which such separation and differentiation itself comes. This notion of the between is itself an essentially topological one. Place is constituted as a between—as a bounded openness and opening. It is out of place that subject and object both arise, and the same is also true of the Midworld. Place, too, is constituted in relation to act and activity. It is our own character, as embodied agents, that is the basis for our engaged being-in-place, and it is through the dynamic character of place that its very relationality plays out. Relation is, to use a Millerian turn of phrase, a verb and not a noun, and one might say something similar of place. In this respect, to reiterate a point already made several times in previous chapters, the language of the event that is so central to later Heidegger is not indicative of a prioritization of the purely temporal but is itself topological. There is not place *and* event—only the event *as* place, place *as* event.

Back into the Brightness of Place

It might be argued that inasmuch as every thinker is a revisionist, arguing for their own philosophical vision of things, so every thinker also looks to another beginning for philosophy—a beginning in their own re-visioned view of the world. Yet what we find in Heidegger is not a new or different view of things (though it does stand apart from the philosophically conventional). On the contrary, it is a re-seeing of what is already before our eyes; a recollection of that with which we are already familiar; a return to the place in which we already are. This is why the *other* beginning is indeed not a *new* beginning; why it is a return to the original place in which thinking has its origin and its ground. Moreover, the place at issue here is not some esoteric "beyond" but, rather, lies in the place that is most immediately present to us—the place in which we act and are acted upon, the place of our very experience of things, the place in which meaning first arises, the place of our own being and of being itself. If we ever seem to leave this place, it is because of thinking's own tendency to forgetfulness and, especially, the forgetfulness that arises through philosophy's own entrapment in its dream-like fantasies.

Heidegger's original account of the two beginnings of thinking, and the need to find our way towards the other beginning as the means also of returning to the first, arises in a time of historical and political crisis in the 1930s—a time of crisis for Germany, for Europe, and for the wider world—and a time of personal crisis for Heidegger himself. In his writing from the 1930s and 1940s, Heidegger sometimes seems to conflate these crises, as if the crisis of thinking and the crisis that erupted into the Second World War were somehow intrinsically connected (it is this that partly underlies his entanglement with Nazism). Yet the core of Heidegger's thinking of the two beginnings and the need for an other beginning, though it is tied to a crisis of modernity, is not based in the historical and political circumstances of the 1930s and 1940s alone, nor in the personal situation in which Heidegger found himself, and this is so in spite of the fact that these may constitute the autobiographical trigger for that thinking. It is not tied to the position of Germany in that period, nor does it depend on the idea of some future German destiny. Indeed, the way in which the figure of the other beginning, or something close to it, can be located elsewhere than in Heidegger's work confirms this very point.

The thinking of the other beginning directs us back to the character of thinking as forgetting and so to the constant need for remembrance. Such remembrance is a task that always lies before us, so long as we are concerned *to think*—which means, so long as we remain concerned with our own human being and, therefore, with our being as given over to the world, given over to place, given over to being. The remembrance at issue here is a remembrance of the place in which thinking begins and so a remembrance of, and a turning back to, the proper place of thinking. That remembrance involves a recognition of what thinking is, of its grounds, and also of its limits. Moreover, this need for remembrance takes on a special character in the face of the philosophical tendency, originating in the very first beginning of philosophy, to turn away from the original and originary place of thinking and instead to immerse itself in a set of fanciful worlds of its own imagining.

This tendency towards forgetfulness and disorientation is indeed reflected in and reinforced by the tendency of our contemporary globalized, corporatized world to position everything within the same homogenized network of connection and flow—to reduce everything to the single currency of the quantifiable, the commoditized, and the countable. Yet, although this may make the task of remembrance harder, it also makes it all the more urgent. The focus on the quantifiable does not obliterate the qualitative; the emphasis on commoditization does not render irrelevant that which cannot be commoditized; the obsession with the countable leaves untouched that which is not countable. Disconnection and discontinuity remain even in the face of the drive toward connection and flow, as the everyday experience of contemporary electronic communication and information technology, with its disjunctions and breakdowns, ably demonstrates.

The possibility of an "other" beginning for philosophy, and so also for thinking, is thus not merely a matter of significance for philosophy alone. The task of finding our way to the other beginning—the task of reorienting thinking—is also the task of finding our way back into the world and back into a mode of being in the world that is neither self-destructive nor self-delusional. *It is the very task of finding a way back into the brightness of place.* This is the task that Heidegger sets before us and of which he constantly reminds us. It is a task that remains regardless of any judgment we might make regarding the stupidity or offensiveness of Heidegger's remarks in the *Notebooks* or elsewhere. It is because this task does indeed remain before us, because it is a task central to thinking and to human being, and because it is Heidegger who more than anyone else has so persistently delineated its character and significance, that we It is because this task does indeed remain before us, because it is a task central to thinking and to human being, and because it is Heidegger who, more than anyone else, has so persistently delineated its character and significance, that we must engage with the topology evident *in* Heidegger's thinking, as well as continuing to think topologically beyond and *after* Heidegger.

Notes

Introduction

1. The distinction of place from space is an important theme in chapter 8; on the relation of place and time, see especially chapter 10.

2. For more on these points, see my discussions in *Place and Experience: A Philosophical Topography*, 2nd ed. (London: Routledge, 2018), 23–41, 161–76, and *Heidegger's Topology: Being, Place, World* (Cambridge, MA: MIT Press, 2006), 27–35, 251–66.

3. "Nature loves to hide"—Heraclitus, B123 DK, in Charles Kahn, *The Art and Thought of Heraclitus* (Cambridge: Cambridge University Press, 1979), 33.

4. I have also used the term "philosophical topography" (notably in *Place and Experience*). I treat the two terms as more or less interchangeable, although "topology" is probably the one I have used more frequently, and where Heidegger is concerned, almost exclusively.

5. See, most notably, Jeff Malpas, *Heidegger's Topology*; and Malpas, *Heidegger and the Thinking of Place* (Cambridge, MA: MIT Press, 2012).

6. See Heidegger, "Seminar in Le Thor 1968," *Four Seminars*, trans. Andrew Mitchell and François Raffoul (Bloomington: Indiana University Press, 2004), 41. Throughout what follows, Heidegger's works are primarily referred to in their English translations, except in those cases where there is no available English translation or where the German is of specific relevance.

7. See Sheehan, *Making Sense of Heidegger: A Paradigm Shift* (London: Rowman and Littlefield International, 2014); and Sheehan, "A Paradigm Shift in Heidegger Research," *Continental Philosophy Review* 34 (2001): 183–202.

8. Joseph P. Fell, *Heidegger and Sartre: An Essay on Being and Place* (New York: Columbia University Press, 1979), xiv. Fell's book first opened the pathway towards the sort of topological reading of Heidegger that has been so central to my work. Although less explicit in its topological orientation, Vincent Vycinas's ground-breaking volume, *Earth and Gods: An Introduction to the Philosophy of Martin Heidegger* (The Hague: Martinus Nijhof, 1961) also deserves notice.

Vycinas was the first, in English, to address Heidegger's later writing, in which topological themes come more explicitly to the fore, and his *Earth and Gods* provides an important point of entry for Heidegger's thinking as a whole—it remains one of the best and most detailed accounts of Heidegger's later thinking. Unfortunately, the work of both Fell and Vycinas seems largely to be neglected by contemporary readers.

9. Heidegger, "*Der Spiegel* Interview with Martin Heidegger," *The Heidegger Reader*, ed. Günter Figal, trans. Jerome Veith (Bloomington: Indiana University Press, 2009), 328.

10. On this see Heidegger, "On the Question of Being," trans. William McNeill, in *Pathmarks*, ed. William McNeill (Cambridge: Cambridge University Press, 1998), esp. 310–11.

Chapter One

1. Edited by Peter Trawny, and published by Klostermann, Frankfurt, these three volumes appear as: *Überlegungen II–VI (Schwarze Hefte 1931–1938)*, *Gesamtausgabe*, vol. 94; *Überlegungen VII–XI (Schwarze Hefte 1938–1939)*, *Gesamtausgabe*, vol. 95; and *Überlegungen XII–XV (Schwarze Hefte 1939–1941)*, *Gesamtausgabe*, vol. 96. Translated by Richard Rojcewicz, and published by Indiana University Press, Bloomington, the first in 2016 and the others in 2017, they appear in English as: *Ponderings II–IV, Black Notebooks 1931–1938*; *Ponderings VII–XI, Black Notebooks 1938–1939*; and *Ponderings XII–XV, Black Notebooks 1939–1941*.

2. As Laurence Hemming argues with respect to some of Heidegger's remarks—see his "Heidegger's Hegel, the Christian Jew: 'Europe' as 'Planetary Criminality and Machination,'" *Heidegger and the Global Age*, ed. Antonio Cerella and Louiza Odysseos (London: Rowman & Littlefield International, 2017), 187–212.

3. Ingo Farin and I have attempted to raise some of these issues in Farin and Malpas, eds., *Reading Heidegger's Black Notebooks* (Cambridge, MA: MIT Press, 2016).

4. My own view is that the *Notebooks* tend to corroborate ideas or to reinforce what is evident from existing sources (even the evidence the *Notebooks* supply regarding the shift to a more explicit focus on place largely reinforces, though in a significant way, what can already be discerned if one looks carefully enough). The anti-Semitic remarks that the *Notebooks* contain are not replicated elsewhere in Heidegger's published works (although the issue of anti-Semitism has certainly arisen elsewhere), but it is not at all clear that those remarks warrant the claim that we must therefore significantly alter the character of our reading of Heidegger's work in its entirety. Indeed, part of the problem

with those remarks is their seeming thoughtlessness. In this regard, I am thus not persuaded by the arguments advanced by Peter Trawny and Donatella di Cesare regarding the essentially anti-Semitic nature of Heidegger's thinking—see Trawny, *Heidegger and the Myth of a Jewish World Conspiracy* (Chicago: University of Chicago Press, 2016); and Di Cesare, *Heidegger and the Jews: The Black Notebooks* (Cambridge: Polity, 2018).

5. *Being and Time*, H369—Heidegger, *Being and Time*, trans. J. Macquarie and E. Robinson (New York: Harper & Row, 1962), 421; see also *Being and Time*, trans. Joan Stambaugh, rev. Dennis Schmidt (Albany: SUNY Press, 2010), 351–52.

6. See Immanuel Kant, *Critique of Pure Reason*, trans. and ed. Paul Guyer and Allen W. Wod, *The Cambridge Edition of the Works of Immanuel Kant* (Cambridge: Cambridge University Press, 1999), B293, A240/B 299.

7. In Malpas, *Heidegger's Topology*, 104–26, I adopt a strong reading of Heidegger's position in *Being and Time* in that I take it to be directed at showing the *derivative* character of spatiality in relation to temporality. It might be argued that talk of derivation is, however, *too* strong (although Heidegger does use language like that of derivation in just this context), but it certainly does seem to be the case that Heidegger argues for spatiality as *secondary* to temporality even though this is a position from which he later retreats.

8. Cartesian spatiality has its own "temporalized" analogue in the leveled-out time of the everyday—the temporality of mere succession—although such "everyday time" can itself be seen as a mode of spatialized time. The tendency to reduce time to space reflects the spatializing tendency that is characteristic of modernity.

9. Which seems confirmed by Heidegger's later comment in "Time and Being," 23.

10. Heidegger, *What Is a Thing?*, trans. W. B. Barton Jr. and Vera Deutsch (Chicago: Henry Regnery, 1967), 16–17.

11. Heidegger, "Time and Being," 23.

12. See *Being and Time*, H54. On the question of dwelling, see Malpas, *Rethinking Dwelling: Heidegger, Place, Architecture* (London: Bloomsbury, 2021).

13. See Martin Heidegger, "Letter on 'Humanism,'" trans. Frank A. Capuzzi, Pathmarks, ed. William McNeill (Cambridge: Cambridge University Press, 1998), 272—the phrase is a central focus for the discussion in chapter 5.

14. See, for example, Heidegger, *Hölderlins Hymne "Andenken,"* Gesamtausgabe, vol. 52, ed. C. Ochtwadt (Frankfurt: Klostermann, 1982), 39–40; and *Hölderlin's Hymn "The Ister,"* trans. William McNeill and Julia Davis (Bloomington: Indiana University Press, 1996), esp. 16–27 and 166.

15. In "Place and World: On Jeff Malpas' Second Edition of *Place and Experience*," *International Journal of Philosophical Studies* 28 (2020): 254–66, Ingo Farin criticizes my claim that Heidegger treats space as secondary in *Being and Time*, arguing that Heidegger does indeed recognize the importance of the spatial

and topological in the early work. It seems likely, however, that there is less of a disagreement here than might first appear. My claim is not that *Being and Time* overlooks the importance of space and place, but rather, as I indicate above, that Heidegger's account in the early work contains divergent and sometimes inconsistent elements such that the real character of place and space, and the relation of both to time, is never clearly worked out.

16. See Heidegger, *Ponderings II–IV*, 76.

17. The hyphenated form does occur in *Being and Time*, but only in a few specific instances, and the unhyphenated form is the one Heidegger standardly employs (though he modifies it later). F.-W. von Herrmann claims that the shift to the hyphenated form as dominant first occurs in the *Contributions*. See von Herrmann, "Dasein and Da-Sein in *Being and Time* and in *Contributions to Philosophy (From Enowning),*" *Heidegger, Translation, and the Task of Thinking: Essays in Honor of Parvis Emad*, ed. F. Schalow (Dordrecht: Springer, 2011), 213–24, esp. 216–17, and if the *Notebooks* are set to one side, then von Herrmann's claim is largely correct.

18. Heidegger, *Ponderings II–IV*, 71.

19. Heidegger, *Ponderings II–IV*, 155.

20. Heidegger, *Contributions*, 247.

21. The term that figures in the third of these, "Beyng," is an attempt to render into English Heidegger's term *Seyn*—an archaic German term form of *Sein* (being).

22. Heidegger, *Contributions*, 7–8.

23. Heidegger, *Contributions*, 205.

24. Heidegger, *Contributions*, 293.

25. Heidegger, "Letter on 'Humanism,'" *Pathmarks*, 241. In another note, at the very beginning of the "Letter," Heidegger writes: "What is said here was not first thought up when this letter was written, but is based on the course taken by a path that was begun in 1936, in the "moment" of an attempt to say the truth of being in a simple manner." See "Letter," 239n.

26. Heidegger, *Anmerkungen I–V*, *Gesamtausgabe*, vol. 94, ed. Peter Trawny (Frankfurt: Klostermann, 2015), 191.

27. Joseph Fell, *Heidegger and Sartre: An Essay on Being and Place*, 221.

28. Heidegger, *Anmerkungen I–V*, 191.

29. Heidegger, *Anmerkungen I–V*, 301, 310, 315, 316, 328.

30. See, for example, Heidegger, *Anmerkungen I–V*, 202.

31. See, for example, Heidegger, *Anmerkungen I–V*, 201–202, 434, and 512.

32. *Ort* appears in the *Contributions* at several places, but never in a way that makes place itself central. See the German original of *Contributions*, *Beiträge zur Philosophie (Vom Ereignis)*, *Gesamtausgabe*, vol. 65, ed. F.-W. von Herrmann (Frankfurt: Kolstermann, 1989), 18, 60, 156, 187, 207, 261, 329, 330, 358. *Ortschaft* seems not to occur at all.

33. See Heidegger, *Beiträge*, 5, 8, 24, 26, 90, 95–98, 155, 228, 234, 237, 238, 242, 243, 255, 260, 277, 285, 322, 384, 397, 407, 412, 413, 417, 486. As with the few appearances of *Ort*, the appearances of *Stätte* are not such as to thematize place in any direct or explicit way.

34. Heidegger, *Ponderings II–IV*, 80 and 82. Heidegger proclaims that it is the *Führer*, Adolf Hitler, who has "awakened a new actuality, giving our thinking a new course and impetus. Otherwise, despite all the thoroughness, it would have remained lost in itself and would only with difficulty have found its way to effectiveness. Literary existence is at an end." See *Ponderings II–IV*, 81.

35. Heidegger, *Ponderings II–IV*, 93.

36. Heidegger, *Ponderings II–IV*, 145–46. Heidegger always maintained a commitment to the value and significance of what the Rectoral Address attempted. Significantly, at the time it was given, the Address also had the strong support of Karl Jaspers. See the discussion in Iain Thomson, *Heidegger on Ontotheology: Technology and the Politics of Education* (Cambridge: Cambridge University Press, 2005), 86–87.

37. The phrase "second beginning" occurs in *Ponderings II–IV*, 153–54, and in several entries in the pages immediately thereafter.

38. Heidegger, *Ponderings II–IV*, 156–57.

39. Heidegger, *Ponderings II–IV*, 159.

40. Heidegger, *Contributions*, 27–28.

41. Heidegger, *Contributions*, 35.

42. On the idea of the "people" in Heidegger's thinking of the 1930s, see James Phillips, *Heidegger's Volk: Between National Socialism and Poetry* (Stanford, CA: Stanford University Press, 2005).

43. Heidegger, "The Origin of the Work of Art," *Off the Beaten Track*, trans. Kenneth Haynes and Julian Young (Cambridge: Cambridge University Press, 2002), 55.

44. *Anmerkungen I–V*, 191.

45. Heidegger, "Seminar in Le Thor 1969," *Four Seminars*, 60–61.

46. Heidegger, *Anmerkungen I–V*, 222–23 and 500. Against this background, one of Heidegger's comments towards the end of "Anaximander's Saying," from 1946, takes on an additional significance. Commenting on the "confusion" that reigns regarding being, Heidegger writes: "Theories of nature, doctrines about history, do not remove the confusion. They further confuse things until they are unrecognizable . . ." See "Anaximander's Saying," *Off the Beaten Track*, 281.

47. Heidegger, *Anmerkungen I–V*, 97, 382.

48. "With *Being and Time* . . . the 'question of Being' . . . concerns the question of being qua being. It becomes thematic in *Being and Time* under the name of 'the question of the meaning [*Sinn*] of being.' Later this formulation was given up in favor of that of 'the question of the truth of Being, and finally in favor of that of 'the question concerning the place or location of Being'

['*Ortschaft des Seins*'], from which the name topology of being arose [*Topologie des Seins*]. Three terms which succeed one another and at the same time indicate three steps along the way of thinking: MEANING—TRUTH—PLACE (τόπος)." See Heidegger, "Seminar in Le Thor 1969," 47, and in the original German, *Seminare (1951–1973), Gesamtausgabe*, vol. 15, ed. C. Ochwadt (Frankfurt: Klostermann, 1986), 344.

49. For instance, "The Thing," *Poetry, Language, Thought*, trans. Albert Hofstadter (New York: Harper & Row, 1971), 180: "The fouring, the unity of the four, presences as the appropriating [*ereignende*] mirror-play of the betrothed, each to the other in simple oneness. The fouring presences as the worlding of world. The mirror-play of world is the round dance of appropriating [*Ereignens*]."

50. See Heidegger, *Contributions*, 246.

51. See, especially, Heidegger, "Time and Being," 19–20.

52. On *chora* and place, see my response to Peter Grattan's attempt to set *chora* against place (or at least against place as *topos*) in "Five Theses on Place (and some associated remarks): A Reply to Peter Gratton," *Il Cannocchiale: rivista di studi filosofici* 42 (2017): 69–81.

53. Daniela Valega-Neu, "The *Black Notebooks* and Heidegger's Writings on the Event (1936–1942)," in *Reading Heidegger's Black Notebooks 1931–1941*, 129.

54. See Valega-Neu, "The *Black Notebooks* and Heidegger's Writings on the Event (1936–1942)," 131–32.

55. This is evident in any number of works from the late 1940s on, but is especially notable in Heidegger, *What Is Called Thinking?*, trans. J. Glenn Gray and F. Wieck (New York: Harper & Row, 1968), particularly with its emphasis on thinking (*Denken*) as thanking (*Danken*).

56. The term is central to Heidegger's discussions in the volume that appeared in German as *Gelassenheit* (Pfullingen: Neske, 1959) and in English as *Discourse on Thinking: A Translation of* Gelassenheit, trans. John M. Anderson and E. Hans Freund (New York: Harper & Row, 1966).

57. The translation here is of Heidegger's German version of the line (rather than being directly from Aristotle's own text). See Heidegger, "Art and Space," *The Heidegger Reader*, 305, and in the original, "Die Kunst und Der Raum," *Aus der Erfahrung des Denkens (1910–1976)*, 203.

58. Heidegger, "Art and Space," 305, "Die Kunst und Der Raum," 203.

Chapter Two

1. Jean Beaufret, "L'entretien sous le marronnier," *L'arc* 22 (1963): 1; quoted in Dominique Janicaud, *Heidegger in France*, trans. François Raffoul and David Pettigrew (Bloomington: Indiana University Press, 2015), 178. Beaufret's essay is a "stylized" account (as Janicaud puts it) of the meeting between Char

and Heidegger that took place under the chestnut tree ("sous le marronnier") at Beaufret's Paris home.

2. See Janicaud, *Heidegger in France*, 90.

3. "Martin Heidegger est mort ce matin. Le soleil qui l'a couché lui a laissé ses outiis et n'a retenu que l'ouvrage. Ce seuil est constant. La nuit qui s'est ouverte aime de preference," Wednesday, 26 May 1976. See René Char, *Oeuvres complètes*, Bibliothèque de la Pléiade, no. 308 (Paris: Éditions Gallimard, 1983), 725.

4. Martin Heidegger, *Acheminement vers la parole* (Paris: Éditions Gallimard, 1976), 8.

5. See Heidegger, "Seminar in Le Thor 1969," 41 and 47.

6. See Peter Caws's discussion in "No Higher than the Mountain Peaks," *World Literature Today* 51 (1977): 358–59. The Lascaux poems are the focus for Maurice Blanchot's discussion of Char in "The Beast of Lascaux," *René Char's Poetry: Studies*, by Maurice Blanchot et al, trans. David Paul (Rome: Editions de Luca, 1956), 29–40.

7. René Char, "The Companions in the Garden," *Furor and Mystery & Other Writings*, trans. Mary Ann Caws and Nancy Kline (Boston, MA: Black Widow Press, 2010), 393. Elsewhere, Char writes that "moving, horrible, exquisite earth and the heterogeneous human condition take hold of each other and are mutually qualified." See Char, "Formal Share," *Furor and Mystery*, 117.

8. Albert Camus, *The Rebel: An Essay on Man in Revolt*, trans. Anthony Bower (New York: Vintage, 1956), 306.

9. Albert Camus, "The Desert," in *Lyrical and Critical Essays*, trans. Philip Thody (New York: Knopf, 1968), 105.

10. In 1949, Camus and Char launched a new magazine, *Empédocle*, that was intended to function as a vehicle for writing in the spirit of this "Mediterranean" sensibility (it ran only until the following year). However, Camus had already set out the basic outlines of the "Mediterraneanism" at issue here in 1937, in a lecture originally titled, "The Native Culture" and, later, "The New Mediterranean Culture." See Camus, "The New Mediterranean Culture," *Lyrical and Critical Essays*, 189–98; and the translation in Neil Foxlee, *Albert Camus's "The New Mediterranean Culture": A Text and its Contexts*, Modern French Identities, vol. 38 (Oxford: Peter Lang, 2010), 37–50. It is also evident in many of his essays before and after the Second World War—especially those in *Noces* (1938) and *L'Eté* (1954) and collected in *Lyrical and Critical Essays*. Camus's Mediterrraneanism (like his stance on Algeria) is not without problems, although, as Foxlee demonstrates, it must be read in its contemporary context (and read thus, many of the usual charges made against the position turn out to be overstated), but, as I argue below, it is perhaps best understood in philosophical terms as conjoining Camus's commitment to a philosophy of limit with his refusal of abstraction. His Mediterraneanism is an expression of

that commitment in the concrete terms of a landscape in which his own life and thought, like that of Char, was deeply embedded.

11. On the topological elements in Nietzsche, see Malpas, "We Hyperboreans: Notes towards a Nietzschean Topography," *Nietzsche: Individual and Community*, ed. Julian Young (New York: Cambridge University Press, 2014), 195–213. The title of the magazine launched by Camus and Char in 1949, *Empédocle*, invokes Nietzsche through the name of the Greek philosopher for whom he had particular admiration. See Nietzsche, *Correspondence 1932–1960: Albert Camus and Jean Grenier*, trans. Jan F. Rigaud (Lincoln: University of Nebraska Press, 2003), 129. The influence of Nietzsche on Camus is noted at various places in Foxlee, *Albert Camus's "The New Mediterranean Culture": A Text and Its Contexts*, esp. 243–46 and 268, but without any mention of the topological elements in Nietzsche's thinking or Nietzsche's own affirmation of the opposition between a southern and northern sensibility.

12. See Annika Döring and Peregrine Horden, "Heidegger as Mediterraneanist," *Critically Mediterranean: Temporalities, Aesthetics, and Deployments of a Sea in Crisis*, ed. yasser elhariry and Edwige Tamalet Talbayev (Cham, Switzerland: Palgrave Macmillan, 2018), 25–43.

13. How did Heidegger first encounter Char's poetry? And through what works? Char's most important publication prior to the 1955 meeting with Heidegger was his *Feuillets d'Hypnos* (Paris: Gallimard, 1946), published in a series edited by Camus and based on the journal Char kept from 1943–44 while a resistance leader in Provence (see Char, *Leaves of Hypnos*, trans. Cid Corman, New York: Grossman, 1973). *Leaves of Hypnos* is also included in *Furor and Mystery & Other Writings*, 133–226. Hannah Arendt famously quotes a line from *Hypnos* as the epigraph to her 1961 collection of essays, *Between Past and Future*. It seems almost certain that Heidegger's reading of Char would have been through *Hypnos* as a key work. Heidegger would surely also have read Char first in French rather than German since the earliest German translation of Char's work (Paul Celan being one of the translators, with the volume also including a preface by Camus) appeared only in the late-1950s as part of a French/German edition—see Char, *Poésies/Dichtungen* (Frankfurt am Main: Fischer, 1959). In any case, Heidegger's sensitivities to matters of language would seem to make it improbable that the sort of close engagement he had with Char's work could have occurred only in translation, and that is all the more so given the character of Char's poetry in particular—the translation of which is no easy task.

14. See Philip Conisbee and Denis Coutagne (with contributions from others), *Cézanne in Provence* (New Haven, CT: Yale University Press, 2006).

15. Heidegger, *Denkerfahrungen 1910–1976*, ed. Hermann Heidegger (Frankfurt: Klostermann, 1983), 163; quoted in Julian Young, *Heidegger's Philosophy of Art* (Cambridge: Cambridge University Press, 2001), 152.

16. It is also, as Heidegger emphasizes in *What Is Called Thinking?*, a thanking, *Danken*, which is to say that it always involved an attending to and acknowledging that out of which it comes. See *What Is Called Thinking?*, 138–47.

17. Joseph Fell, *Heidegger and Sartre*, 266.

18. Heidegger, "Seminar at Le Thor 1969," 77.

19. Heidegger, "Seminar in Le Thor 1966," 1–9.

20. Notably from Char, *Commune présence* (Paris: Gallimard, 1964); and À *la santé du serpent* (Paris: Gallimard, 1954). The published version of the seminar also carries a dedication from Char to Heidegger at its head.

21. See Heidegger, "Moira (Parmenides VIII, 34–41)," *Early Greek Thinking*, trans. David Farrell Krell and Frank Capuzzi (New York: Harper & Row, 1975), 93.

22. See, for instance, Kevin Clinton, "Stages of Initiation in the Eleusinian and Samothracian Mysteries," *Greek Mysteries: The Archaeology and Ritual of Ancient Greek Secret Cults*, ed. Michael B. Cosmopoulos (London: Routledge, 2003), 66–67.

23. Plutarch, *Moralia*, vol. 15 of Loeb Classical Library, trans. F. H. Sandbach (Cambridge, MA: Harvard University Press, 1969), 178, 317–19.

24. Heidegger, *Introduction to Metaphysics*, trans. Gregory Fried and Richard Polt (New Haven, CT: Yale University Press, 2000).

25. Heidegger, "Moira (Parmenides VIII, 34–41)," 79–101.

26. André Laks and Glenn W. Most, eds. and trans., *Early Greek Philosophy*, vol. 5, *Western Greek Thinkers, Part 2*, Loeb Classical Library (Cambridge, MA: Harvard University Press, 2016), 39[B3]. Laks and Most translate the line as: "For it is the same, to think and also to be." Richard McKirahan has "for the same thing is for conceiving as is for being," in A. H. Coxon, ed., *The Fragments of Parmenides* (Las Vegas: Parmenides, 2009), 58. The line is also referred to in "Seminar at Le Thor 1966," *Four Seminars*, 2, where it appears as: "For it is indeed the same: both thinking and being."

27. Heidegger, *Introduction to Metaphysics*, 186. It is very clear throughout Heidegger's exposition here, as it is in many other places outside of *Being and Time*, that the question concerning Dasein is also the question of the human, with Heidegger moving between both terms almost as if they meant the same.

28. See Laks and Most, *Early Greek Philosophy*, vol. 5, *Western Greek Thinkers, Part 2*, 48–49, 30[B8.25]–45[B8.40].

29. The phrase is originally from Burnet's translation—John Burnet, trans., *Early Greek Philosophy*, 4th ed. (1892; repr., London: A. & C. Black, 1930), 176. Laks and Most give the line as "a well rounded ball," *Early Greek Philosophy*, vol. 5, *Western Greek Thinkers, Part 2*, 49; and McKirahan has "a spherical ball," *The Fragments of Parmenides*, 78.

30. A point central to my arguments in both *Place and Experience* and *Heidegger's Topology*. On the issue of sphericity that is invoked here, as it relates

to place and to bound, it is surely no accident that Bachelard ends his own topological investigation, in *The Poetics of Space*, with a discussion of what he calls "a phenomenology of roundness." See Bachelard, *The Poetics of Space*, trans Maria Jolas (Boston: Beacon Press, 1959), 232–41.

31. Heidegger, *Introduction to Metaphysics*, 195.

32. Heidegger, "Moira (Parmenides VIII, 34–41)," 99–100.

33. Heidegger, *Reden und andere Zeugnisse eines Lebensweges (1910–1976)*, Gesamtausgabe, vol. 16, ed. Hermann Heidegger (Frankfurt: Klostermann, 2000), 551. *Bodenständigkeit* appears in the French as "sol original" ["original soil" or "original ground"]. See the text in François Fédier, *Soixante-deux photographs de Martin Heidegger* (Paris: Gallimard, 1999), "Légendes des illustrations" 1.

34. Heidegger's Le Thor seminars took place in the morning, with walks and excursions in the nearby countryside, led by Char, in the afternoon (see *Four Seminars*, esp. 89–90). Thus, Mark Payne writes that "[a]s Char's poems open up their world, they are gateways to the actual landscape, and Heidegger's seminars demand openness to their setting as a condition of participation." See Payne, "The Natural World in Greek Literature and Philosophy," *Oxford Handbooks Online: Classical Studies*, ed. Gareth Williams (Oxford: Oxford University Press, 2014), 12, accessed February 2020.

35. Char writes of Greece that "to imagine you is to reestablish you." See Char, "Hymn in a Quiet Voice," *Furor and Mystery*, 257.

36. Char, "Equal Shares," *Furor and Mystery*, 253. L'Isle-sur-la-Sorgue, about 5 kilometres from Le Thor, was Char's hometown.

37. Camus, "Summer in Algiers," *Lyrical and Critical Essays*, 90.

38. Some have argued that Camus's own talk of place, especially when considered in relation to his native Algeria, is itself associated with an implicit racism and colonialism—see especially Conor Cruise O'Brien, *Camus* (London: Fontana, 1970), and Edward Said, *Culture and Imperialism* (London: Vintage, 1994), 204–24. Whether this is actually the case is arguable, however, and the readings of O'Brien and Said have not gone unchallenged. Yet even were we to accept an element of truth in the charges brought against Camus (which one might argue could also be levelled against elements in Char's thinking), this does not, as I note elsewhere in this discussion, provide any reason to think that talk of place should be abandoned or that it changes the fundamental ontological issues at stake. Indeed, one might argue that such an association is more a reflection of the inevitable limits and failings of the human than it is of the problematic character of place as such. None of us are so transparent to ourselves that we are capable of recognizing or resolving all of our blindnesses and prejudices, and thinking is always subject to the limitations of its time and circumstance.

39. Char, "Leaves of Hypnos," 237; *Furor and Mystery*, 215. The original French reads: "Dans nos tenebres, il n'y a pas une place pour la Beaute. Toute la

place est pour la Beauté" (*Furor and Mystery*, 214). I have modified the published translation to substitute "place" for "space"; a substitution that not only fits with the context in which the line is used here, but also seems to keep closer to the sense in which the French "place" is being employed.

40. For two excellent discussions of the issues here, and of the way that notions of "goundedness," and of home and homecoming, are indeed at work in Heidegger more generally, see Robert Metcalf, "Rethinking 'Bodenständigkeit' in the Technological Age," *Research in Phenomenology* 42 (2012): 49–66; and Robert Mugerauer, *Heidegger and Homecoming: The Leitmotif in the Later Writings* (Toronto: University of Toronto Press, 2008).

41. I would emphasize, once again, that the mere fact that ideas of place and belonging to place may be associated with problematic notions of identity and exclusion (leaving aside the issue as to whether they are so associated in Heidegger, Char, or Camus) is not itself a good reason for abandoning such notions. Any significant notion will carry similar dangers, just as notions of the "good" and the "just" are often drawn upon to justify what is evil and unjust. Significantly, topological ideas and images remain even in the work of thinkers who are critical of Heidegger's own topological language—and this is itself a reflection of the fundamental character of such ideas and images. Thus both "place" and "home" are central in the work of Emmanuel Levinas, for instance, no less than in Heidegger's. Even if sometimes obscured, what is really at issue is how such notions are to be understood. Levinas, for instance, prioritizes the relation to place and home, and the understanding associated with this, that is exemplified by the immigrant rather than the "native" (so much so that it almost seems as if only the immigrant is "fully human"). See Levinas, *Entre Nous: On Thinking-of-the-Other*, trans. Michael B. Smith (New York: Columbia University Press, 1998), 117.

42. See Heidegger, "Hölderlin's Earth and Heaven," in *Elucidations of Hölderlin's Poetry*, trans. Keith Hoeller (New York: Humanity Books, 2000), 182–84.

43. It is this *topological* emphasis that seems largely to be overlooked in Payne's account both of this passage in particular and of Heidegger's position in general (it is present, but never directly taken up). Payne's focus is instead on the experience of the natural world.

44. Heidegger, "Hölderlin's Earth and Heaven," 182–84.

45. See especially Camus, "Helen's Exile," *Lyrical and Critical Essays*, 148.

46. Camus, "Helen's Exile," 148.

47. Char, "Hymn in a Quiet Voice," *Furor and Mystery*, 257.

48. Quoted, from a response by Camus to a critic, by Roger Quilliot in his notes to *The Rebel*. See Camus, *Essais*, ed. Roger Quilliot, Bibliothèque de la Pléiade (Paris: Gallimard, 1965)—originally published 1629.

49. White's thinking is strongly, though not exclusively, oriented towards the North Atlantic environment and culture of Brittany, Scotland, Ireland, Newfoundland, and Labrador.

50. See Jeff Malpas and Kenneth White, *The Fundamental Field: Thought, Poetics, World* (Edinburgh: Edinburgh University Press, 2021). One of White's early books, *Letters from Gourgounel* (London: Jonathan Cape, 1966), written in the Pyrenees, nevertheless draws on a landscape closer to that which appears in Char and Camus.

51. "Seminar in Le Thor 1969," 37–38.

52. In Camus, "La culture indigene. La nouvelle culture mediterranéenne," *Essais*, 1322–23.

53. Foxlee, "'The New Mediterranean Culture': An Annotated Translation," *Albert Camus's "The New Mediterranean Culture": A Text and Its Contexts*, 43–44.

54. Heidegger himself refers to the "aberrations [*Irrgänge*] and attempts [*Versuche*]" in his thinking prior to the late 1940s. See *Anmerkungen I–V*, §125, 191. There are those who have seen Heidegger's later thinking, in particular, as expressive of a romantic rural or "peasant" (*bauerlich*) thought that, because of its connection to landscape, remains within the frame of the thinking that drew Heidegger into proximity with Nazism. For a notable, if early, example, see Robert Minder, "Heidegger und Hebel oder Die Sprache von Messkirch," *Dichter in der Gesellschaft* (Frankfurt: Insel Verlag, 1966), 211–64. Such readings seem to me to fail to engage adequately either with the character of Nazism or with the actual development and character of Heidegger's thinking, especially in the period from the late 1930s onwards (see chapter 1 above). Again, the work of both Robert Metcalf, in "Rethinking 'Bodenständigkeit' in the Technological Age," and Robert Mugerauer, in *Heidegger and Homecoming: The Leitmotif in the Later Writings*, is also relevant here.

55. The shift away from history and from being is itself tied to the more explicit turn to place in Heidegger's thinking—see chapter 1.

56. See Malpas, "Place and Singularity," *The Intelligence of Place: Topographies and Poetics*, ed. Jeff Malpas (London: Bloomsbury, 2015), 65–92.

57. On the importance of the Heraclitean, not only for Heidegger and Char, but also for Blanchot in his own reading of Char, see Lars Iyer, "The Birth of Philosophy in Poetry: Blanchot, Char, Heraclitus," *Janus Head: Journal of Interdisciplinary Studies in Continental Philosophy, Literature, Phenomenological Psychology, and the Arts* 4 (2001): 358–83.

58. Camus, "Helen's Exile," 149.

59. Heidegger, "Seminar in Le Thor 1966," 6.

60. Heidegger, "Der Feldweg" (1948–1949), *Aus der Erfahrung des Denkens, 1910–1976*, 87–90, esp. 89; and in English as "The Pathway," trans. Thomas F. O'Meara, rev. Thomas Sheehan, in *Heidegger, the Man and the Thinker*, ed. Thomas Sheehan (New Brunswick: Transaction Publishers, 1981), 69–72, esp. 71.

61. Camus, "René Char," in *René Char's Poetry: Studies*, 55–59, esp. 56.

62. Char, *Oeuvres complètes*, 757; quoted in Nancy Kline, "Translating Éluard & Char," *Hyperion* 9 (2015): 11.

63. "Seminar in Le Thor 1969," 37–38.

64. Annika Döring and Peregrine Horden argue that the "proximity to Greece" that Heidegger finds in Provence is primarily a matter of Provence's connectedness to Greece by means of the same sea—namely, the Mediterranean—and it is this that is the basis for their characterization of Heidegger as "Mediterraneanist." See Döring and Horden, "Heidegger as Mediterraneanist," 42–43. But this appears too slight as a basis on which to explain the proximity that is at issue here—all the more so when there appear more substantive grounds in Heidegger's own thinking, as well as in that of Char and Camus.

65. René Char, *The Brittle Age and Returning Upland*, trans. Gustaf Sobin (Denver: Counterpath Press, 2009), 27.

66. Char, "Leaves of Hypnos," 61; *Furor and Mystery*, 153.

67. From a letter to René Char, January 1973. See Heidegger, "Andenken an Marcelle Mathieu," *Reden und andere Zeugnisse eines Lebensweges*, 731; quoted in Heidegger, *Four Seminars*, xvi.

68. Heidegger, "Seminar in Le Thor 1969," 63.

69. A theme that is explored in more detail in Malpas, *Place and Experience: A Philosophical Topography*.

70. Heidegger, "Seminar in Le Thor 1969," 63.

Chapter Three

1. See, for example, Hubert L. Dreyfus, *Being-in-the-World: A Commentary on Heidegger's* Being and Time, *Division I* (Cambridge, MA: MIT Press, 1990).

2. See, especially, David E. Storey, *Naturalizing Heidegger: His Confrontation with Nietzsche, His Contributions to Environmental Philosophy* (New York: SUNY Press, 2015).

3. Heidegger, *Being and Time*, Macquarie/Robinson, 100 [§15, H70].

4. Heidegger, *Being and Time*, Stambaugh/Schmidt, 70 [§15, H70].

5. William Wordsworth, "Lines Written a Few Miles above Tintern Abbey, On Revisiting the Banks of the Wye during a Tour, July 13, 1798," *Lyrical Ballads*, vol. I (London: T. N. Longman and O. Rees, 1800), 206–7.

6. This ought also to cast doubt on any simple contrast of countryside and city, although that contrast does appear in Wordsworth—as a poem such as "Michael," mentioned further on in the discussion here (and discussed in chapter 9), indicates.

7. See, for instance, Heidegger, *Being and Time*, §14, H65

8. Gillian Beer, *Darwin's Plots: Evolutionary Narrative in Darwin, George Eliot and Nineteenth-Century Fiction* (Cambridge: Cambridge University Press, 1983), 37.

9. Aristotle, *Metaphysics*, Bk I, 982b9–11, *The Metaphysics Books I–IX*, trans. Hugh Tredennick, Aristotle Volume XVII, Loeb Classical Library (Cambridge MA: Harvard University Press, 1933), 13.

10. Charles Darwin, *On the Origin of Species by Means of Natural Selection, or The Preservation of Favoured Races in the Struggle for Life*, 1st ed. (London: John Murray, 1859), 194; the phrase comes originally from Linnaeus.

11. Seamus Heaney, "The Sense of Place," *Preoccupations: Selected Prose 1968–1978* (London: Faber & Faber, 1984), 145; see also Malpas, *Place and Experience*, 1–3.

12. Hawking made the comments, which were widely reported in online and print media, at the May 2011 Google Zeitgeist conference.

13. E. D. Hirsch, Jr., *Wordsworth and Schelling: A Typological Study of Romanticism* (New Haven, CT: Yale University Press, 1960).

14. Kant, *Critique of Pure Reason*, A216/B263.

15. See Jeff Malpas and Karsten Thiel, "Kant's Geography of Reason," *Kant's Geography*, ed. Stuart Elden and Eduardo Mendieta (New York: SUNY Press, 2011), 195–214.

16. This concern with unity is a key theme in Fell's *Heidegger and Sartre*, although, as I note in the discussion in the epilogue, Fell elaborates upon it without reference to the transcendental—the latter being a notion that he largely rejects.

17. *Being and Time*, H38, Stambaugh/Schmidt.

18. See Malpas, *Heidegger's Topology*, 166–73.

19. See his comments in "Αγχιβασιν. A Triadic Conversation on a Country Path between a Scientist, a Scholar, and a Guide," *Country Path Conversations*, trans. Bret W. Davis (Bloomington: Indiana University Press, 2010), 90. The "Triadic Conversation" was written in 1945 but did not appear in full until 1995. The "Conversation on a Country Path about Thinking" that appears in *Discourse on Thinking* (the original German version of which appeared in 1959) is a revised and abbreviated form of the 1945 "Triadic Conversation."

20. See Heidegger, "The Principle of Identity," *Identity and Difference*, trans. Joan Stambaugh (New York: Harper and Row, 1969), esp. 36–39.

21. Heidegger, "Hebel—Friend of the House," trans. Bruce V. Foltz and Michael Heim, *Contemporary German Philosophy*, vol. 3, ed. Darrel E. Christensen, et al. (University Park: Pennsylvania State University Press, 1983), 97.

22. Aristotle, *Physics IV*, iv, 212a5. See also *Physics IV*, 212a20: "So that is what place is: the first unchangeable limit of that which surrounds," from *Aristotle's Physics Books III and IV*, trans. Edward Hussey (Oxford: Clarendon Press, 1957), 28.

23. *Physics IV*, iv, 208a30, or as Hussey has it, "things that are are somewhere," from *Aristotle's Physics Books III and IV*, 25.

24. W. V. Quine, "On What There Is," *From a Logical Point of View* (New York: Harper & Row, 1953), 14–15.

25. Heidegger, "The Origin of the Work of Art," 53.

26. Heidegger, *Parmenides*, trans André Schuwer and Richard Rojcewicz (Bloomington: Indiana University Press, 1998), 82.

27. Heidegger, "On the Essence and Concept of Φύσις in Aristotle's Physics B, I," *Pathmarks*, ed. William McNeill (Cambridge: Cambridge University Press, 1998), 206.

28. "Matrix" means, originally, "womb"—in Middle English as well as in Latin. The term derives from the Latin *mater* ("mother") from which also comes "material."

29. *Chora* (or *Khôra*, as it is sometimes given) has various meanings, but its primary sense in the original Greek is of the countryside around the *polis* that provides the material sustenance to the city.

30. Heidegger, "The Question Concerning Technology," *The Question Concerning Technology, and Other Essays*, trans. William Lovitt (New York: Harper & Row, 1977), 10–11, 13.

31. Aristotle, *On the Soul*, 2, 1, iii, 413a8–9. "It is also uncertain whether the soul as an actuality (*entelecheia*) bears the same relation to the body as the sailor to the ship"—from *On the Soul/Parva Naturalia/On Breath*, trans. W. S. Hett, Aristotle Volume VIII, Loeb Classical Library (Cambridge, MA: Harvard University Press, 1936), 73.

32. The discussion here essentially summarizes that in chapter 5 of *Heidegger and the Thinking of Place*, 100–103.

33. It might also call be called a "physicalism" (with an emphasis on the physical as pertaining to *physis*), and for the same reason.

Chapter Four

1. See, for example, Heidegger, "Seminar in Le Thor 1969," 60–61; and Heidegger, *The End of Philosophy*, trans. Joan Stambaugh (New York: Harper & Row, 1973), xii–xiii. In both of these passages, Heidegger emphasizes the importance of thinking difference itself in the fashion set out in "The Principle of Identity." In this respect, what becomes less important is the ontological difference as a matter of the separation of the ontological and the ontic (a separation that remains on the side of the metaphysical), and much more important is the belonging together of being and beings, or better, of presence and what presences.

2. At various points, Heidegger is explicit in rejecting "ontology" as a name for the kind of thinking in which he is engaged (see, as noted previously, *Ponderings II–IV*, 71), but typically when this does occur it is in the context of a rejection of ontology as "metaphysics," and especially of ontology as associated with "transcendental philosophy" (a point also made previously, in chapter 3).

If there can be a thinking—and saying—of being that escapes metaphysics, and that also stands apart from the transcendental thinking of which Heidegger is so critical (which, as pointed out previously, need not imply the complete rejection of all that is at issue in the transcendental—again, see chapter 3), then that surely leaves the possibility, of the sort countenanced here, of a legitimate continuation of a form of ontology that is different from what has gone before.

3. See, for instance, the arguments developed in Derrida, *Of Grammatology*, trans. Gayatri Chakravorty Spivak, corr. ed. (Baltimore: Johns Hopkins University Press, 1976), where the understanding at issue is explored in relation to textuality but in a way that also implicates the ontological. See also David Couzen Hoy's discussion in "Forgetting the Text: Derrida's Critique of Heidegger," *Boundary 2*, no. 8 (1979), 223–36.

4. See Gianni Vattimo, *The End of Modernity: Nihilism and Hermeneutics in Postmodern Culture* (Baltimore: Johns Hopkins University Press, 1991).

5. See Hans-Georg Gadamer, "Kant and the Hermeneutical Turn," *Heidegger's Ways*, trans. John W. Stanley (Albany: SUNY Press, 1994), 55. Gadamer does not endorse this characterization but, instead, uses it as a way of capturing the apparent impossibility of the Heideggerian project on a conventional understanding.

6. Käte Bröcker-Oltmanns notes that the use of the term "ontology," in the title of these lectures, is "vague and accidental," since Heidegger would have used the term "logic," except that another course had already been scheduled under that title. See her comments in the "Editor's Epilogue," *Ontology: The Hermeneutics of Facticity*, by Martin Heidegger, trans. John van Buren (Bloomington: Indiana University Press, 1999), 88. Accidental though the circumstances surrounding the use of the term may be, Heidegger's own comments in the lectures, as well as the course of his thinking elsewhere, make clear that his use of the term is far from vague and, in regard to the matters at issue, not at all accidental.

7. Van Buren points out that Heidegger takes logic and ontology to be interconnected. See Heidegger, *Ontology: The Hermeneutics of Facticity*, 91.

8. See Heidegger, "Letter on 'Humanism,'" 239.

9. Christina Lafont has argued, at length, for the problematic character of the hermeneutical transformation that occurs in Heidegger's thinking. See Lafont, *Heidegger, Language, and World-Disclosure* (New York: Cambridge University Press, 2000). Although I will not discuss Lafont's approach in any detail here, I would argue that her approach is limited by its failure to recognize the topological character of the hermeneutical transformation that Heidegger achieves as well as her more strongly analytic reading of the matters at issue.

10. Heidegger, *Ontology: The Hermeneutics of Facticity*, 1.

11. Heidegger's own critiques of ontology are undoubtedly connected with his increasing antagonism to traditional philosophical inquiry as this occurs from the mid-1930s onwards.

12. Heidegger, *Ontology: The Hermeneutics of Facticity*, 11.
13. Heidegger, *Ontology: The Hermeneutics of Facticity*, 6.
14. Heidegger, *Ontology: The Hermeneutics of Facticity*, 8.
15. Heidegger, *Ontology: The Hermeneutics of Facticity*, 7.
16. See van Buren's comments in Heidegger, *Ontology: The Hermeneutics of Facticity*, 102n1.
17. Heidegger, *Ontology: The Hermeneutics of Facticity*, 11.
18. Heidegger, *Ontology: The Hermeneutics of Facticity*, 1.
19. Heidegger, *Ontology: The Hermeneutics of Facticity*, 2.
20. Heidegger, *Ontology: The Hermeneutics of Facticity*, 14.
21. Which is why philosophy is always "of its time"—a point to which Heidegger gives special emphasis (see *Ontology: The Hermeneutics of Facticity*, 14).
22. See Heidegger, *Being and Time*, H37–38. The terms "hermeneutic," "hermeneutics," and "hermeneutical" do appear at other places in the work, but not in such a way that hermeneutics is made an explicit focus of discussion.
23. Heidegger, "A Dialogue on Language," *On the Way to Language*, trans. Peter D. Hertz (New York: Harper & Row, 1971), 29.
24. Plato, *Ion*, 534e—"[T]he poets are but the heralds/interpreters of the gods." See Heidegger, *Ontology: The Hermeneutics of Facticity*, 6; "A Dialogue on Language," 29.
25. Heidegger, "A Dialogue on Language," 29–30.
26. Heidegger, "A Dialogue on Language," 47.
27. Although the English "beckon" is certainly not an exact counterpart to the German *winken*, the etymology of the English terms suggests it may be more appropriate than may first appear. "Beckon," in its modern and older forms, is closely related to "beacon," a term that comes through Middle and Old English, as well as various Germanic forms, from the proto-Indo-European root *bha- meaning "to shine." See Eric Partridge, *Origins: A Short Etymological Dictionary of Modern English*, 2nd ed. (London: Routledge and Kegan Paul, 1959), 42. Such a derivation has obvious resonances in the Heideggerian context.
28. Heidegger, "A Dialogue on Language," 26.
29. Heidegger, "A Dialogue on Language," 40.
30. There is thus an essential indeterminacy that is present throughout Heidegger's thinking (where indeterminacy implies just such a multiplicity of meaning), as well as an inevitable self-referentiality in Heidegger's use of terms (as the use of *winken* itself beckons or hints). The indeterminacy and multiplicity at issue here is what I refer to in chapters 6 and 11 as "iridescence" (see also my *Heidegger's Topology*, 37, 249–50. The presence of such indeterminacy in Heidegger's work—which I would argue carries over into Gadamer's work also—is something Derrida largely ignores or overlooks (a point partly taken up in Hoy, "Forgetting the Text: Derrida's Critique of Heidegger").

31. Although the sense of "relation" at work here is one that must be approached with some care—as Heidegger warns: "We think of [relation] in the sense of relationship [*Wir denken an Beziehung im Sinne der Relation*]. What we know in that way we can identify in an empty, formal, sense, and employ like a mathematical notation. Think of the procedure of logistics. But in the phrase, 'man stands in a hermeneutical relation to the twofold,' we may hear the word 'relation' [*Bezug*] also in a wholly different way. In fact, we must, if we give thought to what was said." See "A Dialogue on Language," 32.

32. Heidegger, "A Dialogue on Language," 41. The characterization of the human as the one who "who walks the boundary of the boundless" is remarkably close to an earlier formulation by Georg Simmel, according to which "the human being is . . . the bordering creature who has no border." See Simmel, "Bridge and Door," *Simmel on Culture*, ed. and trans. David Frisby and Mike Featherstone (London: Sage, 1997), 170—originally published 1909. Simmel's essay contains elements that also seem to reappear in Heidegger, "Building Dwelling Thinking," *Poetry, Language, Thought*, trans. Albert Hofstadter (New York: Harper & Row, 1971), 143–61.

33. Heidegger, *Zollikon Seminars: Protocols, Conversations, Letters*, ed. Medard Boss, trans. Franz May and Richard Askey (Evanston, IL: Northwestern University Press, 2001), 181.

34. Perhaps most notably in P. F. Strawson, *Individuals* (London: Methuen, 1959), chap. 2.

35. Heidegger, "Hebel—Friend of the House," 100–101.

36. Again, see Heidegger, "Hebel—Friend of the House," 100–101.

37. The relation is thus not one in which either term is a sole foundation, but each "founds" the other—thus, the role of language in this regard does not imply any "linguistic idealism" as it is usually understood.

38. See Heinrich Ott's excellent discussion of the idea of the between and its relation to language in "Hermeneutic and Personal Structure of Language," *On Heidegger and Language*, ed. Joseph J. Kockelmans (Evanston, IL: Northwestern University Press, 1972). Ott's work is notable not only for the way in which it implicitly draws out the topology at work in Heidegger's account of language, but also because Ott is so strongly attuned to the hermeneutical as it appears in Heidegger's thought. See also Ott's comments in his "What Is Systematic Theology?," *New Frontiers in Theology*, vol. 1, *The Later Heidegger and Theology*, ed. James M. Robinson and John B. Cobb, Jr. (New York: Harper and Row, 1963), 77–114. Ott's work is especially significant in this context (but like that of Fell and Vycinas, also largely ignored by contemporary readers), not least because of Ott's own hermeneutical orientation, as well as the personal encouragement Heidegger appears to have given to Ott in developing his approach.

39. See Rudolf Carnap, "The Elimination of Metaphysics through Logical Analysis of Language," trans. Arthur Pap, *Logical Positivism*, ed. A. J. Ayer (Glencoe, IL: Free Press, 1959), 60–81—originally published 1932.

40. Heidegger remarks in the Le Thor seminar that it was through Hölderlin that he learned the uselessness of the attempt to coin new words (seemingly confirming Gadamer's claim that it was Hölderlin who first set loose Heidegger's tongue)—or more precisely, "only after *Being and Time* was the necessity of a return to the simplicity of language clear." See Heidegger, *Four Seminars*, 51. One might argue that Heidegger's well-known claims regarding a "neediness" of language (something partially addressed in this same passage from *Four Seminars*) is mistaken if it is taken to imply a limitation in the capacity of language adequately to speak, since this would seem to contradict the character of language as always essentially disclosive. Gadamer may, on such an account, be said to be more in accord with the hermeneutical mode of thinking that appears here through the trust he retains in the capacity of language adequately to speak and to say.

41. Heidegger, "A Dialogue on Language," 42.

Chapter Five

1. See Heidegger, "A Dialogue on Language," 12.

2. See Stuart Elden, "Heidegger's Hölderlin and the Importance of Place," *Journal of the British Society for Phenomenology* 30 (1999): 258–74. Heidegger's increasing engagement with Hölderlin in the thirties is undoubtedly tied to his disengagement from Nazism, but, at the same time, it involves him in attempting to rethink terms that were also at issue in that engagement—including the idea of the German and of Germany. It is only with the end of the war, in the mid- to late forties, that Heidegger's thinking begins to grapple more directly and explicitly with the topological themes that had already emerged as explicit in the thirties, but that were often still addressed, at the earlier stage, in terms that invoked the nation and the people and their role within a certain form of the history of being.

3. Heidegger, "Letter on 'Humanism,'" 239.

4. See Heidegger, "Letter on 'Humanism,'" 257–58.

5. Heidegger lectured on Hölderlin's "The Rhine" and "Germania" in 1934–35; see Heidegger, *Hölderlin's Hymns "Germania" and "The Rhine,"* trans. William McBeill and Julia Ireland (Bloomington: Indiana University Press, 2014). First appearing in 1936, "Hölderlin and the Essence of Poetry" is derived from these lectures—see *Elucidations of Hölderlin's Poetry*, trans. Keith Hoeller (Amherst, NY: Humanity Books, 2000), 51–66. In 1939, Heidegger presented what later appeared as the essay on Hölderlin's "'As When on a Holiday . . . ,'" in *Elucidations of Hölderlin's Poetry*, 67–100. In 1941–42, he lectured on Hölderlin's "'Remembrance,'" an essay derived from this lecture appearing in 1943, and later published in Heidegger, *Hölderlin's Hymne "Andenken," Gesamtausgabe*, vol. 52. In 1942–43, he lectured on Hölderlin's "The Ister," published in *Hölderlin's*

Hymn "The Ister." And, in 1943, he gave a speech in Freiburg on Hölderlin's "Homecoming/To Kindred Ones" to mark the centenary of Hölderlin's death, published in *Elucidations of Hölderlin's Poetry*, 23–50. Heidegger was, of course, familiar with Hölderlin long before the lectures of the 1930s, having been an avid reader of the poet in his schooldays—see Heidegger, *Frühe Schriften, Gesamtausgabe*, vol. 1, ed. Friedrich-Wilhelm von Herrmann (Frankfurt: Klostermann, 1978), 57–59—and finding a renewed enthusiasm for him during his period of military service in the last years of the First World War.

6. Several other essays also testify to Heidegger's ongoing engagement with Hölderlin. Especially notable in this regard is "'. . . Poetically Man Dwells . . . ,'" *Poetry, Language, Thought*, trans. Albert Hofstadter (New York: Harper and Row, 1971), 211–29, in which the idea of "the house of being" is taken up in slightly different terms from those at work in the "Letter on 'Humanism.'" In addition, Hölderlin is the focus for Heidegger's thinking in "Hölderlin's Earth and Heaven," presented in 1959, and "The Poem," from 1968, both in *Elucidations of Hölderlin's Poetry*, 175–208 and 209–20, respectively.

7. Heidegger, "Letter on 'Humanism,'" 254.

8. Heidegger, "'. . . Poetically Man Dwells . . . ,'" 220.

9. Heidegger, "'. . . Poetically Man Dwells . . . ,'" 221.

10. Underlying both the English "dimension" and the German *Dimension* is the Latin *dimensio* ("measurement"), which, in turn, derives from *dimetiri* ("to measure out"), and so from *metiri* ("to measure"). The connection Heidegger makes here between dimension and measure is thus rooted in the terms themselves.

11. Heidegger, "'. . . Poetically Man Dwells . . . ,'" 227. The "building" at issue here is the same "building" that is at issue in "Building Dwelling Thinking," 143–161, but which is here revealed as the taking of measure. It is worth noting that in the "Letter on 'Humanism,'" "building" also appears, although there it is thinking that "builds upon the house of being." See Heidegger, "Letter on 'Humanism,'" *Pathmarks*, 272.

12. Heidegger, "The Nature of Language," *On the Way to Language*, 107.

13. Heidegger, "Hebel—Friend of the House," 100–101.

14. One might argue that this is indeed the very essence of spatiality, and it is largely what leads Günter Figal to argue for the spatial (or a mode of the spatial—what Figal calls "hermeneutical space") as central to the possibility of hermeneutical experience. See Figal, *Objectivity: The Hermeneutical and Philosophy*, trans. T. D. George (Albany: SUNY Press, 2010), 121–53. Figal, however, sees language as a "dimension" of this space, along with two other "dimensions," which he names as freedom and time—see *Objectivity: The Hermeneutical and Philosophy*, 155ff—whereas, on this account, spatiality or, perhaps better, dimensionality (which, as I argue here, is itself directly tied to relationality) emerges as belonging together with language. Additionally, one might argue that inasmuch as dimensionality is both active and open, so it is itself also closely bound to

a mode of temporality and freedom, although not in the sense that the latter two are "dimensions" of the former.

15. Thus, in "A Dialogue on Language," Heidegger talks of the "boundary of the boundless." See "A Dialogue on Language," 41; see also the discussion in chapter 4.

16. Inasmuch as relation encompasses difference, so one might argue that in language is also found the difference of all differences—including even the ontological difference. In Heidegger, *Basic Concepts*, trans. Gary E. Aylesworth (Bloomington: Indiana University Press, 1998), 41, Heidegger talks of the ontological difference—the difference between being and beings—as that in which we have "our domain of residence," prefiguring the idea of the "house of being," but, in so doing, also suggesting the ontological difference as itself given in and through language. In "Language," *Poetry, Language, Thought*, 202–10, Heidegger addresses language in direct connection with difference (here, written by Heidegger in hyphenated form as *Unter-Schied*), although in a way that goes beyond the thinking of the ontological difference alone, and which draws difference into the same constellation of terms that includes the between and the dimension.

17. This might be thought to mark another point of difference from Figal's account in *Objectivity: The Hermeneutical and Philosophy* (since, there, he argues that it is objectivity—"standing over and apart from"—that is basic to the possibility of encounter), except that Figal's notion of objectivity already carries a strong sense of activity within it.

18. Heidegger, *Identity and Difference*, 37–38.

19. Heidegger, "Letter on 'Humanism,'" 254–55.

20. Gaston Bachelard, *The Poetics of Space*, xxxii.

21. Heidegger, "Letter on 'Humanism,'" 272.

22. Heidegger, "Letter on 'Humanism,'" 272.

23. The line alluded to here was first composed in 1947 and appears in Heidegger, "The Thinker as Poet," *Poetry, Language, Thought*, 12: "[P]oetry that thinks is in truth the topology of Being." The phrase "topology of being," which is here understood as the saying of the place of being, also appears in "Seminar in Le Thor 1969," 41, at which point reference is also made back to "The Thinker as Poet" and to the short essay (from the same year as the seminar), "Art and Space," 305–9.

24. See Heidegger, *Being and Time*, esp. §§19–21.

25. Unconcealment is not some abstract "revealing" that belongs nowhere in particular, but is always itself placed. Indeed, the play of concealing and unconcealing belongs essentially to place—it is, one might say, the play of place itself.

26. The event is not to be understood as a merely temporal notion but, as itself, properly topological (as is evident in the discussion below). Joseph Fell describes the event as "the original understanding of place, clearing, abode, home, whole, or totality, worlded 'earth,' ground—all of which mean fundamentally the

same." See Fell, *Heidegger and Sartre: An Essay on Being and Place*, 204. The same is also true, I would argue, of the notion of the "moment" (das *Augenblick*), in *Being and Time*, of which the event can be seen as a development, and of the notion of the *kairos* (the "right" moment in the sense of an "opening"—in Greek, contrasted with *chronos*) that to some extent underpins both. One of the more general shifts in Heidegger's thinking (a shift that is essentially an explication of something already present in his thought) is towards an understanding of the topological character even of temporality itself. For more on the relation between *topos* and the idea of the moment, and between *topos* and time, see chapter 10.

27. Heidegger, "Hölderlin and the Essence of Poetry," 56.

28. "'... Poetically Man Dwells ... ,'" 214.

29. See Davidson, "Seeing Through Language," *Truth, Language, and History* (Oxford: Clarendon Press, 2005), 127–43.

30. In *Heidegger's Topology*, I summarily characterize the event as the "disclosive happening of belonging" as a way of drawing together the notions of "appropriating" (gathering/belonging), happening, and revealing/disclosing that all seem to be involved here—see Malpas, *Heidegger's Topology*, 217–18.

31. Heidegger, *Identity and Difference*, 37–38. The original translation, by Joan Stambaugh, has "appropriation" (or less often "event of appropriation"), rather than "event," for *Ereignis* (so e.g., "to think appropriation as the event of appropriation"), and, instead of "thinking receives the materials" (where "materials" translates *Bauzeug*), Stambaugh has "thinking receives the tools" (*Bauzeug*, *Bau*, and *bauen* all figure in the original passage, although preserving this in the English translation is difficult, and neither Stambaugh's nor the modified translation given here attempts to do this).

32. Heidegger, "'... Poetically Man Dwells ... ,'" 220.

33. Heidegger, "Letter on 'Humanism,'" 254.

34. Heidegger, "Art and Space," 306.

35. Heidegger, "Letter on 'Humanism,'" 254.

36. Heidegger, "'... Poetically Man Dwells ... ,'" 220.

37. Heidegger, "The Nature of Language," 106.

38. The date is significant. As is indicated in an earlier note, this is the same year in which Heidegger talks, in the Le Thor Seminar, of his thinking as a "topology of being," and the seminar makes direct reference to this essay in connection with the idea of such a topology.

39. Heidegger, "Art and Space," 307.

40. Heidegger, "Art and Space," 308.

41. "The question arises: Are places [*Orten*] initially and merely the result and consequence of making-space? Or does making-space acquire its peculiarity from the reign of gathering places? If this were the case, we would have to seek the peculiarity of clearing-away in the grounding of locality [*Ortschaft*] and ponder locality as the combined play of places." See Heidegger, "Art and Space," 308.

Chapter Six

1. See Heidegger, "The End of Philosophy and the Task of Thinking," *On Time and Being*, 57.

2. Heidegger, "Letter on 'Humanism,'" 272. See also Heidegger's comments in *Hölderlin's Hymne "Andenken,"* 39–40; in *Hölderlin's Hymn "The Ister,"* esp. 16–27 and 166; and in "The Nature of Language," 100.

3. Heidegger, *The Principle of Reason*, trans. Reginald Lilly (Bloomington: Indiana University Press, 1996), 48.

4. Joseph Kockelmans writes that "Heidegger's attitude in regard to metaphor is, at first sight at least, very paradoxical. For even though he claims that the language of the thinker cannot be interpreted in such a manner that metaphor would appear to be an important element in philosophical discourse, his later philosophy seems to be metaphorical through and through." See Kockelmans, "Heidegger on Metaphor and Metaphysics," *Martin Heidegger: Critical Assessments*, ed. Christopher Macann, vol. 3 (London: Routledge, 1992), 294.

5. Kockelmans comments that only Derrida seems to have taken this point seriously. See Derrida, "The Retrait of Metaphor," *Psyche: Inventions of the Other*, ed. Peggy Kamuf and Elizabeth G. Rottenberg, vol. 1 (Stanford, CA: Stanford University Press, 2007), 48–80. See Kockelmans, "Heidegger on Metaphor and Metaphysics," 306. Although, as I note below, Derrida's own position on the matter is also somewhat equivocal, nevertheless arguing for a retention of some form of metaphoricity in Heidegger's thinking.

6. Jean Greisch argues, though for somewhat different reasons than those at issue here, that the issue of metaphor is directly implicated with the issue of place, and, more particularly, with place as it appears in both the event [*Ereignis*] and in "discussion" or "placing" [*Erörterung*]—especially in "Language in the Poem," *On the Way to Language*, 159–60—as well as in the event [*Ereignis*]. See Jean Greisch, "Les mots et les roses: La métaphore chez Martin Heidegger," *Revue des sciences philosophiques et theologiques* 57 (1973): 433–55; and also Kockelmans's discussion of Greisch's reading in "Heidegger on Metaphor and Metaphysics," 302–6. The notion of "discussion" or "placing" [*Erörterung*] warrants some further comment here. The way Heidegger himself characterizes the notion explicitly draws out the topological implications present in the German. Thus, Heidegger asserts that the preliminary steps in any "placing" are the directing towards the place and then the heeding of the place. See Heidegger, "Language in the Poem," 159. Here, Heidegger's further characterization of place [*Ort/Ortschaft*] as *gathering* should also be noted. All of Heidegger's later thinking can be construed as just such a "placing"—both a directing towards, and a heeding of, place.

7. Heidegger, "Letter on 'Humanism,'" *Pathmarks*, 272.

8. In this sense, one might also be led to suggest (though perhaps rather polemically) that one of the problems with many readings of Heidegger, early

and late, is that *he is not read "literally" enough*—and this is especially true of the topological vocabulary that he so often employs. Thus, we do not take sufficiently seriously the language of place and space as indeed topological and spatial but instead treat it as if it really referred to something else. Ironically, this may even be true of some of Heidegger's own readings of that language, at least early on. The tendency to deploy topologically and spatial language, and yet to do so in a way that fails to attend to its topological and spatial character, is widespread in the contemporary literature on Heidegger, as well as in philosophy more generally, and across many other disciplines and areas of inquiry. Consequently, the turn towards space and place that is so frequently cited as a characteristic feature of contemporary thought does not represent a new engagement with space and place as such, but rather the deployment of a spatial and topological rhetoric in the service of already existing modes of critique that typically take the social and the political as their primary categories (almost always treating space and place as themselves political or social constructs). What thereby occurs is an obscuring and overlooking of the spatial and the topological in the very proliferation of an apparently spatial and topological language.

9. Derrida seems to take a view of literality along these lines, resisting the treatment of Heidegger's language, and especially its key terms, as reducible to something either purely literal or purely metaphorical, yet nevertheless retaining some sense of metaphoricity in the very withdrawal of metaphor—in its *retrait*. Derrida's approach seems partly to derive both from his own defense of metaphor within the discourse of philosophy—as developed in "White Mythology: Metaphor in the Text of Philosophy," *Margins of Philosophy*, trans. Alan Bass (Chicago: University of Chicago Press, 1982), 207–72—and from his rejection of the notion of that which is "proper to," with which he takes the literal to be at least connected (even if the two notions are not to be identified—see Derrida, "The Retrait of Metaphor," 49—he also seems to associate the "literal" and the "proper" with a certain sense of univocity or monosemy and the metaphoric with the polysemous). Yet, as Derrida recognizes, some sense of the "proper" does indeed remain at work in Heidegger's thinking (it is most obviously present in the notion of the event), even though Derrida contests this very notion (one is tempted to say that he contests its very "propriety"). Here, Derrida's stance on literality and, more importantly, on the "proper," like Heidegger's on metaphor, is itself directly related to a fundamental element within his more general philosophical position and to his critical engagement with Heidegger. What is at issue is the question of being. For Heidegger, the question of being is itself taken up in the question of language (and in the question of the *being of* language), whereas, for Derrida, it is in the face of the question of language that the question of being (especially inasmuch as this is indeed taken to be a question concerning *the proper*), to a large extent, falls away.

10. To some extent, one might argue that this is Kockelmans's view—see "Heidegger on Metaphor and Metaphysics," 316–17—except that Kockelmans makes no reference to the issue of literality but focuses only on the question of metaphor. It is also a view that can be seen as partly at work (and in a slightly different way) in Derrida's reading, and especially in his refusal of the notions of literality and propriety.

11. The idea of the metaphorical and the literal as correlative notions, rather than substantively distinct, seems to me to follow from Donald Davidson's view of metaphor as a particular use of language that always depends upon some prior sense of literality—a view that also involves the denial that there is anything that could be called metaphorical meaning. See Davidson, "What Metaphors Mean," *Inquiries into Truth and Interpretation* (Oxford: Clarendon Press, 1984), 245–64. Davidson's insistence on the primacy of literal meaning should not be construed as somehow turning metaphor into merely a secondary notion, but rather as preserving the character of metaphor as itself a distinctive *use* of language, and not as some special domain of *meaning* within language.

12. Heidegger, "Art and Space," 307. It is such listening that underpins Heidegger's frequent recourse to etymological consideration in his exploration of key terms and concepts. Attending to the origin of a term, and the meanings buried in its history and prior usage, is not only a way of freeing up our linguistic and conceptual preconceptions, but it is also a way of bringing to the fore connections that may otherwise remain implicit in the terms and concepts at issue.

13. See Malpas, *Heidegger's Topology*, 37 and 249–50.

14. Heidegger, *Holderlins Hymne "Andenken,"* 15.

15. See Young, *Heidegger's Philosophy of Art*, 103–4.

16. Given that the two are connected, and given also that Heidegger sees the covering over of this vibrancy as one of the features of modernity—as part of the "emptying out" of language that is a feature of the current age—then one might ask whether modernity is prone to an emptying out of language in the form of a striving for an impossible univocity, but also in the form of a concurrent and persistent *metaphorization*. That the two appear together, even though they also appear in tension with one another, may itself be taken to reflect a deeper contradiction within modernity itself.

17. Heidegger, *Hölderlin's Hymne "Andenken,"* 40.

18. One of the few discussions that directly takes up the idea of literality, as such, is to be found in Owen Barfield, "The Meaning of Literal," *The Rediscovery of Meaning and Other Essays* (Middletown, CT: Wesleyan University Press, 1977), 33–43. Barfield's approach is very different from that pursued here although not entirely incompatible. Following a line of thinking that can be seen as implicitly deriving from Samuel Taylor Coleridge, Barfield argues against the view that metaphor can be seen as arising out of literality (or out of what

he calls the "born literal") and for a view of the fundamental relation of human beings to their world as essentially figurative. One might argue that the rethought conception of the literal advanced here—especially when connected with the idea of the image as developed below (here Bachelard's position is particularly noteworthy)—provides an alternative way of arriving at a similar conclusion to Barfield's, even though in very different terms.

19. See Heidegger's discussion of Trakl's "A Winter Evening" in "Language," *Poetry, Language, Thought*, esp. 198–202.

20. This seems to be present even in Kockelmans's discussion, where the metaphoric and the figurative are treated as roughly equivalent. See "Heidegger on Metaphor and Metaphysics," esp. 297–98. As we shall see in the discussion that follows, however, there is good reason to distinguish these and to treat metaphor as merely one form of figuration, and even to consider the possibility that the figurative and the literal may overlap.

21. See Bachelard, introduction to *The Poetics of Space*, xi–xxxv.

22. Heidegger, "Letter on 'Humanism,'" 272.

23. Heidegger, *Hölderlin's Hymn "The Ister,"* esp. 16–27 and 166.

24. Heidegger, *Hölderlin's Hymne "Andenken,"* 40.

25. Thus, in the discussion that immediately precedes Heidegger's rejection of the "masterkey of all poetics," he directly connects image, symbol, and the movement away from things: "We are tempted to say that Sun and wind are given as natural signs, and this then means something else: they are symbols. In talking and thinking in this way, we assume that the 'Sun' and 'Wind' are known in themselves. We believe that even earlier nations and peoples first came to know the 'Sun' and 'Moon' and 'Wind,' and then, in addition, used these alleged appearances of Nature as images for some world beyond." See Heidegger, *Hölderlin's Hymne "Andenken,"* 39–40.

26. There is an intriguing issue that begins to emerge here, though it cannot be pursued in this discussion, concerning the extent to which Heidegger's antagonism towards the image as symbolic marks an important point of divergence between his position and that of those who take the symbolic image as a central theme—exemplified, perhaps most notably, by Aby Warburg, but also Ernst Gombrich, and perhaps even Walter Benjamin—or at least where it is taken as a theme that extends beyond the confines of cultural history into philosophy and ontology.

27. Heidegger, *Hölderlin's Hymne "Andenken,"* 40.

28. Heidegger, "The Nature of Language," *On the Way to Language*, 82

29. Heidegger, "'. . . Poetically Man Dwells . . . ,'" 225–26.

30. It is just such a rethought conception of metaphor that is to be found in Davidson's "What Metaphors Mean," in which metaphor is a use of language (and not a type of meaning) directed at the opening up of an image.

31. Greisch argues that Heidegger implicitly retains a commitment to a rethought conception of metaphor even as he also rejects metaphor—see Greisch, "Les mots et les roses: La métaphore chez Martin Heidegger"—although Greisch's account moves in a somewhat different direction from that suggested here.

32. Gadamer says of Heidegger that he was a thinker "who sees" and whose thinking took the form, not of a linear progression of ideas, but something more like a spatial exploration approaching the same thing from different angles and directions. See Gadamer, "Martin Heidegger—75 Years," *Heidegger's Ways*, trans. John W. Stanley (Albany: SUNY Press, 1994), 17. For Bachelard, of course, there is a clear sense in which thinking is essentially based in the image—the image, for him, "stems from the logos." See Bachelard, *The Poetics of Space*, xix.

33. See Heidegger, *What Is Called Thinking?*, 44–45; on the connection between representations and images or pictures, see "The Age of the World Picture," *The Question Concerning Technology and Other Essays*, especially 128–34, and 149–50. For more on the issue of representational thinking, see chapters 7 and 8.

34. Bachelard, *The Poetics of Space*, xv.

35. Bachelard, *The Poetics of Space*, xvi, xix.

36. Bachelard, *The Poetics of Space*, xii.

37. Hans-Georg Gadamer, "Reflections on My Philosophical Journey," *The Philosophy of Hans-Georg Gadamer*, ed. Lewis Edwin Hahn, the Library of Living Philosophers (Chicago: Open Court, 1997), 46.

38. Heidegger, "'. . . Poetically Man Dwells . . . ,'" 216.

39. For an exploration of one mode of topology within English literature, see Seamus Heaney, "The Sense of Place," 131–49; for another such exploration (one that is both more far-reaching and attuned to Heidegger), see Kenneth White, *The Wanderer and His Charts: Exploring the Fields of Vagrant Thought and Vagabond Beauty* (Edinburgh: Polygon, 2010). Heaney is a focus for some of my discussion in *Place and Experience*, 2nd ed. (London: Routledge, 2018). On White—and some of the themes explored above—see Malpas, "Between Hegel and the Chinese Gulls," in Malpas and White, *The Fundamental Field: Thought, Poetics, World*, part 2.

40. See Heidegger, "Hölderlin and the Essence of Poetry," *Elucidations of Hölderlin's Poetry*, 60.

41. The essay—"Die Sprache im Gedicht"—has the subtitle "Eine Erörterung von Georg Trakls Gedicht," *Unterwegs zur Sprache*.

42. Heidegger, "Die Sprache im Gedicht," 37. The passage begins: "Originally the word 'place' [*Ort*] meant the point of a spear [*Spitze des Speers*]. In it everything comes together. The place gathers unto itself, in the highest and in the extreme. Its gathering power penetrates and pervades everything." The translation here differs from that given in *On the Way to Language*, which

compresses the first two sentences, omitting the reference to the spear, to give: "Originally the word 'site' suggests a place in which everything comes together, is concentrated." See "Language in the Poem," 159–60. It is worth noting the way in which the English translation here itself serves to obscure the thematization of place—exemplifying the more general tendency to ignore or overlook the topological (whether in Heidegger's work or elsewhere).

Chapter Seven

1. David Hume, *A Treatise of Human Nature*, 2nd ed., ed. L. A. Selby-Bigge, rev. P. H. Nidditch (Oxford: Clarendon Press, 1978), bk. 2, part 3, sec. iii, 413.

2. Peter Singer, "Ethics and Intuitions," *Journal of Ethics* 9 (2005): 331–52.

3. Paul Bloom, *Against Empathy: The Case for Rational Compassion* (New York: HarperCollins, 2016).

4. Matthew Ratcliffe, "Heidegger's Attunement and the Neuropsychology of Emotion," *Phenomenology and the Cognitive Sciences* 1 (2002): 294–95.

5. See also Matthew Ratcliffe, "Why Mood Matters," *Cambridge Companion to Being and Time*, ed. Mark Wrathall (Cambridge: Cambridge University Press, 2013), 157–76; Ratcliffe, "The Feeling of Being," *Journal of Consciousness Studies* 12 (2005): 45–63; and Ratcliffe, *Feelings of Being: Phenomenology, Psychiatry and the Sense of Reality* (Oxford: Oxford University Press, 2008).

6. See Hubert Dreyfus, *Being-in-the-World: A Commentary on Heidegger's Being and Time, Division I* (Cambridge, MA: MIT Press, 1990); and John Haugeland, *Dasein Disclosed: John Haugeland's Heidegger*, ed. Joe Rouse (Cambridge, MA: Harvard University Press, 2013).

7. The gendered treatment of rationality, and particularly the association of reason with the masculine, is the main theme of Genevieve Lloyd's *The Man of Reason: "Male" and "Female" in Western Philosophy* (London: Methuen, 1984).

8. Created by Gene Roddenberry, and starring William Shatner, Leonard Nimoy, DeForest Kelley, and Nichelle Nichols, the original series of *Star Trek* appeared on US television from 1966 to 1969. It has given rise to several subsequent TV series and films.

9. The emphasis on "evidence" being somewhat misleading since it is not evidence as such that is the issue, but certain *kinds* of evidence.

10. See "emotion, n.," *Oxford English Dictionary* (online), Oxford University Press, accessed December, 2020, https://www-oed-com.ezproxy.utas.edu.au/view/Entry/61249?rskey=GOJTbV&result=1. The word derives from both French and Latin origins. In contrast, "passion" is an older term, going back in English to the 12th or 13th centuries, and deriving, via French, from the Latin *pati* meaning, "to suffer." See "passion, n.," *Oxford English Dictionary* (online).

11. See Plato, *Republic*, bk. 4, esp. 436e–441c; *The Republic, Plato: The Collected Dialogues*, ed. Edith Hamilton and Huntington Cairns, Bollingen Series 71 (Princeton: Princeton University Press, 1963), 678–83.

12. See Antonio Damasio, *Descartes' Error: Emotion, Reason, and the Human Brain* (New York: Putnam, 1994).

13. It is common to treat emotions as distinct, for instance, from moods (a distinction relevant to the discussion below), on the grounds that emotions are of shorter duration and a more specific focus—moods being taken to be of longer duration and more diffuse. Such a distinction is not unreasonable, but it is neither precise nor absolute.

14. For an introduction to the field, see Barbara Rosenwein and Riccardo Cristiani, *What is the History of Emotions?* (Cambridge: Polity, 2018).

15. See Charles Darwin, *The Expression of the Emotions in Man and Animals* (London: John Murray, 1872).

16. See "emotion, n." *Oxford English Dictionary*. See also Partridge, *Origins: A Short Etymological Dictionary of Modern English*, in which "emotion" is dealt with under the entry for "move" ("move," para. 12, *Origins*, 419).

17. In this respect, the account here to some extent converges with that of Bennett Helm, *Emotional Reason: Deliberation, Motivation, and the Nature of Value* (Cambridge: Cambridge University Press, 2001). Jan Slaby points out the complementary nature of Helm's and Ratcliffe's accounts (despite what may initially appear as the differences between them). See Slaby, "Emotional Rationality and Feelings of Being," *Feelings of Being Alive*, ed. Joerg Fingerhut and Sabine Marienberg (Berlin: De Gruyter, 2012), 55–78.

18. See Hume, *A Treatise of Human Nature*, bk. 2, part 3, sec. iii, 413–18, esp. 415.

19. See, for instance, Georg Simmel, "Money in Modern Culture," *Simmel on Culture*, ed. and trans. David Fisby and Mike Featherstone (London: Sage, 1997), 243–54; see especially his discussion of what he calls the "blasé attitude." Simmel's account is focused on a set of psychological and mental states and their interconnection with social and economic phenomena. It thus deals with a more varied range of issues than are at stake here and at a very different level of analysis.

20. Thus, Ratcliffe argues for a class of feelings that may be distinct from emotions but are nevertheless, as one might say, existentially situating. See Ratcliffe, "The Feeling of Being," 45–63; and Ratcliffe, *Feelings of Being*. Ratcliffe's discussion of this matter arises explicitly in connection with the question as to the relation between emotions and bodily "feelings." As I have here taken an approach to emotions that treats them as a broad and somewhat indeterminate category, and as I have also emphasized the connection between emotion and bodily feeling, so I would both endorse Ratcliffe's re-evaluation of the character of

bodily feelings and argue that the distinction between emotions and such feelings is not itself clear or absolute. In addition, as I discuss later, my emphasis on the topological means that I do not take the bodily to be primary here; instead, I take it to be embedded in the larger topological structure of worldly situatedness.

21. See Heidegger, *Being and Time*, H133–34.

22. The etymology of *stimmen* and *Stimmung* connects these terms to the mouth—*Stimme* means "voice." See David Wellbery, "Stimmung," trans. Rebecca Pohl, *New Formations* 93 (2018): 6–45, first published 2003.

23. Heidegger, *Being and Time*, Stambaugh/Schmidt, H134.

24. Ratcliffe remarks that "Heidegger does not explicitly distinguish the categories 'mood' and 'emotion.'" See Ratcliffe, "Why Mood Matters," 162.

25. Martin Heidegger, *The Fundamental Concepts of Metaphysics: World, Finitude, Solitude*, trans. William McNeill and Nicholas Walker (Bloomington: Indiana University Press, 1995), 67.

26. Heidegger, *The Fundamental Concepts of Metaphysics*, 65.

27. Martin Heidegger, "Will as Affect, Passion, and Feeling," *Nietzsche*, trans. David Farrell Krell, bk. 1, vols. 1 and 2 (New York: Harper & Row, 1984), 1:44–53.

28. Heidegger, "Will as Affect, Passion, and Feeling," *Nietzsche*, 1:45.

29. Heidegger, *Being and Time*, Stambaugh/Schmidt, H138.

30. Heidegger, "Will as Affect, Passion, and Feeling," *Nietzsche*, 1:49.

31. Heidegger, "Will as Affect, Passion, and Feeling," *Nietzsche*, 1:52. Although "attunement" is here used to translate *Gestimmtheit* rather than *Stimmung*, both terms have the same root.

32. Heidegger, "Will as Affect, Passion, and Feeling," *Nietzsche*, 1:51.

33. Heidegger, "Will as Affect, Passion, and Feeling," *Nietzsche*, 1:51.

34. Heidegger, *Being and Time*, Stambaugh/Schmidt, H134, see also H135, H137, H139.

35. Heidegger, *The Fundamental Concepts of Metaphysics*, 66–67. Heidegger also characterizes attunements as "in each case already there, so to speak, *like an atmosphere* in which we first immerse ourselves in each case and which attunes us through and through . . . [emphasis added]," *The Fundamental Concepts of Metaphysics*, 67.

36. Heidegger, *Being and Time*, Stambaugh/Schmidt, H137.

37. At the end of the section on "Feeling, Passion, and Affect," in the Nietzsche lectures, Heidegger comments that, when judged "by the customary theories of knowledge and consciousness," the Nietzschean understanding of will as feeling "is an emotional one [*sei ein emotionaler*], conceived in terms of our emotional lives, our feelings, and . . . therefore ultimately a biological notion." See Heidegger, "Will as Affect, Passion, and Feeling," *Nietzsche*, 1:45. It might be thought that this indicates that Heidegger takes emotion to be a biological notion. Yet, of course, this is only so on the basis of the same sorts of

"customary theories" against which Heidegger is clearly setting his own account. That emotion is mentioned at all, here, indicates that it is already part of that same constellation to which belong feeling, passion, and affect, but it does not indicate that emotion is to be singled out as *only* or *primarily* a psychological or biological notion (only that it is commonly construed in that way).

38. Heidegger, "Will as Affect, Passion, and Feeling," in *Nietzsche*, 1:45.

39. "Man is not a rational creature who also wills, and addition to thinking and willing, is equipped with feelings . . . [R]ather the state of feeling is original, although in such a way that thinking and willing belong together with it." See Heidegger, "Will as Affect, Passion, and Feeling," *Nietzsche*, 1:51.

40. See Ratcliffe, "Heidegger's Attunement and the Neuropsychology of Emotion," 295.

41. R. J. Dolan, "Emotion, Cognition, and Behavior," *Science* 298 (2002): 1191–94.

42. See Ratcliffe, "Heidegger's Attunement and the Neuropsychology of Emotion," 300–6.

43. See Otto Bollnow, *Das Wesen der Stimmungen* (Frankfurt: Klostermann, 1941).

44. Bollnow, *Human Space*, translated by Christine Shuttleworth (London: Hyphen Press, 2011), 216–17. In this discussion Bollnow also refers both to Heidegger and to Binswanger.

45. See Hermann Schmitz, Rudolf Owen Müllan, and Jan Slaby, "Emotions outside the box: The new phenomenology of feeling and corporeality," *Phenomenology and the Cognitive Sciences* 10 (2011): 241–59 (includes Schmitz, "Entseelung der Gefühle," which first appeared in 2010). See also Schmitz, *System der Philosophie*, 5 vols. (Bonn: Bouvier, 2005), originally published 1964–80.

46. See Gernot Böhme, *Atmospheric Architectures: The Aesthetics of Felt Spaces*, trans. Tina Engels-Schwarzpaul (London: Bloomsbury, 2017); and Böhme, *The Aesthetics of Atmospheres*, ed. Jean-Paul Thibaud (London: Routledge, 2017).

47. Peter Zumthor, *Atmospheres: Architectural Environments, Surrounding Objects* (Basel: Birkhäuser, 2006). See also Tonino Griffero, *Atmospheres: Aesthetics of Emotional Spaces* (London: Routledge, 2016); and Juhani Pallasmaa, "Place and Atmosphere," *The Intelligence of Place: Topographies and Poetics*, ed. Jeff Malpas (London: Bloomsbury, 2015), 129–56.

48. Ratcliffe, "Why Mood Matters," 158.

49. Ratcliffe, "Why Mood Matters," 158.

50. Ratcliffe offers no positive account of the relation between mood and spatiality, not even relation to spatiality understood existentially, let alone to place. However, he does discuss the relation between mood and time. See Ratcliffe, "Why Mood Matters," *Cambridge Companion to* Being and Time, 172–74. In this respect, one might argue that Ratcliffe's account remains too much constrained by the framework of *Being and Time*.

51. To whom Ratcliffe refers (along with Sartre)—see "Why Mood Matters," 170, 171.

52. See Kant, "Concerning the Ultimate Ground of the Differentiation of Directions in Space," *Theoretical Philosophy*, 364–72.

53. A point famously made, even if with a more particular set of issues in mind, in Iris Marion Young, "Throwing Like a Girl: A Phenomenology of Feminine Body Comportment Motility and Spatiality," *Human Studies* 3 (1980): 137–56.

54. This reflects the way in which, in the structure of spatial engagement, situatedness and orientation involve both "objective" and "subjective" components, *including representations*. In relation to the latter, it is important to distinguish between representations as *having a role* in situated engagement and representations *as providing the basis for* that engagement (or as providing the mediating structures that make possible the engagement of a subject with a world). Although implicated in situated engagement, representations are not the primary basis for such engagement.

55. Heidegger, *Being and Time*, H108. See also Heidegger, "Seminar in Le Thor 1968," 32; see also the discussion in Heidegger, *Zollikon Seminars*, 86–87.

56. See Birmingham, *Hannah Arendt and Human Rights*, 29–30.

57. See Malpas, *Rethinking Dwelling*, chaps. 7 and 10.

58. The point here is exactly analogous to that which Heidegger makes, in his 1929 *Kantbuch*, regarding the relation between the character of human intuition as sensible (in other words, as finite) and as operating through the embodied senses: "Human intuition . . . is not "sensible" because its affection takes place through "sense-organs," but rather the reverse." See Martin Heidegger, *Kant and the Problem of Metaphysics*, trans Richard Taft, 5th ed. (Bloomington: Indiana University Press, 1997), 19.

59. Materiality is not something that belongs primarily to the natural sciences. As John William Miller points out, "when one turns to science, supposedly the antagonist of the mental or spiritual, does not come upon 'matter.' One has uniformities and equations expressed in nonmaterial terms. There are numbers, grams, second, centimeters—all 'units of science,' not material objects. Matter is as unknown to science as it was to the passive perceptions of Berkeley." Miller, *The Midworld of Symbols and Functioning Objects* (New York: W. W. Norton, 1982), 151.

60. See Malpas, *Rethinking Dwelling*, chap. 3. Just as important, if not more so, might be the work of Knud Løgstrup (especially given his own engagement with Heidegger); see esp. Løgstrup, *The Ethical Demand*, edited by Hans Fink., introduction by Hans Fink and Alasdair MacIntyre (Notre Dame: University of Notre Dame Press, 1997).

61. See Heidegger, "Letter on 'Humanism,'" 269–71.

62. "Post-truth Politics: Art of the Lie," *The Economist*, September 10, 2016, https://www.economist.com/leaders/2016/09/10/art-of-the-lie.

63. The extremity at issue here is not only evident in relation to emotion and reason—the discussion of "authenticity," in chapter 9, can also be seen as exploring another form of the extremity that characterizes contemporary modernity. Indeed, one might argue that one of the features of the contemporary world is an increasing shift towards more extreme or intensified forms of already existing tendencies and phenomena.

64. See Heidegger, "Will as Affect, Passion, and Feeling," *Nietzsche*, 1:45.

65. See Heidegger, "The Age of the World Picture"; and "What Are Poets For?," *Poetry, Language, Thought*, 124–27. Both essays are also included in *Off the Beaten Track*, 57–72, 200–41.

66. See "The Thing," *Poetry, Language, Thought*, 179, 181–83.

67. See *What Is Called Thinking?*, 26.

68. See "The Age of the World Picture," 129–32.

69. See the discussion in Heidegger, "A Triadic Conversation," 1–104 especially the discussion of representational thinking that takes up much of the first half ("A Triadic Conversation," 1–68). Here the argument does not lead to the abandonment of representational thinking, but rather a recognition of its limits and of the importance of a different and more fundamental kind of thinking.

70. The inquiry into a "basic attunement," *Grundstimmung*, for thinking that is a focus for the early part of the discussion in *The Fundamental Concepts of Metaphysics* is indicative of how Heidegger sees thinking, and even philosophy itself, as dependent on, rather than apart from, mood and emotion. Moreover, it is not only that lack of any proper attunement condemns thinking to "superficiality" (see *The Fundamental Concepts of Metaphysics*, 57), but that without *some* attunement there can be no thinking at all.

71. See especially "A Triadic Conversation," 68ff; See also the version of the conversation in "Conversation on a Country Path," 58–90.

72. The common complaint that Heidegger's thinking is "obscure" often seems to mean little more than that it is a mode of thinking that many readers find difficult to navigate—and that is probably inevitable given the radicality of that thinking and its deliberate attempt to destabilize conventional thinking. "Obscurity" is often counter posed to "clarity," as if the one were always a vice and the other a virtue. But neither obscurity nor clarity is a simple property of thinking or, better perhaps, of the texts in which thinking is expressed, but rather name the way texts appear to readers, and so are a function of what readers bring to texts as much as of what the text brings to the reader. The claim of clarity often made by philosophers in respect of certain texts is frequently a reflection of the way certain texts accord better with the conventions and presuppositions of the specific philosophical context in which they are taken up.

73. See *What Is Called Thinking?*, 208–44.

74. In *What Is Called Thinking?*, 203–4, Heidegger explicates *noein*, often translated as "thinking," in terms of "taking-to-heart," which he further connects with both thanking and remembrance. What is surely implied here also is a sense of affective disposedness, situatedness, and orientation.

Chapter Eight

1. See Stephen Pinker, *Enlightenment Now: The Case for Reason, Science, Humanism, and Progress* (New York: Viking, 2018).

2. A position set out most fully in "The Question Concerning Technology," *The Question Concerning Technology and Other Essays*, 3–35. Heidegger's thinking on technology develops across the course of his thinking, from scattered remarks in *Being and Time* (sometimes the analysis of equipmentality, *das Zeug*, in that work is seen as the precursor to the later account of technology, but it is a mistake to see technology as being at issue in the earlier discussion in the same way as in the later), to the talk of *Machenschaft* in various writings (including the *Notebooks*) from the 1930s and 1940s, to the detailed treatment in the later lectures and essays, including "Insight Into That Which Is" (the 1949 Bremen Lectures). See Heidegger, *Bremen and Freiburg Lectures: Insight Into That Which Is* and *Basic Principles of Thinking*, trans. Andrew Mitchell (Bloomington: Indiana University Press, 1994), 3–76.

3. In response to a question as to whether his position is too pessimistic, Heidegger responds: "Pessimism, no. Pessimism and optimism are positions that do not go far enough." See *"Der Spiegel* Interview with Martin Heidegger," *The Heidegger Reader*, 325.

4. Jean-Jacques Rousseau, *The Discourse Which Carried the Praemium at the Academy of Dijon in MDCCL. On this Question, Proposed by the said Academy, whether the Re-establishment of Arts and Sciences has Contributed to the Refining of Manners* (London: W. Owen, 1751)—first published 1750.

5. The critical appraisal of modernity evident in such writers is not restricted to Continental Europe but is also present, though in different form, in Mohandas K. Ghandi's attack on modernity as embodied in British colonialism, developed in *Indian Home Rule* (Phoenix, Natal: International Printing Press, 1908).

6. See Stephen Hawking, "AI Could Spell End of the Human Race," interview by BBC News, 2 December, 2014, accessed January 2021, https://www.bbc.com/news/av/science-environment-30289705/stephen-hawking-ai-could-spell-end-of-the-human-race; and "An Open Letter: Research Priorities for Robust and Beneficial Artificial Intelligence," Future of Life Institute (website), accessed January 2021, https://futureoflife.org/ai-open-letter—to which Hawking is a signatory.

7. See Mary Shelley, *Frankenstein; or, The Modern Prometheus* (London: Printed for Lackington, Hughes, Harding, Mavor, & Jones, 1818). Shelley's novel is also positioned as a key work within the larger English-language discourse about technology in Mark A. McCutcheon, *The Medium Is the Monster: Canadian Adaptations of Frankenstein and the Discourse of Technology* (Edmonton: Athabasca University Press, 2018). There is no doubt of the significance and influence of Shelley's work, but it is, in many ways, more focused on the moral failings of the scientist, Frankenstein himself, and the problematic character of the scientific hubris he embodies, than on the question of the nature and limits of the technological as such.

8. See Nicholas Maxwell, "The Enlightenment and the Romantic Opposition," *Science and Enlightenment: Two Great Problems of Learning* (Dordrecht: Springer, 2019), 9–20.

9. See for instance, Paul Virilio, *Bunker Architecture*, trans. G. Collins (Princeton: Princeton University Press, 1994)—first published 1975; *Speed and Politics: An Essay on Dromology*, trans. M. Polizzotti (New York: Semiotext(e), 2006)—first published 1977.

10. "Nearness," *Nähe*, is already present in *Being and Time*. See e.g., Heidegger, *Being and Time*, Stambaugh/Schmidt, H105: "*An essential tendency toward nearness lies in Dasein*" [emphasis in original]. See also, Emil Kettering, *Nähe, das Denken Martin Heideggers* (Pfullingen: Neske, 1987).

11. See "The Thing," 163.

12. Aaron James Wendland, Christopher Merwin, and Christos Hadjioannou, *Heidegger on Technology* (London: Routledge, 2019). The same is true in Don Idhe, *Heidegger's Technologies: Postphenomenological Perspectives* (New York: Fordham University Press, 2010). Andrew Feenberg's discussion, in *Questioning Technology* (London: Routledge, 1999), esp. 183–99, neglects most of the details of Heidegger's analysis, even as it complains about the abstraction and nostalgia of Heidegger's approach. Feenberg also seems to assume (partly as a result of his reliance on Albert Borgmann's work) that Heidegger's critique of technology is largely about the loss of *meaning* (despite the fact that meaning largely disappears as a significant category in Heidegger's later thinking) and pays no attention to any possible spatial or topological dimension.

13. See Andrew Mitchell, "Translator's Foreword," *Bremen and Freiburg Lectures*, xi; and Mitchell, *The Fourfold* (Evanston: Northwestern University Press, 2015), esp. 49–62. Despite its exclusive focus on Heidegger's later thinking, Mitchell's *The Fourfold* not only ignores the topological aspect of Heidegger's critique of technology, yet also pays no explicit attention to the topological character of the later thinking more generally. Mitchell's focus is on the relationality at work in the later thinking—and there is no doubt that this is important—but such relationality can only adequately be understood in the context of Heidegger's topology.

14. David Harvey, *The Condition of Postmodernity: An Enquiry into the Origins of Cultural Change* (Cambridge, MA: Blackwell, 1990), part 3, 201–326.

15. See Barney Warf, "Excavating the History of Time-Space Compression," *Geographical Review* 101 (2011): 435–46.

16. See Karl Marx, *Grundrisse: Foundations of the Critique of Political Economy (Rough Draft)*, trans. Martin Nicolaus (Harmondsworth: Penguin Books, 1973), 538–39.

17. This reflects the prominence of spatial and topological analyses in contemporary thought more generally—part of the so-called "spatial turn" (or occasionally the "topological" or "topographical" turn) in contemporary theory; although, once again, this is a prominence that characterizes approaches outside of philosophy more than within it.

18. See Reiner Schürmann's discussion of *Geviert* in *Heidegger on Being and Acting: From Principles to Anarchy*, trans. Christine-Marie Gros (Bloomington: Indiana University Press, 1987), 348n158.

19. This is very clear, in the case of *Wohnen*, from the discussion in "Building Dwelling Thinking," 143–61, esp. 155–58. In the case of *Gelassenheit*, it is evident from the situated character of the "Memorial Address" and the "Conversation on a Country Path," both included in *Discourse on Thinking*, in which the notion is most directly taken up. For more on *Gelassenheit*, see the discussion in chapter 9.

20. The Enlightenment is as much an ideal as it is a historical phenomenon—as historical, there are, of course, several enlightenments (rather than a single encompassing movement), and many different strands within it. Moreover, the criticism of the Enlightenment as it has come to epitomize, in the work of thinkers like Pinker, a certain optimistic progressivism need not entail a rejection of the Enlightenment in its entirety or of any and every ideal associated with it. There are also important questions about how the Enlightenment is itself to be understood from a topological perspective. See Charles W. J. Withers, *Placing the Enlightenment: Thinking Geographically about the Age of Reason* (Chicago: University of Chicago Press, 2007).

21. See Pinker, *Enlightenment Now*, 8–11.

22. The classic statement of this is found, of course, in Immanuel Kant, "An Answer to the Question: What Is Enlightenment?" (1784), *Practical Philosophy*, ed. and trans. Mary J. Gregor (Cambridge: Cambridge University Press, 2012), 11–22.

23. The first book to argue for such a claim, in detail, was Jeffrey Herf, *Reactionary Modernism: Technology, Culture, and Politics in Weimar and the Third Reich* (Cambridge: Cambridge University Press, 1984).

24. For Goebbels's account of the importance of the radio, see Josef Goebbels, "Der Rundfunk als achte Großmacht," *Signale der neuen Zeit: 25 ausgewählte Reden von Dr. Joseph Goebbels* (Munich: Zentralverlag der NSDAP, 1938), 197–207.

25. See Peter Linebaugh, "Ned Ludd & Queen Mab: Machine-Breaking, Romanticism, and the Several Commons of 1811–12," *Stop Thief! The Commons, Enclosures, and Resistance* (Oakland, CA: PM Press, 2014), 77–107. For a broader discussion of Luddism, in both its historical and contemporary contexts, see Steven E. Jones, *Against Technology: From the Luddites to Neo-Luddism* (London: Routledge, 2006).

26. See, for instance, Feenberg, *Questioning Technology*, 15. Feenberg also refers to Heidegger (and Habermas) as committed to an "unhistorical understanding" of essence in *Questioning Technology*, 201.

27. See Heidegger, "The Question Concerning Technology," 29.

28. Heidegger, *Being and Time*, Stambaugh/Schmidt, H42.

29. Heidegger, *Being and Time*, Stambaugh/Schmidt, H42.

30. In this respect, such a topological understanding draws on the idea of place, in the terms of Greek thinking, as both *topos* and *chora*.

31. The term is most directly translated as "ownmost." See the discussion in chapter 9.

32. See Davidson, "The Folly of Trying to Define Truth," *Truth, Language, and History* (Oxford: Clarendon Press, 2005), 19–20. Davidson talks of "concepts," but this should not be too quickly identified with talk of concepts or representations in the Heideggerian context.

33. Davidson, "On the Folly of Trying to Define Truth," 35. The strategy is "to trace the connections between the concept of truth and the human attitudes and acts that give it body."

34. On this basis, one might also revise one's understanding of the traditional "what is . . ." question, so that it too becomes a question that looks to relational or contextual connection rather than reductive definition.

35. See Malpas, *Heidegger and the Thinking of Place*, 199–224.

36. Of course, technology does not just happen of its own accord, as it were, and so there is an important story to tell about how the development of technological systems occurs through the way those systems connect with human actions and intentions. In this respect, there is a connection between technology and subjectivity (one that might well be developed with reference to Nietzsche's will to power), and so, too, between subjectivity and spatialization, but this does not mean that technology is, after all, grounded in subjectivity or is an outcome or function of subjectivity.

37. "Technology is a means to an end [and] . . . a human activity. The two definitions . . . belong together." See Heidegger, "The Question Concerning Technology," 4.

38. See José Ortega y Gassett, "Der Mythus des Menschen hinter der Technik" [The Myth of Humanity Outside Technology], *Mensch und Raum*, ed. Otto Bartning (Darmstadt: Neue Darmstaedter Verlangsanstalt, 1952), 111–17— presented by Ortega at the 1951 Darmstadt meeting, immediately following Heidegger's "Building Dwelling Thinking"; and Ortega y Gassett, "Man the

Technician," *History as a System and Other Essays Toward a Philosophy of History*, trans. Helene Weyl (New York: Norton, 1961), 85–161.

39. Heidegger, "The Question Concerning Technology," 12.

40. "The Question Concerning Technology," 12. In the *"Der Spiegel* Interview," 325, Heidegger insists that "technology . . . no longer has anything to do with tools," thereby indicating the extent to which his rejection of an instrumental view of technology almost certainly means that technology cannot be understood through an analogy with the account of equipmentality developed in *Being and Time*, §§15–16.

41. See Heidegger, "The Question Concerning Technology," 14, 21–22. Notice that, in the discussions of the matter here, Heidegger emphasizes the interdependence of science and technology (specifically of physics and its technical apparatus), but he also makes what is seen by some as an odd claim. He asserts that although "modern physical science" arose before modern "machine-power technology" (p. 22), modern technology precedes modern science in terms of its essence. This may indeed seem odd if read purely in terms of two discrete historical phenomena (although that this is not a historical claim is indicated precisely by the emphasis on essence), but it is not at all odd if it is read in terms of the way *spatialization*, which comes more fully into view only with the technological ordering of things as it develops in the eighteenth and nineteenth centuries, and which is a mode of ordering and not a mode simply of knowing or inquiring, is indeed already presaged in the science of the seventeenth century. Modern technology is thus the unfolding of a mode of ordering and revealing that is already present in modern science, but its unfolding is indeed not a consequence of science.

42. See, e.g., Heidegger, *Contributions*, 293–306.

43. On the empirical evidence for a connection between space and number, see the useful opinion article by Maria Dolores De Hevia, Luisa Girelli, and Viola Macchi Cassia, "Minds without Language Represent Number through Space: Origins of the Mental Number Line," *Frontiers in Psychology* 3 (2012): 466, accessed December 2020, https://www.frontiersin.org/articles/10.3389/fpsyg.2012.00466/full.

44. The displacement of place by space is a central part of the narrative in Edward S. Casey, *The Fate of Place: A Philosophical History* (Berkeley: University of California Press, 1997).

45. The work of Michel Foucault's work is particularly relevant here, especially the later writings and lectures on governmentality. See, for instance, *Security, Territory, Population: Lectures at the Collège de France, 1977–1978*, trans. Graham Burchell (New York: St. Martin's Press, 2007). The close relationship between Heidegger's topological thinking and the emphasis on space and place that appears in Foucault is explored in Stuart Elden, *Mapping the Present: Heidegger, Foucault, and the Project of a Spatial History* (London: Continuum, 2001).

46. Although, in his discussion in "The Question Concerning Technology," Heidegger seems to focus on technology as exemplified by the industrial technology that starts to appear in the eighteenth century (as already indicated in a previous note), in the "Memorial Address," it is quite clear that he sees forms of modern planning and organization as no less a part of modern technology than are radio, television, and the atomic bomb. See Heidegger, "Memorial Address," 48–52. Does Heidegger's thinking of technology shift between the 1950 essay and the 1955 address? The fact that Heidegger also talks of the of "human resources" and "the supply of patients for a clinic," in "The Question Concerning Technology" (see p. 18), suggests that he already has in mind, in 1950, the way *Gestell* plays out in organizational practices and structures, and it would probably be surprising if he did not. But whether Heidegger does shift his thinking on this matter is not a question of great significance. It would certainly be mistaken to suppose that Heidegger's thinking did not exhibit changes or shifts, or even mistakes and inconsistencies. Heidegger is no different, in this respect, from any other thinker.

47. Heidegger, "Memorial Address," 50.

48. On the importance of the numerical and calculative, see Stuart Elden, *Speaking against Number: Heidegger, Language, and the Politics of Calculation* (Edinburgh: Edinburgh University Press, 2006), esp. 121–38, where Elden makes explicit connections to issues of space and place.

49. See Heidegger, "The Question Concerning Technology," 20.

50. In this context, however, the etymology of the English "frame" is worth noting since it comes from a set of older terms associated with notions of use and usefulness or the making ready of things for use. See, for instance, the entry in Eric Partridge, *Origins: A Short Etymological Dictionary of Modern English*, 233. In this respect, the translation of *Gestell* as "enframing" or "framework" captures something not explicitly captured in the translation as "positionality." In earlier times, a "frame" could also mean a machine, particularly of the sort used in textile production. Thus, the "machine breakers" of the early nineteenth century—the original Luddites—were also "frame-breakers."

51. Heidegger, "The Question Concerning Technology," 16.

52. Feenberg, *Questioning Technology*, 195.

53. Feenberg, *Questioning Technology*, 196.

54. See especially, Hubert Dreyfus and Charles Spinosa, "Highway Bridges and Feasts: Heidegger and Borgmann on How to Affirm Technology," *Man and World* 30 (1997): 159–77.

55. See Jeff Malpas, "The Place of Mobility: Individualization, Relationality, and Contemporary Technology," *Mobile Technology and Place*, ed. Rowan Wilken and Gerard Goggin (London: Routledge, 2012), 26–38.

56. See Heidegger, "Seminar in Le Thor 1969," 61.

57. See Heidegger, "*Der Spiegel* Interview," 325.
58. See Heidegger, *Parmenides*, 82, 85.
59. On the primacy of failure in respect of governmental systems (but which is applicable to technological systems more generally), see Jeff Malpas and Gary Wickham, "Governance and the World: From Joe DiMaggio to Michel Foucault," *The UTS Review* 3 (1997): 91–108.
60. See, for instance, Paul Virilio, *The Original Accident* (Cambridge: Polity Press, 2007).
61. On the problematic character of neoliberalism, see, among many other works, Dominique Lévy and Gérard Duménil, *The Crisis of Neoliberalism* (Cambridge, MA: Harvard University Press, 2011).
62. One might argue that the Heideggerian point at issue here is just another way of talking about the ideological structures with which modern technology is embedded. Yet while ideology and ideology-critique do provide a way of taking up some of what is at issue here, what they leave out is precisely the ontological dimension that is required to ground any such critique and without which it can never escape a certain arbitrariness.

Chapter Nine

1. It is the poem that begins my discussion of place and the self in *Place and Experience*, 1–3, and to which I have also returned in discussions elsewhere. It is also briefly mentioned in chapter 3.
2. Seamus Heaney, "The Sense of Place."
3. William Wordsworth, "Michael," *Lyrical Ballads*, II: 203.
4. Guignon, "Authenticity," *Philosophy Compass* 3 (2008), 281. What Guignon presumably means here is that it is Heidegger who brings the term into common *philosophical* parlance since, as Guignon's own work indicates, "authenticity" was common in English well before the term was used in relation to Heidegger.
5. Lionel Trilling, *Sincerity and Authenticity* (Cambridge, MA: Harvard University Press, 1971), 93.
6. Trilling, *Sincerity and Authenticity*, 92.
7. Trilling, *Sincerity and Authenticity*, 94.
8. Trilling, *Sincerity and Authenticity*, 94.
9. Trilling, *Sincerity and Authenticity*, 131. The derivation is briefly alluded to in the *Oxford English Dictionary* (online) entry for "authentic": "ancient Greek αὐθέντης perpetrator," although the entry for "authentic" in the reissued first edition of the *Dictionary* contains a longer reference to the Greek that includes the essentials of Trilling's derivation (though without the reference to murder). See "authentic," *Oxford English Dictionary* (Oxford: Oxford University Press, 1933). Partridge gives a very short etymology that connects "authenticity" with

authentes in the sense of "one who acts on his own authority, a chief," in *Origins: A Short Etymological Dictionary of Modern English*, 33.

10. Including in contemporary management and leadership literature. See W. L. Gardner, C. C. Cogliser, K. M. Davis, and M. P. Dickens, "Authentic leadership: A review of the literature and research agenda," *The Leadership Quarterly*, 22, 1120–45—where there is a plethora of popular and more academic treatments. See also Katrina P. Jongman-Sereno and Mark R. Leary, "The Enigma of Being Yourself: A Critical Examination of the Concept of Authenticity," *Review of General Psychology* 23 (2019) 133–42, for a useful survey, not only of some of the difficulties with the idea of authenticity, particularly from a psychological perspective, but also of the various ways in which it has been deployed in psychological and behavioral research. Guignon provides a more philosophical overview, though oriented to his own reading, in his "Authenticity." The slippages in the idea of authenticity that are a major theme in the discussion in this chapter appear throughout much of the contemporary literature.

11. Charles Guignon, *On Being Authentic* (New York: Routledge, 2004), 161.

12. See Charles Taylor, *The Ethics of Authenticity* (Cambridge, MA: Harvard University Press, 1991); Bernard Williams, "From Sincerity to Authenticity," *Truth and Truthfulness: An Essay in Genealogy* (Princeton, NJ: Princeton University Press, 2002), 172–205. Guignon's "Authenticity" provides a survey of some of the larger body of literature here.

13. Guignon, *On Being Authentic*, ix. Taylor also asserts, as a key premise of his account, that "authenticity is a valid ideal." See Taylor, *The Ethics of Authenticity*, 23.

14. Guignon, *On Being Authentic*, 167.

15. As noted previously, the term is closely associated with the work of Meister Eckhart. For a useful introduction to Eckhart in his relation to Heidegger (and in the context of Heidegger's relation to mysticism), see Hans Ruin, "The Inversion of Mysticism—*Gelassenheit* and the Secret of the Open in Heidegger," *Religions* 10 (2019), https://www.mdpi.com/2077-1444/10/1/15?type=check_update&version=1, accessed October 2021. *Gelassenheit* is employed by Heidegger as a key term in the "Memorial Address" and "Conversation on a Country Path about Thinking" (and in the original "A Triadic Conversation"). The term "releasement" is introduced by Guignon into his discussion early on (as "self-loss or releasement")—*On Being Authentic*, 5—where it is set against authenticity characterized as "enownment" (the latter being the term Guignon uses for *Eigentlichkeit*). See, *On Being Authentic*, 7.

16. Guignon, *On Being Authentic*, 167.

17. *The Prelude* (named as such by Wordsworth's wife, Mary) was intended as the introduction to Wordsworth's great unfinished work, *The Recluse*.

18. See especially Geoffrey Hartmann, "A Poet's Progress: Wordsworth and the *Via Naturaliter Negativa*," *Modern Philology* 59 (1962): 214–24; the essay also forms a central part of Hartmann, *Wordsworth's Poetry, 1787–1814* (New

Haven, CT: Yale University Press, 1964). Guignon refers (*On Being Authentic*, chap. 4, n12) to another of Hartmann's essays, "The Romance of Nature and the Negative Way," *Romanticism and Consciousness: Essays in Criticism*, ed. Harold Bloom (New York: Norton, 1979), 287–305. Jonathan Bate points to the connection to Paul de Man—specifically to de Man, "Intentional Structure of the Romantic Image," first published in 1960, and reprinted in De Man, *The Rhetoric of Romanticism* (New York: Columbia University Press, 1984), 1–17. See Bate, *Romantic Ecology: Wordsworth and the Environmental Tradition* (London: Routledge, 1991), 7–8. Hartman's reading, in conjunction with that of Harold Bloom, is one that aimed, as Jonathan Bate puts it, "to bring philosophy, and in particular that philosophical tradition which ran from Kantian idealism to Husserlian phenomenology, to the centre of Romantic studies." See Bate, *Romantic Ecology*, 7.

19. Guignon, *On Being Authentic*, 51.

20. Guignon, *On Being Authentic*, 65.

21. By way of contrast, see, for instance, E. D. Hirsch Jr., *Wordsworth and Schelling: A Typological Study of Romanticism*.

22. In Heaney's words, the Westmoreland landscape that appears here is "both humanized and humanizing." See Seamus Heaney, "The Sense of Place," 145.

23. Trilling, *Sincerity and Authenticity*, 11.

24. Although Guignon does say that what is crucial about authenticity "is not just the intensity or fervour of the expression it carries with it." See *On Being Authentic*, 158.

25. Guignon, *On Being Authentic*, 156–57.

26. Guignon, *On Being Authentic*, 157–63.

27. Guignon, *On Being Authentic*, 158.

28. *Hamlet*, 1.3.

29. Hence the appearance of the discussion of authenticity, in Williams, "From Sincerity to Authenticity," *Truth and Truthfulness*.

30. Trilling, *Sincerity and Authenticity*, 93.

31. The entry for "authentic" in the *Oxford English Dictionary* (online) thus includes, among various senses, "Genuine; not feigned or false. Now the usual sense . . . Of a document, artefact, artwork, etc.: having the stated or reputed origin, provenance, or creator; not a fake or forgery," and the entry in the reissued first edition of the *Dictionary* includes the following: "a. OF. *authentique* (13th c.), ad Latin *authentic-us*, a. Gr. αὐθεντικύς 'of first-hand authority, original,' f. αὐθεντία 'original authority,'" at the same time connecting back to "αὐθέντης 'one who does a thing himself, a principal, a master, an autocrat.'"

32. See, for instance, Simon Feldman, *Against Authenticity: Why You Shouldn't Be Yourself* (Lanham, MD: Lexington Books, 2014).

33. I would argue, therefore, that there is no viable task that corresponds to a genuine *rethinking* of authenticity. Such rethinking can never take the form

merely of a stipulative redefinition, but must always be a turn back to, hence a retrieval of, something significant that is already present but is obscured or forgotten. Rethinking is, as noted elsewhere, a matter of the overcoming of forgetting—of recollection. Perhaps, if we follow Trilling, however, then we could say that what is to be recollected or retrieved in relation to authenticity it is precisely its implication with extremity and exceptionality.

34. Guignon, *On Being Authentic*, 167.

35. Guignon, *On Being Authentic*, 167.

36. See especially Immanuel Kant's elaboration of this point in "Concerning the Ultimate Ground of the Differentiation of Directions in Space," 364–72.

37. See Gadamer, *Truth and Method*, trans. Joel Weinsheimer and Donald Marshall (New York: Crossroad, 2nd rev. edn., 1989), esp. 383–88.

38. See Heidegger, "Memorial Address," 49–57.

39. Something a little clearer, perhaps, in the German *Gelassenheit*, from *lassen*, let or allow, as well as *gelassen*, calm or calmly, than in the English "releasement."

40. See Malpas, *Rethinking Dwelling*, chap. 10 and epilogue.

41. See also the discussion in Ingo Farin and Jeff Malpas, "On Overestimating Philosophy: Lessons from Heidegger's *Black Notebooks*," *Journal of Aesthetics and Phenomenology* 4 (2017): 183–95.

42. See the cautious note appended to the first appearance of *eigentlich* in the Macquarie and Robinson translation of *Being and Time*, 24, n.3 in which the translators try to differentiate some of the senses at issue in the term, as well as to explain their use of "authentic."

43. Husserl, *Cartesianische Meditationen und Pariser Vorträge*, *Husserliana* vol. I, see esp. §44, ed. S. Strasseer (The Hague, Martinus Nijhoff, 1950); see also the English translation by Dorian Cairns, *Cartesian Meditations: An Introduction to Phenomenology* (The Hague: Martinus Nijhof, 1960). The original text was from 1929, appearing in French in 1931, but not in German until the 1950 *Husserliana* edition.

44. See Adorno, *The Jargon of Authenticity*, trans. Knut Tarnowski and Frederic Will (Evanston: Northwestern University Press, 1973); *Jargon der Eigentlichkeit: Zur deutschen Ideologie* (Frankfurt: Suhrkamp, 1964). Adorno's critique, the main thrust of which is repeated by a host of other commentators, is largely a rejection of the very project of ontological inquiry, whether in Heidegger or elsewhere, on the grounds of its concealed ideological character. Yet not only is that critique dependent on a set of highly contentious assumptions, but it is entirely unable to provide any account of its own grounds since any such account would be forced back to a set of considerations that must, in some sense, be ontological in character.

45. *Being and Time*, Stambaugh/Schmidt, H130. The account of *Eigentlichkeit* given here is necessarily brief and is not intended to cover all aspects

of the term as it operates in Heidegger. For a fuller account, see, for instance, Stephan Käufer, "Authenticity," *The Cambridge Heidegger Lexicon*, ed. Mark Wrathall (Cambridge: Cambridge University Press, 2021), 7177. Like almost every discussion of authenticity in Heidegger, the adequacy of "authenticity" as a translation of *Eigentlichkeit* is effectively treated as a given in Käufer's discussion.

46. Heidegger, *Zu eigenen Veröffentlichungen*, §23a, ed. F.-W. von Herrmann, Gesamtausgabe 82 (Frankfurt: Klostermann, 2018), 58.

47. See Moore, *Eckhart, Heidegger, and the Imperative of Releasement* (Albany: SUNY Press, 2019), 4; see also Bret Davis, *Heidegger and the Will* (Evanston, IL: Northwestern University Press, 2007).

48. *Being and Time*, H145—in German, "Werde, was du bist!" See Nietzsche, *The Gay Science*, trans. Walter Kaufmann (New York: Vintage, 1974), 219, §270: "What does your conscience say? — 'You shall become the person you are.'" The original is in Pindar, 2nd Pythian Ode.

49. *Being and Time*, Stambaugh/Schmidt trans., H145n. In an outline for a proposed, but never taught, course on the philosophical foundations of medieval mysticism in the 1918–1919 semester at Freiburg, that would have focused on Meister Eckhart, in whose work *Gelassenheit* figures prominently, Heidegger writes of Eckhart's "fundamental conception": "[Y]ou can only know what you are." Heidegger, *The Phenomenology of Religious Life*, trans. Matthias Fritsch and Jennifer Anna Grosetti-Ferencei (Bloomington: Indiana University Press, 2010), 240. The comment seems to prefigure the connection indicated by the later annotated comment on the passage from *Being and Time*.

50. *Eigentlichkeit* is thus also tied to a fundamental questioning of one's own being. Such ontological questioning is just what is at issue in the fundamental ontology of *Being and Time* and connects directly to the idea developed in the earlier *Hermeneutics of Facticity* (explored in chapter 4) of the essence of human being as always given over to the task of self-understanding or self-interpretation—to an engagement with the possibilities of its own being (see Heidegger, *Ontology: The Hermeneutics of Facticity*, 11).

51. See "Conversation on a Country Path," 58–90; and "A Triadic Conversation," 1–104.

52. See also Heidegger, "The Principle of Identity," 37–38.

53. See especially, as noted above, Heidegger, "Conversation on a Country Path"; and Heidegger, "A Triadic Conversation."

54. Wordsworth, "Michael," *Lyrical Ballads*, II: 200.

55. Nostalgia is thus misunderstood when construed in terms of the pleasant, backward-looking feeling with which it is now all too commonly associated, but which is really a form of *mythophilia*.

56. See Bate, *Romantic Ecology*, 8.

57. Wordsworth, "Michael," *Lyrical Ballads*, II: 223.

58. John Kerrigan writes that "Wordsworth's entire career was shaped by his need to find a dwelling-place which would not fade." See Kerrigan, "Wordsworth and the Sonnet: Building, Dwelling, Thinking," *Essays in Criticism* 35 (1985): 50.

59. See, for instance, Christian Norberg-Schulz, *The Concept of Dwelling: On the Way to Figurative Architecture* (New York: Electa/Rizzoli, 1985). Massimo Cacciari has been one of Norberg-Schulz's strongest critics, as evident in "Eupalinos or Architecture," *Oppositions* 21 (1980): 106–16. Cacciari sees Norberg-Schulz as committed to a "nostalgic" attempt (I would argue that it is better characterized as utopic) to recapture a pure relation to place that is impossible, and that Cacciari argues Heidegger himself rejects.

60. See J. B. Jackson's analysis and critique of the idea of wilderness in his "Beyond Wilderness," in *A Sense of Place, A Sense of Time* (New Haven, CT: Yale University Press, 1994), 71–92.

61. Wordsworth, *The Prelude, or Growth of a Poet's Mind*, ed. Ernest de Selincourt, rev. Helen Darbishire, 2nd ed. (Oxford: Clarendon Press, 1959), 409.

Chapter Ten

1. Hannah Arendt, *Thinking*, in *The Life of the Mind*, one-volume ed., ed. Mary McCarthy (San Diego: Harcourt, Brace and Co., 1971), 1:1. See Heidegger, *What Is Called Thinking?*, trans. J. Glenn Gray (New York: Harper and Row, 1968), 159. Arendt's only deviation from J. Glenn Gray's translation is in the third line, which Gray gives as: "Thinking solves no cosmic riddles."

2. Arendt, *Thinking, The Life of the Mind*, 1:197–200.

3. See Malpas, "We Hyperboreans: Notes towards a Nietzschean Topography," 195–213.

4. See Arendt, "Walter Benjamin, 1892–1940," *Men in Dark Times* (New York: Harcourt Brace Jovanovich, 1968), 176 and 194.

5. See Arendt, *Thinking, The Life of the Mind*, 1:71.

6. See Arendt, *Thinking, The Life of the Mind*, 1:197. The story from Xenophon to which Arendt alludes is repeated by Rüdiger Safranski in direct response to the question, as he puts it: "Where are we actually when we think?" Safranski uses the story to contrast Socrates with Heidegger—the latter being described as "a particularly place-bound philosopher." See Safranski, *Martin Heidegger: Between Good and Evil*, trans. Ewald Osers (Cambridge, MA: Harvard University Press, 1990), 276–77.

7. Arendt, *Thinking, The Life of the Mind*, 1:197.

8. Arendt, *Thinking, The Life of the Mind*, 1:197.

9. Arendt, *Thinking, The Life of the Mind*, 1:199. This third point appears, to some extent, to underlie the first two. Arendt remarks that "these oddities

of the thinking activity arise from the fact of withdrawal," which is associated with a focus on the "essential," and "essences cannot be localized."

10. Arendt, *Thinking*, *The Life of the Mind*, 1:201.

11. See the discussion in Jeff Malpas and Günter Zöller, "Reading Kant Geographically: From Critical Philosophy to Empirical Geography," *Contemporary Kantian Metaphysics: New Essays on Space and Time*, ed. Roxana Baiasu, Graham Bird, and A. W. Moore (London: Palgrave Macmillan, 2012), 146–66.

12. See especially, Heidegger, "Art and Space," 305–9.

13. See Heidegger, *Being and Time*, §§19–21. Heidegger's account of existential spatiality, and the world of practical involvement with which it is associated, does involve notions of position (*Platz*) and region (*Gegend*), but these tend to operate within a larger structure of ends that itself seems embedded in the structure of temporality. In general, Heidegger's account of existential spatiality, although important, is not entirely consistent or fully worked out. See Malpas, *Heidegger's Topology*, 126–46. Peg Birmingham treats Heidegger's account of existential spatiality as essentially an account of Dasein's *embodiment*. See Birmingham, *Hannah Arendt and Human Rights: The Predicament of Common Responsibility* (Bloomington: Indiana University Press, 2006), 29–30. Birmingham's reading is an important corrective to the standard criticism that Heidegger neglects the body—something previously touched on in chapter 7—but it also indicates how existential spatiality already includes a more topologically oriented mode of thinking. If it is a mode of embodiment, and embodiment is certainly at issue, then it is a mode of embodiment extended into the world (Heidegger thus has an "extended" view of body, no less than of mind), in which the body is understood as a mode of placedness.

14. Arendt, *Thinking*, *The Life of the Mind*, 1:6, 1:31, 1:122, 1:190; see also "Personal Responsibility under Dictatorship," *Responsibility and Judgment*, ed. J. Kohn (New York: Schocken, 2003), 45.

15. See, for instance, the discussions in Richard Menary, ed., *The Extended Mind* (Cambridge, MA: MIT Press, 2010).

16. See "A Triadic Conversation," 22. The refusal of the distinction is not peculiar to this discussion alone.

17. See Eugene T. Gendlin, "Time's Dependence on Space: Kant's Statements and Their Misconstrual by Heidegger," *Kant and Phenomenology*, ed. Thomas Seebohm and Joseph Kockelmans (Washington, DC: Center for Advanced Research in Phenomenology and University Press of America, 1984), 147–60.

18. Arendt, *Thinking*, *The Life of the Mind*, 1:202.

19. Franz Kafka, "He: Notes from the Year 1920," *The Great Wall of China: Stories and Reflections*, trans. Willa Muir and Edwin Muir (New York: Schocken Books, 1946), 141. The passage in question is the very last in the series of brief stories, notes, and aphorisms.

20. See Hannah Arendt, *Between Past and Future: Eight Exercises in Political Thought* (New York: Penguin, 2006), esp. 7–14.

21. Arendt, *Between Past and Future*, 14–15. Peg Birmingham also refers to the essay "No Longer and Not Yet," *Essays in Understanding, 1930–1954*, ed. Jerome Kohn (New York: Schocken Books, 1994), 158–62, as another instance in which Arendt invokes this Kafkaesque notion of temporality. See Birmingham, *Hannah Arendt and Human Rights*, 17. However, the essay to which Birmingham draws attention (actually a review of the English translation of Hermann Broch's *Death of Virgil*) contains no direct reference to Kafka's parable, and it deploys the idea of the "no longer and not yet" in a way that connects only partially with the way past and future are dealt with in *The Life of the Mind*, or in *Between Past and Future*. It also does so in a way that seems deliberately ambiguous. So, for instance, the idea refers to the "empty space" that has arisen in the twentieth century with the loss of historical continuity (Arendt, "No Longer and Not Yet," *Essays in Understanding*, 158), to the past and the future as exemplified in the work of Proust and Kafka (159), and also to the "no longer alive and not yet dead" (161).

22. Arendt, "Preface: The Gap between Past and Future," *Between Past and Future. Eight Exercises in Political Thought*, 3.

23. Arendt, *Thinking*, *The Life of the Mind*, 1:210. The same line is repeated, along with the passage in which it is embedded, in *Between Past and Future*, 13.

24. Arendt, *Between Past and Future*, 13.

25. Birmingham, *Hannah Arendt and Human Rights*, 17–23.

26. Arendt, *Thinking*, *The Life of the Mind*, 1:204.

27. See Nietzsche, "Of the Vision and the Riddle," *Thus Spoke Zarathustra*, trans. R. J. Hollingdale (Harmondsworth: Penguin, 1969), part 3, 176–180.

28. Arendt, *Thinking*, *The Life of the Mind*, 1:204. The quotation is not directly referenced but appears to be from *Nietzsche I* (Stuttgart: Neske, 1961), 278. The passage appears in David Farrell Krell's English translation as: "That is what is peculiar to, and hardest to bear in, the doctrine of eternal return—to whit, that eternity *is* in the moment, that the Moment is not the fleeting 'now,' not an instant of time whizzing by a spectator, but the collision of future and past." See Heidegger, *Nietzsche*, trans. David Farrell Krell, 2:57. (Note that bk. 1 of Krell's translation—i.e., what is there designated as vols. 1 and 2—corresponds, in its entirety, to *Nietzsche I* in the original German.)

29. Arendt, *Thinking*, *The Life of the Mind*, 1:210.

30. Arendt, *Thinking*, *The Life of the Mind*, 1:85–86.

31. Arendt writes that "neither the word 'willing' nor the word 'thinking' occurs in Heidegger's early work before the so-called 'reversal' (*Kehre*) or 'turn-about' that occurred in the mid-thirties," adding "and Nietzsche's name is nowhere mentioned in *Being and Time*." See Arendt, *Willing*, *The Life of the*

Mind, 2:172. (Arendt's attached note cites Hildegard Feick, *Index zu Heideggers Sein und Zeit*, Tübingen: Niemeyer, 1961.) However, there is an especially pertinent mention of Nietzsche's name in *Being and Time*, §76, H396. There, Heidegger refers to the second of Nietzsche's *Untimely Meditations*, "On the Use and Disadvantage of History for Life," and to its threefold characterization of historiography. See Nietzsche, *Untimely Meditations*, trans. R. J. Hollingdale (Cambridge: Cambridge University Press, 1998), 57–124. Heidegger relates this directly to his own account of ownmost temporality, adding, "The beginning of [Nietzsche's] *Untimely Meditations* makes us suspect he understood more than he made known." The discussion of Nietzsche is followed immediately by a passage that essentially summarizes the character of ownmost temporality and its relation to Dasein, including the idea of the now or the *Augenblick*. There are few studies that consider the relation between Heidegger's account of temporality and Nietzsche's treatment of the *Augenblick*, but for one that does, and that also attends to some of the spatial and topological elements, see Rachel Aumiller, "Dasein's Shadow and the Moment of its Disappearance," *Human Studies: A Journal for Philosophy and the Social Sciences* 40 (2016): 25–41.

32. It is one of the notable features of Birmingham's account that not only does she draw attention to the way natality itself figures in Heidegger's discussion in *Being and Time* but that she does indeed make the explicit connection back to Heidegger's discussion, including his discussion of the *Augenblick* as well as of spatiality and temporality, when this is so clearly absent from Arendt's treatment in *The Life of the Mind*, as well as in *Between Past and Present*. See Birmingham, *Hannah Arendt and Human Rights*, esp. 28–33.

33. See Arendt, *Willing*, *The Life of the Mind*, 2:172–194, §15. Arendt reads the course of Heidegger's work as moving from an emphasis on "willing," in the early work, to "thinking," in the later.

34. See Heidegger, *Being and Time*, §§65–83.

35. See Heidegger, *Being and Time*, H427n13. See also Heidegger's comments in *The Concept of Time*, trans. W. McNeill (Oxford: Basil Blackwell, 1992), 1E, where he argues against eternity as relevant to the understanding of time.

36. Heidegger, *Being and Time*, H17; Stambaugh/Schmidt, 17.

37. Nader M. El-Bizri refers to Heidegger's "temporocentric interpretation of space"—see El-Bizri, "On kai khôra: Situating Heidegger between the *Sophist* and the *Timaeus*," *Studia Phaenomenologica* 4 (2002), 79–80.

38. The idea of such a "between" is denoted in Greek by *diastēma*. The term has an obvious spatial sense, meaning extension, distance, or dimension, and it thus appears at several points, for instance, in the discussions in Keimpe Algra, *Concepts of Space in Greek Thought* (Leiden: Brill, 1992). However, the term can also be used to refer to a *temporal* interval—as Anthony Preus notes in his *Historical Dictionary of Ancient Greek Philosophy* (Lanham, MD: Scarecrow Press, 2009), 86–87. The entanglement of spatial and temporal notions that

diastēma or "interval" exemplifies is a long-standing and widespread feature of philosophical thought.

39. Arendt, *Thinking, The Life of the Mind*, 1:211.
40. Arendt, *Thinking, The Life of the Mind*, 1:205–6.
41. Heidegger, *What Is Called Thinking?*, 244.
42. Heidegger, *Basic Concepts*, 78.
43. *Ereignis* and its verb form, *sich ereignen*, derive from an older term, *eröugnis*, meaning "what is shown," "what can be seen," which, like *Augenblick*, contains a reference to the eye—*Auge*. See Friedrich Kluge, *An Etymological Dictionary of the German Language*, trans. John Francis Davis (London: George Bell & Sons. 1891).
44. Fell, *Heidegger and Sartre*, 221.
45. See Arendt, *Thinking, The Life of the Mind*, 1:3–5, and also 179–80.
46. Arendt, *Thinking, The Life of the Mind*, 1:179–93 (chap. 3, §18, "the two-in-one.")
47. Arendt, *Thinking, The Life of the Mind*, 1:191.
48. Arendt, *Thinking, The Life of the Mind*, 1:187.
49. See Emmanuel Levinas, *Totality and Infinity*, 291. The limitation in Levinas's thinking, noted previously, is that it assumes (but never addresses) an essentially Cartesian understanding of spatiality. See again, the discussion in Malpas, *Rethinking Dwelling*, chap. 3.
50. See Plato, *Timaeus* 49a–52d, trans. Benjamin Jowett, *Plato: The Collected Dialogues*, ed. Edith Hamilton and Huntington Cairns, Bollingen Series 71 (Princeton, NJ: Princeton University Press, 1963), 1176–79.
51. See Birmingham, *Hannah Arendt and Human Rights*, 31.
52. Birmingham, *Hannah Arendt and Human Rights*, 33.
53. Birmingham, *Hannah Arendt and Human Rights*, 32.
54. Heidegger, "Hebel—Friend of the House," 100–101.
55. Heidegger, "Memorial Address," 45.

Epilogue

1. There is a clear sense of the teleological at work here, yet in a different sense from that which is normally taken for granted. Though the argument is too long to put here, it is a sense of *telos* as *topos*—or, perhaps more accurately, of the structure of the teleological as itself topological (the character of orientation is an instructive and relevant example).
2. See Thomas Sheehan, *Making Sense of Heidegger: A Paradigm Shift*, 231–48.
3. As was noted previously (in chapter 4), Heidegger remarks on this in one of the Le Thor seminars—see Heidegger, *Four Seminars*, 51.

4. See William J. Richardson, *Heidegger: Through Phenomenology to Thought*, Phenomenologica 13 (The Hague: Martinus Nijhoff, 1963).
5. See Arendt, *Willing, The Life of the Mind*, 2:172.
6. See Arendt, *Willing, The Life of the Mind*, 2:172–94, §15.
7. Sheehan, *Making Sense of Heidegger*, xiii.
8. The basic idea at issue here is at the heart of Donald Davidson's thinking, in which a similar interpretive (or implicitly hermeneutical) focus is also allied with a topological mode of thinking that remains in play even though it is never, by Davidson himself, brought directly to the fore—see my discussion in *Heidegger and the Thinking of Place*, chap. 10.
9. See the various discussions of this in Ingo Farin and Jeff Malpas, eds., *Reading Heidegger's Black Notebooks 1931–1941*.
10. Fell, *Heidegger and Sartre*, xiv.
11. See Heidegger, *Being and Time*, Macquarie/Robinson, esp. §38, H175–80.
12. Fell, *Heidegger and Sartre*, 266.
13. Fell, *Heidegger and Sartre*, 266.
14. Fell, *Heidegger and Sartre*, 238, quoted from Heidegger, *Identität und Differenz* (Pfullingen: Neske, 1957), 25, in the English edition, *Identity and Difference*, 33.
15. Fell, *Heidegger and Sartre*, 258.
16. The iridescence that belongs both to Heidegger's language and to language as such involves an irreducible equivocity or multivocity that is not merely linguistic, but is itself tied to an equivocity or multivocity *of being*. As indicated earlier, this equivocity takes the form of a unified multiplicity whose character as a unity is itself complex and thereby mirrors aspects of the specific form of equivocity (that of so-called focal meaning or *pros hen* equivocation) that Aristotle associates with being. The understanding of unity that appears here is central to much of Fell's discussion in *Heidegger and Sartre*—a topic that resurfaces briefly in chapter 9.
17. The phrase is used with a deliberate nod to the work of John William Miller, a key figure for Fell and discussed further in the discussion that follows here. Miller writes that "Language of all sorts is not the means of communication, but the actuality of communication" (*The Definition of the Thing with Some Notes on Language* [New York: W.W. Norton, 1980], 189). Here, however, language itself has to be understood in terms of its own actuality rather than its abstract conceptualisation. The primacy of act, and so of actuality, is a central theme throughout Miller's work.
18. Thomas Sheehan, "A Paradigm Shift in Heidegger Research," 193; and also, *Making Sense of Heidegger*, 136–38. Sheehan is certainly not alone in reading Dasein in this way, and the issue is discussed further in Malpas, *Heidegger's Topology*, 47–51; see also Fell, *Heidegger and Sartre*, 38–48. Although Fell distinguishes between the "there" and the "here," he is quite clear on the

topological character of Dasein, noting: "Dasein is place, and place is orientation," 48. There are passages in which Heidegger warns against treating the *Da* in terms of the "there" or "here," but when he does so, the warning is directed against readings that would focus on mere location or spatial position (i.e., readings that assume an essentially derivative notion of spatiality). The line Sheehan takes from Stein itself plays on the distinction between the different senses of "there" that are at issue, yet Sheehan gives no attention to what is at issue in those different senses.

19. See Casey, *The Fate of Place: A Philosophical History*.

20. Fell, *Heidegger and Sartre*, xiii. Hegel appears throughout Fell's discussion but given the emphasis to Hegel in Fell's opening comments, there is surprisingly little specific focus on Hegel within the body of Fell's main text. The entry for Hegel in the index, however, is the largest for any philosopher other than Heidegger or Sartre.

21. Not only because of the way in which, for Heidegger, Hegel's thinking remains thoroughly "metaphysical," but also because of the clear proximity between important elements in the Hegelian and Heideggerian approaches alongside Heidegger's own equally clear desire to set himself apart from Hegel (Heidegger does, of course, set himself apart from the philosophical tradition in general, but especially so in relation to Hegel).

22. See Dean W. Bond, "Hegel's Geographical Thought," *Environment and Planning D: Society and Space* 32 (2014): 179–98; see also, Stephan Günzel, "Philosophische Geographien: Nietzsche und Hegel," *Hegel-Jahrbuch, Phänomenologie des Geistes* 2, ed. A. Arndt, K. Bal, H. Ottmann (Berlin: Akademie Verlag, 2002), 294–302.

23. See for example, Terry Pinkard, *Hegel's Phenomenology: The Sociality of Reason* (Cambridge: Cambridge University Press, 1994); and Robert R. Williams, *Hegel's Ethics of Recognition* (Berkeley: University of California Press, 2000).

24. Despite the fact that he is often seen as an adherent to the view that gives priority to relations over relata, F. H. Bradley directed his famous regress argument against that very idea as well as against the attempt to found relations in the relata. See Bradley, *Appearance and Reality* (Oxford: Clarendon Press, 1893), chaps. 2 and 3. One might say that what Bradley demonstrates is thus the impossibility both of founding the relational in the nonrelation or of the nonrelational in the relational. In fact, the problems at issue here are just those that attend upon any version of what Heidegger calls "subjectivism."

25. Robert Brandom, *Making It Explicit: Reasoning, Representing, and Discursive Commitment* (Cambridge, MA: Harvard University Press, 1994). Brandon dedicated *Making It Explicit* to Wilfrid Sellars and Richard Rorty and has been very ready to acknowledge the significance of Davidson's influence in his work.

26. Davidson is an especially interesting figure, having assimilated, like Miller, a range of different influences, including those emanating from Quine,

and therefore Lewis, but also G. H. Mead and Alfred North Whitehead (working closely with the latter as an undergraduate at Harvard). The result is also a highly original and radical position. Not surprisingly, Richard Rorty was the contemporary figure with whom Davidson acknowledged the greatest degree of philosophical connection and sympathy. There is a story, which could also be told, that would weave Davidson into the topological picture that I have here sketched in relation to Heidegger, Miller, and Fell (in Davidson's case, the German influence is more directly Kantian than it is Hegelian). For a somewhat summary and programmatic account of the topological elements in post-Kantian thinking, including Davidson, see Malpas "Self, Other, Thing: Triangulation and Topography in Post-Kantian Philosophy."

27. As in the title of Miller's *The Midworld of Symbols and Functioning Objects*.

28. John William Miller, *The Midworld of Symbols and Functioning Objects* (New York: Norton, 1982), 7.

29. Heidegger, "Building Dwelling Thinking," 154; see also Heidegger, *Parmenides*, 82.

30. See especially Paul Redding, *Hegel's Hermeneutics* (Ithaca, NY: Cornell University Press, 1996).

31. At least if one interprets the topological character of the transcendental to also entail the transcendental character of the topological—something already touched upon in chapter 3. It is notable that the term "transcendental" does not appear in the index to Fell's *Heidegger and Sartre*, and, when Fell does use the term, it is viewed as a problematic notion (so Fell writes of "how one cannot really begin anew or construct an ontology on the basis of either a transcendental or a natural ground," *Heidegger and Sartre*, 425). Fell implicitly assumes, however, a very different reading of the transcendental than do I—although one undoubtedly closer to Heidegger's.

32. Fell, *Heidegger and Sartre*, xiii.

33. It is also a notion directly invoked by the supposed connection of hermeneutics with Hermes—the one who mediates between gods and mortals. Every form of meaningful engagement involves just such a between.

34. It is important to note here that the relational approach that characterizes hermeneutics is not such that it requires a simple prioritization of relation over thing. When understood topologically, the emphasis on relationality necessarily draws together the ideas of both relation and thing. Nowhere is this clearer than in Heidegger, for whom the thing is that which gathers (see especially "The Thing," 163–86).

35. Including both the specific form of "subjectivism" that prioritizes the human subject and the broader "subjectivism" (of which the former is an instance) that looks to some form of underlying *subiectum* or substrate.

36. Hegel's relation to hermeneutics is certainly not straightforward (although see, once again, Redding's discussion in *Hegel's Hermeneutics*), but it is significant—as the role accorded to Hegel within Gadamer's thinking (and especially the way Gadamer contrasts Hegel with Schleiermacher in his critique of "romantic hermeneutics") would alone suggest. See Gadamer, *Truth and Method*, esp. 164–69.

37. See, especially, Miller, *The Midworld of Symbols and Functioning Objects*, chap. 1.

Bibliography

Adorno, Theodor. *The Jargon of Authenticity*. Translated by Knut Tarnowski and Frederic Will. Evanston: Northwestern University Press, 1973. Originally published 1964 as *Jargon der Eigentlichkeit: Zur deutschen Ideologie* by Surkamp (Frankfurt).

Algra, Keimpe. *Concepts of Space in Greek Thought*. Leiden: Brill, 1992.

"An Open Letter: Research Priorities for Robust and Beneficial Artificial Intelligence." Future of Life Institute (website). Accessed January 2021. https://futureoflife.org/ai-open-letter.

Arendt, Hannah. *Between Past and Future: Eight Exercises in Political Thought*. New York: Penguin, 2006.

Arendt, Hannah. *The Life of the Mind*. One-volume ed., edited by Mary McCarthy. San Diego: Harcourt, Brace and Co., 1971.

Arendt, Hannah. "No Longer and Not Yet." In *Essays in Understanding, 1930–1954*, edited by Jerome Kohn, 158–162. New York: Schocken, 1994.

Arendt, Hannah. "Personal Responsibility Under Dictatorship." In *Responsibility and Judgment*, edited by Jerome Kohn, 17–48. New York: Schocken, 2003.

Arendt, Hannah. "Walter Benjamin, 1892–1940." Translated by Harry Zohn. In *Men in Dark Times*, 153–206. New York: Harcourt Brace Jovanovich, 1968.

Aristotle. *Aristotle's Physics, Books III and IV*. Translated by Edward Hussey. Oxford: Clarendon Press, 1957.

Aristotle. *The Metaphysics Books I-IX*. Translated by Hugh Tredennick. Aristotle Volume XVII, Loeb Classical Library (Cambridge MA: Harvard University Press, 1933).

Aristotle. *On the Soul/Parva Naturalia/On Breath*. Translated by W. S. Hett. Aristotle, Volume VIII, Loeb Classical Library. Cambridge, MA: Harvard University Press, 1936.

Aumiller, Rachel. "Dasein's Shadow and the Moment of its Disappearance." *Human Studies: A Journal for Philosophy and the Social Sciences* 40 (2016): 25–41.

Bachelard, Gaston. *The Poetics of Space*. Translated by Maria Jolas. Boston: Beacon Press, 1959.

Barfield, Owen. "The Meaning of Literal." In *The Rediscovery of Meaning and Other Essays*, 33–43. Middletown, CT: Wesleyan University Press, 1977.

Bate, Jonathan. *Romantic Ecology: Wordsworth and the Environmental Tradition*. London: Routledge, 1991.

Beaufret, Jean. "L'entretien sous le marronnier." *L'arc* 22 (1963): 1–7.

Beer, Gillian. *Darwin's Plots: Evolutionary Narrative in Darwin, George Eliot and Nineteenth-Century Fiction*. Cambridge: Cambridge University Press, 1983.

Birmingham, Peg. *Hannah Arendt and Human Rights: The Predicament of Common Responsibility*. Bloomington: Indiana University Press, 2006.

Bloom, Paul. *Against Empathy: The Case for Rational Compassion*. New York: HarperCollins, 2016.

Böhme, Gernot. *The Aesthetics of Atmospheres*. Edited by Jean-Paul Thibaud. London: Routledge, 2017.

Böhme, Gernot. *Atmospheric Architectures: The Aesthetics of Felt Spaces*. Translated by Tina Engels-Schwarzpaul. London: Bloomsbury, 2017.

Bollnow, Otto. *Das Wesen der Stimmungen*. Frankfurt: Klostermann, 1941.

Bollnow, Otto. *Human Space*. Translated by Christine Shuttleworth. Edited by Joseph Kohlmaier. London: Hyphen Press, 2008.

Bond, Dean W. "Hegel's Geographical Thought." *Environment and Planning D: Society and Space* 32 (2014): 179–198.

Bradley, F. H. *Appearance and Reality*. Oxford: Clarendon Press, 1893.

Brandom, Robert. *Making It Explicit: Reasoning, Representing, and Discursive Commitment*. Cambridge, MA: Harvard University Press, 1994.

Bröcker-Oltmanns, Käte. "Editor's Epilogue." In *Ontology: The Hermeneutics of Facticity*, by Martin Heidegger, edited by John van Buren, 88–90. Bloomington: Indiana University Press, 1999.

Burnet, John, trans. *Early Greek Philosophy*. 4th ed. London: A. & C. Black, 1930. Originally published 1892.

Cacciari, Massimo. "Eupalinos or Architecture." *Oppositions* 21 (1980): 106–116.

Camus, Albert. *Essais*. Edited by Roger Quilliot. Bibliothèque de la Pléiade. Paris: Gallimard, 1965. Originally published 1629.

Camus, Albert. *Lyrical and Critical Essays*. Edited by Philip Thody. Translated by Ellen Conroy Kennedy. New York: Knopf, 1968.

Camus, Albert. *The Rebel: An Essay on Man in Revolt*. Tranlsated by Anthony Bower. New York: Vintage, 1956.

Camus, Albert. "René Char." In *René Char's Poetry: Studies*, by Maurice Blanchot et al., translated by David Paul, 55–59. Rome: Editions de Luca, 1956.

Carnap, Rudolf. "The Elimination of Metaphysics Through Logical Analysis of Language." Translated by Arthur Pap. In *Logical Positivism*, edited by A. J. Ayer, 60–81. Glencoe, IL: Free Press, 1959. Originally published 1932.

Casey, Edward S. *The Fate of Place: A Philosophical History*. Berkeley: University of California Press, 1997.

Caws, Peter. "No Higher than the Mountain Peaks." *World Literature Today* 51 (1977): 357–365.
Char, René. *À la santé du serpent*. Paris: Gallimard, 1954.
Char, René. *The Brittle Age and Returning Upland*. Translated by Gustaf Sobin. Denver: Counterpath Press, 2009.
Char, René. *Commune présence*. Paris: Gallimard, 1964.
Char, René. *Feuillets d'Hypnos*. Paris: Gallimard, 1946.
Char, René. *Furor and Mystery & Other Writings*. Translated by Mary Ann Caws and Nancy Kline. Boston, MA: Black Widow Press, 2010.
Char, René. *Leaves of Hypnos*. Translated by Cid Corman. New York: Grossman, 1973.
Char, René. *Oeuvres complètes*. Bibliothèque de la Pléiade, no. 308. Paris: Éditions Gallimard, 1983.
Char, René. *Poésies/Dichtungen*. Frankfurt am Main: Fischer, 1959.
Clinton, Kevin. "Stages of Initiation in the Eleusinian and Samothracian Mysteries." Chap. 3 in *Greek Mysteries: The Archaeology and Ritual of Ancient Greek Secret Cults*, edited by Michael B. Cosmopoulos. London: Routledge, 2003.
Conisbee, Philip, and Denis Coutagne (with contributions by others). *Cézanne in Provence*. New Haven, CT: Yale University Press, 2006.
Coxon, A. H., ed. *The Fragments of Parmenides*. Las Vegas: Parmenides, 2009.
Damasio, Antonio. *Descartes' Error: Emotion, Reason, and the Human Brain*. New York: Putnam, 1994.
Darwin, Charles. *The Expression of the Emotions in Man and Animals*. London: John Murray, 1872.
Darwin, Charles. *On the Origin of Species by Means of Natural Selection, or The Preservation of Favoured Races in the Struggle for Life*. 1st ed. London: John Murray, 1859.
Davidson, Donald. "The Folly of Trying to Define Truth." In *Truth, Language, and History*, 19–37. Oxford: Clarendon Press, 2005.
Davidson, Donald. "What Metaphors Mean." In *Inquiries into Truth and Interpretation*, 245–264. Oxford: Clarendon Press, 1984.
Davis, Bret W. *Heidegger and the Will*. Evanston, IL: Northwestern University Press, 2007.
de Man, Paul. *The Rhetoric of Romanticism*. New York: Columbia University Press, 1984.
Derrida, Jacques. *Of Grammatology*. Translated by Gayatri Chakravorty Spivak. Corr. ed. Baltimore: Johns Hopkins University Press, 1976. Originally published, in French, 1967.
Derrida, Jacques. "The Retrait of Metaphor." In vol. 1 of *Psyche: Inventions of the Other*, edited by Peggy Kamuf and Elizabeth G. Rottenberg, 48–80. Stanford, CA: Stanford University Press, 2007.

Derrida, Jacques. "White Mythology: Metaphor in the Text of Philosophy." In *Margins of Philosophy*, translated by Alan Bass, 207–272. Chicago: University of Chicago Press, 1982.

di Cesare, Donatella. *Heidegger and the Jews: The Black Notebooks*. Cambridge: Polity, 2018.

Dolan, R. J. "Emotion, Cognition, and Behavior." *Science* 298 (2002): 1191–1194.

Döring, Annika, and Peregrine Horden. "Heidegger as Mediterraneanist." In *Critically Mediterranean: Temporalities, Aesthetics, and Deployments of a Sea in Crisis*, edited by yasser elhariry and Edwige Tamalet Talbayev, 25–43. Cham, Switzerland: Palgrave Macmillan, 2018.

Dreyfus, Hubert L. *Being-in-the-World: A Commentary on Heidegger's* Being and Time, *Division I*. Cambridge, MA: MIT Press, 1990.

Dreyfus, Hubert L. and Charles Spinosa. "Highway Bridges and Feasts: Heidegger and Borgmann on How to Affirm Technology." *Man and World* 30 (1997): 159–77.

El-Bizri, Nader M. "On kai khôra: Situating Heidegger between the *Sophist* and the *Timaeus*." *Studia Phaenomenologica* 4 (2002): 73–98.

Elden, Stuart. "Heidegger's Hölderlin and the Importance of Place." *Journal of the British Society for Phenomenology* 30 (1999): 258–274.

Elden, Stuart. *Mapping the Present: Heidegger, Foucault, and the Project of a Spatial History*. London: Continuum, 2001.

Farin, Ingo. "Place and World: On Jeff Malpas' Second Edition of *Place and Experience*." *International Journal of Philosophical Studies* 28 (2020): 254–266.

Farin, Ingo, and Jeff Malpas. "On Overestimating Philosophy: Lessons from Heidegger's *Black Notebooks*." *Journal of Aesthetics and Phenomenology* 4 (2017): 183–195.

Farin, Ingo, and Jeff Malpas, eds. *Reading Heidegger's Black Notebooks*. Cambridge, MA: MIT Press, 2016.

Fédier, François. *Soixante-deux photographs de Martin Heidegger*. Paris: Gallimard, 1999.

Feenberg, Andrew. *Questioning Technology*. London: Routledge, 1999.

Feick, Hildegard. *Index zu Heideggers* Sein und Zeit. Tübingen: Niemeyer, 1961.

Fell, Joseph P. *Heidegger and Sartre: An Essay on Being and Place*. New York: Columbia University Press, 1979.

Figal, Günter. *Objectivity: The Hermeneutical and Philosophy*. Translated by T. D. George. Albany: SUNY Press, 2010.

Foucault, Michel. *Security, Territory, Population: Lectures at the Collège de France, 1977–1978*. Translated by Graham Burchell. New York: St. Martin's Press, 2007.

Foxlee, Neil. *Albert Camus's "The New Mediterranean Culture": A Text and its Contexts*. Modern French Identities, vol. 38. Oxford: Peter Lang, 2010.

Gadamer, Hans-Georg. "Kant and the Hermeneutical Turn." In *Heidegger's Ways*, translated by John W. Stanley, 49–60. Albany: SUNY Press, 1994.

Gadamer, Hans-Georg. "Martin Heidegger—75 Years." In *Heidegger's Ways*, translated by John W. Stanley, 15–28. Albany: SUNY Press, 1994.
Gadamer, Hans-Georg. "Reflections on My Philosophical Journey." In *The Philosophy of Hans-Georg Gadamer*, edited by Lewis Edwin Hahn, 3–63. The Library of Living Philosophers. Chicago: Open Court, 1997.
Gadamer, Hans-Georg. *Truth and Method*. Translated by Joel Weinsheimer and Donald Marshall. 2nd rev. ed. New York: Crossroad, 1992.
Gendlin, Eugene T. "Time's Dependence on Space: Kant's Statements and Their Misconstrual by Heidegger." In *Kant and Phenomenology*, edited by Thomas Seebohm and Joseph Kockelmans, 147–160. Washington, DC: Center for Advanced Research in Phenomenology and University Press of America, 1984.
Ghandi, Mohandas K. *Indian Home Rule*. Phoenix, Natal: International Printing Press, 1908.
Goebbels, Josef. "Der Rundfunk als achte Großmacht." In *Signale der neuen Zeit: 25 ausgewählte Reden von Dr. Joseph Goebbels*, 197–207. Munich: Zentralverlag der NSDAP, 1938.
Greisch, Jean. "Les mots et les roses: La métaphore chez Martin Heidegger." *Revue des sciences philosophiques et theologiques* 57 (1973): 433–455.
Griffero, Tonino. *Atmospheres: Aesthetics of Emotional Spaces*. London: Routledge, 2016.
Guignon, Charles. "Authenticity." *Philosophy Compass* 3 (2008): 277–290.
Guignon, Charles. *On Being Authentic*. New York: Routledge, 2004.
Günzel, Stephan. "Philosophische Geographien: Nietzsche und Hegel." In *Hegel-Jahrbuch, Phänomenologie des Geistes* 2, edited by A. Arndt, K. Bal, and H. Ottmann, 294–302. Berlin: Akademie Verlag, 2002.
Hartmann, Geoffrey. "A Poet's Progress: Wordsworth and the *Via Naturaliter Negativa*." *Modern Philology* 59 (1962): 214–224.
Hartmann, Geoffrey. "The Romance of Nature and the Negative Way." In *Romanticism and Consciousness: Essays in Criticism*, edited by Harold Bloom, 287–305. New York: Norton, 1979.
Hartmann, Geoffrey. *Wordsworth's Poetry, 1787–1814*. New Haven, CT: Yale University Press, 1964.
Harvey, David. *The Condition of Postmodernity: An Enquiry into the Origins of Cultural Change*. Cambridge, MA: Blackwell, 1990.
Haugeland, John. *Dasein Disclosed: John Haugeland's Heidegger*. Edited by Joe Rouse. Cambridge, MA: Harvard University Press, 2013.
Hawking, Stephen. "AI Could Spell End of the Human Race." Interview by BBC News, 2 December, 2014. Accessed January 2021. https://www.bbc.com/news/av/science-environment-30289705/stephen-hawking-ai-could-spell-end-of-the-human-race.
Heaney, Seamus. "The Sense of Place." In *Preoccupations: Selected Prose 1968–1978*, 131–149. London: Faber & Faber, 1984.

Heidegger, Martin. *Acheminement vers la parole*. Paris: Éditions Gallimard, 1976.
Heidegger, Martin. *Anmerkungen I–V (Schwarze Hefte 1942–1948)*. *Gesamtausgabe*, vol. 97, edited by Peter Trawny. Frankfurt: Klostermann, 2015.
Heidegger, Martin. *Aus der Erfahrung des Denkens, 1910–1976*, edited by Hermann Heidegger. *Gesamtausgabe*, vol. 13. Frankfurt: Klostermann, 1983.
Heidegger, Martin. *Basic Concepts*. Translated by Gary E. Aylesworth. Bloomington: Indiana University Press, 1998.
Heidegger, Martin. *Being and Time*. Translated by J. Macqaurie and E. Robinson. New York: Harper & Row, 1962.
Heidegger, Martin. *Being and Time*. Translated by Joan Stambaugh. Revised by Dennis Schmidt. Albany, NY: SUNY Press, 2010.
Heidegger, Martin. *Beiträge zur Philosophie (Vom Ereignis)*. *Gesamtausgabe*, vol. 65, edited by F.-W. von Herrmann. Frankfurt: Kolstermann, 1989.
Heidegger, Martin. *Bremen and Freiburg Lectures: Insight Into That Which Is* and *Basic Principles of Thinking*. Translated by Andrew Mitchell. Bloomington: Indiana University Press, 1994.
Heidegger, Martin. *The Concept of Time*. Translated by W. McNeill. Oxford: Basil Blackwell, 1992.
Heidegger, Martin. *Contributions to Philosophy (Of the Event)*. Translated by Richard Rojcewicz and Daniela Valega-Neu. Bloomington: Indiana University Press, 2012.
Heidegger, Martin. *Country Path Conversations*. Translated by Bret W. Davis. Bloomington: Indiana University Press, 2010.
Heidegger, Martin. *Denkerfahrungen 1910–1976*. Edited by Hermann Heidegger. Frankfurt: Klostermann, 1983.
Heidegger, Martin. *Discourse on Thinking: A Translation of* Gelassenheit. Translated by John M. Anderson and E. Hans Freund. New York: Harper & Row, 1966. First published 1959, in German, as *Gelassenheit* by Neske (Pfullingen).
Heidegger, Martin. *Early Greek Thinking*, translated by David Farrell Krell and Frank Capuzzi. New York: Harper & Row, 1975. First published in 1954.
Heidegger, Martin. *Elucidations of Hölderlin's Poetry*. Translated by Keith Hoeller. Amherst, NY: Humanity Books, 2000.
Heidegger, Martin. *The End of Philosophy*. Translated by Joan Stambaugh. New York: Harper & Row, 1973.
Heidegger, Martin. *Four Seminars*. Translated by Andrew J. Mitchell and François Raffoul. Bloomington: Indiana University Press, 2004.
Heidegger, Martin. *Frühe Schriften*. *Gesamtausgabe*, vol. 1, edited by Friedrich-Wilhelm von Herrmann. Frankfurt: Klostermann, 1978.
Heidegger, Martin. *The Fundamental Concepts of Metaphysics: World, Finitude, Solitude*. Translated by William McNeill and Nicholas Walker. Bloomington: Indiana University Press, 1995.

Heidegger, Martin. *Gelassenheit*. Pfullingen: Günter Neske, 1959.
Heidegger, Martin. "Hebel—Friend of the House." Translated by Bruce V. Foltz and Michael Heim. In *Contemporary German Philosophy*, vol. 3, edited by Darrel E. Christensen et al., 89–101. University Park: Pennsylvania State University Press, 1983.
Heidegger, Martin. *The Heidegger Reader*. Edited by Günter Figal. Translated by Jerome Veith. Bloomington: Indiana University Press, 2009.
Heidegger, Martin. *Hölderlin's Hymn "The Ister."* Translated by William McNeill and Julia Davis. Bloomington: Indiana University Press, 1996.
Heidegger, Martin. *Hölderlins Hymne "Andenken." Gesamtausgabe*, vol. 52, edited by C. Ochtwadt. Frankfurt: Klostermann, 1982.
Heidegger, Martin. *Hölderlin's Hymns "Germania" and "The Rhine,"* trans. William McBeill and Julia Ireland (Bloomington: Indiana University Press, 2014).
Heidegger, Martin. *Identität und Differenz*. Pfullingen: Neske, 1957.
Heidegger, Martin. *Identity and Difference*. Translated by Joan Stambaugh. New York: Harper and Row, 1969.
Heidegger, Martin. *Introduction to Metaphysics*. Translated by Gregory Fried and Richard Polt. New Haven, CT: Yale University Press, 2000. Originally published 1953.
Heidegger, Martin. *Kant and the Problem of Metaphysics*. Translated by Richard Taft. 5th ed. Bloomington: Indiana University Press, 1997.
Heidegger, Martin. *Nietzsche*. Translated by David Farrell Krell. Bk. 1, vols. 1 and 2. New York: Harper & Row, 1984. This corresponds to the original German version, *Nietzsche I*, parts 1 and 2.
Heidegger, Martin. *Nietzsche I*. Stuttgart: Neske, 1961.
Heidegger, Martin. *Off the Beaten Track*. Edited and translated by Kenneth Haynes and Julian Young. Cambridge: Cambridge University Press, 2002.
Heidegger, Martin. *On the Way to Language*. Translated by Peter D. Hertz. New York: Harper & Row, 1971.
Heidegger, Martin. *On Time and Being*. Translated by Joan Stambaugh. New York: Harper and Row, 1972.
Heidegger, Martin. *Ontology: The Hermeneutics of Facticity*. Translated by John van Buren. Bloomington: Indiana University Press, 1999.
Heidegger, Martin. *Parmenides*. Translated by André Schuwer and Richard Rojcewicz. Bloomington: Indiana University Press, 1998.
Heidegger, Martin. *Pathmarks*. Edited by William McNeill. Cambridge: Cambridge University Press, 1998.
Heidegger, Martin. "The Pathway." Translated by Thomas F. O'Meara. Revised by Thomas Sheehan. In *Heidegger, the Man and the Thinker*, edited by Thomas Sheehan, 69–72. New Brunswick: Transaction Publishers, 1981.
Heidegger, Martin. *Poetry, Language, Thought*. Translated by Albert Hofstadter. New York: Harper & Row, 1971.

Heidegger, Martin. *Ponderings II-IV, Black Notebooks 1931–1938*. Translated by Richard Rojcewicz. Bloomington: Indiana University Press, 2016.

Heidegger, Martin. *The Principle of Reason*. Translated by Reginald Lilly. Bloomington: Indiana University Press, 1996.

Heidegger, Martin. *The Question Concerning Technology and Other Essays*. Translated by William Lovitt. New York: Harper & Row, 1977.

Heidegger, Martin. *Reden und andere Zeugnisse eines Lebensweges (1910–1976)*. *Gesamtausgabe*, vol. 16, edited by Hermann Heidegger. Frankfurt: Klostermann, 2000.

Heidegger, Martin. *Seminare (1951–1973)*. *Gesamtausgabe*, vol. 15, edited by C. Ochwadt. Frankfurt: Klostermann, 1986.

Heidegger, Martin. *Überlegungen II–VI (Schwarze Hefte 1931–1938)*. *Gesamtausgabe*, vol. 94, edited by Peter Trawny. Frankfurt: Klostermann, 2014.

Heidegger, Martin. *Überlegungen VII–XI (Schwarze Hefte 1938–1939)*. *Gesamtausgabe*, vol. 95, edited by Peter Trawny. Frankfurt: Klostermann, 2014.

Heidegger, Martin. *Überlegungen XII–XV (Schwarze Hefte 1939–1941)*. *Gesamtausgabe*, vol. 96, edited by Peter Trawny. Frankfurt: Klostermann, 2014.

Heidegger, Martin. *Unterwegs zur Sprache*. *Gesamtausgabe*, vol. 12, edited by F.-W. von Herrmann, Frankfurt: Klostermann, 1985.

Heidegger, Martin. *Vorträge und Aufsätze (1936–1953)*. *Gesamtausgabe*, vol. 7, edited by F.-W. von Herrmann. Frankfurt: Klostermann, 2000.

Heidegger, Martin. *Vorträge und Aufsätze*. Pfullingen: Neske, 1954.

Heidegger, Martin. *What Is a Thing?* Translated by W. B. Barton, Jr. and Vera Deutsch. Chicago: Henry Regnery, 1967.

Heidegger, Martin. *What Is Called Thinking?* Translated by J. Glenn Gray and F. Wieck. New York: Harper & Row, 1968. First published as *Was heisst denken?* (Tubingen: Niemeyer, 1954).

Heidegger, Martin. *Zollikon Seminars: Protocols, Conversations, Letters*. Edited by Medard Boss. Translated by Franz May and Richard Askey. Evanston, IL: Northwestern University Press, 2001.

Heidegger, Martin. *Zu eigenen Veröffentlichungen*. *Gesamtausgabe* vol. 82, edited by F.-W. von Herrmann. Frankfurt: Klostermann, 2018.

Helm, Bennett. *Emotional Reason: Deliberation, Motivation, and the Nature of Value*. Cambridge: Cambridge University Press, 2001.

Hemming, Laurence. "Heidegger's Hegel, the Christian Jew: 'Europe' as 'Planetary Criminality and Machination.'" In *Heidegger and the Global Age*, edited by Antonio Cerella and Louiza Odysseos, 187–212. London: Rowman & Littlefield International, 2017.

Herf, Jeffrey. *Reactionary Modernism: Technology, Culture, and Politics in Weimar and the Third Reich*. Cambridge: Cambridge University Press, 1984.

Hirsch, E. D., Jr. *Wordsworth and Schelling: A Typological Study of Romanticism*. New Haven, CT: Yale University Press, 1960.

Hoy, David Couzen. "Forgetting the Text: Derrida's Critique of Heidegger." *Boundary 2*, no. 8 (1979): 223–236.
Hume, David. *A Treatise of Human Nature*. 2nd ed. Edited by L. A. Selby-Bigge. Revised by P. H. Nidditch. Oxford: Clarendon Press, 1978.
Idhe, Don. *Heidegger's Technologies: Postphenomenological Perspectives*. New York: Fordham University Press, 2010.
Iyer, Lars. "The Birth of Philosophy in Poetry: Blanchot, Char, Heraclitus." *Janus Head: Journal of Interdisciplinary Studies in Continental Philosophy, Literature, Phenomenological Psychology, and the Arts* 4 (2001): 358–383.
Jackson, J. B. "Beyond Wilderness." In *A Sense of Place, A Sense of Time*, 71–92. New Haven, CT: Yale University Press, 1994.
Janicaud, Dominique. *Heidegger in France*. Translated by François Raffoul and David Pettigrew. Bloomington: Indiana University Press, 2015.
Jones, Steven E. *Against Technology: From the Luddites to Neo-Luddism*. London: Routledge, 2006.
Jongman-Sereno, Katrina P., and Mark R. Leary, "The Enigma of Being Yourself: A Critical Examination of the Concept of Authenticity." *Review of General Psychology* 23 (2019): 133–142.
Kafka, Franz. "He: Notes from the Year 1920." In *The Great Wall of China: Stories and Reflections*, translated by Willa Muir and Edwin Muir, 263–277. New York: Schocken Books, 1946.
Kahn, Charles. *The Art and Thought of Heraclitus*. Cambridge: Cambridge University Press, 1979.
Kant, Immanuel. "An Answer to the Question: What is Enlightenment?" (1784). In *Practical Philosophy*, edited and translated by Mary J. Gregor, 11–22. Cambridge: Cambridge University Press, 2012.
Kant, Immanuel. "Concerning the Ultimate Ground of the Differentiation of Directions in Space." In *Theoretical Philosophy, 1755–1770*, translated and edited by David Walford, in collaboration with Ralf Meerbote, 364–372. Cambridge: Cambridge University Press, 1992.
Kant, Immanuel. *Critique of Pure Reason*. Translated and edited by Paul Guyer and Allen W. Wood. In *The Cambridge Edition of the Works of Immanuel Kant*. Cambridge: Cambridge University Press, 1999.
Käufer, Stephan. "Authenticity," In *The Cambridge Heidegger Lexicon*, edited by Mark Wrathall, 71–77. Cambridge: Cambridge University Press, 2021.
Kettering, Emil. *Nähe, das Denken Martin Heideggers*. Pfullingen: Neske, 1987.
Kerrigan, John. "Wordsworth and the Sonnet: Building, Dwelling, Thinking." *Essays in Criticism* 35 (1985): 45–75.
Kline, Nancy. "Translating Éluard & Char." *Hyperion* 9, no. 1 (2015): 6–12.
Kluge, Friedrich. *An Etymological Dictionary of the German Language*. Translated by John Francis Davis. London: George Bell & Sons. 1891.

Kockelmans, Joseph. "Heidegger on Metaphor and Metaphysics." In vol. 3 of *Martin Heidegger: Critical Assessments*, edited by Christopher Macann, 293–320. London: Routledge, 1992.

Lafont, Christina. *Heidegger, Language, and World-Disclosure*. New York: Cambridge University Press, 2000.

Laks, André, and Glenn W. Most, eds. and trans. *Early Greek Philosophy*. Vol. 5, *Western Greek Thinkers, Part 2*. Loeb Classical Library. Cambridge, MA: Harvard University Press, 2016.

Levinas, Emmanuel. *Entre Nous: On Thinking-of-the-Other*. Translated by Michael B. Smith. New York: Columbia University Press, 1998.

Levinas, Emmanuel. *Totality and Infinity: An Essay on Exteriority*. Translated by Alphonso Lingis. 1961. Reprint, Pittsburgh: Duquesne University Press, 1969.

Lévy, Dominique, and Gérard Duménil. *The Crisis of Neoliberalism*. Cambridge, MA: Harvard University Press, 2011.

Linebaugh, Peter. "Ned Ludd & Queen Mab: Machine-Breaking, Romanticism, and the Several Commons of 1811–12." In *Stop Thief! The Commons, Enclosures, and Resistance*, 77–107. Oakland, CA: PM Press, 2014.

Lloyd, Genevieve. *The Man of Reason: "Male" and "Female" in Western Philosophy*. London: Methuen, 1984.

Løgstrup, Knud, *The Ethical Demand*, edited by Hans Fink, with introduction by Hans Fink and Alasdair MacIntyre. Notre Dame: University of Notre Dame Press, 1997.

Malpas, Jeff. "The Beckoning of Language." In *Hermeneutic Heidegger*, edited by Ingo Farin and Michael Bowler, 203–221. Evanston: Northwestern University Press, 2016.

Malpas, Jeff. "The Beginning of Understanding: Event, Place, Truth." In *Consequences of Hermeneutics: Fifty Years after Gadamer's* Truth and Method, edited by Jeff Malpas and Santiago Zabala, 261–280. Chicago: Northwestern University Press, 2010.

Malpas, Jeff. *Donald Davidson and the Mirror of Meaning*. Cambridge: Cambridge University Press, 1992.

Malpas, Jeff. "Five Theses on Place (and some associated remarks): A Reply to Peter Gratton." *Il Cannocchiale: rivista di studi filosofici* 42, no. 1–2 (2017): 69–81.

Malpas, Jeff. *Heidegger and the Thinking of Place*. Cambridge, MA: MIT Press, 2012.

Malpas, Jeff. "Heidegger, Space and World." In *Heidegger and Cognitive Science*, edited by Julian Kiverstein and Michael Wheeler, 309–342. London: Palgrave-Macmillan, 2012.

Malpas, Jeff. *Heidegger's Topology: Being, Place, World*. Cambridge, MA: MIT Press, 2006.

Malpas, Jeff. "New Media, Cultural Heritage, and the Sense of Place: Mapping the Conceptual Ground." *International Journal of Heritage Studies* 14, no. 3 (2008): 197–209.

Malpas, Jeff. "On Human Being as Placed Being." *Environmental & Architectural Phenomenology* 25 (2014): 11–12.

Malpas, Jeff. *Place and Experience: A Philosophical Topography.* 2nd ed. London: Routledge, 2018.

Malpas, Jeff. "Place and Singularity." In *The Intelligence of Place: Topographies and Poetics*, edited by Jeff Malpas, 65–92. London: Bloomsbury, 2015.

Malpas, Jeff. "Place and Situation." In *Routledge Companion to Hermeneutics*, edited by Jeff Malpas and Hans-Helmuth Gander, 354–366. London: Routledge, 2015.

Malpas, Jeff. "The Place of Mobility: Individualization, Relationality, and Contemporary Technology." In *Mobile Technology and Place*, edited by Rowan Wilken and Gerard Goggin, 26–38. London: Routledge, 2012.

Malpas, Jeff. "Putting Space in Place: Relational Geography and Philosophical Topography." *Planning and Environment D: Space and Society* 30 (2012): 226–242.

Malpas, Jeff. *Rethinking Dwelling: Heidegger, Place, Architecture.* London: Bloomsbury, 2021.

Malpas, Jeff. "Self, Other, Thing: Triangulation and Topography in Post-Kantian Philosophy." *Philosophy Today* 59 (2015): 103–126.

Malpas, Jeff. "Thinking Topographically: Place, Space, and Geography." *Il Cannocchiale: Revista di studi filosofici* 42, no. 1–2 (2017): 25–53.

Malpas, Jeff. "We Hyperboreans: Notes Towards a Nietzschean Topography." In *Nietzsche: Individual and Community*, edited by Julian Young, 195–213. New York: Cambridge University Press, 2014.

Malpas, Jeff, and Karsten Thiel. "Kant's Geography of Reason." In *Kant's Geography*, edited by Stuart Elden and Eduardo Mendieta, 195–214. New York: SUNY Press, 2011.

Malpas, Jeff, and Kenneth White. *The Fundamental Field: Thought, Poetics, World.* Edinburgh: Edinburgh University Press, 2021.

Malpas, Jeff, and Gary Wickham. "Governance and the World: From Joe DiMaggio to Michel Foucault." *The UTS Review* 3 (1997): 91–108.

Malpas, Jeff, and Günter Zöller. "Reading Kant Geographically: From Critical Philosophy to Empirical Geography." In *Contemporary Kantian Metaphysics: New Essays on Space and Time*, edited by Roxana Baiasu, Graham Bird, and A. W. Moore, 146–166. London: Palgrave Macmillan, 2012.

Marx, Karl. *Grundrisse: Foundations of the Critique of Political Economy (Rough Draft).* Translated by Martin Nicolaus. Harmondsworth: Penguin Books, 1973.

Maxwell, Nicholas. "The Enlightenment and the Romantic Opposition." In *Science and Enlightenment: Two Great Problems of Learning*, 9–20. Dordrecht: Springer, 2019.

McCutcheon, Mark A. *The Medium Is the Monster: Canadian Adaptations of Frankenstein and the Discourse of Technology*. Edmonton: Athabasca University Press, 2018.

Menary, Richard, ed. *The Extended Mind*. Cambridge, MA: MIT Press, 2010.

Metcalf, Robert. "Rethinking 'Bodenständigkeit' in the Technological Age." *Research in Phenomenology* 42 (2012): 49–66.

Miller, John William. *The Definition of the Thing with Some Notes on Language*, New York: W. W. Norton, 1980.

Miller, John William. *The Midworld of Symbols and Functioning Objects*. New York: W.W. Norton, 1982.

Minder, Robert. "Heidegger und Hebel oder Die Sprache von Messkirch." In *Dichter in der Gesellschaft*, 211–264. Frankfurt: Insel Verlag, 1966.

Mitchell, Andrew. *The Fourfold*. Evanston: Northwestern University Press, 2015.

Mugerauer, Robert. *Heidegger and Homecoming: The Leitmotif in the Later Writings*. Toronto: University of Toronto Press, 2008.

Nietzsche, Friedrich. *Correspondence 1932–1960: Albert Camus and Jean Grenier*. Translated by Jan F. Rigaud. Lincoln: University of Nebraska Press, 2003.

Nietzsche, Friedrich. *The Gay Science*, trans. Walter Kaufmann. New York: Vintage, 1974.

Nietzsche, Friedrich. *Untimely Meditations*. Translated by R. J. Hollingdale. Cambridge: Cambridge University Press, 1998.

Nietzsche, Friedrich. "Of the Vision and the Riddle." In part 3 of *Thus Spoke Zarathustra*, translated by R. J. Hollingdale, 176–180. Harmondsworth: Penguin, 1969.

Norberg-Schulz, Christian. *The Concept of Dwelling: On the Way to Figurative Architecture*. New York: Electa/Rizzoli, 1985.

O'Brien, Conor Cruise. *Camus*. London: Fontana, 1970,

Ortega y Gassett, José. "Man the Technician." In *History as a System and Other Essays Toward a Philosophy of History*, translated by Helene Weyl, 85–161. New York: Norton, 1961.

Ortega y Gassett, José. "Der Mythus des Menschen hinter der Technik" [The Myth of Humanity Outside Technology]. In *Mensch und Raum*, edited by Otto Bartning, 111–117. Darmstadt: Neue Darmstaedter Verlangsanstalt, 1952.

Ott, Heinrich. "Hermeneutic and Personal Structure of Language." In *On Heidegger and Language*, edited by Joseph J. Kockelmans, 169–194. Evanston, IL: Northwestern University Press, 1972.

Ott, Heinrich. "What Is Systematic Theology?" In *New Frontiers in Theology*, vol. 1 of *The Later Heidegger and Theology*, edited by James M. Robinson and John B. Cobb, Jr., 77–114. New York: Harper and Row, 1963.

Pallasmaa, Juhani. "Place and Atmosphere." In *The Intelligence of Place: Topographies and Poetics*, edited by Jeff Malpas, 129–156. London: Bloomsbury, 2015.
Partridge, Eric. *Origins: A Short Etymological Dictionary of Modern English*. 2nd ed. London: Routledge and Kegan Paul, 1959.
Payne, Mark. "The Natural World in Greek Literature and Philosophy." In *Oxford Handbooks Online: Classical Studies*, edited by Gareth Williams, 12. Oxford: Oxford University Press, 2014. doi: 10.1093/oxfordhb/9780199935390.013.001.
Phillips, James. *Heidegger's Volk: Between National Socialism and Poetry*. Stanford, CA: Stanford University Press, 2005.
Pinkard, Terry. *Hegel's Phenomenology: The Sociality of Reason*. Cambridge: Cambridge University Press, 1994.
Pinker, Stephen. *Enlightenment Now: The Case for Reason, Science, Humanism, and Progress*. New York: Viking, 2018.
Plato. *Plato: The Collected Dialogues*. Edited by Edith Hamilton and Huntington Cairns. Bollingen Series 71. Princeton, NJ: Princeton University Press, 1963.
Plutarch. *Moralia*. Vol. 15, Loeb Classical Library, translated by F. H. Sandbach. Cambridge, MA: Harvard University Press, 1969.
Preus, Anthony. *Historical Dictionary of Ancient Greek Philosophy*. Lanham, MD: Scarecrow Press, 2009.
Quine, W. V. "On What There Is." In *From a Logical Point of View*, 1–19. New York: Harper & Row, 1953.
Ratcliffe, Matthew. "The Feeling of Being." *Journal of Consciousness Studies* 12 (2005): 45–63.
Ratcliffe, Matthew. *Feelings of Being: Phenomenology, Psychiatry and the Sense of Reality*. Oxford: Oxford University Press, 2008.
Ratcliffe, Matthew. "Heidegger's Attunement and the Neuropsychology of Emotion." *Phenomenology and the Cognitive Sciences* 1 (2002): 287–312.
Ratcliffe, Matthew. "Why Mood Matters." In *Cambridge Companion to* Being and Time, edited by Mark Wrathall, 157–176. Cambridge: Cambridge University Press, 2013.
Redding, Paul. *Hegel's Hermeneutics*. Ithaca, NY: Cornell University Press, 1996.
Richardson, William J. *Heidegger: Through Phenomenology to Thought*. Phenomenologica 13. The Hague: Martinus Nijhoff, 1963.
Rosenwein, Barbara, and Riccardo Cristiani. *What is the History of Emotions?* Cambridge: Polity, 2018.
Rousseau, Jean-Jacques. *The Discourse Which Carried the Praemium at the Academy of Dijon in MDCCL. On this Question, Proposed by the said Academy, whether the Re-establishment of Arts and Sciences has Contributed to the Refining of Manners*. London: W. Owen, 1751. Originally published 1750, in French.

Ruin, Hans. "The Inversion of Mysticism—*Gelassenheit* and the Secret of the Open in Heidegger," Religions 10 (2019). Accessed January 2021. https://www.mdpi.com/2077-1444/10/1/15?type=check_update&version=1.

Said, Edward. *Culture and Imperialism*. London: Vintage, 1994.

Safranski, Rüdiger. *Martin Heidegger: Between Good and Evil*. Translated by Ewald Osers. Cambridge, MA: Harvard University Press, 1990.

Schmitz, Hermann. *System der Philosophie*. 5 vols. Bonn: Bouvier, 2005. Originally published 1964–1980.

Schmitz, Hermann, Rudolf Owen Müllan, and Jan Slaby. "Emotions Outside the Box: The New Phenomenology of Feeling and Corporeality." *Phenomenology and the Cognitive Sciences* 10 (2011): 241–259.

Schürmann, Reiner. *Heidegger on Being and Acting: From Principles to Anarchy*. Translated by Christine-Marie Gros. Bloomington: Indiana University Press, 1987.

Sheehan, Thomas. *Making Sense of Heidegger: A Paradigm Shift*. London: Rowman and Littlefield International, 2014.

Sheehan, Thomas. "A Paradigm Shift in Heidegger Research." *Continental Philosophy Review* 34 (2001): 183–202.

Shelley, Mary. *Frankenstein; or, The Modern Prometheus*. London: Printed for Lackington, Hughes, Harding, Mavor, & Jones, 1818.

Simmel, Georg. *Simmel on Culture*, edited and translated by David Frisby and Mike Featherstone. London: Sage, 1997.

Singer, Peter. "Ethics and Intuitions." *Journal of Ethics* 9 (2005): 331–352.

Slaby, Jan. "Emotional Rationality and Feelings of Being." In *Feelings of Being Alive*, edited by Joerg Fingerhut and Sabine Marienberg, 55–78. Berlin: De Gruyter, 2012.

Storey, David E. *Naturalizing Heidegger: His Confrontation with Nietzsche, His Contributions to Environmental Philosophy*. New York: SUNY Press, 2015.

Strawson, P. F. *Individuals*. London: Methuen, 1959.

Taylor, Charles. *The Ethics of Authenticity*. Cambridge, MA: Harvard University Press, 1991.

Thomson, Iain. *Heidegger on Ontotheology: Technology and the Politics of Education*. Cambridge: Cambridge University Press, 2005.

Trawny, Peter. *Heidegger and the Myth of a Jewish World Conspiracy*. Chicago: University of Chicago Press, 2016.

Trilling, Lionel. *Sincerity and Authenticity*. Cambridge, MA: Harvard University Press, 1971.

Valega-Neu, Daniela. "The *Black Notebooks* and Heidegger's Writings on the Event (1936–1942)." In *Reading Heidegger's Black Notebooks 1931–1941*, edited by Ingo Farin and Jeff Malpas, 127–143. Cambridge, MA: MIT Press, 2016.

Vattimo, Gianni. *The End of Modernity: Nihilism and Hermeneutics in Postmodern Culture*. Baltimore: Johns Hopkins University Press, 1991.

Virilio, Paul. *Bunker Architecture*. Translated by George Collins. Princeton: Princeton University Press, 1994.
Virilio, Paul. *The Original Accident*. Translated by Julie Rose. Cambridge: Polity, 2007.
Virilio, Paul. *Speed and Politics: An Essay on Dromology*. Translated by M. Polizzotti. New York: Semiotext(e), 2006. Originally published 1977, in French.
von Herrmann, F.-W. "Dasein and Da-Sein in *Being and Time* and in *Contributions to Philosophy (From Enowning)*." In *Heidegger, Translation, and the Task of Thinking: Essays in Honor of Parvis Emad*, edited by F. Schalow, 213–224. Dordrecht: Springer, 2011.
Vycinas, Vincent. *Earth and Gods: An Introduction to the Philosophy of Martin Heidegger*. The Hague: Martinus Nijhof, 1961.
Warf, Barney. "Excavating the History of Time-Space Compression." *Geographical Review* 101 (2011): 435–46.
Wellbery, David. "Stimmung." Translated by Rebecca Pohl. *New Formations* 93 (2018): 6–45. Originally published, in German, 2003.
Wendland, Aaron James, Christopher Merwin, and Christos Hadjioannou. *Heidegger on Technology*. London: Routledge, 2019.
White, Kenneth. *Letters from Gourgounel*. London: Jonathan Cape, 1966.
White, Kenneth. *The Wanderer and His Charts: Exploring the Fields of Vagrant Thought and Vagabond Beauty*. Edinburgh: Polygon, 2010.
Williams, Bernard. "From Sincerity to Authenticity." In *Truth and Truthfulness: An Essay in Genealogy*, 172–205. Princeton, NJ: Princeton University Press, 2002.
Williams, Robert R. *Hegel's Ethics of Recognition*. Berkeley: University of California Press, 2000.
Withers, Charles W. J. *Placing the Enlightenment: Thinking Geographically about the Age of Reason*. Chicago: University of Chicago Press, 2007.
Wordsworth, William. *Lyrical Ballads*. 2 vols. London: T. N. Longman and O. Rees, 1800.
Wordsworth, William. *The Prelude, or Growth of a Poet's Mind*. Edited by Ernest de Selincourt. Revised by Helen Darbishire. 2nd ed. Oxford: Clarendon Press, 1959.
Young, Iris Marion. "Throwing like a Girl: A Phenomenology of Feminine Body Comportment Motility and Spatiality." *Human Studies* 3 (1980): 137–156.
Young, Julian. *Heidegger's Philosophy of Art*. Cambridge: Cambridge University Press, 2001.
Zumthor, Peter. *Atmospheres: Architectural Environments, Surrounding Objects*. Basel: Birkhäuser, 2006.

Index

abode/dwelling-place, see *Aufenthalt*
abstraction, 42–43, 62, 119, 128, 132, 133; refusal of, 233–234
acceleration, 139
accident, 158
Acheminement vers la parole, see *On the Way to Language*
action, 113, 119, 125, 128, 131, 147, 148, 214
activism, 144
actuality, 165, 220, 276
Adorno, Theodore, 138, 177, 269
affect, 121–122
affectivity/affectedness, 117, 124–125
agency, 223
AI, *see* artificial intelligence
aletheia, 33, 44, 58–59, 73, 75, 80, 90, 92, 149, 209; *see also* unconcealing/unconcealment
Aletheia, 32
Algeria, 233, 236
Andenken, 31; 200; *see also* remembrance
animal communication, 92
anthropologism, 148
anthropology of the world, 46–48
antinaturalism, 55, 61–62
anti-Nazism, 20
anosognosia, 125–126
anthropocentrism, 64

antimodernism, 141, 143
anti-Semitism, 5, 8, 20, 213, 228–229
apathy, emotional, 124–125
appearing, 34, 50, 55–56, 58, 74, 80, 84, 92, 107, 206, 222; *see also* showing
appearance, *see* appearing
appropriation, 93, 248; *see also* event
Arendt, Hannah, 138, 139, 185–208, 211, 234; topology in, 186, 198, 201–202, 204
argument, 115
Aristotle, 59, 60–62
art, 7–8
"Art and Space," 24, 96–97
artificial intelligence, 138
Atlanticism, 41
atmosphere, 127
attachment, 37
attunement, see also *Grundstimmung*, mood, tuning, *Stimmung*
Aufenthalt, 21, 34, 132, 185; *see also* dwelling
Augenblick, 3, 195–196, 197–198, 201, 202, 204, 205, 248, 274, 273; *see also* moment/now
authentication, 172
authentes, 176, 267; *see also* authentic, authenticity

297

authentic, 145, 166, 170, 171, 174, 175, 177, 182, 183, 184; see also *eigentlich*, ownness/owned
authentic temporality, *see* temporality (ownmost)
authenticity, 117, 163–184, 268–269; instability of, 173, 182–183; and management, 267; polemical sense, 165, 178; as social virtue, 166, 179; see also *Eigentlichkeit*, ownness/owned, self-expression
authoritarianism, 175
authority, 172
available, *see* ready-to-hand
awareness, 73

beauty, 37
Bachelard, Gaston, 89, 105, 108, 236, 253
Barfield, Owen, 251–252
Bate, Jonathan, 181
Beaufret, Jean, 27, 232–233
beckon, 76, 78, 243
beckonings, see *Winke*
becoming native, *see* native
Befindlichkeit, 120, 121
beginning, 17, 30–32, 45, 99, 195, 204, 208, 209, 214–216, 220, 222–225; of philosophy, 45, 99, 209, 220, 222–225; of thinking, 17, 30–32, 209, 214–216, 224–225; *see also* first beginning, natality, other beginning
being, 6, 14, 15–24, 33–34, 47–48, 52, 57, 63, 68, 70, 73, 74, 82, 84, 88, 89, 101–102, 145, 168–169, 241, 250; *see also* presencing
Being and Time, 9–12, 50, 56, 57, 72, 120–121, 122–123, 130, 176–177, 178, 179, 185–186, 198, 199, 201, 215, 220, 229
being authentic, 167

being-historical, *see* thinking
being in, 130
being-in-place, 37, 38, 131, 180–181, 182, 183, 192, 204
being-in-the-world, 38, 119, 124, 131, 140
being there/here, *see* Dasein
belonging, 37, 237
beyng, 230; *see also* being
benefits, technological, *see* technology (benefits of)
Benjamin, Walter, 187, 252
Bergson, Henri, 199
Bestand, 140, 153
bestimmen, *see* tuning
between, 76, 79, 82, 84, 90, 205, 222, 223, 274–275; *see also* dimensionality, *distema*, gap, space, *Zwischen*/*zwischen*
bildlich, *see* language (figurative)
Birmingham, Peg, 130, 194–195, 204–206, 272, 274
birth, 205, 206, 208; *see also* natality, native
Black Notebooks, 7–9, 12–13, 16–17, 19, 21, 26, 213, 225, 228
Bloom, Paul, 113, 132
Bodenständigkeit, 35; *see also* groundedness
bodily differentiation, 128–129
bodily spatiality, *see* spatiality (bodily)
body, 128–130, 131, 256, 272
Bollnow, Otto, 126–127
Bordeaux, 39
boredom, 119
Borgmann, Albert, 154
bound/boundary, 43, 56, 59–61, 76, 77–78, 79, 87, 179, 192, 206, 212, 220, 222
boundedness, *see* bound/boundary
boundlessness, 77–78, 78, 87

Bradley, Francis Herbert, 277
Brandom, Robert, 219, 277
Braque, Georges, 27–28
breakdown, see technological breakdown
brightness, 1–2, 225
bringing-forth, see *poiesis*
building, 246

Cacciari, Massimo, 271
calculation/calculative, 113, 114, 117, 134, 144, 152, 154, 265
calculative reason, 113, 114, 117, 119, 134
calculative thinking, see thinking (calculative)
Camus, Albert, 36–37, 39, 40–43, 138, 139, 233–234, 234
Capgras's syndrome, 125–126
capitalism, 158
care, 120
Carnap, Rudolf, 71, 81
Cartesian spatiality, see spatiality (Cartesian)
Casey, Edward, 218
cause, 61
Cézanne, Paul, 29, 36
challenging, 141
Char, René, 27–30, 32, 36–37, 40–42, 45–46, 105, 193, 232–233, 233–234, 234, 236; "Hymn in a Quiet Voice," 40; *Leaves of Hypnos*, 45–46
Chora/Khôra, 23, 60, 204, 232, 241, 263
circularity, see hermeneutical circularity
city and countryside, 239
Clare, John, 110
clarity, 259
clearing, 3, 13, 59, 64, 78–79, 87, 92; see also *Lichtung*

cognition, 114, 125, 131
cognitive emotion, see emotion
colonialism, 236
combat of reason and passion, 113–119
commitment, 170
commodification, 225
common life, 115
common presence (*commune présence*), 32
commune présence, see common presence
communication, 69, 92, 276
communication technology, 143, 154, 155, 225
concealing/revealing, see unconcealing/unconcealment
concept, 134, 144, 146–147
conceptual image, see image (conceptual/representational)
conceptual thinking, see thinking (conceptual/representational)
concreteness, 42–43, 165
connection/connectivity, 154–155, 225
Conrad, Joseph (*Heart of Darkness*), 165
consequentialism, 114
conservatism, 137, 138, 142, 144
constructionism, 92
content, 192
Contributions to Philosophy, 9, 13, 14–16, 18–19
control, 176
convergence, 155–156
convergent connectivity, 156; see also connection/connectivity, convergence
conversation, 69, 76, 176
corporatization, 224
counting/countable, 225
countryside and city, 239
crisis, 224

critique, 211

Da, 3, 12–13, 22, 33, 59, 91, 124, 198, 218, 277; see also there/here
Da-sein, 12, 13, 14, 16, 230; see also Dasein
Damasio, Antonio, 116–117, 125
Danken, 232, 235; see also thank/thanking
Denken, 31, 200, 232; see also thinking
Darwin, Charles, 53–54, 117–118
Dasein, 9–10, 13, 70, 124, 130, 198, 215, 235; and human being, 33, 235
Davidson, Donald, 146–147, 219, 251, 276, 277–278
death, 206
decision, 113
definition, 146
democracy, 43
Derrida, Jacques, 66, 242, 243, 249, 250, 251
Descartes, René, 116–117, 152, 199
"Descartes' error," 116
development, technological, see technological development
devices, see technological devices
dialogue, 76, 77, 203
"Dialogue on Language," 67, 72–73, 74–76, 77
diastema, 76, 274–275; see also between, dimensionality, space, Zwischen/zwischen
difference/differentiation, 58, 60, 79, 80, 86, 87, 92, 93, 153, 219, 241, 247; and identity, 43, 58, 79, 80, 203, 219, 241; in space, 129, 176, 203, 223; see also sameness
digital technology, see technology
dimensio, 246; see also dimension/dimensionality

Dimension, 84, 246; see also dimension/dimensionality
dimension/dimensionality, 30–31, 34–35, 76–77, 84, 86–87, 89, 90, 94–97, 108, 205, 246–247; see also space
dimetiri, 246; see also dimensionality
disclosure, 2
disconnection, 225
discourse, 72
disorientation, 102, 133, 224–225
displacement, 189, 203, 207–208
disposedness, 135
disruption, 142, 194, 203
distance, 119, 135, 139, 130, 145, 207
Dolan, Ray, 125
Dreyfus, Hubert, 49, 154
dwelling, 11–12, 46, 83, 85, 86, 88, 89, 94, 101, 217, 262; see also Aufenthalt, Wohnen

Early Greek Thinking, 34
earth, 29, 37, 79, 85, 87, 91
earth, seen from space, 157
Eckhart, Meister, 24, 267
Eichmann, Adolf, 207
Eichmann trial, 202
eigentlich, 145, 269; see also authentic
eigentliche Zeitlichkeit, see temporality (ownmost)
Eigentlichkeit, 163, 177–179, 270; see also authenticity, ownness/owned
Eindeutigkeit, see univocity
Einräumen, see spacing/making space
ek-stasis, 84, 198
Eleusis, 32
Eleusian mysteries, 32–33
embodiment, see body
emergence, 31, 61, 64, 204, 206, 220; see also physis, poiesis
emotion, 113–136, 256–257; as biological/psychological, 124,

256–257; bodily character of, 129; cognitive, 125–126, 135; as disclosive, 123; as distinct from feeling, 255–256; as distinct from mood, 255, 256; empirical approaches to, 125–126; etymology of term, 118, 254; ontological/phenomenological approaches to, 123–127
emotional apathy, *see* apathy
emotional expression, 117–118
emotional engagement, 120
empathy, 113
Empédocle, 233, 234
emptying out of language, 251
encounter, 3, 63, 64, 222, 247
end, 3, 99, 119, 143, 148–149, 209, 214, 220; *see also* beginning, means/ends
Enlightenment, 139, 142, 148, 159, 262
enownment, 267; *see also* authenticity, *Eigentlichkeit*
environment/environmental, 133, 160
epistemology, 215
equiprimordiality, 219
equivocity, 1, 103, 104, 110, 210, 276; *see also* iridescence, vibrancy
Erde, *see* earth
Ereignis, 3, 13, 14, 15, 18, 19, 20, 21, 58, 59, 93, 177, 179, 202, 203, 205, 212, 248, 249, 275; *see also* appropriation, event
Erörterung, 110, 249; *see also* placing
Es gibt, 23; *see also* givenness
essence, 144–146
essentialism, 144, 150
eternal recurrence, 195
ethics, 113, 114, 132, 133; topological, 131–132
ethical thinking, 113, 114
ethos, 132

etymology, 218; of authentic/authenticity, 166, 266–267, 268; of beckon, 243; of emotion, 118; of *Ereignis* 275; of frame, 265; of hermeneutics, 269; of nature and place, 60; of relation, 145; of *stimmen/Stimmung*, 256
Europe, 213, 214, 224
European thought, 214, 215
event, 3, 15, 18, 19, 22, 87–88, 91, 93–94, 177, 179, 202, 203, 205, 223, 247–248, 249, 275; *see also* appropriation, *Ereignis*
evidence, 254
evil, 202, 207, 232
everyday/ordinary, 183, 188
exceptionalism, philosophical, 6
exceptionality, 165, 173, 177, 178, 183–184
excess, 44, 45, 169
exclusion/exclusionary, 38, 237
existential spatiality, *see* spatiality (existential)
existentiale Räumlichkeit, *see* spatiality (existential)
exteriority, 203
externality, 130, 180
extremity, 173, 177, 259

facticity, 70–71, 73, 80, 222
failure, 25–26, 158–159
falling, 215
feeling, 120, 121, 122–123, 255–256
Feenberg, Andrew, 154, 261
Der Feldweg, 44
Fell, Joseph, 4, 202, 213, 215–216, 218–219, 221, 222, 227, 240
Figal, Günter, 246, 247
figuration, 252
figurative language, *see* language (figurative)
finitude, 48, 196, 197, 222

first beginning, 30–31, 37, 45, 209, 212, 215
flow, 225
focal meaning, 276; *see also* equivocity, iridescence
forgetting, 63, 64, 101, 207, 209, 212–213, 214–215, 224; *see also Seinsvergessenheit*
formal indication, 68
Foucault, Michael, 264
fourfold, 3, 22–23, 47, 49, 77, 85–86, 91, 96, 108–109, 154–155, 216, 219, 261; *see also Geviert*
fouring, *see* fourfold
frame/framework, 153, 265
frame-breakers, 265
freedom, 142, 148, 211
Friedrich, David Casper, 41
fundamental attunement, see *Grundstimmung*
futurity, 215
The Fundamental Concepts of Metaphysics, 121, 122–123

Gadamer, Hans-Georg, 66, 109, 179, 245, 253
gap between past and future, 185, 193, 201, 205
gathering, 22, 34, 40, 108–109, 111, 154, 155, 203
Gefühl, 121; *see also* feeeling
Gegend, 272
gelassen, 269
Gelassenheit, 24, 135, 140, 167, 175, 178, 262, 267, 269, 270; *see also* releasement
gender, 254
genealogy, 214
Genoa, 41
German idealism, *see* idealism
Germany, 40, 213, 224, 245
Gebirg, 153

Gemüt, 153
Gestell, 63, 139, 140, 152, 161; *see also* frame/framework, position/positionality, *stellen, thesis*
Geviert, 3, 22, 47, 59, 140; *see also* fourfold
Ghandi, Mohandas K., 260
givenness, 23; *see also Es gibt*
glance, 87
Gleichursprünglichkeit, *see* equiprimordiality
globalization, 224–225
Goebbels, Josef, 143
Gombrich, Ernst, 252
Greece, 36, 39–41, 45, 239
Greeks, 39–40, 43, 214, 215
grief, 164–165, 180, 184
ground/groundedness, 35–36, 37, 236
Grundstimmung, 121, 259
Guignon, Charles, 166–168, 169–170

Hartmann, Geoffrey, 167
Harvey, David, 140
Hawking, Stephen, 54
"He" (in Kafka's *Notes from the Year 1920*), 193
Heaney, Seamus, 57, 163
heartfeltness, 136
Hebel, Johan Peter, 78
Hegel, Georg Wilhelm Friedrich, 218, 221, 222, 277, 279
Heidegger studies, 4
Heidegger, Martin: and anti-Nazism, 20; and anti-Semitism, 5, 8, 20, 213; friendship with René Char, 27–30, 43, 232–233, 234; and Hitler, 5, 20, 43, 231; and irrationalism, 114–115, 134, 135; and nationalism, 5, 20, 213; and Nazism (National Socialism), 5, 8, 16, 20, 138–139, 166, 238;

obscurity of, 259; reading of, 3–5, 7–9, 49, 75–76, 114–115; and rectorate (Freiburg), 16, 17; shifts in thinking of, 9, 11–12, 12–13, 14–24, 35–36, 65–66, 71, 80–81, 83, 90–91, 99–100, 109, 115, 145, 176–177, 200–201, 210–211, 217, 248, 265, 273
Heraclitus, 2
Herausforderung, see challenging
hermeneueien, 69, 72, 74
hermeneutical circularity, 135
hermeneutical space, 246
hermeneutics, 65–82, 83, 135, 221–223, 246, 278, 279; as "bearing of message or tidings," 75, 76; of facticity, 70, 80; as methodology, 69; as theory of interpretation, 69
Hermes, 278
Himmel, see sky
hints and beckonings, see *Winke*
Hirsch, E. D., 54
historicality, 215
history of being, 16–17, 20–22, 23–24, 177, 213–214
history of emotions, 117
history of forgetting, 214–215
history of philosophy, 215
Hitler, Adolf, 5, 20, 43, 231
Hölderlin, Friedrich, 12, 30, 38–40, 83–84, 91, 109, 245–246
homecoming, 237
homeland, 36, 42
homelessness, 88–89
house/home, 38, 87, 88, 89, 94, 101, 102, 105, 108, 217, 237
"house of being," 12, 68, 84, 86, 88, 89, 97, 99, 105, 217, 247
human/human being, 19, 20–21, 28–29, 37, 40, 41, 46–48, 52–54, 64, 77–78, 79, 84–86, 88–90, 92–93, 105, 124, 130, 140, 147, 163, 168, 180, 193–194, 206, 224, 235; and Dasein, 33, 235; essence of, 47–48; and language, 46, 64, 78, 86, 88–89, 91–94, 103, 105; and limit, 37, 40; and place, 20–21, 28–29, 37–38, 41, 46–48, 52, 64, 77–79, 84–86, 88–90, 124, 130, 163, 168, 180, 206, 224, 235; and technology, 147–150
human condition, 193, 194
humanism, 142
Hume, David, 113
Husserl, Edmund, 177
hypokeimenon, 130; see also *subiectum*

idea, 147
idealism, 56, 168, 219, 244
identity, 37, 38–39, 58, 79, 80, 183, 203, 219, 237; and difference, 43, 58, 79, 80, 203, 219, 241; see also sameness
ideology/ideology critique, 266, 269
image, 12, 105–109, 134, 217, 252, 253; conceptual/representational, 134; poetic, 134
immanence, 40
inclusion, 38
indeterminacy, 105, 134, 135, 146, 211, 243
indifference, 119–120; see also apathy
inhumanity, 119–120
initiation, 32–33
inner, 128, 190–192, 207
instrumentalism/instrumentality, 147–148, 158–159
intellect/rational insight, 116
intentionality, 147
internality, 130, 180
interpretation, 7–8, 69, 72, 73, 213; methodology of, 69; theory of, 69

interval, see *diastema*, *see also* between, dimension/dimensionality, space, *Zwischen/zwischen*
An Introduction to Metaphysics, 33, 34
irrationality/irrationalism, 114–115, 121, 134, 135, 144
iridescence, 1–2, 104, 110, 210, 276; *see also* equivocity, vibrancy
Islamic State (ISIL/DAESH), 142, 143
L'Isle-sur-la-Sorgue, 36, 236

jug, 154
Jünger, Ernst, 139

Kafka, Franz, 193–194, 198
Kafka's parable, 193–194, 195, 198, 273
Kairos, 247
Kant, Immanuel, 10, 54–55, 55–59, 190, 192, 201, 203, 221; *Critique of Pure Reason*, 55–56
Kampf, see struggle
Kehre, 209, 210, 273; *see also* return, turning
Kierkegaard, Søren, 138
knowledge, 148, 215
Kockelmans, Joseph, 251
Kurtz (in Conrad's *Heart of Darkness*), 166, 170, 171

Lafont, Christina, 242
landscape, 29, 37, 38, 40–41, 44, 52, 54, 147, 163, 180, 181, 234, 238
language, 6, 10, 12–13, 25, 67, 71, 74, 79–80, 81, 83–97, 101, 103–104, 205–206, 210, 217, 247, 250, 251; difficulty (neediness) of, 110–111, 245; and event, 93–94; figurative, 12, 106–107, 252; and human being, 46, 64, 78, 86, 88–89, 92–94, 103, 105; metaphorical, 12, 101, 103–104, 198–199, 217, 252; and

natality, 205–206; as natural, 92; ontological, 92; and place, 12, 81, 87, 97, 101, 205–206; and poetry, 45–46, 83–84, 104–109, 110; and space/dimensionality, 9–10, 76–77, 81, 85–87, 89, 94–97, 199; topological, 14, 15–16, 76, 77, 90, 101–102, 147, 198, 199, 217–218, 250; *see also logos*, Saying
lassen, 269
Le Thor, *see* Seminars in Le Thor
"Letter on 'Humanism,'" 84, 94–95, 100–101, 133
letting be/letting go, 176, 178
Levinas, Emmanuel, 131, 203, 237, 275
Lewis, Clarence Irving, 219
liberalism, 137, 139
library, 187
Lichtung, 3, 13, 59; *see also* clearing
life, 37, 40
liminality, 41
limit, 37, 40, 41, 44, 59–61, 62, 149, 153, 158, 212, 224, 233–234; as delimitation, 87
linearity of time, 193–194
linguistic idealism, 244
listening, 251
literality, 102–104, 217, 250, 251–252
lived space, 126
location, *see* physical location
logic, 70, 242
logos, 43, 67, 72, 74, 90; *see also* language
loss, 180
love for place, 36–37
Luddism/Luddites, 144, 263

machine, 138
making-space, *see* spacing
das Man, *see* One
management, 159, 267

Marcuse, Herbert, 138
Marx, Karl, 140
mastery, 176
materialism, nonreductive, 151; romantic, 53, 131–132, 151; see also naturalism
materiality, 132, 181, 258
mathematical, 151
matrix, 241
meaning, 8, 79, 86, 206, 251
means-ends, 147–150
measure, 37, 40, 85, 108, 152, 246
meditative thinking, see thinking
Mediterranean, 39, 40, 239
Mediterraneanism, 29, 40, 41, 42–43, 233, 239
memory, 200
Messkirch, 44
Merleau-Ponty, Maurice, 128
metaphor, 12, 99–111, 218, 251, 249, 250–251, 252, 253; and image, 105–109; and metaphysics, 101–102; and place, 101, 249; and poetry, 103–104; as transfer/carrying across, 101; see also language (metaphorical), literality
metaphora/metaphero 101; see also metaphor
metaphorical language, see language (metaphorical); see also metaphor
metaphorization, 251
metaphysics, 71, 81, 101–102, 151, 168, 195, 241–242; see also thinking, representational/conceptual
metiri, 246; see also measure
Michael (in Wordsworth's "Michael"), 163, 164–165, 166, 180–181, 183–184
Midworld, 220, 223
Miller, John William, 219–220, 222–223, 276
mindfulness, 136

Mitchell, Andrew, 139–140, 261
moderation, 37, 44
modernism, 143
modernity, 44, 63, 90, 117, 137–140, 141–144, 151, 152, 154, 167, 214, 224, 259; project of, 141–142, 143, 148, 251, 260
moment/now, 3, 15, 193–198, 201, 204, 205, 206, 230, 248, 273, 274; see also *Augenblick*
monetization, 119, 159
monosemy, see univocity
mood, 120–121, 122–123, 126–127, 128, 130, 134; see also *Stimmung*
moral decision-making, 113
moral value, 181–181
motivation, 118, 119–120
movement, 61, 87, 118, 139, 210
mutuality, 57, 219; see also reciprocity
mysteries, see Eleusian mysteries
mythophilia, 270

Nähe, see nearness
natality, 195, 204–206, 274
nationalism, 5, 20, 35, 37, 43, 175, 213, 245
National Socialism, see Nazism
native, 36, 204
naturalism, 49, 53–55, 62–63; nonreductive, 64, 131; see also antinaturalism, materialism, physicalism
nature, 38, 41, 49–64, 152, 153, 181; and empirical science, 53–55; and human being, 52, 53–54; as poetic, 51–52, and Romanticism, 53–55; see also physis
"The Nature of Language," 96, 106
Nazism, 5–8, 16, 20, 142, 143, 166, 224, 238, 245; see also anti-Nazism
nearness, 85, 92, 96, 99, 135, 139, 145
need, 47, 247

neediness/difficulty of language, *see* language (neediness/difficulty of)
neoliberal economics, 159
Nietzsche, Friedrich, 41, 138, 187, 195, 198, 234, 273–274
Nietzsche lectures, 121, 122, 124, 195–197
noein, 260
nonlinguistic, 92
Norberg-Schulz, Christian, 271
North Atlantic, 237
nostalgia, 180, 270
nous, *see* intellect/rational insight
now, *see Augenblick*, moment
number/numerical, 151, 152, 154
nunc stans (standing present), 196, 197, 201

object/objective/objectivity, 58, 113, 116, 119, 127, 131, 192, 222, 247, 258
obscurity, 259
occurrent, *see* present-at-hand
ocean, 41
Offene, 25, 90; *see also* opening/openness
on the way, 110–111
On the Way to Language, 28
One, 178
onefold (*Einfalt*), 80; *see also* being, presencing, twofold
ontological difference, 21, 66, 80, 102, 241, 247
ontology, 5, 65–69, 70, 80, 81–82, 89, 90, 92, 103, 150, 177, 178, 179, 219–220, 241–242
Ontology—The Hermeneutics of Facticity, 66–71, 73–74
open, *see* opening
opening/openness, 1, 2, 13, 25, 30–31, 59, 61, 64, 71, 76, 78, 79, 81, 84, 86, 87, 90, 92, 93, 135, 151, 201, 203, 204, 223

opposites, unity of, 43–44
optimism, 138
ordering of world, 147, 151, 152
ordinary, *see* everyday
orientation, 73, 118, 119–120, 124, 128–129, 133, 210–211
origin 172
Ortega y Gasset, José, 148
"The Origin of the Work of Art," 19
Ort/Ortschaft, 15–16, 22, 24, 25, 77, 90, 185, 190, 202, 230, 231; *see also place*
Ortschaft des Denkens, *see* thinking (place of)
Orwell, George, 175
other beginning, 17, 30–31, 37, 209, 212, 215, 222–225; *see also* first beginning
Ott, Heinrich, 244
outer, 190–192
ownmost temporality, *see* temporality (ownmost)
ownness/owned, 93, 177–178

Parmenides, 30, 31–34
patrie, *see* homeland
Payne, Mark, 237
passion, 113, 254
past, 180, 193–194; and future, 185, 193–194
peasant thought, *see* rural thought
Peirce, Charles Sanders, 222
People (*Volk*), 19, 21–22, 245
peras, 59; *see also* bound/boundary, limit
personal and philosophical, 7–8
pessimism, 138
phenomenology, 124, 219, 221
philosophical hermeneutics, *see* hermeneutics
philosophical topography, 227
philosophical topology, 2, 219, 227; *see also* topology
photograph, 157

philosophy, 4, 5, 6, 16–17, 18–19, 45, 54, 70, 71, 99, 151, 152, 215, 218, 220, 222, 223–224, 225
physical location, 181
physicalism, 241
physis, 38, 58, 60–62, 149, 209
picture, 157
Pinker, Stephen, 137, 142
place, 1–4, 6, 9–10, 11–13, 15–16, 19–24, 24–25, 26, 28, 30, 31, 33–35, 37–38, 43–44, 46, 47–48, 57, 59, 62, 64, 67, 74, 76, 77–78, 80, 84, 90, 97, 102, 105, 109, 110–111, 126, 127, 133, 135–136, 147, 151, 152, 155, 160–161, 179, 180, 181–184, 185–186, 187–189, 190, 192–193, 203–204, 210–211, 215–216, 217, 220, 221–222, 223, 236, 237, 247; and atmosphere, 127; of being, 16, 21, 22, 74, 84, 87, 88–90, 109–111; and essence, 145–146; and human being, 20–21, 28–29, 37–38, 41, 46–48, 52, 64, 77–79, 84–86, 88–90, 124, 130, 163, 168, 180, 206, 224, 235; and identity, 37–38, 237; and language, 12, 81, 87, 97, 101, 205–206; and loss, 180; love for, 36–37; and natality, 204; neglect of, 2, 128, 140, 186, 187, 216, 218; and self, 130–131, 168, 179, 180–184, 203, 207; sense of, 133, 163, 189; and space, 1, 24, 25, 76, 90, 127, 129, 151–152, 190, 220–221; of thinking, 15, 24, 31, 37, 81, 135–136, 186–190, 192, 193, 195, 202, 206–208, 210, 211–212, 223–224; and time, 90, 185, 198, 199–202; *see also* chora, Ort/Ortschaft, Stätte, topos
placing, 14, 15, 74, 88, 90–91, 108, 109–111, 145–146, 203, 208, 249; *see also* placedness/being-placed

placelessness, 185, 187–189, 207
placedness/being-placed, 3, 90, 105, 109, 124, 126, 130, 131, 134, 135, 145, 183, 187, 204, 206; *see also* being-in-place
Plato, 116
Platz, 272
plurality, 203
"'. . . Poetically Man Dwells . . . ,'" 84–85, 95
poetic image, *see* image (poetic)
poetic thinking, *see* thinking (poetic/meditative)
poetry, 29–31, 45–46, 83–84, 85, 88, 89, 99, 101, 103–109, 163, 217, 234
poiesis (bringing-forth), 61, 103, 149
polemos (strife), 23
politics, 16–17
Polonius (in Shakespeare's *Hamlet*), 171, 173–174
polysemy, *see* equivocity
position/positionality, 62–63, 70–71, 128, 139, 152, 153, 155, 215, 272; and *Gestell*, 63, 139–140, 153, 265; *see also* Stelle, thesis
post-truth, 133
pragmatism, 219
prelinguistic, 92
premodern, 142, 156
premodern technology, *see* technology
presencing, 33–35, 48, 58, 73, 74, 84, 92, 145, 149, 200, 241; *see also* being, twofold
presence, *see* presencing
present-at-hand (occurrent), 50
"The Principle of Identity," 58
priority: of empirical/natural science, 214; of *physis*, 61; of quantitative, 214; of reason, 115–117; of space/spatiality, 9–10, 90, 229–230; of technology, 151; of temporality/time, 10–11, 185–186, 192, 198, 201, 223; of transcendental, 56

progress, 137, 141, 148
progressivism, 135, 139, 141–142, 157
proper, 93, 97, 177–178, 250
properties, 144, 145
pros hen, see focal meaning; see also equivocity
Provence, 28–30, 35–36, 39, 45, 239
psyche, 116

quantity/quantitative, 151, 152, 215, 225–226
"The Question Concerning Technology," 140, 149
question of being, 33, 68–73, 80, 90, 103, 250
questioning, 68, 70, 270
quidditas, 144
quietism, 23
Quine, W. V. O., 59

racism, 236; see also anti-Semitism
radio, 143
Ratcliffe, Matthew, 114, 125, 127–128, 255–256, 257
rationality, 114–116, 133, 134, 138, 144
rationalization, 119
Raum, 10, 24, 190; see also space
Räumlichkeit, 10, 11, 190; see also spatiality
ready-to-hand (available), 50
reason, 113–120, 133, 134–136, 137, 142, 144, 148, 254
reciprocity, 57, 136; see also mutuality
recognition, 219, 221
Rectoral Address, see "The Self-Assertion of the German University"
rectorate (Freiburg), see Heidegger, Martin
region, 147

relation/relating, 86, 87, 145, 219, 220, 244, 277, 278
relational ontology, 131
relationality, 39, 87, 131–132, 145, 179, 219–221, 222, 223, 278
releasement, 24, 135, 167, 175–179, 183; see also *Gelassenheit*
remembrance/recollection, 31, 200, 207, 215–216, 223, 224–225, 269
reorientation, 225
repetition, 32, 80, 194, 195
representation/representational, 10, 105, 108, 144, 153, 154, 203, 258
representational image, see image
representational thinking, see thinking
resource/standing reserve, see *Bestand*
responsibility, 64
responsiveness, 24, 64, 117, 125
rethinking, 6, 90, 269
retrieval, 6, 269
return, 18, 100, 109, 180, 200, 207, 208, 209, 216, 223–224, 225, 269
revealing, 44, 92, 149, 150, 154; see also unconcealing/unconcealment
revenge against time, 195
reversal, see *Kehre*, return, turning
Richardson, William, 211
romantic image, 183
Romanticism, 53–55, 56, 139, 167; scientific, 53–54
romantic materialism, see materialism
romantic materiality, 132
Rorty, Richard, 278
Rousseau, Jean-Jacques, 138, 165
Royce, Josiah, 219, 222
rupture, 203
rural thought, 238

sameness, 38, 79–80, 86, 93; see also difference, identity
Sartre, Jean-Paul, 218

Saying (as essence of language), 74–75, 78, 79–80, 81, 88, 109, 110–111
saying of being, see ontology
saying of place, see topology
Schelling Friedrich, 54, 57
Schmitz, Hermann, 127
science, empirical/natural, 54, 61–62, 63, 137, 142, 151, 152, 214, 215, 264
scientific Romanticism, see Romanticism
sea, 41
Second World War, 224
seeing, 108
Seinsgeschichte, 213; see also history of being
seinsgeschichtliche/seynsgeschichtliche Denken, see thinking (being-historical)
Seinsvergessenheit, 63; see also forgetting of being
self, 130, 131, 165, 167–168, 172–175, 176, 178–179, 180, 203; dialogical, 179, 181; individual, 178, 199; and place, 41, 130–131, 168, 179, 180–184, 203, 207; social, 169, 175, 179
"The Self-Assertion of the German University" (Rectoral Address), 17, 231
self-emergence, 62
self-expression, 117
self-help movement, 175
self-identity, 219
self-interpretation, 71, 73
self-possession, 167, 170, 171
self-presencing, 64
self-realization, 167
self-release, 167, 176, 180, 183
self-understanding, 69–70, 270
Seminar/Seminars in Le Thor, 28, 31, 35–36, 43, 236

sense of place, see place
sensibility, 258
sensuousness, 79, 86
Seyn, see beyng
Shakespeare, William (*Hamlet*), 171, 173–174
Sheehan, Thomas, 4, 210–211, 218, 277
Shelley, Mary (*Frankenstein*), 138, 261
showing, 73, 74, 75, 76, 80, 81, 108; see also appearing, seeing
signless cloud, 158
Simmel, Georg, 119, 244, 255
sincerity, 169, 171
Singer, Peter, 113, 132
singular/singularity, 30–31, 37, 38, 42–43, 165, 211–212
site, see *Stätte*
situatedness/situation, 70–71, 73–74, 76, 122, 126, 147, 176, 179, 181, 198, 206, 210, 222; see also placedness/being-placed
situational awareness, 167, 176, 179
skepticism, see technological skepticism
sky, 77–78, 85, 87, 91
social, 92, 117, 165, 166, 169, 171, 173, 175, 181, 214, 250
social constructionism, 92
sociopolitical, 133
Socrates, 188, 207
sophrosune, see moderation
soul, see *psyche*
soul, divisions of, 117
sound, 78
space, 1, 9–13, 24, 25, 34–35, 76–77, 78, 81–82, 89–90, 95, 126–127, 140, 151–152, 153, 185–186, 190, 220–221, 229–230, 317; annihilation of, 140; and extension/extendedness, 152; and

space *(continued)*
  language, 9–10, 76–77, 81, 85–87, 89, 94–97, 199; and modernity, 152; and mood, 126–127; and place, 1, 24, 25, 76, 90, 127, 151, 190, 220–221; and time, 1, 10–11, 95, 151, 186, 201–202, 229–230; *see also* between, *diastema*, dimensionality, opening/openness, *Raum*
spacing/making space, 87, 96–97; *see also* clearing, openness/opening, dimensionality
spatial difference/differentiation, *see* difference/differentiation
spatial engagement, 258
spatial turn, 154
spatiality, 9–11, 78, 84, 94–97, 139–140, 153, 176, 192, 246; bodily, 128–130, 272; Cartesian, 11, 90, 190; existential, 11, 130, 190, 272; founded in temporality, 11; topological, 126; *see also Räumlichkeit*
spatialization, 139, 151–160, 199, 220
speed, 139
sphericity, 33, 235–236
Der Spiegel interview, 157–158
standing-out, see *ek-stasis*
standing present, see *nunc stans*
standing reserve/resource, see *Bestand*
Star Trek, 115, 254
state, modern, 152
Stätte, 16, 231
Stein, Gertrude, 218
Stelle, 63; *see also* position/positionality, thesis
stellen, 63, 140, 153; *see also Gestell*, thesis
Stimme, see voice

Stimmung, 120–121, 134; *see also* mood
strife, see *polemos*
struggle, 23
subjectivism, 18, 222, 278
subject/subjectivity/subjective, 55–56, 113, 124, 131, 192, 222, 258, 263
subiectum, 130, 220, 278
superabundance, 45
switching/switching point, 154, 155
symbol, 105–106, 252
systems, *see* technological systems

Taylor, Charles, 166, 169
techne, 61, 149
technicality, philosophical, 210, 217
technological breakdown, 158–159
technological continuity, 156
technological development, 155–156, 263
technological devices, 149, 154
technological modernity, 141
technological skepticism, 138
technological systems, 155–156
technology, 137–161, 176, 213, 225; benefits of, 159–160; digital, 157; essence of, 150–152, 160; and human being, 147–150; industrial, 265; instrumentalist construal of, 147–150; and limit, 158; modern, 141, 155–159, 160–161; and modernity, 137–141, 143–144, 148, 150–152, 154–155, 156–159; as obscuring, 158–159; as ordering, 147, 151, 152; planning/organizational, 152, 265; premodern, 156; and science, 264; topological analysis of, 160–161
teleology, 275
telos, 275
temporalism, 186, 198
temporocentrism, 198

temporality, 9–11, 16, 95, 186, 192–194, 193–194, 197, 201, 205, 248; ordinary, 197; ownmost (authentic), 197
territory, 152
thank/thanking, 200, 232, 235, 260
there/here, 3, 12–13, 16, 20, 22, 23, 33, 59, 70, 71, 73, 76, 91, 130, 131, 198, 218, 276–277
there is/it gives, see *Es gibt*
thesis, 62–63, 140; see also position/positionality
thing, 105, 106, 108, 135, 145, 154, 222, 223
thinker, 187–188
thinking, 3–4, 5–6, 15–20, 21–22, 24–26, 29–31, 33, 53–55, 63–64, 81, 109, 134–136, 185–208, 209, 210, 211–213, 215, 217, 223–224; being-historical, 16–20, 21; calculative, 134; conceptual/representational, 134, 135, 144, 151, 152, 259; context of, 212; as event, 195, 202, 203; failure of, 25–26; and forgetting, 214–215; and place, 15, 24, 31, 81, 135–136, 186–190, 192, 193, 195, 202, 206–208, 210, 211–212, 214–215, 223–224; poetic/meditative, 29–31, 109, 111, 134, 135, 217; as recuperative, 6; scientific, 53–55; and time, 186, 194–199, 200–202; world-historical, 212, 213, 214; *see also* topology
Thoreau, Henry David, 187
thoughtlessness, 207
threshold, 41
time, 1, 10–11, 90, 95, 151, 185–186, 192–202; and place, 90, 185, 198, 199–202; and space, 1, 10–11, 95, 151, 186, 201–202, 229–230

time-space compression, 140
timespace, see *Zeit-raum*
Todtnauberg, 187
topography, see philosophical topography
topological ethics, see ethics
topological reason, see reason
topological relationality, 131
topological thinking, see topology
topological/topographical turn, 262
topology (thinking of place)/topological, 2–3, 5, 6, 9, 15–16, 20, 21–22, 24–25, 32–34, 77, 84, 88, 89–90, 91, 101–102, 109–110, 126, 127–132, 135, 139, 140, 145, 147, 155, 160–161, 179, 186, 198–199, 200–201, 203, 204–208, 210–211, 213, 215–216, 216–218, 219, 220, 222, 223, 250, 253, 278; of being (*Topologie des Seyns*), 3, 15, 20, 21, 24, 28, 74, 79, 90, 109, 247, 248; in English literature, 253; and natality, 204; neglect of, 128, 140, 186, 216, 218, 249–250, 253; and technology, 160–161; and transcendental, 58, 221, 278
topos, 1–2, 22, 24, 34, 59, 62, 79, 80, 81, 91, 189–190, 200, 205–206, 207, 210, 220, 248; *see also* place
totalitarian state, 175
tradition, 5–6
tragedy, 39–40
transcendence, 40, 57; *see also* immanence
transcendental, 55, 55–59, 221, 240, 241–242, 278; and topological, 58, 221, 278
triangulation, 147
Trilling, Lionel, 164–165, 168–170, 171–172
Trump, Donald, 133

truth, 33, 133, 146, 147, 174; see also unconcealing/unconcealment, alétheia
truthfulness, 171, 172–174
tuning (bestimmen), 78; see also Stimmung
turning (Kehre, Wendung), 83, 209, 210–212, 273; see also return
twentieth-century, 142
two-in-one, 203
twofold (Zweifalt) of presence and presencing, 33, 35, 73, 74, 75, 76, 80, 81, 200, 241

unconcealing/unconcealment, 33, 58, 44, 58–59, 72, 73, 75, 76, 80, 81, 90, 92, 149, 209, 247; see also alétheia
understanding, 69–70, 206
unifying-differentiating, 80
unity, 33, 43, 56–57, 58, 74, 203, 223
univocity, 102–103, 104, 251
unterwegs, see on the way
urban, 41
utilitarianism, 114

value, 125
Vattimo, Gianni, 66
Venice, 41
vibrancy, 80, 104, 105, 108, 251
Vieldeutigkeit, see equivocity
violence, in interpretation, 4, 213
Virilio, Paul, 139, 158, 161
voice, 78
Volk, see people
vorhanden, see present-at-hand
Vycinas, Vincent, 227–228

wakefulness, 73

Warburg, Aby, 252
weak thought, 66
Weber, Max, 138
Wendung, see turning
Western philosophy, 36, 215, 218
What Is Called Thinking?, 33, 134, 185, 200
White, Kenneth, 40–41, 237, 238
Williams, Bernard, 166, 169, 171
willing, 122
Winke, 69, 75, 76, 92, 243; see also beckon, hints
withdrawal, 188–189, 203–204
Wittgenstein, Ludwig, 187
Wohnen, 12, 94, 140, 217, 262; see also Aufenthalt, dwelling
wonder, 53
wooden iron, 66, 80
word, 79, 86
Wordsworth, William, 51–52, 53–55, 63–64, 110, 163, 167–168, 180–184; "Michael," 163, 180–184; The Prelude, 168; "Tintern Abbey," 51–52
world, 2, 3, 13, 40, 46–47, 50, 54, 56, 78, 79, 80, 85, 91, 109, 123, 124, 131, 133, 140, 152, 154, 184, 203, 207
world ordering, see ordering
world-history, 214
worldhood, 50
writing under erasure, 6

Zeit-Spiel-Raum, 151, 216
Zeit-raum, 13, 90, 151
zuhanden, see ready-to-hand
Zwischen/zwischen, 13, 25, 90; see also between, dimensionality, diastema, space, spatiality

www.ingramcontent.com/pod-product-compliance
Lightning Source LLC
Chambersburg PA
CBHW021648230426
43668CB00008B/556